THE SOUTHWEST HISTORICAL SERIES

EDITED BY

RALPH P. BIEBER

VIII

JOSEPH GEITING McCOY
From a photograph

HISTORIC SKETCHES OF
THE CATTLE TRADE
OF THE WEST AND
SOUTHWEST

by

JOSEPH G. McCOY

edited by

RALPH P. BIEBER

Associate Professor of History, Washington University, St. Louis

*with additional illustrations
from the original 1874 edition*

PORCUPINE PRESS
Philadelphia
1974

First edition 1940
(Glendale: The Arthur H. Clark Co., 1940)

Reprinted 1974 by
PORCUPINE PRESS, INC.
Philadelphia, Pennsylvania 19107

Library of Congress Cataloging in Publication Data

McCoy, Joseph Geiting, 1837-1915.
    Historic sketches of the cattle trade of the West
and Southwest.

    (The Southwest historical series, 8)
    Reprint of the 1940 ed. published by A. H. Clark Co.,
Glendale, Calif.
    Includes bibliographical references.
    1. Cattle trade--Southwest, Old--History. I. Title.
F786.S752 vol. 8 [HD9433]   917.9'03'2s
ISBN 0-87991-311-8   [338.1'7'62130976]   74-7160

Manufactured in the United States of America

CONTENTS

PREFACE

PREFACE

In 1874, Joseph G. McCoy, then residing in Kansas City, Missouri, published his *Historic Sketches of the Cattle Trade of the West and Southwest,* an invaluable contribution to the literature of the Texas cattle drives. The original edition has become scarce and seldom occurs for sale. Although the book was reprinted in 1932, more than a year after it was announced for republication in this series, it appeared without any editorial additions whatever. The editor, therefore, feels justified in proceeding with his original plans. The material which he used in writing the introduction and footnotes to the present volume is located in various parts of the country and has been gathered at intervals over a period of approximately sixteen years.

The editor has reproduced the text of the first edition in its entirety, but has omitted the advertisements and most of the crude illustrations which have little or no historic value. On account of the inaccuracies and inconsistencies in the original, he has corrected capitalization, paragraphing, spelling, punctuation, hyphenization, typographical errors, and the excessive use of quotation marks and abbreviations. He has made no changes in word order, sentence structure, or grammar. Additions have been made solely to clarify the meaning of the author, and these, as well as the pagination of the original edition, have been enclosed in brackets.

The editor is under obligations to many individuals for aid given in the preparation of this work. He is especially indebted to George A. Root and Nyle H. Miller, of the Kansas State Historical Society, and Hortense B. C. Gibson, of Wichita, Kansas. He also desires to express his sincere appreciation to Kirke Mechem and his staff, Kansas State Historical Society; Mrs. A. B. Seelye, John B. Edwards, Homer W. Wilson, M. E. Calkins, and Mary Shirley, Abilene, Kansas; Emma B. Scott, Illinois State Historical Library; Purd B. Wright and Irene Gentry, Kansas City Public Library; Roy T. King, State Historical Society of Missouri; Stella M. Drumm, Missouri Historical Society; Joseph J. Hill, formerly of the Bancroft Library, University of California; Winnie Allen, library of the University of Texas; and James A. McMillen, library of Louisiana State University. For valuable assistance in editorial work and in preparing the manuscript for publication, the editor is indebted to his wife, Ida Parker Bieber.

RALPH P. BIEBER

Washington University
St. Louis, Missouri
July 25, 1939

INTRODUCTION

INTRODUCTION

Driving longhorns out of Texas to the cow towns of the northern plains is one of the most significant and colorful subjects in the annals of the Southwest. It is the narrative of a frontier industry that pointed the way to the occupation of a vast empire previously considered a great desert. From the close of the Civil war until the early nineties it attracted the attention of the whole nation, which became familiar with the terms cowboy, stampede, six-shooter, round-up, lariat, chaps, sombrero, and others connected with trailing stock over the open range. Nor have the cattle drives, although coming to an end nearly fifty years ago, ceased to interest the American people, since novels, songs, and moving pictures concerning them continue to have a popular appeal. The most important work pertaining to this subject, and the only book ever written by an eyewitness and participant, is Joseph G. McCoy's *Historic Sketches of the Cattle Trade of the West and Southwest*.

Joseph Geiting McCoy was born on a farm in Sangamon county, Illinois, about ten miles west of Springfield, on December 21, 1837. His father, David McCoy, was a native of Georgia who had migrated to Tennessee, thence to Ohio, and, shortly after the War of 1812, to Montgomery county, Illinois; his mother, Mary Kilpatrick, was born in Fayette county, Kentucky, and moved to Montgomery county, Illinois, in 1817. There, in the fall of the following year, David McCoy and Mary Kilpatrick were married, and in the spring of 1819 removed to a tract of land on the south side of Richland creek, Sangamon county, being among the pioneer settlers in that region. After residing there four years, the couple moved five miles south and settled on the north side of Spring creek, about ten miles west of Springfield. David and Mary had eleven children, three of whom were born at Richland creek and eight at Spring creek. Joseph was among the latter. Little is known of his early life except that he spent his youth on the farm, went to the district school, and attended the academy of Knox College at Galesburg during the school year, 1857-1858. On October 22, 1861, at the age of twenty-three, he married Sarah Epler, of Pleasant Plains, Sangamon county, the ceremony being performed at the home of the bride by Rev. Newton Cloud. She was born in Cass county, Illinois, January 16, 1837, a daughter of Jacob and Mary Beggs Epler, natives of Indiana.[1] Joseph and Sarah made their home near Springfield. They had seven children, two of whom — Florence and David — are still living today.[2]

Joseph made his first commercial venture away from home shortly before his marriage, when he transported a carload of mules of his own raising over five different railroads to Paris, Kentucky, and disposed of them at a substantial profit. He was so encouraged by the success of this undertaking that in 1861 he decided to embark in the business of feeding cattle and shipping them to market, which was then a thriving industry in central Illinois.[3] Two older

[1] Tombstone Inscription, Joseph Geiting McCoy, Maple Grove Cemetery, Wichita, Kansas; Florence L. McCoy to Hortense B. C. Gibson, Oct. 24, 1938, MS., Kansas State Historical Society (hereafter cited as K.S.H.S.); *Daily Illinois State Journal* (Springfield), Oct. 23, 1861; John Carroll Power, *History of the Early Settlers of Sangamon County, Illinois* (Springfield, 1876), 487-488; *History of Sangamon County, Illinois* (Chicago, 1881), 817-818, 913; *Portrait and Biographical Album of Sedgwick County, Kan.* (Chicago, 1888), 676-677; Edwin H. Van Patten, "A Brief History of David McCoy and Family," *Journal of the Illinois State Historical Society*, XIV, 122-127.

[2] Owen was born in Sangamon county, Illinois, and died there at the age of six months. Troy was born in Sangamon county and died there at the age of a year and a half. Mary E. (in later years called Mayme) was born in Sangamon county, September 7, 1866, and died in Wichita, Kansas, February 24, 1939. David B. was born in Sangamon county, June 21, 1869, and is now living in Atlanta, Georgia. Doctor Florence L. was born in Abilene, Kansas, October 10, 1871, and is now residing in Wichita. Eugene M. was born in Kansas City, Missouri, June 23, 1874, and died in Wichita, May 7, 1894. Ada was born in Westport, Missouri, and died in infancy. Joseph's wife, Sarah Epler, died in Kansas City, Missouri, November 10, 1911, and was buried in Maple Grove Cemetery, Wichita. Florence L. McCoy to Hortense B. C. Gibson, Oct. 24, 1938, MS., K.S.H.S.; *Wichita Evening Eagle* (Wichita, Kan.), Feb. 24, 1939; *Portrait and Biographical Album of Sedgwick County, Kan.*, 677.

[3] *Proceedings of the Second Annual Convention of the National Live Stock*

brothers, William and James, were already following this occupation. At that time Illinois produced more beef cattle than any other state in the union except Texas, and ranked first in the number of such live stock shipped from the western prairies to the eastern markets.[4] In 1862, Joseph also made a venture in woolgrowing, which, however, was not very profitable. Expanding his interests at the close of the Civil war, he engaged extensively in purchasing and feeding cattle, mules, hogs, and sheep and in transporting them to the various packing centers. During the years 1866 and 1867 he shipped mules to Cairo, Illinois, and New Orleans, and cattle, hogs, and sheep to New York and Chicago. The principal towns in central Illinois from which he sent live stock were Springfield, Bates, Alexander, Berlin, Bement, Sanger, and Tolono. In 1866 and early in 1867 he transacted business without a partner or under the name of J. G. McCoy & Company; but in the latter year he joined the firm that his brothers, William and James, had already established – William K. McCoy & Brother – which was then renamed William K. McCoy & Brothers.[5] It was while he was a member of this company that he decided to provide a place in the North to which Texas cattle might be driven without molestation, and from which they could be shipped or driven to the farmers or packers of the northern and eastern states.

Cattle were not indigenous to Texas but were introduced by the Spaniards at least by the latter part of the seventeenth century. General Alonso de León, governor of Coahuila, who made four expeditions north of the Río Grande between 1687 and 1690, and who established the first missions in that region during the latter year, brought live stock with him; so did Domingo Terán de los Ríos, who, in 1691, was made governor of the newly created province

Association (Denver, 1899), 323; Arthur Charles Cole, The Era of the Civil War, 1848-1870 (Centennial History of Illinois, III, Springfield, 1919), 83-85.

[4] Eighth Census of the United States, Agriculture, 184, 192; New York Times, Dec. 27, 1860.

[5] Daily Illinois State Journal, May 12, June 9, 13, 20, July 4, 11, 23, 28, Aug. 13, 15, 29, Dec. 29, 1866, Feb. 9, Apr. 20, May 1, 4, 8, 11, 15, 22, 23, June 5, 15, 19, 26, 29, Oct. 29, 1867; Proceedings of the Second Annual Convention of the National Live Stock Association, 323.

of Texas. When the province was abandoned in 1693, some of the stock was left behind.[6] On June 22, 1715, St. Denis, a Frenchman, asserted that the Indians had been afraid to kill the live stock left by the Spaniards and that as a result it had "increased to thousands of cows, bulls, horses, and mares, with which the whole country is covered." [7] Fray Francisco Céliz, chaplain of the Alarcón expedition to Texas, noted in his diary on March 12, 1718, that they saw a "black Castilian bull" near the Colorado river, a discovery which led them to believe that the trails of stock seen recently had been made "by cattle which General Alonso de León left exhausted on the return from his first trip to Texas." [8] When the Spaniards began their permanent occupation of Texas during the eighteenth century, they brought along additional cattle, thus laying the foundation for a great industry of a future day. Athanase de Mézières, lieutenant-governor of Natchitoches, wrote that he saw "an incredible number of Castilian cattle" while crossing the Brazos and Colorado rivers early in March, 1778.[9] Throughout the century, cattle were raised on scattered ranches and at missions, but many ran wild. Having a limited market, they were of little value; they were principally slaughtered for their hides or to supply the local demand for beef, although a few were driven overland to New Orleans.[10]

[6] *Pichardo's Treatise on the Limits of Louisiana and Texas* (Charles Wilson Hackett, editor and translator, Austin, 1931, 1934), I, 181, II, 525-526; Fray Juan Agustín Morfi, *History of Texas, 1673-1779* (Carlos Eduardo Castañeda, editor and translator, *Quivira Society Publications*, VI, Albuquerque, 1935), 241; Elizabeth Howard West, "De León's Expedition of 1689," *Quarterly of the Texas State Historical Association*, VIII, 205.

[7] *Pichardo's Treatise on the Limits of Louisiana and Texas* (Hackett, ed.), II, 526.

[8] Fray Francisco Céliz, *Diary of the Alarcón Expedition into Texas, 1718-1719* (Fritz Leo Hoffmann, editor and translator, *Quivira Society Publications*, V, Los Angeles, 1935), 52.

[9] *Athanase de Mézières and the Louisiana-Texas Frontier, 1768-1780* (Herbert Eugene Bolton, editor and translator, Cleveland, 1914), II, 187.

[10] *Ibid.*, I, 276, II, 112, 242, 281, 293; *Pichardo's Treatise on the Limits of Louisiana and Texas* (Hackett, ed.), II, 106, 204; Herbert Eugene Bolton, *Texas in the Middle of the Eighteenth Century* (Berkeley, 1915), 6, 85, 99,

When the Spanish regime in Texas was replaced by Mexican rule in 1821, Anglo-americans started to migrate to the province and occupy agricultural land, bringing some cattle with them. This stock was crossed with some of the Spanish breed. Picturesque and unique in appearance, the Spanish and hybrid types had similar characteristics,[11] which were described as follows: "The bodies had an emphasized lankiness and were raised high from the ground by the long legs; the head was elongated, and in many of the animals the long, narrow face had a sinister and sullen expression. The wide-spreading curved horns, unlike those of most very long-horned varieties of cattle, generally had a horizontal trend, and not uncommonly their spread from tip to tip was as much as five feet; and in some rather exceptional cases reached six." [12] Herding stock on the open range as an industry distinct from farming was gradually developed into a well-organized business by the Anglo-americans, although military activities during the Texan struggle for independence and depredations of Indian tribes retarded its growth. But the market for cattle continued to be limited. Many of them were still slaughtered mainly for their hides and tallow, which were exported in sailing vessels from ports on the Gulf of Mexico. Some were killed to supply the local demand for beef; others to provide smoked or salted meat for shipment to the West Indies. A small number were sold locally as work oxen. About 1837 and 1838 cowboys began to round up wild, unbranded cattle between the Nueces river and the Río Grande and drive them in herds of three hundred to a thousand to towns in the interior. Besides, probably as early as 1842, a few began to be driven overland to Shreveport, Louisiana, whence

100, 300-302, 418; Clara M. Love, "History of the Cattle Industry in the Southwest," *Southwestern Historical Quarterly*, XIX, 372.

[11] *Report of the Commissioner of Agriculture for the year 1870*, pp. 346-347; *Texas Almanac for 1861*, pp. 148-149; *Burke's Texas Almanac and Immigrant's Handbook for 1885*, p. 147; *Prose and Poetry of the Live Stock Industry of the United States* (Denver and Kansas City, 1905), I, 390, 441-442; Edward Everett Dale, *The Range Cattle Industry* (Norman, 1930), 21.

[12] *Prose and Poetry of the Live Stock Industry*, I, 441. See also Ernest Staples Osgood, *The Day of the Cattleman* (Minneapolis, 1929), 26-27.

they were shipped in flatboats down the Red and Mississippi rivers to New Orleans, then the greatest cattle market in the South.[13]

But the greatest expansion in the Texas cattle industry began with the annexation of the republic to the United States in 1845. Thereafter and until the outbreak of the Civil war thousands of Anglo-americans moved into the state and engaged in the live stock business. The number of cattle increased at a tremendous rate, so that by 1860 there were more in Texas than in any other state in the union.[14] Its attractions as a cattle-producing region were widely advertised during the fifties. There, it was stated, they multiplied rapidly, the net increase being about thirty per cent annually; the expense of feeding and wintering them was negligible; the grazing lands were the finest in the world; and only a few hands had to be hired to do the work. It was argued, in short, that raising cattle in Texas was a sure and quick way to wealth.[15] One writer claimed that "there innumerable herds of cattle, happier and prettier than ever was pastured by Virgil in his pastorals, enliven the otherwise oppressive loneliness of the scene." [16] Another asserted: "Texas is, beyond all comparison, the best grazing country in the United States. . . Nature, all-bountiful and propitious, spreads out upon the prairies her carpet of perennial greenness, and there they roam, lowing and feeding, fat and sleek." [17] The editor of the *Indianola Bulletin* declared that every possible encouragement should be given to cattle rais-

---

[13] *Prose and Poetry of the Live Stock Industry*, I, 387-391; *Tenth Census of the United States*, III (*Agriculture*), 965; *DeBow's Commercial Review of the South and West*, III, 238, 240; *Carl, Prince of Solms-Braunfels, Texas, 1844-1845* (Houston, 1936), 27; *Texas Almanac for 1861*, pp. 148-149; *Burke's Texas Almanac for 1885*, pp. 147-148; Dale, *op. cit.*, 24.

[14] *Eighth Census of the United States, Agriculture*, 148, 184, 192; *Prose and Poetry of the Live Stock Industry*, I, 390-391.

[15] *Valley Farmer*, VIII, 282; Melinda Rankin, *Texas in 1850* (Boston, 1850), 91-92; J. D. B. DeBow, *The Industrial Resources, etc., of the Southern and Western States* (New Orleans, 1853), III, 341; John C. Reid, *Reid's Tramp; or, a Journal of the Incidents of Ten Months Travel* (Selma, Ala., 1858), 33-35; *Texas Almanac for 1861*, pp. 151-152.

[16] *DeBow's Review of the Southern and Western States*, IX, 196.

[17] *DeBow's Review and Industrial Resources, Statistics, etc.*, XVIII, 334-335.

ing and that the interests of the stockmen should be pro-
tected by law. "No State in the Union can begin to compete
with Texas in raising cattle, mules, horses, sheep and hogs,"
he proudly boasted.[18] Writing from Lamar, Refugio county,
on June 17, 1860, another Texan claimed: "Every person
in this section of country who has given his attention to
stock-raising has become well off by it, and some have made
handsome fortunes." [19]

Raising longhorns in Texas between the Mexican and
Civil wars was a profitable business not only because an
ever-increasing number were slaughtered for their hides and
tallow, but also because a limited quantity of beeves began
to find a regular market outside the state. During this period
cattle were driven to southern, northern, and western states,
or shipped by boat to New Orleans, Mobile, and the West
Indies. Nevertheless, the supply of stock in Texas continued
to exceed the demand – a condition that was not changed
until after the Civil war.

New Orleans offered the most reliable market for Texas
beeves between 1848 and 1860. Some reached there by
routes that were primarily overland; others came by way of
the Gulf of Mexico. The first shipments by boat were made
from Indianola (at the entrance to Lavaca bay), Texas, as
early as 1849. On April 26 of that year W. H. Foster inserted a "cattle wanted" advertisement in the Houston
Democratic Telegraph and Texas Register, asserting that
he was building a wharf on Lavaca bay for the purpose of
transporting "live cattle" from that place to New Orleans,
that he would continue to operate there for six weeks or
two months, and that thereafter he would conduct the business from Galveston. Commenting in a later issue upon the
beginning of this commerce from Indianola, the newspaper
remarked: "We hope that the new trade that has thus been
opened under favorable auspices will become a source of
wealth to our citizens and will induce thousands of settlers
to locate in the beautiful and healthy prairies of the west.
These extensive and luxuriant pastures might sustain herds

18 *Texas State Gazette* (Austin), May 27, 1854.
19 *Texas Almanac for 1861,* p. 151.

and flocks sufficient to supply all the markets of the Atlantic cities." [20] Throughout the fifties steamers of light draft transported emigrants, their agricultural implements, and merchandise from New Orleans to Texas ports, and on the return trip took aboard cattle, hides, tallow, cotton, and other products. Most of this trade was monopolized by the Morgan line of steamers. Indianola was the principal port from which stock were shipped to New Orleans, but some were also exported from Galveston, Corpus Christi, Port Lavaca, and Sabine Pass. [21] The total number transported by boat cannot be stated accurately. The *Galveston Civilian* estimated that about 10,000 head had been shipped from Texas to New Orleans between October, 1850, and October, 1851. [22] From 1850 to 1856, according to the *Galveston Commercial and Weekly Prices Current,* between 2900 and 6000 were transported annually from Galveston to New Orleans; however, part of this number may have included cattle shipped originally from Indianola which had merely stopped at Galveston on their way to New Orleans. [23]

But most Texas cattle reached New Orleans during this period by routes that were primarily overland. Some drovers proceeded from western and southern Texas to Liberty on the Trinity river, thence to Beaumont on the Neches, and from there, after passing the Sabine into Louisiana, across the Calcasieu and Mississippi to New Orleans. Since there were few bridges along these trails, most rivers were crossed by swimming, fording, or ferrying. Other cattlemen drove longhorns from central and eastern Texas across the Sabine

---

[20] *Democratic Telegraph and Texas Register,* Aug. 30, 1849. See also *ibid.,* Sept. 13, Oct. 11, 1849; *Colorado Tribune* (Matagorda, Tex.), May 3, 1852; *Texas State Gazette,* Oct. 12, 1850; *Historical and Biographical Record of the Cattle Industry and the Cattlemen of Texas and Adjacent Territory* (Saint Louis, 1895), 35.

[21] *Texas State Gazette,* Oct. 12, 1850, Oct. 11, 1851; *Colorado Tribune,* May 3, 1852; *Texas Monument* (La Grange), May 19, Sept. 29, 1852; D. E. Braman, *Braman's Information about Texas* (Philadelphia, 1858), 61-71; *Texas Almanac for 1860,* pp. 224-225; *ibid., 1861,* p. 237; *Tenth Census of the United States,* III (*Agriculture*), 976; *Prose and Poetry of the Live Stock Industry,* I, 392-393; Dale, *op. cit.,* 24; *Historical and Biographical Record of the Cattle Industry,* 35, 57.

[22] *Colorado Tribune,* Nov. 3, 1851.

[23] *Galveston Commercial and Weekly Prices Current,* Sept. 1, 1856.

to Shreveport, Natchitoches, or Alexandria, Louisiana, and then shipped them by boat down the Red and Mississippi rivers to New Orleans.[24] The overland drives assumed rather large proportions in the fifties. A citizen of Beaumont estimated that about 40,000 head crossed the Neches river there in 1853.[25] A resident of Liberty who kept a record of all cattle using the Trinity river ferry at that place during 1855 and 1856, listed twenty-five droves with a total of 5834 head in the former year, and thirty-one droves with 6869 head in the latter.[26] The *Galveston Weekly News* asserted that during the first ten months of 1856 as many as 32,412 beeves from western Texas passed the Sabine into Louisiana, most of which were destined for New Orleans.[27] Texas cattle arriving in that city by the overland routes, as well as those coming by the Gulf of Mexico, were either slaughtered for local consumption or were shipped to various parts of Louisiana, Alabama, or the West Indies.[28]

A desire to obtain higher prices for stock than could be realized in New Orleans or the West Indies resulted in the long drive to California after the Mexican war. Although the first Texas cattle were driven to the Pacific coast by gold seekers in 1849,[29] not many herds were started in that direction until 1853 and 1854. During the early fifties returning argonauts brought news to Texas that beeves commanded high prices in Los Angeles and San Francisco, because the large and constant influx of population was making a heavy drain upon the meat supply. To many drovers this was good news indeed. Hence in 1853 and 1854 thousands of cattle were headed west in the hope that fortunes could be realized in the new El Dorado. Following the Whiting-Smith route of 1849, the main trail began at San Antonio

[24] *Texas Monument,* Nov. 16, 1853; *Texas State Gazette,* Apr. 29, 1854, May 26, 1855; *Galveston Weekly News,* Dec. 4, 1855, July 22, 1856; Edward Smith, *Account of a Journey through North-eastern Texas, Undertaken in 1849* (London, 1849), 28-34; Dale, *op. cit.,* 24.

[25] *Texas Monument,* Nov. 16, 1853.

[26] *Galveston Weekly News,* Nov. 18, 1856.

[27] *Ibid.,* Aug. 4, 1857.

[28] Smith, *Account of a Journey through North-eastern Texas,* 34.

[29] James G. Bell, *A Log of the Texas-California Cattle Trail, 1854* (J. Evetts Haley, ed., Austin, 1932), 4.

and extended west and northwest to Franklin (the present El Paso), Texas; another trail started at Clarksville in eastern Texas and led across the northern part of the state to Franklin. From the latter place the route proceeded to a point north of Doña Ana, New Mexico, and thence southwest through the Guadalupe pass, Santa Cruz, Tucson, Pima Indian villages, Fort Yuma, Warner's Ranch, and San Diego or Los Angeles. In the latter cities the drovers either sold their stock to California buyers, or continued their journey by boat or overland trails to the San Francisco or Sacramento markets.[30] Longhorns purchased in Texas at from $5 to $15 a head were sold in California for $60 to $150 each.[31] The *Sacramento State Journal* estimated that in 1854 about 9000 cattle came into the state by the southern route;[32] the San Antonio *Western Texan* on June 1, 1854, asserted that "between seven and eight thousand head of cattle and stock of all kinds" were then on the way to the "Modern Ophir." Other estimates were somewhat higher.[33] Stock continued to be driven from Texas to California until 1860, although after 1854 the numbers were usually smaller.[34]

This journey of fifteen hundred or two thousand miles

---

[30] *Ibid.*, 7-78; Ignatius Erskine, Journals and Other Memoranda, California, 1854, MS., University of Texas Library; James Bell, "A Diary Kept on the Overland Trail in 1854," *Frontier Times*, IV, 28-39; *Texas State Gazette,* June 18, 1853, July 29, 1854; *The Standard* (Clarksville, Tex.), May 28, 1853; *Texas Monument,* June 22, 1853; *Galveston Journal,* May 22, 1854; *Colorado Tribune,* July 21, 1854; *Western Texan* (San Antonio), June 1, 1854; *St. Joseph Commercial Cycle* (St. Joseph, Mo.), June 24, 1853; *Daily Alta California* (San Francisco), Aug. 10, Nov. 1, 2, 1853, Mar. 5, Aug. 16, 1854; *San Diego Herald,* Oct. 22, 1853, Dec. 9, 1854; *Historical and Biographical Record of the Cattle Industry,* 35.

[31] *Daily Missouri Republican* (St. Louis), Apr. 26, 1854; *Daily Alta California,* Mar. 25, 1854; *Standard,* May 28, 1853; *Texas State Gazette,* Apr. 21, 1855.

[32] *Daily Alta California,* Dec. 25, 1854.

[33] *Ibid.*, Aug. 16, 1854.

[34] *Texas State Gazette,* Apr. 21, 1855; *Daily Alta California,* Aug. 7, 1855; *Galveston Weekly News,* Aug. 31, 1858; *San Antonio Daily Herald,* Oct. 23, 1858; *San Francisco Daily Herald,* Oct. 8, 1858, Sept. 9, 1859; Frederick Law Olmsted, *A Journey through Texas* (London, 1859), 273-275; Louis Pelzer, *The Cattlemen's Frontier* (Glendale, 1936), 37.

was the first really long drive of Texas cattle. Hot winds, dusty trails, and hostile Apache were among the obstacles encountered. Some cattle had to be left behind because they were footsore; others died on the way due to the scarcity of water and absence of proper grazing facilities. Hundreds of carcasses were strewn along the trail — mute evidences of the hazardous nature of the long journey.[35] "From end to end it was a trail of dangers and uncertainties — long dry drives that set cattle mad with thirst and drew saddle horses to 'skin and bones'; alkaline lakes that poisoned and killed thirsting herds; *malpais* ridges that cut hoofs to the quick and set the riders afoot; and the eternal threat of loss to white and Indian thieves." [36] Very few drovers arrived in California with their herds intact; hence the high prices they obtained for cattle were essential to compensate them for losses on the long and hazardous drive.[37]

Between 1848 and 1860 an additional outlet was found for Texas cattle by driving them to the North. The nature and extent of this early drive has never been appreciated, since most authorities have relied upon McCoy's statement that "but few attempts were ever made before the war to drive cattle north." However, evidence has been discovered that longhorns from Texas and the Indian Territory found their way to the principal live stock markets of the Middle West and East, and that this traffic was interrupted only by the outbreak of the Civil war. Prior to 1861, Texas developed a regular cattle trade with the North, which was resumed on a much larger scale after the close of the conflict.

Many Texas cattle trailed north during this period were driven into or through Missouri. An early contemporary reference to this traffic is found in an issue of the *Dallas*

---

[35] *Texas State Gazette,* June 18, 1853, July 29, Aug. 5, Nov. 4, 1854; *Daily Alta California,* Aug. 16, Sept. 3, 1854, July 27, 1855; *San Francisco Daily Herald,* Sept. 5, 16, Nov. 19, 1854; *Galveston Weekly News,* Aug. 31, 1858; Bell, *A Log of the Texas-California Cattle Trail* (Haley, ed.), 3-78.

[36] Bell, *A Log of the Texas-California Cattle Trail* (Haley, ed.), 3-4.

[37] During 1853 and 1854 numerous herds of cattle were driven to California from Missouri, Illinois, Arkansas, and Indian Territory. *Daily Missouri Republican,* Jan. 27, Mar. 14, Apr. 16, May 12, 20, 27, 1853, Apr. 29, May 30, 1854; *Daily Alta California,* May 20, 1854; *Quincy Whig* (Quincy, Ill.), Sept. 8, 1853.

Herald in June, 1850: "Several large droves of cattle have passed through this place during the present season en route to Missouri. They are brought mostly from the upper Brazos and carried to Missouri, to be sold for beef, or to furnish teams for California emigrants. This, we have no doubt, might afford a very considerable and lucrative item of trade to the people of this section of country, if they should give it their attention." [38] Nor did this prophecy fail to materialize, for during the following decade tens of thousands of cattle passed through Dallas and its vicinity on their way to Missouri and other northern states. The main trail crossed the Red river at Preston, Grayson county, Texas, led northeast through or near Boggy Depot and Fort Gibson, Indian Territory, continued in the same direction to the western boundary of Arkansas or Missouri, and then entered the latter state at various points along its southern or western border. [39] The *Texas State Gazette* asserted that in 1854 about fifty thousand cattle were reported to have crossed the Red river at Preston on their way to northern states and territories. [40]

The principal markets for Texas cattle in Missouri were Independence, Westport, and Kansas City, the starting points of the great overland trails to the West. Passing north through the western tier of counties in Missouri or through the eastern part of the present state of Kansas, longhorns from Texas and the Cherokee Nation and short-horns from western Arkansas and southwestern Missouri finally reached those thriving frontier towns and found a ready sale at good prices. Although a few longhorns were driven there immediately before and during the Mexican war, not until after the conflict did they arrive in any great quantity. Beginning about 1849 and continuing until the outbreak of the Civil war, they reached those markets in

---

[38] *Texas State Gazette,* July 6, 1850.

[39] *Ibid.,* Aug. 5, 1854; *Weekly Independent* (Belton, Tex.), May 2, 9, 23, 1857; *Galveston Weekly News,* May 10, 1859; *Dallas Herald,* May 18, June 8, 1859; *Border Sentinel* (Mound City, Kan.), Feb. 1, 1867; W. B. Parker, *Notes Taken during the Expedition Commanded by Capt. R. B. Marcy* (Philadelphia, 1856), 48-49, 75; Cuthbert Powell, *Twenty Years of Kansas City's Live Stock Trade and Traders* (Kansas City, 1893), 120-121.

[40] *Texas State Gazette,* Aug. 5, 1854.

ever-increasing numbers. Independence and Westport did the largest Texas cattle business before about 1855; after that time Westport and Kansas City — especially the latter — became the principal markets. Work oxen were sold to emigrants to California, Utah, Oregon, Colorado, and Kansas, to fur traders and Santa Fé traders, to overland freighters, and to the quartermaster's department of the United States army. Stock cattle for farms or ranches were disposed of to drovers from Missouri, Kansas, Iowa, Nebraska, Illinois, Minnesota, and California. Beeves were purchased by local butchers, by such military posts as Fort Leavenworth, Fort Riley, Fort Kearny, and Fort Laramie, by the commissary department of the army for military expeditions across the plains, and by beef packers and stock dealers from Quincy and Chicago, Illinois. Kansas City became the largest live stock market on the western frontier during the later fifties.[41] Approximately 9000 Texas horses and cattle were sold in or near the city in 1857, according to an estimate made by an informant of the *Galveston Civilian*.[42] The Kansas City *Western Journal of Commerce* stated that in 1857 about 52,000 stock cattle from Texas, the Cherokee Nation, Arkansas, and Missouri, and 14,700 horses, mules, and work oxen were disposed of in that market.[43] According to the same newspaper, the following live stock were sold there in 1858: 48,000 stock cattle from Texas, the Cherokee Nation, Arkansas, and Missouri, and 16,600 horses, mules, and work oxen.[44] It estimated that two-thirds of all the live stock which reached Kansas City came from

41 *Kansas City Enterprise,* July 26, 1856, May 30, June 6, 1857; *Western Journal of Commerce* (Kansas City, Mo.), Jan. 9, Aug. 14, 1858; *Kansas City Daily Western Journal of Commerce,* June 16, 18, 20, 22, July 7, Aug. 10, 17, 31, 1858, Jan. 1, 1859, Nov. 17, 1860, Jan. 1, 1861; *Daily Missouri Republican,* Aug. 28, 1855, Sept. 13, 26, 1858, Sept. 4, 1859; *Washington Telegraph* (Washington, Ark.), Aug. 21, 1859; *Border Sentinel,* Feb. 1, 1867; W. H. Miller, *The History of Kansas City* (Kansas City, 1881), 164; Powell, *op. cit.,* 120-121.

42 *Western Journal of Commerce,* Nov. 14, 1857.

43 *Ibid.,* Jan. 9, 1858. The *Western Journal of Commerce* used the term "stock cattle" rather loosely, since it intended to include both beeves and stock cattle in that classification. Likewise, the work oxen it listed comprised some Texas cattle.

44 *Kansas City Daily Western Journal of Commerce,* Jan. 1, 1859.

Texas.[45] During 1858, according to the same newspaper, about 11,000 stock cattle were driven from that point to Chicago.[46] All longhorns destined for Chicago and points north and east of Kansas City crossed the Missouri river at Randolph ferry, about three miles east of the city.[47] That the lucrative traffic in Texas cattle was in no way affected by the increasing tension between the North and the South over the slavery issue is evidenced by the following terse statement of the *Dallas Herald:* "Yesterday, a drove of two thousand beef cattle passed through Dallas, en route for the North, to feed our abolition neighbors. We hope that southern diet may agree with them." [48]

St. Louis was another market for Texas cattle during the fifties. Prior to 1845 its live stock business was transacted at Papstown, a small place east of the present site of East St. Louis, Illinois; but in that year St. Louis began to have its own stockyards.[49] During the Mexican war and afterward cattle from Missouri, Iowa, and Illinois were driven to the city, where a small number were packed, others were sold to emigrants and traders to the Far West, but most were shipped down the Mississippi river to New Orleans. By 1852, when about fifteen thousand head were sent south, the *Daily Missouri Republican* claimed that St. Louis was "one of the greatest points for the shipment of cattle in the West." [50] As early as September, 1853, ninety-seven cattle from the Cherokee Nation reached the city.[51] The first Texas longhorns arrived during the summer of 1854. In the middle of August of that year George W. McClure disposed of twenty-four head, which were described as "good for nothing" and brought only two cents a pound. About the same time A. W. Ramsay, of Pettis county, Missouri,

[45] *Ibid.*, June 20, 1858.

[46] *Western Journal of Commerce*, Sept. 25, 1858.

[47] *Kansas City Daily Western Journal of Commerce*, June 22, 26, July 3, 9, Aug. 10, 17, 27, 31, 1858; Miller, *op. cit.*, 164. During the summer of 1858 this ferry began to be called the "lower ferry."

[48] *Dallas Herald*, May 18, 1859.

[49] *The Live Stock Market of the Western, Southern and Middle States* (St. Louis, 1875), 7.

[50] *Daily Missouri Republican*, Jan. 3, 1853.

[51] *Ibid.*, Sept. 26, 1853.

marketed fifty-five longhorns at from $22 to $30 each.[52]
Throughout the rest of the year additional sales of Texas
cattle were made at $15 to $19 a head.[53] Commenting upon
the sale of twenty-six steers from Holland county, Texas,
at $15 each on October 27, 1854, a St. Louis newspaper
observed: "They were driven nearly or quite 500 miles, and
it may be a matter of astonishment how they could be sold
for so small a price. The thing is explained when we say
they subsisted all the way on grass, and kept in tolerable
order, and what is more, they never eat a ear of corn in
their lives. An attempt was made to feed them with corn
and provender at the stock yards, but they ran away from
it. Texas cattle are about the nearest to 'wild animals' of
any now driven to market. We have seen some Buffaloes
that were more civilized." [54]

From 1855 to 1860, Texas and Indian cattle continued to
come to St. Louis, although in what numbers has not been
ascertained. Most of them were driven all the way, but a
few arrived by rail from Tipton, Missouri, and other points
on the Pacific Railroad. The stockyards at which the longhorns were sold were the Wedge House, the Bellevue
House on Manchester road, Baldwin's on Broadway, and
Ashbrook's on Commercial street; the price per head ranged
from $10 to $35.[55] Some were not ready for market. Thus
in 1857, when Ashbrook's recorded the arrival of a drove
from Texas and the Indian Territory, it noted that they
were "not fit for people to eat: they will do to bait traps
to catch wolfs in." [56] A few longhorns were packed or
slaughtered locally, many were sent to Illinois for feeding,
and others were shipped by boat to New Orleans.

Thousands of cattle from Texas and the Indian Territory
were trailed through Missouri to Illinois during the fifties.

52 *Ibid.*, Aug. 24, 1854.

53 *Ibid.*, Sept. 25, Oct. 9, 30, 1854; *Daily St. Louis Intelligencer*, Oct. 30, 1854.

54 *Daily St. Louis Intelligencer*, Oct. 30, 1854.

55 *Daily Missouri Republican*, Mar. 19, July 9, 1855, June 29, July 13, 20, 27, Nov. 9, 1857, July 19, Aug. 9, 1858, June 7, 12, July 4, 11, 25, 1859; *St. Louis Daily Evening News*, July 9, 1859; *Weekly California News* (California, Mo.), June 11, 1859, Oct. 6, 1860; J. de Cordova, *Texas: Her Resources and her Public Men* (Philadelphia, 1858), 54.

56 *Daily Missouri Republican*, July 20, 1857.

Entering the former state along its western or southern boundary, they were driven north and northeast by various routes, crossing the Missouri river by ferry at Kansas City, Independence, Lexington, Boonville, Rocheport, and other places. The most important crossings were Kansas City and Boonville; numerous trails from western and southwestern Missouri converged near the latter town.[57] After ferrying the Missouri, the herds continued to move northeast over various roads to the Mississippi river, crossing it at Quincy, Illinois, Hannibal, Missouri, and other towns farther south.[58] Beginning in 1859, when the Hannibal and St. Joseph Railroad was completed across the state, some longhorns were trailed north through western Missouri or eastern Kansas to St. Joseph, Missouri, whence they were transported to Hannibal and Chicago by rail. At the same time a number were shipped east from intermediate points on this railroad.[59] Practically all of the Texas cattle that were driven across Missouri to Illinois were grazed on the prairies of the latter state before they were sent to market.

Driving longhorns into or through Missouri met with considerable opposition during the latter half of the decade. The ravages of the so-called Texas fever, which killed thousands of native live stock, were the principal reason. Although the disease was not unknown during the early fifties, the first real epidemic in Missouri occurred in 1855. During August, September, and October of that year many shorthorns died of the malady in the counties of St. Clair, Cedar, Benton, Henry, Howard, and Cooper, as well as in other parts of central and western Missouri through which Texas cattle had been driven.[60] In the absence of any

[57] *Kansas City Enterprise*, July 25, 1856; *Kansas City Daily Western Journal of Commerce*, June 22, 1858; *Marshall Democrat* (Marshall, Mo.), Sept. 3, 24, 1858, May 20, 1859; *Weekly Missouri Statesman* (Columbia, Mo.), Sept. 17, 1858; Powell, *op. cit.*, 120; *Prose and Poetry of the Live Stock Industry*, I, 393.

[58] *Cattle Industry Clippings*, I, 85, K.S.H.S.; *Tri-Weekly Messenger* (Hannibal, Mo.), Sept. 27, 1855, Nov. 7, 1857; *Daily Quincy Whig*, Sept. 11, 1854, Sept. 13, 1855; *Daily Missouri Republican*, June 12, 1859.

[59] *Cattle Industry Clippings*, I, 85, K.S.H.S.; *Hannibal Daily Messenger*, May 5, 29, Sept. 22, 1859; *Daily Missouri Republican*, Sept. 4, 1859.

[60] *Boonville Weekly Observer* (Boonville, Mo.), Sept. 7, Oct. 6, Nov. 17,

legislation on the subject, a number of farmers took the law into their own hands. They held conventions at several county seats, where resolutions were adopted condemning the passage of longhorns through their midst and appointing vigilance committees to organize the citizens to prevent it. As a result, in a few counties the farmers and their friends armed themselves, stopped the progress of the drovers, and threatened to kill any Texas steers that crossed the county boundaries. Popularly this action was known as the "war" on Texas cattle.[61] Writing in a jocular vein, the *Warsaw Democrat,* of Benton county, observed: "We have heard some enquiry as to whether the soldiers in the 'late war' against Texas cattle are not entitled to land warrants under an amended act of Congress, granting bounty lands to soldiers in any war since 1790." [62] The final outcome of this agitation was the introduction of a bill into the lower house of the Missouri legislature on November 17, 1855, "to prevent diseased stock from being brought into the state." After some alterations this measure, under the title "Noxious Animals," became a law on December 13, 1855.[63] It stipulated that no person should "willfully and knowingly drive any diseased or distempered cattle, affected with what is commonly known as Texas or Spanish fever, or any other infectious disease, into or through this State, or from one part thereof to another, unless it be to remove them from one piece of ground to another of the same owner." The penalty for violation, upon conviction, was a forfeiture of twenty dollars for each cow thus driven, the offender being made liable for all damages. When a justice of the peace had proof that the act was being broken in the county, he was to order the owner or his agent to impound the cattle; and

1855; *Weekly Missouri Statesman,* Aug. 24, 31, 1855; *Tri-Weekly Messenger,* Nov. 6, 10, 1855.

61 *Glasgow Weekly Times* (Glasgow, Mo.), Sept. 27, 1855; *Boonville Weekly Observer,* Sept. 7, Oct. 6, 1855; *Weekly Missouri Statesman,* Aug. 31, 1855; William Renick, *Memoirs, Correspondence and Reminiscences* (Circleville, Ohio, 1880), 25-26.

62 *Boonville Weekly Observer,* Oct. 6, 1855.

63 Missouri, *House Journal,* 18 Gen. Assem., adjourned sess., pp. 87, 111, 112; Missouri, *Senate Journal,* 18 Gen. Assem., adjourned sess., p. 255; *Revised Statutes of the State of Missouri, 1855,* II, 1104-1105.

if either failed to comply, or permitted the longhorns to escape from the pound after complying, the justice was to direct the stock to be killed. The constable or any other person who was ordered by the justice of the peace to dispatch the cattle was to be compensated for their services at the rate of a dollar per head, which was to be paid by the owner if he was known, and if not, by the county. Any officer who failed to execute the order of the justice of the peace was to forfeit a sum of money equal to the fees he would have received had he performed his duty. All fines and forfeitures under the statute were to "be recovered by indictment." [64] This law had the distinction of being the first passed by a state legislature to restrict the driving of Texas cattle.

Since practically no Texas fever existed in Missouri during 1856 and 1857, the effectiveness of this legislation was not tested for several years; meanwhile longhorns were allowed to pass into or through the state without opposition. [65] But in 1858 the disease broke out over a large area, exceeding in virulence the epidemic of 1855. It killed thousands of cattle in the counties of Vernon, Cass, Benton, Henry, Johnson, Lafayette, Ray, Pettis, Boone, and Cooper, and caused heavy financial losses to the farmers. [66] The act of 1855 proved to be totally inadequate to stem the spread of the malady, partly because it did not provide the proper machinery of enforcement, but also because Texas cattle, apparently in a healthy condition, transmitted the disease in a way undiscoverable by the most careful observers. Consequently the farmers and their friends once more took the law into their own hands and turned back the southern herds at the county boundaries. Conventions again assembled in various parts of the state, at which vigilance committees were appointed to detect the arrival of the longhorns and

---

[64] *Revised Statutes of the State of Missouri, 1855,* II, 1104-1105.

[65] *Marshall Democrat,* Sept. 10, 1858.

[66] *Daily Missouri Republican,* Aug. 29, Sept. 13, 17, 23, 26, 1858; *Saint Louis Daily Evening News and Intelligencer,* Aug. 30, 1858; *Marshall Democrat,* Sept. 10, 24, 1858, May 20, 1859; *Weekly Missouri Statesman,* Sept. 1, 17, 1858; *Weekly California News,* Oct. 9, 1858; *Valley Farmer,* X, 372.

to call out volunteers to stop them.[67] "This course of proceeding may be considered illegal," admitted one local newspaper, "but our farmers have their rights as well as the Texas drovers."[68] The action of a convention held in Nevada, Vernon county, on September 6, 1858, may be given as a typical example of the attitude of such gatherings. Unanimously adopting a series of thirteen resolutions, this body declared the act of 1855 entirely inadequate to deal with the epidemic, called upon the legislature to pass a law prohibiting the driving of all Texas cattle into the county from April to October, asserted that "after mature deliberation" it decided to prevent the passage of any "southern cattle" through the county "lawfully and peaceably if we can, forcibly and at whatever consequences, if we must," and appointed a central committee of six to organize the citizens to turn back all Texas cattle. The convention ordered that the resolutions be published in the St. Louis *Daily Missouri Republican,* hoping that the newspapers of Arkansas and Texas would copy them and thereby "do a favor to their own citizens."[69] The passage of these and similar resolutions in central and western Missouri resulted in some violence, and during the latter part of 1858 many drovers found it difficult if not impossible to travel through the state over the usual highways.

A number of cases of Texas fever occurred in Missouri during 1859 and 1860, but the disease was not so prevalent as in 1858. The driving of longhorns through the state, although not stopped entirely, was made more difficult because of the alertness of the farmers, who continued to hold conventions and turn back the herds at the county boundaries.[70] Some drovers, as already pointed out, took their

---

[67] *Daily Missouri Republican,* Aug. 29, Sept. 13, 26, 1858; *Marshall Democrat,* Sept. 3, 10, 1858.

[68] *Clinton Journal* in *Weekly California News,* July 2, 1859. Although this statement was made in 1859, it also represents the point of view of the farmers in 1858.

[69] *Daily Missouri Republican,* Sept. 13, 1858.

[70] *Ibid.,* June 7, 12, July 8, Sept. 4, 1859; *Marshall Democrat,* May 20, 1859, July 25, 1860; *Weekly California News,* July 2, Aug. 13, 1859; *Liberty Weekly Tribune* (Liberty, Mo.), Aug. 16, 1859.

stock north through eastern Kansas to St. Joseph, Missouri, and shipped them to Illinois by railroad. On the eve of the Civil war the Missouri legislature responded to repeated protests of the farmers and took action to meet their complaints. A petition from some citizens of Cass and Jackson counties was presented to the lower house on February 20, 1861, asking for the enactment of a law to prevent the driving of Texas cattle into or through those districts. It was referred to the committee on the judiciary, which reported a bill that became a law on March 27, 1861.[71] The statute, entitled "Diseased Cattle," authorized each county court to appoint three "competent and discreet persons" in every township to serve as a board of cattle inspectors. This body was given the power to examine all Texas, Mexican, and Indian stock driven into the township, and if it discovered that any were afflicted with Texas fever or liable to transmit the disease, it was authorized to declare them a public nuisance and order them to leave the state by the same route over which they had entered it. If the owner failed to comply with this demand, the president of the board was to issue a writ to a sheriff or constable, who, with the aid of citizens summoned for the purpose, was to kill the cattle or drive them "out of the county." The secretary of state was directed to transmit a copy of the act to the governor of Texas and to the chiefs of the Indian tribes living beyond the southwestern border of Missouri.[72] This statute, although not immediately applicable because of the outbreak of the Civil war, became of great importance at the close of the conflict.

During the fifties cattle from Texas and the Indian Territory were also driven into or through Kansas, both before and after it was organized as a territory. Instead of entering southwest Missouri, they proceeded north along or near the military trail through Fort Scott to Fort Leavenworth. They used many other routes after 1854, when the territory was organized and began to be settled. Some were purchased

71 Missouri, *House Journal*, 21 Gen. Assem., 1 sess., pp. 349, 568, 612, 669; Missouri, *Senate Journal*, 21 Gen. Assem., 1 sess., p. 517; *Missouri Laws, 1860-1861*, pp. 25-28.

72 *Missouri Laws, 1860-1861*, pp. 25-28.

by newly arrived emigrants to help stock their ranches, others were disposed of to overland freighters or Santa Fé traders at Wyandotte, Leavenworth, Atchison, and other towns, and still others were sold to the United States army for beef or work oxen at Forts Leavenworth and Riley. But many Texas cattle were driven on through Kansas to Nebraska, Iowa, Illinois, or Minnesota, some of which proceeded through the eastern part of the territory in the late fifties to avoid the irate Missouri farmers. The stock that crossed the Missouri river usually ferried or forded it at St. Joseph, Missouri, White Cloud, Kansas, or other towns to the north and west.[73]

In 1858 and afterward Texas fever broke out in Kansas. The immediate result was the passage of an act by the territorial legislature, February 1, 1859, which stipulated that no person would be permitted to drive any cattle infected with this disease into or through Kansas. Identical in practically every respect with the Missouri law of 1855, from which it was undoubtedly copied, it contained an additional section prohibiting Texas, Arkansas, and Indian stock from entering the counties of Bourbon, Linn, Lykins (the present Miami), and Johnson between June 1 and November 1.[74] This act was openly violated during 1859 and 1860, with the result that thousands of Kansas cattle died of Texas fever. Angry farmers in Linn, Bourbon, Leavenworth, Allen, and other counties organized themselves into companies with the ostensible purpose of enforcing the Kansas statute. However, they passed resolutions which went beyond the provisions of the act, declaring that they would resist the passage of all droves of Texas cattle through their townships between April 1 and November 1, "peaceably if we can, forcibly if we must." As a result some longhorns were shot down, and bloody encounters between Kansas farmers armed with rifles and Texas drovers armed

[73] *Galveston Weekly News*, May 25, June 1, 1858; *Dallas Herald*, Apr. 11, 1860; *Lawrence Republican* (Lawrence, Kan.), June 30, 1859, May 24, July 12, 19, 1860, Jan. 31, 1861; *Fort Scott Democrat* (Fort Scott, Kan.), Aug. 4, 1859, Aug. 11, 1860; *Report of the Commissioner of Agriculture, 1885*, p. 539; *Historical and Biographical Record of the Cattle Industry*, 391.
[74] *General Laws of the Territory of Kansas, 1859*, pp. 621-622.

with revolvers were narrowly averted.[75] On May 1, 1861, the legislature passed another act making it illegal to drive Texas, Arkansas, or Indian cattle into any part of Kansas between April 1 and November 1, but the Civil war broke out before its effectiveness could be tested.[76]

Many Texas and Indian cattle which passed through Arkansas, Kansas, Nebraska, Missouri, or Iowa were destined for Illinois, where they were fed upon the prairies before being sent to market. As early as the summer of 1852, Joseph Mallory, of Piatt county, Illinois, brought a herd of Cherokee cattle into the state, where he fed them for almost a year and then sent them to New York.[77] T. C. Ponting, of Christian county, Illinois, and W. Malone, of Vermilion county, Indiana, purchased some longhorns in Fanning county, Texas, in April, 1853, drove them to Illinois in four months, and, after grazing them a year, sent them east to the New York market.[78] On July 16, 1854, a hundred head of Cherokee stock "of the large broad horned order" were driven through Springfield, Illinois, on their way to the pasture lands northwest of Bloomington in the same state.[79] Thirteen days later a drove of about eleven hundred Texas cattle, "with very little Spanish blood in them," were brought to Springfield by William Renick, who had purchased them in northern Texas the previous spring. He placed them on sale, claiming that they were "in fine order and well broke." Whether he disposed of any in Springfield has not been ascertained, but it is known that he sold some in Chicago during the same year and others in New York City during the spring of 1855.[80] On September 11, 1854, Cecil & Brown inserted an advertisement in the *Daily Quincy Whig* offering to sell six hundred Texas cattle at Douglasville, Illinois, opposite Hannibal, Missouri. The

[75] *Fort Scott Democrat*, July 28, Aug. 4, 1859, Jan. 5, 19, Feb. 2, 16, Sept. 29, 1860; *Liberty Weekly Tribune*, July 15, 1859; *Lawrence Republican*, May 24, July 19, 1860.

[76] *General Laws of Kansas, 1861*, pp. 279-281.

[77] *New York Semi-Weekly Tribune* (New York City), July 12, 1853.

[78] *New York Daily Tribune*, July 4, 1854.

[79] *Illinois Daily Journal*, July 17, 1854.

[80] *Ibid.*, July 28, 1854; *New York Daily Tribune*, Apr. 19, 1855; Renick, *Memoirs*, 24-25.

first longhorns to reach Chicago appear to have arrived late in September or early in October, 1854. They were a drove of six hundred which had started from Texas the previous April. "They are described as very fine looking cattle," asserted a Chicago newspaper, "and remarkable for their sleek appearance and very long horns. The prices at which they sold, however, would argue no superiority in point of fact to those raised upon our own prairies." [81] They were disposed of at the Bull's Head Stockyards, Madison street and Ashland avenue, the purchase price ranging from $2.50 to $2.75 a hundred pounds.[82] Some of the Texas cattle driven to Illinois during 1854 were not marketed in Chicago until the following year, when, as a result of a longer period of feeding, they fetched higher prices.[83]

Cattle from Texas and the Indian Territory continued to arrive in Illinois until the beginning of the Civil war. They crossed the Mississippi river at Clinton, Iowa, Quincy, Illinois, Hannibal or St. Louis, Missouri, and at other towns in Iowa, Missouri, and Illinois. They were usually fed upon the Illinois prairies from a few months to a year before they were ready for sale, but a number were immediately driven or shipped by rail from the Mississippi to Chicago. Being the principal packing center, the latter city was the main market for Texas beeves; however, Quincy and Springfield packed a limited quantity. The cattle were disposed of in the Chicago market at prices ranging from $25 to $66 a head, depending upon their weight and condition. Some of them were driven and shipped to the eastern cities.[84] No accurate figures can be given concerning the number driven

81 *Daily Democratic Press* (Chicago, Ill.), Oct. 11, 1854. See also *ibid.*, Oct. 4, 1854.

82 *Ibid.*, Oct. 11, 1854; Rudolf Alexander Clemen, *The American Livestock and Meat Industry* (New York, 1923), 83-84.

83 *Daily Democratic Press,* May 23, 1855.

84 *Ibid.*, Sept. 10, 12, 1855, Jan. 1, 1856; *Chicago Daily Journal,* May 20, 1857; *Chicago Daily Press and Tribune,* July 27, Aug. 10, Sept. 13, 24, 29, Oct. 6, Nov. 2, 1858, Jan. 1, 1859; *Daily Illinois State Journal,* Oct. 27, Nov. 9, 1855; *Daily Quincy Whig,* Oct. 30, Nov. 10, 1855; *Hannibal Tri-Weekly Messenger,* Sept. 27, 1855, July 10, Nov. 9, 1858; *Galveston Weekly News,* June 10, 1856, May 19, 1857; *Daily Missouri Democrat* (St. Louis, Mo.), Aug. 22, 1857; Cole, *op. cit.,* 83; Dale, *op. cit.,* 26.

into or through Illinois during this period. In September, 1855, a correspondent of a Chicago newspaper reported that on a recent visit to Lasalle he had been informed that "a gentleman resident there named McCoy, formerly of Kenosha, with three or four other persons in that neighborhood, is concerned in driving cattle from Texas and Mexico, and that they now have 20,000 on the way, which will probably arrive within the next two or three weeks." [85] This number may have been an exaggeration, but it seems clear that thousands of Texas and Indian cattle were driven into or through the state during the later fifties. John T. Alexander, a large stock dealer near Jacksonville, engaged in the business of feeding longhorns for sale, and beginning about 1856 drove them to Logansport, Indiana, whence they were shipped by rail and lake steamer to the live stock markets of the East. [86]

Texas and Indian cattle reached New York City at an early date. The first of the latter type — seventy-four Cherokee longhorns — arrived during the second week of July, 1853. They were part of the herd which Joseph Mallory had brought to Illinois the year previous and which he had later sold to Seymour G. Renick, of Darby creek, Ohio. Grazed in Illinois until the middle of June, 1853, they were driven to Laporte, Indiana, whence Renick shipped them by rail to Toledo, Ohio, thence by boat over Lake Erie to Buffalo, New York, and thence by rail to Albany and New York City. There he sold them at from $65 to $78 each. [87] Commenting on their appearance, the *New York Tribune* stated: "They all bear their original owner's brand, some of the figures of which may belong to the Cherokee alphabet — certainly they do not to ours. These cattle are rather coarse, many have the long horns peculiar to the 'Spanish Cattle,' once a very fine breed in Louisiana and Texas. All

---

85 *Daily Democratic Press*, Sept. 10, 1855.

86 *Daily Inter-Ocean* (Chicago, Ill.), Aug. 25, 1876; Frederic L. Paxson, "The Cow Country," *American Historical Review*, XXII, 67; Logan Esarey, *A History of Indiana from 1850 to the Present* (Indianapolis, 1918), 730-731. Professor Paxson states inaccurately that Alexander "had driven Texas cattle to Logansport, Ind., about 1848."

87 *New York Semi-Weekly Tribune*, July 12, 1853; *Daily Missouri Republican*, Aug. 2, 1853.

of them show at a glance that they come from among the 'outside barbarians' somewhere." [88] The first Texas long-horns reached New York City on or shortly before July 3, 1854; they were part of the herd which Ponting and Malone had driven from Fanning county, Texas, to Illinois the year before.[89] In the summer of 1854 they were driven to Marion, Indiana, whence they were shipped by rail to Cleveland, Ohio, Erie, Pennsylvania, and Dunkirk, New York, coming from the latter place to New York City over the Erie Railroad. They had traveled 1500 miles on foot and 600 by rail. The expense of driving them from Texas to Illinois was $2 a head, whereas the cost of driving and shipping them from Illinois to New York City was $17 each. A number were sold for $80 apiece at Allerton's Washington Drove Yards, Fourth avenue and Forty-fourth street.[90] The *New York Tribune* observed: "These cattle are generally 5, 6 and 7 years old, rather long-legged, though fine horned, with long taper horns, and something of a wild look. . . It is said that the meat of this description of stock is fine-grained and close, somewhat like venison, and apt to be a little tough cooked in the ordinary way, and therefore not as good to eat fresh as that of cattle of a more domestic character. This will be somewhat changed by purchasing them young and feeding them two years as well as this drove has been fed for one year." [91]

Longhorns from Texas and the Cherokee Nation continued to reach Allerton's Washington Drove Yards in New York City from 1855 to 1860. Most of them had been fed one or two years on the prairies of Illinois. A good shipping route was from Chicago to Detroit over the Michigan Central Railroad, thence to Suspension Bridge over the Great Western, and thence to Albany and New York City over the New York Central. Some Texas cattle were driven overland all the way. Although longhorns commanded fairly sub-

---

[88] *New York Semi-Weekly Tribune,* July 12, 1853.

[89] *New York Daily Tribune,* July 4, 1854; *New York Herald,* July 4, 1854; *New York Daily Times,* July 4, 1854. Clemen erroneously asserts that "in 1850 a few Texas cattle were sold in New York." Clemen, *op. cit.,* 174; *Prairie Farmer,* xv, 248.

[90] *New York Daily Tribune,* July 4, 1854.

[91] *Ibid.*

stantial prices in New York City, they were never shipped
there in large numbers, principally because they were not in
great demand for beef.[92] In 1855 about 750 head reached
Allerton's; from 1856 to 1859 probably 1000 to 2000 a
year; and in 1860, only 99.[93] The city newspapers made
occasional comments on their appearance and quality. On
July 31, 1856, the *New York Daily Times* observed: "These
would about balance, if suspended by the neck, as the horns
were nearly large enough to 'equipoise' the rest of the animal." On August 19, 1858, the same journal asserted:
"These were barely able to cast a shadow, and according to
the opinion of the sellers would not weigh anything, were
it not for their horns, which were useful also in preventing
them from crawling through the fences." A week later the
Times remarked: "Among these were 140 from Texas,
said to have been grazed in Illinois, but it must have been
by the roadside, as they came along, for their appearance
indicated that they had tasted very little even of prairie
grass, as any other fat-producing material."

A few cattle were also driven north from Texas to the
Pike's Peak region just before the Civil war. Beeves and
work oxen were taken to the South Platte mines during the
gold rush of 1858 and 1859, but they were mostly shorthorns from Kansas, Missouri, Iowa, and Illinois. An establishment known as the "Texas Ranch" had been located
about thirty-five miles south of Denver by February, 1860;[94]
whether it had any relationship to cattle driving from Texas
has not been determined. Among the first – if not the first –
longhorns to reach Colorado directly from Texas were those
which arrived during the latter part of 1860. On August
29 of that year Oliver Loving, John Dawson, Sylvester
Reed, and J. W. Curtis started a herd from northern Texas,
crossed the Red river into Indian Territory, struck the
Santa Fé trail some distance east of the present Great Bend,

92 *New York Daily Times*, July 3, 31, Aug. 21, 28, Sept. 11, Oct. 2, 9, 16,
30, Dec. 4, 1856, Aug. 5, 19, 26, Sept. 2, 9, 16, 23, 1858, Aug. 4, 25, 1859; *New
York Herald*, June 28, 1855; *New York Daily Tribune*, Apr. 19, 1855; *Daily
Illinois State Journal*, Aug. 5, Sept. 23, 1856, Sept. 15, 1857; Cordova,
Texas, 54; *Prairie Farmer*, xv, 248.
93 *New York Times*, Dec. 27, 1860; *Daily Democratic Press*, Jan. 8, 1856.
94 *Rocky Mountain News* (Denver, Colo.), Feb. 29, 1860.

Kansas, followed that route west to Pueblo, and spent the winter a few miles west of the latter place.[95] During the following spring Loving went north to Denver and sold some of the cattle to miners and speculators. After having been forcibly detained there during the early part of the Civil war, he left his companions and traveled by stage to St. Joseph, Missouri, finally reaching his home in Texas on August 9, 1861.[96]

The next period in the history of the Texas cattle drives extends from 1861 to 1865 – the era of the Civil war. During that time most of the markets that had been opened in the previous decade were closed. On April 19, 1861, President Lincoln declared a blockade of the coasts of Texas, Louisiana, Mississippi, Alabama, and other southern states, and on August 16 of the same year prohibited all commercial intercourse with the seceding commonwealths.[97] One of the results of these proclamations was the termination of stock exportation from Texas ports, as well as the cessation of all drives to California, Colorado, and most of the northern states. A small amount of illegal traffic in Texas and Indian cattle was done with Kansas during the war. Besides, longhorns were driven from Texas to supply both the Confederate and Union armies in the South.

The largest outlet for Texas cattle during the war was in the southern states. In 1861, after the federal blockade in the Gulf of Mexico began to take effect, Texas stockmen drove their herds overland to New Orleans and other parts of the South, disposing of them to the civilian population or to the Confederate soldiers. This movement continued unabated until the spring of 1862, when the capture of New Orleans by Farragut caused it to decline.[98] But, tempted by high prices, Texas ranchmen persisted in bringing some stock to New Orleans, where they were sold for "federal

---

[95] Dawson may have driven Texas cattle to Denver over the same route in 1859. *Tenth Census of the United States*, III (*Agriculture*), 974.

[96] *Ibid.; Historical and Biographical Record of the Cattle Industry*, 306; J. Evetts Haley, *Charles Goodnight* (Boston and New York, 1936), 20-21.

[97] James D. Richardson, *A Compilation of the Messages and Papers of the Presidents*, VI, 14-15, 37-38.

[98] *Historical and Biographical Record of the Cattle Industry*, 57; *Prose and Poetry of the Live Stock Industry*, I, 394.

gold." The Houston *Tri-Weekly Telegraph* vigorously objected to this traffic with the Yankees: "This thing must be stopped. Will the people, particularly the Provost Marshals of the various counties attend to these speculators? Let not a hoof of these cattle now on the road, ever pass out of the State, except in charge of men of known patriotism and integrity who will take them to Corinth. Being destined for New Orleans, they are subject to confiscation. Let them be confiscated at once." [99] However, longhorns continued to be brought to New Orleans during the rest of the conflict, and in June, 1864, were selling at from $40 to $60 a head.[100] Texas beeves in limited numbers also helped to supply the Confederate armies throughout the war. On October 11, 1862, a statute of the Confederate congress exempted from the draft a certain number of individuals engaged exclusively in raising stock – "one male citizen for every five hundred head of cattle." [101] Late in the following February, George W. White, Confederate commissary agent for Texas, issued a circular to the cattlemen of the state in which he asserted that the soldiers "must have a large portion of the beef cattle of Texas." He declared that he was authorized by the Secretary of War and the Commissary General to impress the required number of cattle, and that he would pay "$25 per head for cattle 4 years old and upward, where the owner or agent gathers them; or $22 per head where the owner or agent refuses to gather, and the same has to be collected at the expense of the Government." [102] The stock thus obtained were driven through Louisiana or southern Arkansas, crossed the Mississippi river, and were then hurried east to the Confederate forces. But the increasing vigilance of the federal gunboats on the Mississippi and the

---

99 *Tri-Weekly Telegraph* (Houston), June 18, 1862.

100 *New Orleans Times,* June 12, 1864.

101 *The War of the Rebellion: A Compilation of the Official Records of the Union and Confederate Armies,* ser. IV, vol. II, pp. 160-162 (hereafter cited as *Official Records of the Rebellion*); Albert Burton Moore, *Conscription and Conflict in the Confederacy* (New York, 1924), 67-68. "The exemption of stock-raisers from serving in our armies should have been sooner acted upon," asserted one Texas periodical. *Texas Almanac—Extra,* Nov. 15, 1862.

102 *Tri-Weekly Telegraph* (Houston), Feb. 27, 1863.

difficulty of swimming or ferrying the cattle across the river made this traffic more and more hazardous.[103]

Some longhorns were driven from northern Texas and the Indian Territory to Kansas between 1862 and 1865. On account of the unsettled conditions in the former regions during the Civil war, many residents of Kansas engaged in the business of stealing cattle from the Cherokee, Creek, Choctaw, Seminole, and Chickasaw Indians, as well as from the rebels in northern Texas, and driving them north to sell at a profit. Among them were prominent citizens, federal soldiers, provost marshals, Indian agents, traders, and others, who usually employed lawless whites, negroes, and Kickapoo, Shawnee, Delaware, and other Indians to do the pilfering for them.[104] One of those who was actively engaged in this nefarious traffic was the mayor of Leavenworth, who found it an easy way to supplement his meager salary.[105] Emporia and other towns in southern Kansas profited considerably from this business.[106] However, on August 9, 1864, the citizens of Morris county held a meeting in Council Grove at which resolutions were adopted condemning the trade, declaring it a violation of the Kansas statute of May 1, 1861, and calling upon the state and federal authorities to suppress it.[107] Kansas responded with an act on February 11, 1865, which prohibited any person except immigrants from driving cattle out of Texas and the Indian Territory into or through any county in the state.[108] On the following March 3 the United States Congress passed a law making

[103] *Prose and Poetry of the Live Stock Industry*, I, 394; *Historical and Biographical Record of the Cattle Industry*, 306; *The Trail Drivers of Texas* (J. Marvin Hunter, ed., Nashville, 1925), 96, 267-269, 571, 633, 723-724, 741.

[104] *House Ex. Docs.*, 38 cong., 2 sess., no. 1, pp. 449-450, 456, 464; *ibid.*, 39 cong., 1 sess., no. 1, pp. 200-201, 436-437, 446-447, 449-450, 455-456, 470-471, 473; *Official Records of the Rebellion*, ser. 1, vol. xxxiv, pt. 3, p. 598; *Kansas Tribune* (Lawrence), Mar. 11, 1865; *Smoky Hill and Republican Union* (Junction City, Kan.), July 9, Aug. 20, 1864; *Leavenworth Daily Conservative* (Leavenworth, Kan.), Nov. 8, 27, 1864; Annie Heloise Abel, *The American Indian under Reconstruction* (Cleveland, 1925), 73-97.

[105] *Leavenworth Daily Conservative*, Nov. 8, 27, 30, 1864.

[106] *Smoky Hill and Republican Union*, July 9, 1864.

[107] *Ibid.*, Aug. 20, 1864.

[108] *Kansas Laws, 1865*, pp. 159-160.

cattle stealing a felony punishable by a heavy fine or impris-
onment or both.[109] In the same year Lieutenant Williams,
who had made an investigation in compliance with instructions from the War Department, reported that in his opinion
at least three hundred thousand cattle had been stolen from
the Indian Territory since 1862.[110]

The period of the Civil war was a disastrous one for most
Texas cattlemen. During the first two years many of them
enlisted in or were drafted into the Confederate army,
leaving their ranches in charge of women and children. Only
a limited number of stock found a market. Besides, a number of severe drouths swept through the ranch country, resulting in the death of thousands of longhorns from thirst
or disease. Prices of cattle fell to a low level, ranging from
$1 to $2 a head; and even at such low figures there were
few purchasers. Some drovers took herds across the Río
Grande into Mexico but without much success.[111] "Then
dawned a time in Texas," wrote McCoy, "that a man's
poverty was estimated by the number of cattle he possessed."
Conditions such as these made possible the great cattle
drives after the Civil war.

The final period of the Texas cattle drives extends from
1866 until the latter part of the century. These years, as is
well known, were the heyday of the long drive. High prices
of beef in the North, the construction of railroads across
the Great Plains, and the demand for cattle to stock the
newly established ranches of the northern prairies were the
principal causes for the marked increase in this business.
Hundreds of thousands of longhorns annually passed over
the trails to the North and West. Indeed the traffic assumed
such proportions that it attracted the attention of the whole
country and even of foreign countries.

In 1866 the driving and shipping of stock out of Texas
was resumed with renewed vigor. The routes used were primarily those that had been blazed before the Civil war or
that were variations or extensions of these routes. The

109 United States, *Statutes at Large*, XIII, 563; Abel, *op. cit.*, 92-93.

110 *House Ex. Docs.*, 39 cong., 1 sess., no. 1, p. 201.

111 *Prose and Poetry of the Live Stock Industry*, I, 395, 527-528; *Historical and Biographical Record of the Cattle Industry*, 57, 330.

principal exception was the Goodnight-Loving trail, opened by Charles Goodnight and Oliver Loving, which extended southwest from Fort Belknap, Texas, to the Horsehead crossing of the Pecos river, thence northwest and north along that river to Fort Sumner, New Mexico, and thence northwest to Denver, Colorado.[112] But the main trail to the northern states, over which most of the cattle were driven out of Texas, crossed the Red river at Preston, Texas, and then proceeded by way of Boggy Depot and Fort Gibson to the northeastern corner of Indian Territory or into southwestern Missouri.[113] Beyond the latter districts the drovers found their progress halted or greatly impeded. Although Kansas, on February 16, 1866, had repealed its statute of February 11, 1865,[114] the law of May 1, 1861, still remained in effect, stipulating that no Texas, Arkansas, or Indian cattle could be driven into any part of the state between April 1 and November 1.[115] In western Missouri many county courts had appointed boards of cattle inspectors for the various townships in accordance with the law of March 27, 1861, which authorized these bodies to order all longhorns out of the state that were afflicted with Texas fever or liable to transmit the disease. Moreover, a few bands of Jayhawkers and lawless whites, survivals of the Civil war period and before, roamed through western Missouri and

[112] *Daily Herald* (San Antonio, Tex.), Aug. 28, 1866; Haley, *Charles Goodnight*, 121-140, 209.

[113] *Dallas Herald*, Apr. 28, 1866; George C. Duffield, "Driving Cattle from Texas to Iowa, 1866" (W. W. Baldwin, ed.), *Annals of Iowa*, third series, vol. XIV, pp. 246-256; *Trail Drivers of Texas* (Hunter, ed.), 114, 696-699. During 1866 a number of Texas cattle were driven to shipping points on the Red river, transported down that stream by boat to the Mississippi, and thence north to Cairo, Illinois, or St. Louis. *Daily Missouri Republican*, July 20, 1866; Dale, *op. cit.*, 54.

[114] *Kansas Laws, 1866*, p. 248.

[115] However, early in October, 1866, the following item appeared in a Kansas newspaper: "We see from our exchanges that Judge Watson has decided that the law of 1861, prohibiting the driving of cattle through the State from the country south of us at certain seasons of the year was repealed by implication by a law of 1865, and that the law of 1865 having been repealed by a law of 1866, there is now no law on the subject." *Leavenworth Daily Conservative*, Oct. 6, 1866. John H. Watson was a judge of the district court of the state of Kansas.

eastern Kansas, molesting the southern drovers or stealing their herds under the guise of preventing the introduction of Texas fever.[116]

Confronted with these and other obstacles, the drovers pursued different courses. A number decided to proceed into Kansas or Missouri, despite the legislation and prejudice against them. Many who entered the latter state were anxious to reach Sedalia, whence they might ship their stock to St. Louis over the Pacific Railroad. However, due to the vigilance of the cattle inspectors, who turned back the drovers whether they possessed diseased longhorns or not, they were unable to reach their objective, and were either forced south into the Indian Territory or compelled to travel poor and little-used roads in Missouri. One of the latter routes extended east along or near the southern boun-dary of the state, through a remote and mountainous region, and then turned north to some point on the Pacific Railroad east of Sedalia, whence the stock were shipped to St. Louis and Chicago. A number of cattlemen brought their herds all the way to St. Louis on foot.[117] The drovers who entered Kansas either sold their longhorns surreptitiously at Baxter Springs, Fort Scott, and other places in the eastern part of the state,[118] or trailed them west of the settlements and thence east into Missouri, Nebraska, or Iowa. Those who chose the latter course traveled west along or south of the southern boundary of Kansas until they reached a point close to the Arkansas river, thence north to the Santa Fé trail at or near Lost Spring, thence east over the trail through Diamond Spring and Council Grove, and thence north to the Kansas river, crossing it at St. Mary's. There the trail forked, one part proceeding east to Elwood, and the other north through the towns of America and Seneca, and thence

[116] Border Sentinel, Feb. 1, 1867; Independent Press (Sedalia, Mo.), Nov. 15, 1866; Trail Drivers of Texas (Hunter, ed.), 590-591, 696-699; History of Vernon County, Missouri (St. Louis, 1887), 347.

[117] Tenth Census of the United States, III (Agriculture), 975; Daily Missouri Republican, July 17, 28, Aug. 1, 2, 3, 6, 13, 18, Sept. 11, 1866; Independent Press, Nov. 15, 1866; History of Vernon County, Missouri, 347.

[118] Olathe Mirror (Olathe, Kan.), Aug. 9, 1866; Powell, op. cit., 121; Trail Drivers of Texas (Hunter, ed.), 696-699; Historical and Biographical Record of the Cattle Industry, 352-353.

northeast to Brownville or Nebraska City, Nebraska. The drovers who reached Elwood ferried the Missouri river to St. Joseph, Missouri, whence they shipped their stock over the Hannibal and St. Joseph Railroad to Hannibal, Missouri, and thence over the Chicago, Burlington, and Quincy Railroad to Quincy and Chicago. Those who crossed the Missouri river at Brownville or Nebraska City trailed their herds into Iowa and either sold them to farmers or shipped them from Ottumwa or other towns over the Chicago, Burlington, and Quincy to Burlington and Chicago.[119]

Many drovers, instead of taking their cattle immediately into or through Missouri or Kansas, decided to herd them on the Cherokee Strip or on the unsettled lands in southwestern Missouri until November 1, when they could begin to enter Kansas legally. On July 9, 1866, a newspaper correspondent at Fort Scott estimated that between 80,000 and 100,000 cattle were then grazing on the Cherokee Strip alone.[120] Starting on November 1, these drovers proceeded into Kansas or Missouri, following, in a general way, the trails used by those who had entered earlier in the year. But the season was so far advanced that many of the longhorns never reached a market in 1866, and if they did, they arrived in an emaciated condition and were sold at low prices. Some cattlemen, in despair, wintered their stock in central Illinois, southwestern Missouri, southern Kansas, or the Cherokee Strip, and sent them to market early in 1867.[121]

The number of longhorns driven from Texas to the northern states in 1866 has usually been estimated at 260,000 head. In an article penned at Abilene on September 24,

[119] *Daily Morning Herald* (St. Joseph, Mo.), Sept. 7, 11, 16, Oct. 13, 1866; *Daily Missouri Republican*, Dec. 9, 17, 1866; *Daily Quincy Herald*, Aug. 28, Sept. 14, 20, 25, Nov. 17, 1866; *Daily Illinois State Journal*, Sept. 5, 6, 8, 12, 26, 1866; *Chicago Tribune*, Oct. 12, 17, Nov. 3, 1866; Duffield, *loc. cit.*, 256-262; *Trail Drivers of Texas* (Hunter, ed.), 114; Pelzer, *op. cit.*, 38-40; Frank S. Popplewell, "St. Joseph, Missouri, as a Center of the Cattle Trade," *Missouri Historical Review*, XXXII, 447-448.

[120] *Leavenworth Daily Conservative*, Aug. 11, 1866; *Independent Press*, Nov. 15, 1866; *Border Sentinel*, Feb. 1, 1867; *Daily Missouri Republican*, July 17, 1866; *Trail Drivers of Texas* (Hunter, ed.), 590-591.

[121] *Daily Missouri Republican*, Dec. 9, 12, 24, 27, 1866, Apr. 1, 5, 13, 27, 29, 1867; *Daily Illinois State Journal*, Dec. 8, 1866; *Daily Quincy Whig*, Dec. 6, 1866; Dale, *op. cit.*, 53.

1867, a correspondent of the *New York Daily Tribune*, who had just questioned McCoy about the Texas cattle drives, asserted that "about 250,000 head crossed the Red River, destined for Northern and Eastern States" in 1866.[122] Writing from Newton, Kansas, in August, 1871, another newspaper correspondent, who had recently interviewed McCoy there, stated: "In 1866 attempts were made to drive two hundred and sixty thousand head of Texas cattle through southern Kansas and southwestern Missouri to eastern markets." [123] McCoy, in his own book, published three years afterward, asserted: "We have heard the number of cattle that had crossed the Red river in 1866 put down as high as 260,000 head." The United States Census of 1880, which employed McCoy as a "special investigator as to the drives into Kansas," stated that 260,000 longhorns started for Sedalia, Missouri, during 1866.[124] In 1885, Joseph Nimmo, chief of the bureau of statistics of the Treasury Department, gave the same figures, which he obtained from the annual report of the board of trade of Kansas City, Missouri; but the latter probably derived its information about the drive in 1866 from the census lists.[125] McCoy, therefore, seems to have been directly or indirectly responsible for the accepted estimate of 260,000. However, a resident of Belton, Texas, in February, 1867, asserted: "From the best data I have, not less than 200,000 head of stock and beef cattle were driven out of Texas" [in 1866]. This figure, which was practically contemporary, included the longhorns trailed out of Texas in all directions.[126]

One of the results of the drive of 1866 was the outbreak of Texas fever in Missouri, Kansas, Nebraska, Colorado, Kentucky, Tennessee, and Illinois.[127] Farmers in those states claimed that most of the longhorns themselves were healthy but in some way spread the fatal disease among the native

---

122 *New York Daily Tribune*, Nov. 6, 1867.

123 *Kansas Daily Commonwealth* (Topeka), Aug. 15, 1871.

124 *Tenth Census of the United States*, III (*Agriculture*), 955, 975.

125 *House Ex. Docs.*, 48 cong., 2 sess., no. 267, p. 31.

126 *Daily Herald* (San Antonio), Mar. 3, 1867.

127 *Report of the Commissioner of Agriculture for the Year 1866*, pp. 73-75; *General Laws and Private Acts of the Territory of Colorado, 1866-1867*, pp. 86-87; *Nebraska Laws, 1867*, p. 74; *Daily Missouri Republican*, Sept. 13, 1866.

cattle. A major cause for opposition to the drives in 1866, as in previous years, was the recurrence of this epidemic. One newspaper asserted: "We should keep out the Texas cattle on the same principle that we would the small pox or the cholera. They are pestilential." [128] A physician and farmer of Nevada, Vernon county, Missouri, suggested that the legislature either enact a law to exclude all longhorns or buy a right of way from the state's southern and western boundaries to the Pacific Railroad, over which Texas cattle might be driven at all times.[129] Additional suggestions were made in other states, most of them urging the legislatures to take action to exclude the longhorns. As a result of this agitation, between January and June, 1867, Missouri, Kansas, Nebraska, Kentucky, Colorado, and Illinois passed laws prohibiting or restricting the trailing of Texas cattle across their boundaries.[130] The Kansas statute of February 26, 1867, is of special significance. It repealed certain sections of the law of 1861 and stipulated that no person should drive Texas or Indian cattle into the state between March 1 and December 1, except into that part of southwestern Kansas which lay west of the sixth principal meridian and south of township 18 — a region corresponding roughly to the district south and west of the present city of McPherson.[131] However, any individual or company who gave a bond for $10,000 to guarantee the payment of all damages to native stock might select a route from any place in southwestern Kansas, west of the sixth principal meridian and south of township 18,[132] to some point on the Union Pacific Railroad, Eastern Division, north of township 19

---

[128] *Border Sentinel*, Feb. 1, 1867.

[129] *Ibid.*

[130] *Missouri Laws, 1867*, pp. 128-130; *Kansas Laws, 1867*, pp. 263-267; *Nebraska Laws, 1867*, p. 74; *General Laws and Private Acts of the Territory of Colorado, 1866-1867*, pp. 86-87; *Kentucky Acts, Adjourned Session, 1867*, I, 53-54; *Public Laws of Illinois, 1867*, p. 169; Osgood, *op. cit.*, 36.

[131] The sixth principal meridian runs about sixteen miles east of McPherson; the southern boundary of township 18 is about four miles north of the city.

[132] The sixth principal meridian crosses the southern boundary of the state about two and a half miles east of the present town of Hunnewell, Sumner county.

and "west of the first guide meridian west from the sixth principal meridian," [133] over which he might drive Texas cattle at any season of the year. The only restrictions were that the route was not to be located within five miles of any settler without his consent in writing, that the longhorns were not to be driven or fed along a public highway, and that they were to be transported from the shipping point on the railroad to some destination outside of the state.[134]

The difficulties encountered by the Texas drover in 1866 and the legislation of certain northern states and territories early in the following year made the outlook for a successful drive in 1867 very dark indeed. The only ray of light was the provision in the Kansas law of February 26, 1867, which authorized any individual or company, upon certain conditions, to drive Texas cattle to some point on the Union Pacific Railroad, Eastern Division, west of "the first guide meridian west from the sixth principal meridian." At this juncture McCoy, taking advantage of the statute, made plans to locate a shipping point on the railroad to which longhorns might be driven without molestation and from which they could be transported to the eastern live stock markets.

But McCoy was not the first person to conceive the idea of establishing such a shipping point. As early as March 9, 1867, a firm in Topeka, Kansas, known as the "Kansas Live Stock Company," issued a circular, signed by Chester Thomas, president, and W. W. H. Lawrence, secretary, informing stockmen that as a result of the passage of the law of February 26, 1867, cattle could "be driven into Kansas without being subjected to the annoying difficulties that dealers in Southern and Texas cattle were subjected to last year." The company claimed that it was laying out a route in Kansas west of the point where the sixth principal meridian intersected the southern boundary of the state, over

---

[133] The first guide meridian west from the sixth principal meridian runs about a mile west of the present city of Ellsworth; the northern boundary of township 19 is about twenty-one miles south of the city. Ellsworth was founded during the spring of 1867, several months after the passage of this act. The Union Pacific Railroad, Eastern Division, was opened for business to Ellsworth about July 1, 1867.

[134] *Kansas Laws, 1867,* pp. 263-267.

which longhorns might pass without hindrance. By the time drovers reached the southern limits of Kansas, agents of the firm would meet them and conduct them to a depot on the Union Pacific Railroad, Eastern Division, the name of which was not disclosed. The company agreed to purchase, on its own account, 50,000 head of cattle for packing in the fall, as well as 5000 work oxen, provided it could obtain them by June 1. Besides, it promised to sell all grades of stock placed in its hands for disposal. The firm asserted that it was erecting corrals and shipping yards on the railroad – again not specifying the place. It urged cattlemen to drive their stock slowly, so as to get them into Kansas in a healthy condition. It advised all drovers, after crossing the Red river into Indian Territory, to take a direct route to "Forts Arbuckle, Holmes, and from thence a due northerly course to the southern boundary of Kansas." The company claimed to be capitalized at $100,000.[135]

This circular, which was distributed through the mails and published in Texas newspapers, induced some drovers to start out on the trail indicated. The first herd reached Fort Arbuckle by July, 1867.[136] But a number of cattlemen, lacking confidence in the company's promises and fearing Indian depredations along the new route, turned east to the old trail from Preston to Fort Gibson, hoping to market their longhorns at Baxter Springs, Kansas. Writing from Boggy Depot, Indian Territory, on June 2, 1867, one of these drovers asserted: "The only market that Texans can rely on at present for their stock is Bakster Springs, Kansas, unless there can be a route opened from Fort Gibson to the 6th principal meridian as designated by the circular from the Kansas Live Stock Company, thence north to some point on the Pacific Railroad. This, I fear, will not be a success this year. . . I fear there are many like myself who have listened too much to the flattering reports of Kansas sharpers, whose whole soul and principle is constructed of greenbacks, and are prompted by no other motives." [137]

---

[135] *Daily Herald* (San Antonio), May 17, 1867.

[136] *Ibid.*, June 28, 1867; *Wichita Daily Eagle*, Mar. 1, 1890; *Prose and Poetry of the Live Stock Industry*, I, 285.

[137] *Daily Herald* (San Antonio), June 28, 1867.

This drover's lack of faith in the integrity of the "Kansas Live Stock Company" was entirely justified, for nothing further is heard of its activities. In the meantime, while the cattlemen were trailing their herds northward to an uncertain market, McCoy carried into execution plans that were practically identical with those projected by the abortive live stock firm. Sometime in 1866, in conversations with Charles F. Gross, of Springfield, Illinois, who had recently returned from an extended visit to Texas, he learned of the large number of cattle grazing on the prairies of that state and of the low prices at which they could be purchased.[138] During the early spring of 1867 he went on a business trip to Christian county, Illinois, where he bought some longhorns from W. W. Sugg, who had driven them from Texas the previous year. Sugg likewise told him of the large number of cattle in Texas, and in addition described the obstructions encountered by the drovers in southwestern Missouri and southeastern Kansas. Conversations with these two men, as well as information obtained from other sources, gave McCoy the idea of establishing "at some accessible point a depot or market to which a Texan drover could bring his stock unmolested, and there, failing to find a buyer, he could go upon the public highways to any market in the country he wished." This idea, he admitted in later years, became an obsession with him – "a waking thought, a sleeping dream." [139]

At first he thought of building a shipping yard on the Arkansas river near Fort Smith, Arkansas, and of transporting Texas cattle by boat to Cairo, Illinois, whence they could be sent by railroad to the pastures of that state. But before proceeding to carry out this plan, he made a journey to Kansas City, Missouri, where he made the acquaintance of Marsh & Coffy, a firm which was then engaged in trading goods for Texas and Indian cattle. After Marsh informed him that the Union Pacific Railroad, Eastern Division, had been constructed up the Kaw river as far west as Salina, McCoy began to think of the possibility of establishing a

138 *Abilene Weekly Reflector* (Abilene, Kan.), Apr. 30, 1925.

139 Joseph G. McCoy, "Historic and Biographic Sketch," *Kansas Magazine,* vol. ii, no. 6, p. 49.

shipping point on that railroad instead of near Fort Smith. Marsh gave him a letter of introduction to the freight agent at Wyandotte (the modern Kansas City), Kansas, to whom he presented his plan. That official received him cordially, gave him a pass to Salina and return, and encouraged him to find a suitable location on the railroad where cattle yards might be built. When the train reached Abilene, a small town on the road, it was delayed about an hour to await the repair of a bridge. During that time McCoy made inquiries of the few inhabitants and began to give serious consideration to this place as a possible location for a shipping point. He continued his journey to Salina and on his return stopped at Junction City, where he met J. J. Myers, a Texas cattle-man, who encouraged him to carry out his ideas.[140] He began to consider the vicinity of Junction City as a possible shipping point and made tentative plans to build cattle yards at Kansas Falls, six miles southwest of that place.[141] But this scheme did not materialize.

"Failing to obtain a location but fully decided to select the prairies of the West instead of the banks of the southern rivers," McCoy returned to Wyandotte and attempted to make an agreement with the freight agent, who, however, referred him to the president of the railroad in St. Louis. He immediately traveled to that city and interviewed the president, John D. Perry, and also members of the executive committee.[142] After about three days, during which he made a hurried trip to his home near Springfield, he was informed by Perry: "I do not believe that you can, to any extent, establish or build up a cattle trade on our road. It looks too visionary, too chimerical, too speculative, and it would be altogether too good a thing to ever happen to us, or to our road. . . But Mr. McCoy, if you think you can get cattle freighted over our road (it is just the thing we want), and are willing to risk your money in a stock yard and other necessary appendages, we will put in a switch and, if you succeed, I will pledge that you shall have full and fair recom-

---

140 *Ibid.*, pp. 49-50; Joseph G. McCoy, "How Abilene was Made in Early Days," *Dickinson County Clippings*, 174, K.S.H.S.

141 *Junction City Weekly Union* (Junction City, Kan.), June 8, 1867.

142 McCoy, "Historic and Biographic Sketch," *loc. cit.*, p. 50.

pense." [143] No written contract was drawn up between Mc-Coy and the railroad; only a verbal agreement was made. At the same time, or shortly afterward, Perry promised him about five dollars for each carload of cattle sent from his proposed stock depot to the eastern markets. [144] McCoy immediately proceeded to make a second visit to the West, and about the middle of June, 1867, selected Abilene as his shipping point. [145]

Abilene was barely six years old when McCoy chose it as a shipping point for Texas cattle. The first settler in the immediate vicinity of the later town site was Timothy Fletcher Hersey, of Jo Daviess county, Illinois, who, with a companion, located a farm along the west bank of Mud creek in July, 1857. About a hundred feet west of the creek Hersey built a log cabin, to which he brought his wife and two small children in March, 1858. [146] During the spring of 1860 or 1861, Charles H. Thompson, of Leavenworth, Kansas, purchased a tract of land east of Mud creek, and in the latter year decided to lay out a town on part of his property. [147] In May or early in June, 1861, Robert S. Miller, justice of the peace and deputy recorder of deeds, surveyed the village site, dividing it into blocks and lots; [148] he may have been aided in this work by Hersey. [149] It was located

---

[143] Joseph G. McCoy vs. the Kansas Pacific Railway Company, *Copy of the Record of the Judgment and Proceedings of the District Court for Davis County, Kansas, 1871*, p. 59, MS., Supreme Court of Kansas, Topeka (hereafter cited as McCoy vs. the Kansas Pacific Railway Company).

[144] Martin, Burns, and Case, *Brief of the Defendant in Error, Kansas Pacific Railway Company vs. Joseph G. McCoy, Supreme Court of Kansas*, 10 (hereafter cited as *Brief of the Defendant in Error, Kansas Pacific Railway Company vs. McCoy*).

[145] Dickinson County (Kan.), Deed Record A, 496, MS., Recorder of Deeds Office, Abilene; McCoy, "Historic and Biographic Sketch," *loc. cit.*, p. 52.

[146] *Jewell County Republican* (Jewell, Kan.), Oct. 7, 1904; Sylvia Hersey Barger, "Timothy F. Hersey," *Dickinson County Clippings*, III, Mrs. A. B. Seelye, Abilene; T. F. Hersey to H. L. Humphrey, 1904, *ibid.*

[147] *Abilene Chronicle*, Mar. 3, 1870; *History of the State of Kansas* (A. T. Andreas, Chicago, 1883), 685.

[148] Dickinson County, Deed Record A, 70-71, 96, MS., Recorder of Deeds Office, Abilene; Dickinson County, Plat Book A, 1, MS., *ibid.*

[149] In a letter written to John Beach Edwards, of Abilene, during 1904 or 1905, Hersey stated: "As a surveyor, I laid out the original Abilene town site." J. B. Edwards, "T. F. Hersey, First Settler of Abilene," *Dickinson*

on the north half of the northwest quarter of section 21, township 13, range 2 east of the sixth principal meridian. The blocks measured 295 by 400 feet, the lots 50 by 140 feet, and most of the streets were 80 feet wide. The plat of the town was filed in the office of the recorder of deeds on June 7, 1861.[150] At the suggestion of Findlay Patterson, of Pennsylvania, Thompson named the town "Abilene," after the tetrarchy of Abilene, a small kingdom between Palestine and Syria during the first century B.C. which was mentioned in the Bible.[151] The new settlement grew slowly. On February 1, 1862, Thompson, in an advertisement entitled "Ho! Ho! for the West," claimed that over a hundred lots had been sold and that the town consisted of "a store, blacksmith shop, hotel, Post Office, and several families." As an inducement to attract settlers, he offered to give two to five lots to anyone who located there and made improvements. He also promised to make liberal donations for churches, schools, and public improvements.[152] Later the town was selected as the permanent seat of Dickinson county.[153]

County Clippings, III, Mrs. A. B. Seelye, Abilene. However, the manuscript records of the recorder of deeds demonstrate that Robert S. Miller was the surveyor, although Hersey may have helped him. On November 8, 1861, when Thompson sold some of his lots in the town, they were described as being located "in the Town of Abilene according to the plat as surveyed by Robert S. Miller and Recorded in the office of Register of Deeds for the County of Dickinson . . . on the 7th day of June A.D. 1861." Dickinson County, Deed Record A, 96, MS., Recorder of Deeds Office, Abilene. As early as June 26, 1861, certain Abilene lots sold by Thompson were described "as shown upon the plat of said town as surveyed by Robert S. Miller and now on file in the Recorder's office of Dickinson County." *Ibid.,* 70-71.

[150] *Ibid.,* 96; Dickinson County, Plat Book A, 1, MS., Recorder of Deeds Office, Abilene.

[151] St. Luke, chapter III, verse 1. Mrs. Hersey is usually given the credit for naming the town, the main basis for this belief being a state history published in 1883. *History of the State of Kansas* (1883), 685. However, on March 3, 1870, when Charles H. Thompson was still residing in or near Abilene, the *Abilene Chronicle* declared: "The name of the village was suggested to Mr. Thompson by a Mr. Patterson, of Pennsylvania." In 1902 the Kansas State Historical Society, with H. R. Thompson as authority, stated that the name had been "suggested to C. H. Thompson, the founder, in 1861, by Mr. Findlay Patterson, from Pennsylvania." Kansas State Historical Society, *Transactions,* VII, 475.

[152] *Smoky Hill and Republican Union,* Feb. 6, 1862.

[153] *General Laws of Kansas, 1862,* pp. 441-442; *Smoky Hill and Republican Union,* Feb. 6, 1862; *History of the State of Kansas* (1883), 685.

Because of the Civil war and Indian hostilities, the growth of Abilene was retarded, and by the late spring of 1867, according to McCoy, it consisted of only "about one dozen log huts." At that time, immediately west of the town, and west of Mud creek, were two log cabins of Timothy F. Hersey, one of which was used as a dwelling and the other as a storeroom or stage station. On the second floor of the latter, dances were occasionally held.[154] In a dugout on the east bank of the creek was a blacksmith shop operated by Thomas McLean.[155] A short distance east of the dugout was a log house containing six rooms, called the Bratton Hotel, of which John P. Simpson was the proprietor. Southwest of it, and near the creek, was its horse stable.[156] East of the hotel was a saloon operated by Josiah Jones, who also trapped prairie dogs and sold them at five dollars or more a pair.[157] Still farther east was the Frontier Store, owned by William S. Moon. Consisting of one room eighteen feet wide and thirty feet long, it served as a grocery, dry-goods store, post office, and office of the recorder of deeds. Moon lived in a log house about a block south of the store.[158] All of these buildings were constructed of logs and had dirt roofs, except the hotel and the store, which had roofs made of shakes, or shingles.[159]

Abilene remained the principal shipping point for Texas cattle from 1867 until 1871, and in that time grew rapidly in size and importance. A number of additions were made to the original town during these years, the first of which — Thompson & McCoy's Addition — was laid out in December,

[154] "Recollections of Melvina Moon Quinn," *Dickinson County Clippings*, IV, Mrs. A. B. Seelye, Abilene; M. Hoffman, "Abilene's Early History," *Dickinson County Clippings*, VIII, *ibid.*

[155] "Recollections of John P. Simpson," *Dickinson County Clippings*, VI, *ibid.*

[156] *Ibid.;* "Recollections of Melvina Moon Quinn," *Dickinson County Clippings*, IV, *ibid.; Daily Missouri Republican*, June 10, 1867.

[157] *Daily Missouri Republican*, June 10, 1867; *Historical and Biographical Record of the Cattle Industry*, 494; "Recollections of John P. Simpson," *Dickinson County Clippings*, VI, Mrs. A. B. Seelye, Abilene.

[158] *Daily Missouri Republican*, June 10, 1867; "Recollections of Melvina Moon Quinn," *Dickinson County Clippings*, IV, Mrs. A. B. Seelye, Abilene; Mrs. Elizabeth Ross, "Early Days in Abilene," *Dickinson County Clippings*, VI, *ibid.*

[159] "Recollections of John P. Simpson," *Dickinson County Clippings*, VI, *ibid.*

1867.[160] By the latter part of July, 1870, when the United States census was taken, Abilene had acquired a resident population of seven or eight hundred,[161] most of whom were born in approximately twenty-seven different states in the Union, and a little over a hundred in about thirteen foreign countries. The Americans were principally natives of Ohio, Indiana, Illinois, Kentucky, Tennessee, New York, Pennsylvania, Kansas, and Missouri; the foreigners were primarily natives of Ireland, England, Canada, Germany, Sweden, and Scotland.[162] The cattle trade gave color to Abilene, largely determined the character of its growth between 1867 and 1871, and made it one of the best-known small towns in the United States during these years. By 1871, the last and most important year of this trade in Abilene, the town could boast of a two-story brick courthouse; a stone schoolhouse; a railroad depot; the Great Western Stockyards, built by McCoy in 1867 but now owned by John Freeland; a weekly newspaper, the *Abilene Chronicle*, owned and edited by Vear Porter Wilson; a large number of frame residences; two churches – the Baptist Chapel and the Universalist Chapel; a calaboose; the Novelty Theater, owned by Fuller & Mitchell and managed by George Burt; two banks – Kellogg, Newman & Company, and the Abilene Bank owned by W. B. Clarke & Company; four hotels – the Drover's Cottage (built by McCoy in 1867 but now owned by Moses B. George), Gulf House, American House, and Planter's House; at least seven saloons (in addition to those in the hotels) – the Alamo, Bull's Head, Elkhorn, Pearl, Old Fruit, Jim Flynn's, and Tom Downey's; several boarding-houses, including the Huff House; three or more restaurants – the Eureka, Eugene

---

[160] Dickinson County, Deed Record J, 172, MS., Recorder of Deeds Office, Abilene; *History of the State of Kansas* (1883), 688.

[161] Since the census returns in 1870 made no distinction between the city of Abilene and Grant township, the number of inhabitants in the former can only be estimated from the vocations given. The township had a total population of 849. Ninth Census of the United States, Dickinson and Doniphan Counties, Kansas, MS., K.S.H.S.; *Ninth Census of the United States*, I (*Population*), 143.

[162] Ninth Census of the United States, Dickinson and Doniphan Counties, Kansas, MS., K.S.H.S.

Kellogg's, and B. F. Smith's; the Twin Livery Stables, operated by Edward H. Gaylord; two lumber yards – Alexander and Larimer's, and Theophilus Little's; W. H. Eicholtz's furniture store and undertaking establishment; Trott's Photograph Gallery; Bascom & Smith's tinshop; and at least one blacksmith shop – W. H. Whitehurst & Company. At the same time Abilene possessed a great many stores, most of which owed their existence to the cattle trade: a large number of establishments dealing in general merchandise or clothing – H. H. Hazlett's Farmer's and Drover's Supply Store, Jacob Karatofsky's Great Western Store, Reuben & Ringolsky's, G. A. Wills's Texas Store, George B. Seely's, J. S. Durkee's, M. Goldsoll's Texas Store, and others; a hardware store – J. M. Hodge & Company; a firm selling farm machinery – J. E. Bonebrake & Company; the Drover's Boot Shop of T. C. McInerney; several fruit stores; a number of grocery stores, including Hoffman's, Johntz Brothers', and P. Taylor's; Charles Jones's jewelry store; and a firm selling guns, pistols, ammunition, and sewing machines – P. Hand & Company. The town also had three or four real estate houses, including Shane & Henry, Augustine & Lebold, and Mahan & Cox, and several lawyers, ministers, school teachers, and musicians. To the southeast of Abilene was the Beer Garden, or Devil's Addition to Abilene, or Fisher's Addition, as it was variously called, a group of houses occupied by prostitutes during the cattle trading season.[163]

---

[163] *Ibid.; Abilene Chronicle*, Apr. 21, 1870, Mar. 23, May 4, 18, 25, June 1, July 6, 13, 20, 27, 1871; *Kansas Daily Commonwealth*, May 19, July 2, 1870; *Junction City Weekly Union*, Oct. 1, 1870, Aug. 19, 1871; *Kansas Daily Tribune*, June 23, 1868; *Republican Daily Journal* (Lawrence, Kan.), Feb. 21, 1871; *Leavenworth Times & Conservative*, June 25, 1869, June 21, 1870; *Daily Kansas State Record* (Topeka), Aug. 5, 1871; *Leavenworth Times and Bulletin*, May 4, 1871; J. B. Edwards, "History of Early-day Abilene," *Abilene Daily Chronicle*, June 12, 19, 26, July 3, 1938; J. B. Case, "Early Days in Abilene," *Dickinson County Clippings*, I, Mrs. A. B. Seelye, Abilene; H. L. Humphrey, "William Bascom Smith," *Dickinson County Clippings*, VI, *ibid.;* M. Hoffman, "Abilene's Early History," *Dickinson County Clippings*, VIII, *ibid.;* E. C. Little, "A Son of the Border," *Dickinson County Clippings*, X, *ibid.;* Theophilus Little, "Early Days of Abilene and Dickinson County," in Adolph Roenigk, *Pioneer History of Kansas* (1933), 35-38; *Trail Drivers of Texas* (Hunter, ed.), 456-457; *History of the State of Kansas* (1883), 689-

During the early years of its existence as a cattle depot Abilene was one of the roughest towns in the United States in the summer months. Since it was unincorporated, the county officials had the sole responsibility for the maintainance of law and order, but these officers found it impossible to cope with the lawless elements.[164] Determined to end this chaotic condition, the inhabitants made plans to establish a municipal government. A Kansas statute of February 25, 1868, stipulated that whenever a majority of the inhabitants of any town or village presented a petition to the probate court asking to be incorporated, the judge was to grant their request, provided he was convinced that a majority of the taxable citizens had signed the petition.[165] Accordingly, on September 3, 1869, John H. Mahan, attorney, and forty-three other residents of Abilene presented a petition to the probate court, of which Cyrus Kilgore was judge and ex-officio clerk, asking that the town be incorporated. Since a majority of the tax-paying citizens had signed the document, and since favorable action on the petition would be for the best interests of the inhabitants as a whole, the judge granted the request, creating a corporation known as the "Inhabitants of the Town of Abilene." The court also appointed a board of five trustees to exercise the corporate powers of the town: James B. Shane, Theodore C. Henry, Thomas Sherran, Timothy F. Hersey, and Joseph G. McCoy. These officials were to serve until their successors were "elected and qualified." [166]

Shortly after Abilene was incorporated as a town, its board of trustees organized and elected Theodore C. Henry chairman.[167] A native of the state of New York, he had

691; Floyd Benjamin Streeter, *Prairie Trails & Cow Towns* (Boston, 1936), 81-83.

164 *Abilene Chronicle*, Apr. 6, 1871; *Prose and Poetry of the Live Stock Industry*, I, 507-508.

165 *General Statutes of Kansas, 1868*, pp. 1064-1071.

166 Abilene, Ordinance Book, 3-4, MS., Mayor's Office.

167 Henry's office, chairman of the board of trustees, was created by the act of February 25, 1868. In the minutes of the last two meetings of the board on April 3 and 5, 1871, Henry was incorrectly styled mayor; there was no such official until Abilene became a city of the third class on April 7, 1871, when McCoy, who had been elected mayor on April 3, took the oath of office.

moved to Alabama and then to Springfield, Illinois, where he had been persuaded by McCoy to seek his fortune in Abilene during the latter part of 1867. The organization and personnel of the board of trustees remained the same until the first Monday in April, 1870, when an election appears to have been held in which Doctor H. C. Brown and C. H. Lebold were chosen trustees in place of Hersey and McCoy. The board reëlected Henry chairman. It also selected G. L. Brinkman as its clerk, but on June 13 he was replaced by W. Fancher. George B. Seely, a merchant, appears to have been the town treasurer.[168] One of the board's most important actions for the good order and name of Abilene was the appointment of Thomas James Smith as chief of police on June 4, 1870, at a salary of $150 for the first month; on August 9 his compensation was increased to $225 per month, effective from July 4. Highly respected by cowboys and citizens alike, he was very proficient in the performance of his difficult duties and served Abilene faithfully until November 2, 1870, when he was killed by a man whom he was attempting to arrest near the town. The last meeting of the board of trustees was held on April 5, 1871.[169]

Meanwhile, Abilene's growth in population entitled it to organize as a third class city. In preparation for such action, the trustees, on March 8, 1871, employed Mr. McBenson to take a census of the town, paying five dollars for his services.[170] On April 3, 1871, in accordance with a Kansas act of March 2 of the same year, an election was held which resulted in Abilene starting its existence as a city of the third class. Joseph G. McCoy was elected mayor, G. L. Brinkman, Doctor Lucius Boudinot, S. A. Burroughs, Samuel Carpenter, and W. H. Eicholtz councilmen, and Eliphalet

Abilene, Minute Book of the City Council, 29-52, MS., Mayor's Office; *General Statutes of Kansas, 1868,* p. 1065. The minutes of the board of trustees are recorded in the same book as those of its successor, the city council.

[168] Abilene, Minute Book of the City Council, 31, MS., Mayor's Office; *Abilene Chronicle,* May 12, 1870; Kansas State Historical Society, *Transactions,* IX, 528; Stuart Henry, *Conquering Our Great American Plains* (New York, 1930), viii, 32.

[169] Abilene, Minute Book of the City Council, 29, 37, 51, MS., Mayor's Office; Kansas State Historical Society, *Transactions,* IX, 527-531.

[170] Abilene, Minute Book of the City Council, 47, MS., Mayor's Office.

Barber police judge.[171] Thus McCoy became the first mayor of Abilene. The initial meeting of the mayor and councilmen was held in the office of S. A. Burroughs on April 7. At a session on April 15 the mayor, with the approval of the council, appointed A. A. Hurd clerk of the council, J. H. McDonald street commissioner, C. H. Lebold city treasurer, and James Butler Hickok city marshal, and the council itself chose Doctor Boudinot president of the council and James Culbertson city attorney. The only change in the personnel of the council during the year occurred when the vacancies caused by the resignations of Brinkman and Eicholtz on May 24 were filled by the election of Ira L. Smith and J. A. Gauthie on June 13. Culbertson resigned as city attorney on May 24 and E. H. Kilpatrick was chosen to replace him on June 14. Two weeks later – June 28 – Kilpatrick was also made clerk in place of Hurd, although the former had served as clerk pro tem. since June 14. On June 16 the mayor, at the unanimous request of the council, appointed James Gainsford and J. H. McDonald policemen to assist Marshal Hickok.[172] Among the many problems that had to be solved during McCoy's term of office were the maintainance of law and order, the rate of taxation, the price of licenses to sell liquor, and the regulation or elimination of prostitutes. He was fortunate in his selection of Hickok as city marshal, for "Wild Bill," as he was universally called, was a genius in the use of pistols and kept order in the city by overawing potential lawbreakers. Wild Bill was discharged on December 13, 1871, because his services were no longer needed. McCoy's term of office expired early in April, 1872, when Samuel Carpenter, who had been elected mayor on April 1, assumed the duties of his office.[173]

McCoy's activities in the cattle trade at Abilene are related in his book and need not be repeated here. As for his real estate transactions, he purchased his first land from

---

[171] *Ibid.*, 51; *Kansas Laws, 1871*, pp. 118-142; *Abilene Chronicle*, Apr. 6, 1871.

[172] Abilene, Minute Book of the City Council, 52, 55, 57, 65, 69, 71-73, MS., Mayor's Office; *Abilene Chronicle*, Apr. 6, June 15, 1871.

[173] Abilene, Minute Book of the City Council, 52-126, MS., Mayor's Office; *Abilene Chronicle*, Apr. 4, 1872.

Charles H. Thompson on June 18, 1867, paying $1953.50 for 250 acres. One hundred acres of this tract were located south of the railroad tracks and immediately east of the town, and the rest lay north of the tracks, adjoining the town on the north.[174] Between July 1 and December 25, 1867, he bought more land in the immediate vicinity of Abilene from Elias Drake, Christian Hoffman, William C. Bean, Edson W. Dow, and Charles H. Thompson, for which he paid $3900 all-told.[175] On December 26, 1867, he joined with Thompson to make the first addition to the town, called Thompson & McCoy's Addition, most of which lay north of the railroad tracks and immediately north of Abilene. Comprising 80 acres, the addition was divided into blocks that measured 295 by 400 feet, and into lots 40 by 140 feet. It was situated on the south half of the southwest quarter of section 16, township 13, range 2 east of the sixth principal meridian.[176] On October 8, 1868, McCoy disposed of 480 acres of land in Sangamon county, Illinois, to his brothers, William and James, for $40,000, and during the same year or the next brought his family to Abilene.[177] In the fall of 1869 he moved into the new house which he had built north of the tracks in Thompson & McCoy's Addition.[178] Between December 25, 1867, and March 24, 1870, he sold most of his land to Jacob Augustine, John Kuney, Charles H. Thompson, Samuel N. Hitt, Theodore C. Henry, Jacob Ringolsky, Jonathan B. Warfield, William H. Whitehurst, William Sirmott, William Mullen, and Henry Huff, disposing of much of it in 1869 to meet his financial obligations. The greater portion of this property was located in Thompson & McCoy's Addition.[179] During the summer of 1871, while

174 Dickinson County, Deed Record A, 496, MS., Recorder of Deeds Office, Abilene.

175 *Ibid.*, 518, 528, 546, 566; *ibid.*, Deed Record B, 44.

176 Dickinson County, Plat Book A, 2, MS., Recorder of Deeds Office, Abilene; Dickinson County, Deed Record J, 172, MS., *ibid.*

177 Sangamon County (Ill.), Deed Record No. 36, pp. 15-16, MS., Recorder of Deeds Office, Springfield; *Abilene Weekly Reflector*, Apr. 30, 1925; McCoy vs. the Kansas Pacific Railway Company, 7, MS., Supreme Court of Kansas; Dickinson County, Deed Record B, 386, MS., Recorder of Deeds Office, Abilene.

178 McCoy vs. the Kansas Pacific Railway Company, 7, MS., Supreme Court of Kansas; *Republican Daily Journal*, Oct. 19, 1869.

179 Dickinson County, Deed Record B, 32-34, 308, 386, 432, 473, 485, MS.,

he was still mayor of Abilene, he went to Newton, Kansas, to design and supervise the construction of stockyards about a mile and a half from that town.[180]

In the latter part of April, 1872, McCoy, although still a resident of Abilene, journeyed to Wichita as a salesman for a wrought-iron fence, which was "the most durable and cheap fence ever invented," and would not "rot, burn, blow or fall down." [181] However, he could not completely detach himself from the cattle business. Wichita was eager to attract the Texas drive to its yards, and during the latter part of May the city council employed James Bryden to go south and induce drovers to direct their herds to that point. At the same time, in order to supplement Bryden's activities, a number of citizens hired McCoy to journey north and east to advertise Wichita to prospective cattle buyers.[182] He traveled through Kansas, Iowa, Missouri, and other states, spreading the news about the great depot for Texas cattle. The efforts of Bryden and McCoy were so successful that Wichita became the largest market for longhorns in 1872. On August 2 the latter wrote a letter to the *Wichita City Eagle* summarizing his accomplishments and thanking the citizens who had contributed to his compensation.[183]

McCoy left Abilene permanently in the spring of 1873 and moved to Kansas City, Missouri, in or near which he was to reside for about eight years. There he established a commission house for the sale of live stock, with branches in St. Louis and Chicago. His firm, Joseph G. McCoy & Company, also provided cattlemen and newspapers with reports of live stock sales at the principal markets.[184] In September, 1873, he helped to organize the Live Stock Men's National Association at Kansas City and became its first corresponding secretary. Collaborating with J. Parker Mitchner, he wrote a series of articles for *The Cattle Trail,*

Recorder of Deeds Office, Abilene; *ibid.,* Deed Record C, 241-242, 311, 336, 340; *ibid.,* Deed Record J, 173.

180 *Kansas Daily Commonwealth,* Aug. 15, 1871.

181 *Wichita City Eagle,* Apr. 26, 1872.

182 *Ibid.,* May 3, 24, 1872.

183 *Ibid.,* June 7, 14, July 12, Aug. 2, Sept. 19, Oct. 24, 1872.

184 *Kansas Daily Commonwealth,* May 4, 1873; *Wichita City Eagle,* May 15, June 12, 1873.

a weekly Kansas City newspaper edited by H. M. Dickson, which, with additions, he published as a book in 1874 under the title of *Historic Sketches of the Cattle Trade of the West and Southwest*.[185] The volume issued from the press of Ramsey, Millett & Hudson, of Kansas City, and sold at three dollars a copy.[186] In 1880 and 1881 he was employed by the United States Census Bureau to gather statistics of the number of live stock on ranges, his district including northwestern Texas, Indian Territory, southeastern New Mexico, and western Kansas. He traveled through the country on a spring wagon drawn by a team of mules, and camped at night on the open prairie. He was also employed by the census bureau as "special investigator as to the drives into Kansas," and the statistics which he compiled became the basis for the estimates of the number of longhorns driven north between 1866 and 1880.[187] During 1881 the Cherokee Nation obtained his services to systematize the collection of the tax on cattle grazed within its boundaries.[188]

In November, 1881, while in the employ of the Cherokee, he moved to Wichita and rented a house, intending to remain there only during the winter.[189] But he made his permanent residence in that city, which was destined to be his home for most of the remaining years of his life. In 1883 he was living on the west side of Lawrence avenue (now called Broadway); but sometime within the next two years he moved into a new house that he had built at 433 North Fourth avenue (renamed North St. Francis avenue about 1900), which has remained in the possession of his family ever since.[190] Between 1885 and 1899 he was listed in the Wichita city directories at various times as grocer, real

---

185 *Trail Drivers of Texas* (Hunter, ed.), 15.

186 *Wichita City Eagle*, May 28, 1874.

187 *Tenth Census of the United States*, III (*Agriculture*), 955, 965-977; *Wichita City Eagle*, Apr. 7, 1881; McCoy, "Historic and Biographic Sketch," *loc. cit.*, p. 54; "Joseph G. McCoy," *Kings and Queens of the Range*, vol. II, no. 13, p. 8.

188 *Wichita City Eagle*, Nov. 10, 1881; *Portrait and Biographical Album of Sedgwick County, Kan.*, 677.

189 *Wichita City Eagle*, Nov. 10, 1881.

190 *Directory of the City of Wichita for 1883*, p. 80; *ibid.*, *1885*, p. 128; *Wichita Evening Eagle*, Feb. 24, 1939.

estate agent, speculator, stockman, and proprietor of a flour and feed store.[191] An ardent advocate of opening Indian Territory to white settlement, he moved to Oklahoma as a Sooner in 1889, although his name continues to appear in the Wichita directories. He first settled at Reno City and then at El Reno, and took an active part in the political life of the new territory. Early in October, 1890, at a Democratic convention held at Norman, he was nominated territorial delegate to Congress, but in the first regular election on the following November 4 he was defeated by his Republican adversary, David A. Harvey.[192] McCoy came back to Wichita shortly afterward and was again employed by the census bureau to gather statistics on the number of live stock on ranges. In 1893 he was appointed an inspector by the Treasury Department and sent to the Pacific Northwest to detect opium smuggling from China. Returning to Wichita after a brief employment, he took an active part in the election of 1896. In the following year Governor Leedy made him cattle inspector at the Kansas Stockyards, Kansas City, Kansas.[193] From 1900 until 1913 the Wichita city directories list him at different times as retired, cattleman, book agent, and canvasser.[194] He was a member of the First Presbyterian Church and of the Independent Order of Odd Fellows. About 1914 he removed to Kansas City, Missouri, but by that time his health was failing. He was taken seriously sick during the late summer of the following year and died on October 19, 1915, at 1315 Broadway, where he was

[191] *Directory of the City of Wichita for 1885*, p. 128; ibid., *1886*, pp. 149, 204; ibid., *1887*, p. 246; ibid., *1888*, p. 284; ibid., *1889*, p. 241; ibid., *1890*, p. 225; ibid., *1891*, p. 154; ibid., *1892*, p. 227; ibid., *1894*, p. 228; ibid., *1898-1899*, p. 280.

[192] *Ibid., 1889*, p. 241; ibid., *1890*, p. 225; *Wichita Eagle*, May 6, 1894; Joseph B. Thoburn, *Standard History of Oklahoma* (Chicago and New York, 1916), II, 690; Sam P. Ridings, *The Chisholm Trail* (Guthrie, 1936), 97-98; Dan W. Peery, "The First Two Years," *Chronicles of Oklahoma*, VII, 321-322.

[193] McCoy, "Historic and Biographic Sketch," *loc. cit.*, pp. 54-55; "Joseph G. McCoy," *Kings and Queens of the Range*, vol. II, no. 13, p. 8; *Proceedings of the Second Annual Convention of the National Live Stock Association*, 324.

[194] *Directory of the City of Wichita for 1900*, p. 198; ibid., *1902*, p. 226; ibid., *1903-1904*, p. 242; ibid., *1904-1905*, p. 274; ibid., *1906*, p. 386; ibid., *1907*, p. 435; ibid., *1910*, p. 465; ibid., *1912*, p. 361; ibid., *1913*, p. 343.

rooming. The cause of his death, according to his physician, Doctor Lane, was acute oedema of the lung. His body was taken to Wichita and interred in Maple Grove Cemetery, where he had buried his wife scarcely four years before.[195]

[195] Maple Grove Cemetery, Record of Interment No. 5035, MS., Wichita; Gill Mortuary Records, MSS., Wichita; *Kansas City Star*, Oct. 19, 1915; *Wichita Eagle*, Oct. 20, 1915; *Portrait and Biographical Album of Sedgwick County, Kan.*, 677.

HISTORIC SKETCHES

OF THE

CATTLE TRADE

OF THE

WEST AND SOUTHWEST.

By JOSEPH G. McCOY,

THE PIONEER WESTERN CATTLE SHIPPER.

ILLUSTRATED BY PROF. HENRY WORRALL, TOPEKA, KAS.
ENGRAVED BY BAKER & CO., CHICAGO, ILL
ELECTROTYPED BY J. T. RETON & CO., KANSAS CITY. MO.

PUBLISHED BY
RAMSEY, MILLETT & HUDSON. KANSAS CITY, MO.,
PRINTERS, BINDERS, ENGRAVERS, LITHOGRAPHERS & STATIONERS.
1874.

To the half-score of kind-hearted gentlemen, residents of Kansas City, who generously sustained the writer in the darkest hour and hardest struggle of his existence, this book is gratefully inscribed by its

AUTHOR

Courteously Yours

Jos. G. McCoy

[McCOY'S] PREFACE

The aim and purpose of the author in publishing this work is to convey in simple, unpretentious language, practical and correct information upon the opening, development, and present status of the live stock trade of the Great New West, and to put into existence, he believes, the first and only work devoted exclusively to a plain exposition of the manner of growing and marketing common live stock, and the modes of preparation of the various articles of product made therefrom, with brief historic sketches of leading and characteristic men of the present day engaged in the business.

No claim or pretense whatever is made to literary merit or even correct language and syntax. It has been the author's lot in his brief life to do, to act, and not to write. With a deep conviction that in the work a hundred errors and imperfections exist to each single merit, it is diffidently submitted to the reading, but not to the critic, world.

JOS. G. McCOY

I. THE LIVE STOCK INDUSTRY IN TEXAS

Among the earliest vocations spoken of by the sacred historian is that of the producers of live stock, the herdsmen, or, as would be styled by western men, the ranchmen. The word "rancho" is a Spanish term meaning a "farm," and the "farm" may be used for any purpose; whatever that may be, the prefix will indicate. Thus it is common to hear of a corn ranch, a wheat ranch, a sheep ranch, a horse ranch, a cattle ranch. Sacred writ plainly tells us that Abel's offering, being the product of his stock ranch, was more acceptable to Deity than that of his agricultural brother, but it is painful to learn that the Granger Cain should get so choleric and jealous of his brother as to let murderous thoughts take possession of him. Every Bible reader (and what stockman doesn't read his Bible) knows full well that the great wealth and possessions of the patriarchs consisted principally in live stock, and the inspired writer tells us that among other mentioned assets belonging to Deity, "the cattle upon a thousand hills" are his. Noah was an ancient and extensive live stock shipper; but had the congressional legislation of the present day prescribing twenty-six hours as the limit of time that a stock shipper [2] shall keep his animals aboard been in force then, Mr. Noah would certainly have been put in the lockup, or in the basement of the capitol with the contumacious witness, for he kept his first shipment aboard forty days without unloading it for rest or feed. However, he must have done well, for history tells us that he straightway got on a spree and went for the ladies in true cattleman's style. Nevertheless he seems to have become disgusted with the business of live stock shipping, and quit it entirely.

To the superior skill of ancient Jacob as a successful

breeder of speckled cattle was he indebted for his great success in acquiring wealth; but the less said about the morals of that speckled-cattle operation the better, perhaps, for the reputation of Jacob. Nevertheless, he seems to have enjoyed special favor and frequent communications from Deity. Indeed it seemed Deity's special pleasure to make his will toward mankind known through the medium of live stock men more than any other class. It was to a refugee herdsman attending his father-in-law's flocks that he appeared in the burning bush and held audible converse with that modest shepherd, who was there told of the high duties and destinies that were upon him – nothing less than to deliver his people from the iron hand of bondage and lead them through great trials and tribulations unto the promised land that "flowed with milk and honey."

Great as was his diffidence and humble as was the estimate he put upon his own abilities, believing himself too obscure and slow of speech to stand before Egypt's opulent king, yet with the unmistakable assurances given him of Divine support and assistance, he went forth in full confidence to the accomplishment of the greatest task ever imposed on mortal man – the faithful unfolding of the will and promises of God to his people, and the laying down in tablets of stone and imperishable parchment the foundation of all civilized, just human jurisprudence. It is a remarkable fact that both Jacob and Moses had such special notice by Providence whilst [3] in the service of their father-in-laws; in this day and generation it is supposed to be the mother-in-laws who make a double portion of Providence indispensable to family quietude.

It was a herdsman fresh from tending his father's flock that God chose to designate as being one after his own heart, and to inspire to write the richest strains of sacred poetry e'er chanted by earth's worshipping millions. It was the herdsmen upon the hills of Judea that first heard the angelic tidings of "Peace on earth and good will to man," and they alone had the honored guidance of a brilliant star specially deputed to guide them to where lay, in the ox's manger, the being "before whom every knee shall bend and every tongue confess." We deem it time idly spent to farther show, what all must acknowledge, that the vocation of live stock is not only ancient, but of old, as now, altogether honorable in the highest degree.

The live stock business, or the breeding, rearing, and marketing of cattle, hogs, and sheep, is a subject of peculiar interest to almost every man of all vocations of life. The western man is interested in it, for it is largely his business, his means of making money. The western merchant, tradesman, and mechanic are interested in it, for upon its pecuniary prosperity depend, in a large degree, his own. The eastern man is interested in it, for it is a part of his living, and, with a part of the laboring classes of the East, its products, namely animal flesh, is one of their rare luxuries. The importer looks to the export of barreled pork and beef for the exchange to pay his debtor balance. The accountant at his desk, weary and careworn, deprived of his liberty, looks wistfully forward to the day when with ample means he can retire to some villa and enjoy himself in unrestrained freedom among a troupe of favorite domestic animals. In short, we believe the love of domestic animals is universal, and we believe that that love is elevating when indulgence is guided by proper intelligence. At all events, those whom we most [4] revere in high stations of life, at present and in the past, were lovers of domestic animals.

As all trades have pecularities which mark them in different sections, so the cattle trade of the West and Southwest has traits distinctive and peculiar to itself, some of which we propose to note as we attempt a brief history of its early development; and our effort shall be more especially directed to what is familiarly known as the western and southwestern cattle trade, which is an interest, a commerce, that has not received the attention its magnitude and importance deserved.

The area of the American continent situated east of the Rocky mountains that is especially adapted to the production of live stock is very great, and embraces the western and larger halves of Texas, the Indian Territory, Kansas, Nebraska, Dakota, all of Wyoming, the eastern half of Colorado, and nearly all of New Mexico, aggregating many hundreds of thousands of square miles and many millions of acres. Each of the above-mentioned territories will receive special attention in its turn. Texas, being not only the largest but the first one settled, will receive first attention. The Gulf of Mexico and the Río Grande river form its southern and southwestern boundaries; the Territory of New Mexico forms its western boundary; the Red river is its northern line; and Louisiana bounds it on the east. Its area is over 237,000 square miles, or over 152,000,000 of acres, one hundred and fifty millions of which are devoted principally to the production of live stock. From its near geographical location to Old Mexico, from whence a supply of live stock for ranching purposes was early obtained, and owing to its excellent climate— being almost destitute of winter weather – and its unlimited grazing facilities, Texas first attracted settlers from Mexico, as well as from all parts of the New World.

Texas was originally a part of the domain of Mexico, and from that country was at first sparsely stocked up with Spanish cattle of similar blood and quality to those originally placed in Mexico [5] by Cortes, the conqueror.[196] But a brave and hardy class of white men soon came to the control of political affairs in Texas and struck for freedom. So self-reliant and daring a race of people as then constituted the white population of Texas could not be conquered, nor fail to obtain any reasonable object for which they might unitedly make an effort to attain. After many bloody struggles victory perched upon the independent banner and the independence of Texas was acknowledged by the mother country. For a few years Texas was an independent republic, but believing that in union there is strength, she cast her lot with the United States, but retained the ownership of her public domain; so that an emigrant locating upon her public lands looks to the state government for a title instead of the United States, as is the case in other states and territories. The admission of Texas into the Union was the cause[197] of the Mexican war, the history and results of which are familiar to most readers.

---

196 For an account of the early cattle industry of Texas, see Dobie, "The First Cattle in Texas and the Southwest Progenitors of the Longhorns," *Southwestern Historical Quarterly*, XLII, 171-197.

197 One of the causes.

The state of Texas is watered and drained by the Río Grande, Pecos, Colorado, Brazos, Trinity, and Red rivers. The eastern portion is heavily timbered with immense forests of pitch or hard pine; the central portion of the state is more diversified with prairie and timber, and its soil and climate conspire to make it the very best agricultural country; the western portion of Texas, and by far the largest half, is as well adapted to stock raising as any portion of the globe, and like any other portion that is well adapted to that business, it is fit for little else than stock raising. For a distance of fully five hundred miles east of the Rocky mountains the grasses are different in character and appearance to those found in the balance of the Mississippi valley. It is a fine, soft, velvety species, seldom growing over three or four inches long, and has a mild, sky-bluish, green color. It is familiarly known as buffalo grass. It usually attains its full growth in the spring months during the rainy season, and when the dry, heated months of summer approach, it cures or dries up, but retains all the nutritious qualities originally possessed. In fact, many [6] stockmen regard it as superior feed, making more fat or tallow when it has attained its growth and is cured by the sun's hot rays than when it is in process of growing and is fresh and green. Western Texas is covered with species of grass nearly akin to the buffalo grass, one of which is called grama grass; also, another variety is called mesquite grass. Both varieties cure up in summer and constitute excellent food for stock during the winter. It is too short of growth to make much of a fire. In fact, a person unaccustomed to it would be loath to think that there was so much as bare sustenance in it, much less good living and thick tallow. There are several varieties of mesquite grass, one of which is noted for its disposition to run over the ground much like a miniature watermelon vine. It is considered the best grass that grows in Texas. From sections of that state where the vining mesquite grass abounds comes the heaviest and fattest Texan cattle, and in the mesquite regions the cattle grow larger than in any other portion of Texas. In 1870, according to the census, Texas had three and one-half millions of cattle, three-fourths of a million of sheep, and one-half mil-

lion of horses, the aggregate value of which would fall little
short of thirty-five millions of dollars.[198] The largest live
stock owners in the United States are residents of Texas.
Several individuals owning from twenty-five to seventy-five
thousand head of cattle each, with horses in proportion, are
to be found in southwestern Texas.

If it was true in the past political history of our country
that there was "an irrepressible conflict" between the ideas
and domestic institutions of the two sections of our nation,
it is none the less true now that there is a similar "conflict"
between those interests denominated or dubbed "shorthorn"
and "longhorn," or Texas cattle and Durham cattle. Both
breeds, we believe, sprang from Europe – the first from
Spain, the latter from England. Neither, strictly speaking,
is native, nor do we know of any record of cattle of any
description being found on this continent at its discovery.
The Spanish [7] cattle were introduced into Mexico by
Cortes, the conqueror.[199] Although he may have destroyed
and despoiled a rich government and a happy people, and
sewn the seeds of despotism, discord, and revolution by an
unfit amalgamation of races, so that in that land of perpetual
summer nothing human is permanent, yet he did confer a
good and enduring benefit by the introduction of a stock
of cattle peculiarily adapted to that clime and people.

Before we go any farther in tracing the history of the
southwestern cattle trade, let us look into the life of the
producer, the owner, the ranchman, their manner of life,
and their labor – in short, how the cattle are raised. In
Texas, perhaps not one owner in ten lives upon his stock

198 According to the census of 1870, Texas had 3,494,043 neat cattle on
farms (428,048 milch cows, 132,407 working oxen, and 2,933,588 "other
cattle"), 496,115 neat cattle not on farms, 424,504 horses on farms, 150,137
horses not on farms, and 714,351 sheep. *Ninth Census of the United States,*
III (*Wealth and Industry*), 75, 251.

199 According to a statement made in Mexico City on October 22, 1554,
Gregorio de Villalobos, lieutenant governor of Veracruz, brought "a number
of calves" from Santo Domingo to Mexico about 1521, "so that there might
be cattle, he being the first to bring them to New Spain." Adolph F. A.
Bandelier and Fanny R. Bandelier, *Historical Documents Relating to New
Mexico, Nueva Vizcaya, and Approaches Thereto, to 1773* (Charles Wilson
Hackett, ed., Washington, D.C., 1923), I, 40-41.

ranch, but usually in some near post office village; occasionally one is found living in a city. In choosing a location for a stock ranch, a point centrally situated as to grazing lands and an abundance of living water is selected for headquarters of the ranch. Here is erected, usually of logs, a rude house and corrals, with capacity in proportion to the herd, with a small pound or chute for branding of large cattle, such for instance, as a drove of beeves, preparatory to starting them to market. The slight brand put on the stock at that time is called a "road brand," in contradistinction to the "ranch brand," which is usually put on the animal when young.

We will suppose a man to be just commencing in the stock business. After having purchased enough land to give him a footing whereon to build the above houses and corrals, with sufficient water and timber for his purposes, he then decides what his ranch brand and earmarks shall be, and whatever device or letter or figure he selects, he is careful to have it differ from all other brands and marks in that portion of the state. Then he goes before an officer of the county or district and places upon record his brand and earmarks, filing a copy thereof; also a statement of the number of cattle and horses he has at that time bearing that brand and marks, taking from the recorder a certificate of his action. From [8] thenceforward all stock found bearing that brand and earmarks are his, and by him can be taken possession of by summary process wherever found in the state.

The stock laws of Texas are very complete and provide ample penalties for violation. When a stockman sells his entire cattle or horses, he gives the purchaser articles of writing, which are proper subjects of record, conveying all right and title to all stock bearing the brands and earmarks therein described. The conveyance is as absolute and complete as is a deed to a piece of land in the northern states, and, as has been said, like deeds, should be recorded. The ownership of a stock of cattle in Texas is determined in a legal contest by the records, just as we determine the ownership of a piece of land. When a stock is purchased, it is usual, if it be not very large, that each animal is counterbranded; i.e., the first brand burned out and the purchaser's brand burned on instead. The purchaser has the right to continue the same brand if he so chooses, not only upon those he buys but upon their increase; for he not only by his purchase becomes the owner of the stock but of the brand also, and has all the rights thereunto pertaining of the original owner. It is customary to brand the increase whilst quite young, which is often done by the men from the various ranches of the neighborhood working in concert, driving to some one of the corrals all the stock in a given district, and when they are safely enclosed, proceed to catch the calves or colts with the lasso and draw them outside the corral; where is provided a fire for heating the branding irons, which are quickly put on after the proper cutting of the ears.

The ownership of the young animal is determined by the brand of its mother. When this process is completed, the little frightened animal is let run free, and human hand is not placed upon it again for years – perhaps not until it is full grown and sold to go to market, when it is necessary to road brand it. After all has been done by coöperation that can be advantageously, the "cowboys," as the common [9] laborers are termed, go in squads of four or five, scouting over the entire range, camping wherever night overtakes them, catching with the lasso upon the prairie every young animal found whose mother bears their employer's brand. It is legal and a universal practice to capture any unmarked and unbranded animal upon the range, and mark and brand the same in their employer's brand, no matter to whom the animal may really belong, so be it is over one year old and is unbranded.

It is easy to see that any energetic, enterprising ranchman can greatly increase the number of his stock by this means; in fact, to this opportunity is the rapid increase of many stockmen's herds owing. Unbranded animals over a year old are, in ranchmen's parlance, called "Mauvrics," which name they got from a certain old Frenchman of that name who began stock raising with a very few head and in a very brief space of time had a remarkably large herd of cattle. It was found that he actually branded fifty annually for each cow he owned. Of course he captured the un-branded yearlings.[200]

To supply a ranch whereon a stock of ten thousand head of cattle are kept, with the necessary saddle horses, a stock of at least one hundred and fifty brood mares should be

[200] McCoy's definition of the term "maverick" and his explanation of its origin are not entirely accurate. The meaning of the term varied with the time and place of usage, signifying either an unbranded motherless calf, or an unbranded yearling, or any unbranded cow over a year old. Condemning the practice of "maverick branding," a San Antonio newspaper asserted in 1867: "The term maverick which was formerly applied to unbranded year-lings is now applied to every calf which can be separated from the mother cow—the consequence is, the fastest branders are accumulating the largest stocks." During the seventies, in the Territory of Colorado, the Bent County Stock Association defined mavericks as "unbranded motherless calves over one month old." Samuel Augustus Maverick, after whom this class of stock was named, was born at Pendleton, South Carolina, July 23, 1803. After graduating from Yale College in 1825, he studied law at Winchester, Virginia, and was then admitted to the bar in his native state of South Carolina. Later he moved to Alabama, but in 1835 migrated to San Antonio, Texas. He was one of the signers of the Texas Declaration of Independence on March 2, 1836. Returning to Alabama, he married Mary Ann Adams near Tuskaloosa, August 4, 1836, and two years afterward came back to San Antonio, where he practiced law and speculated in land. In 1842, apprehending an invasion of Mexican troops, he moved to a tract of land on the west bank of the Colorado river near Lagrange, Texas. Mrs. Maverick becoming ill during 1844, he removed to Decrow's Point, at the southwestern tip of Matagorda Peninsula, where, it was hoped, she would regain her health. On March 16, 1847, he purchased four hundred cattle at three dollars a head from Mr. Tilton, who resided on Matagorda Peninsula about twenty-five miles northeast of Decrow's Point. Maverick named the place "Tiltona Ranch" and placed it in charge of a negro called Jack, whom he had brought from South Carolina to Texas in 1838. During October, 1847, he left Decrow's Point and returned to San Antonio, where he continued to practice law and speculate in land; besides, he served in the Texas legislature for a time. Meanwhile, his cattle at Tiltona Ranch were not properly cared for by the negro, many of them remaining unbranded. On July 24, 1852, a prospective buyer from Matagorda wrote Maverick that his stock had been "awfully neglected, not branded ever since you left." In May, 1853, a friend in Matagorda informed Mrs. Maverick: "It is said and that by some of our most respectable citizens that yearlings and calves may be seen by dozens following and sucking your cows and branded in other people's brands." During the spring of 1854, Maverick brought his stock north to a point about forty-five miles southeast of San Antonio and named the place "Conquista Ranch." Jack, despite his bad record, remained in charge of the cattle.

kept. The geldings only are used for the saddle. This class of horses are small, hardy animals, bordering on the pony closely, and are of Spanish origin. Their food is grass exclusively, and many of them are as utterly unfamiliar with the use of grain as they are of Latin, and will often, when kept in the North, starve to death before they will eat grain. Almost everyone has to be taught to eat corn or oats by placing a quantity in a small muzzle-shaped sack and fastening it over the animal's nose.

If anyone imagines that the life of a ranchman or cowboy is one of ease and luxury, or his diet a feast of fat things, a brief trial will dispel the illusion, as is mist by the sunshine. True, his life is one of more or less excitement and adventure, and much of it is spent in the saddle, yet it is a hard life and his daily fare will never give you the gout. [10] Corn bread, mastfed bacon, and coffee constitute nine-tenths of their diet; occasionally they have fresh beef and less often they have vegetables of any description. They do their own cooking in the rudest and fewest possible vessels, often not having a single plate or knife and fork other than their pocketknife, but gather around the camp kettle in true Indian style, and with a piece of bread in one hand, proceed to fish up a piece of sow belly and dine sumptuously, not forgetting to stow away one or more quarts of

The negro continued to neglect the stock and permitted many calves to go unbranded. Finally, in September, 1856, Maverick sold his cattle to Mr. A. Toutant (or Mr. A. Toutant Beauregard), at which time Mrs. Maverick stated that they were "at Conquista Ranch and scattered over the country around there." Toutant (or Beauregard) marked as many unbranded cattle as he could locate, believing them to be Maverick's. Since so many of Maverick's calves at Tiltona Ranch and Conquista Ranch went unbranded and wandered over the range, many people near those places began to call all unbranded calves or cattle "mavericks"—a practice that spread throughout Texas and the West in the course of time. Maverick died at San Antonio, September 2, 1870. *Memoirs of Mary A. Maverick* (Rena Maverick Green, ed., San Antonio, 1921), 7-23, 60, 78, 84-85, 92, 96, 115-117, 122-133; *Daily Herald* (San Antonio), June 20, 1867; *Texas Live Stock Journal* (Fort Worth), Apr. 21, 1883; *Historical and Biographical Record of the Cattle Industry*, 65-66, 594-595; *Prose and Poetry of the Live Stock Industry*, I, 629; Pelzer, *op. cit.*, 75, 101-103; Ora Brooks Peake, *The Colorado Range Cattle Industry* (Glendale, 1937), 106-107; Philip Ashton Rollins, *The Cowboy* (New York, 1936), 247.

the strongest coffee imaginable, without sugar or cream; indeed you would hesitate, if judging it from appearance, whether to call it coffee or ink. Of all the vegetables, onions and potatoes are the most desired and the oftenest used, when anything more than the "old regulation" is had. Instead of an oven, fireplace, or cooking stove, a rude hole is dug in the ground and the fire made therein, and the coffee-pot, the camp kettle, and the skillet are the only culinary articles used.

The life of the cowboy is one of considerable daily danger and excitement. It is hard and full of exposure, but is wild and free, and the young man who has long been a cowboy has but little taste for any other occupation. He lives hard, works hard, has but few comforts and fewer necessities. He has but little, if any, taste for reading. He enjoys a coarse practical joke or a smutty story; loves danger but abhors labor of the common kind; never tires riding; never wants to walk, no matter how short the distance he desires to go. He would rather fight with pistols than pray; loves tobacco, liquor, and women better than any other trinity. His life borders nearly upon that of an Indian. If he reads anything, it is in most cases a blood and thunder story of the sensation style. He enjoys his pipe, and relishes a practical joke on his comrades, or a corrupt tale wherein abounds much vulgarity and animal propensity. His clothes are coarse and substantial, few in number, and often of the gaudy pattern. The sombrero hat and large spurs are inevitable accompaniments. Every house has the appearance of a lack of convenience and [11] comfort, but the most rude and primitive modes of life seem to be satisfactory to the cowboy. His wages ranges from fifteen to twenty dollars per month in specie. Mexicans can be employed for about twelve dollars per month. The cowboy has few wants and fewer necessities, the principal one being a full supply of tobacco. The desire for anything to read is very limited.[201]

---

[201] In 1882 a Fort Worth newspaper gave the following description of a cowboy: "The average cowboy is not a bad man in any sense of the term. . . In the first place they are almost universally men of intelligence. It is a rare thing to find a cowboy that is a fool, or even a near approach to a fool. The life he is compelled to lead calls for the constant exercise of good judgment,

We will here say for the benefit of our northern readers that the term "ranch" is used in the Southwest instead of "farm"; the ordinary laborer is termed a "cowboy"; the horse used, a "cow horse"; and the herd of horses, a "caviyard."

The fame of Texas as a stock-growing country went abroad in the land, and soon after her admission to the Union, unto her was turned the eyes of many young men born and reared in the older southern states, who, being poor in this world's goods, but were ambitious to make for themselves a home and a fortune. Many of this class went to Texas, then a new and comparatively thinly settled country, and began in humblest manner, perhaps for nominal wages, to lay the foundation of future wealth and success. Time and space will not suffice for us to mention all who are worthy examples of what young men of energy and enterprise have accomplished in Texas, but we will present one as a worthy and fair example of a large class.

Mr. William Peryman, now a ranchman and drover, of Frio county, Texas, began business life by caring for his father's stock of cattle, which was not large, for one-third of the increase. In a few years he was able to buy out his father's stock and then set out exclusively for himself. He has now been ranching for seventeen years and has acquired a fortune of princely magnitude. His ranches aggregate fully twenty-five thousand acres of land, all under fence, of which he cultivates but few acres, only sufficient for the necessities of his own house and one or two fancy saddle horses kept

and if a fool starts in as a 'cow-puncher,' he is soon made to understand that he has mistaken his calling. . . In the next place, he is emphatically an enterprising 'cuss,' and is ever on the alert for opportunities to put into exercise enterprising schemes. He will figure on futures in beef steers as if he was a millionaire, and can clearly demonstrate that in just so many years a four-year-old beef steer will necessarily be worth so much, and that a present investment of so many thousands will inevitably 'pan out' to his figures in a given length of time. This sometimes looks like a very foolish employment for men who are proverbially minus bank accounts. . . The cattle kings of Texas today were, most of them, Texas cowboys a few years since. . . We deem it hardly necessary to say in the next place that the cowboy is a feerless animal. A man wanting in courage would be as much out of place in a cow-camp, as a fish would be on dry land." *Texas Live Stock Journal,* Oct. 21, 1882.

L. B. HARRIS.

WM. PERYMAN.

WM. PERRYMAN'S RANCHE.

for his own private use. The balance of his lands are devoted to grazing. His stock of [13] cattle numbers twenty-
five thousand head, and the annual increase varies from four
to five thousand. Mr. Peryman keeps a stock of one thousand
horses and annually brands about three hundred colts. Upon
his premises may also be found from five to six hundred
hogs, which live and fatten upon the nuts found in abundance in the timber belts which skirt almost every stream.
Mr. Peryman has declined seventy-five thousand dollars
specie for his stock of cattle, and his horses are worth perhaps fully twenty thousand dollars. His ranch would be
cheap at fifty thousand dollars. Near one hundred and fifty
thousand dollars is found to be the net results of seventeen
years' ranching under the management of Mr. Peryman.
For the first five years after the close of the Civil war,
New Orleans and Old Mexico afforded market for a limited
number of cattle, and to those points Peryman was a constant drover. But finding that the plains of western Kansas
afforded a field for much larger operations, he has of late
years turned his droves northward, and for four years has
driven annually from three to five thousand head of beeves;
yet he is particular to keep his stock on the ranch intact and
fully cared for in his absence. His principal ranch is on the
San Miguel,[202] a lively stock stream affording plenty of
water and abounding with sufficient timber for ranch purposes. The timber affords an abundance of mast for his
hogs, a part of which are always fat and ready for the knife.
Mr. William Peryman is an Alabamian by birth, but has
spent most of his youth in the state of his adoption. He is
a finely proportioned, muscular fellow, fond of his friends,
courteous, kind-hearted, and chivalrous — a fine type of a
southern gentleman. If in his power, he will make you happy;
is warm and impulsive in temperament; shrewd in business
transactions; in his leisure moments jovial and convivial.
His extensive business is conducted with Mexican help exclusively, and although often one hundred men may be seen
employed on his ranch, not a single female can be seen to

---

[202] San Miguel creek, in the eastern part of Frio county. Peryman drove
about five thousand longhorns to Ellsworth in 1873. *Ellsworth Reporter,* June
26, 1873.

grace the premises with [14] her presence; for although
young, Peryman is what the ladies term an "Old Bach."

There are many men now in Texas engaged in ranching
who went to the state before it was detached from Mexico,
and when the struggle for independence began, entered
heartily into the war for liberty and freedom. Perhaps history gives account of no more hardy, self-reliant, daring,
and brave soldiers than were marshaled under the Lone Star
banner in the bloody war for the independence of Texas.

L. B. Harris, of San Antonio, has been a resident of
Texas for forty years, coming from Georgia at the age of
six years. At an early age he was thrown upon his own
resources, which were nothing more than a clear head, a
stout, fearless heart, an abundance of energy, and a pair
of hands not [15] afraid of work. There are few points,
indeed, few hills or hollows in Texas or Old Mexico that
he has not roamed over. If there are privations and hardships that he is not familiar with, they are few. When but
a boy his hard experience learned him full well the intrinsic
value of a dollar, and today Texas has few more shrewd
and successful ranchmen and drovers than Mr. Harris. Beginning life, as we have said, penniless, it was just to his
hand to take part in the Mexican war, and was among the
first to take up and the last to lay down arms in that struggle,
which grew out of, if not caused by, the admission of his
state into the Federal Union. At the close of the Mexican
war, Mr. Harris turned his attention to civil pursuits, and
began ranching with only one hundred and fifty head of
cattle and a few horses, which business he has continued for
seventeen successive years and, we need not add, with a
reasonable degree of success. His ranches [16] (two in
number) contain about thirty-four hundred acres of land.
As he has been for the last five years driving north to market
annually about five thousand head of cattle, mostly of his
own raising, his stock has become reduced to about two
thousand head of cattle, but he still maintains a stock of
twelve hundred horses. The surplus horses are sold at home
to stockmen and drovers. Mr. Harris has lived an active,
outdoor life, always ready for any emergency, and never
afraid to help himself or his neighbors; but of late years

he has concluded to reduce his business into a smaller compass that he may enjoy the comforts of his beautiful home and interesting family in San Antonio, Texas. There are few markets for Texan cattle that he has not been in with his own stock. But in 1867 he turned from the limited and uncertain demand in New Orleans and Old Mexico to the larger and more reliable market found in western Kansas. Whoever becomes intimately acquainted with L. B. Harris will recognize in him a kind-hearted, true man, whose every impulse is honest, and who would disdain to do a mean act or oppress a man when in his power to do so. Quick, wiry, shrewd, always ahead of his appointments, and never tardy; does his own thinking and acts on his own judgment, and seldom fails to do better than those who make far greater pretensions. It is said that he made the largest single sale of cattle during the year of 1873, which was to one firm, of seven thousand head for the snug sum of $210,000.[203]

But we will close this chapter and pass to the history of the cattle trade of the West by presenting sketches of one or more Texan ranchmen, such as are not only producers and drovers, but farmers also.

James F. Ellison,[204] of San Marcos, Texas, left his native Alabama home at the age of twenty-one, and turned his face toward the Lone Star State to make for himself a home and fortune. No sooner did he land in the state of his adoption than he engaged in marketing stock. For nearly twenty years he was a constant drover to Orleans and Mexico, but [17] finding western Kansas afforded a more inviting market, the last five years has found him making

---

203 Harris drove cattle to Wichita in 1872. In 1873 and 1874 he trailed his longhorns to Ellsworth. *Wichita City Eagle,* May 24, 1872; *Ellsworth Reporter,* May 1, 29, 1873, May 28, 1874.

204 James F. Ellison, born in Winston county, Mississippi, November 6, 1828, moved to Caldwell county, Texas, in 1850, and in 1869 made his first drive to the North. He continued in this business until the early eighties, trailing his herds to Abilene, Ellsworth, and Dodge City, Kansas, and Ogallala, Nebraska. For a time he operated as a partner of John O. Dewees. He died at San Marcos, Texas, November 13, 1904. *Abilene Chronicle,* Apr. 6, 1871; *Ellsworth Reporter,* June 20, 1872; *Dodge City Times,* May 26, 1877; *Trail Drivers of Texas* (Hunter, ed.), 92-93, 476-478, 538-540, 940-941; Pelzer, *op. cit.,* 47-48, 58-59, 63.

an annual drive of from four to twelve thousand head
thereto. Mr. Ellison is a solid, substantial man, one who
thinks for himself and looks upon life as a great, solid real-
ity; but little given to frivolity; is sober, honest, upright, and
true hearted; is shrewd and energetic in business, and always
manages to sell out in good time and at fair prices; is public
spirited and wide-awake, full of resources; and withal a
genuine, good cattleman, and belongs to that type of men
of which any country may be proud.

But perhaps no more appropriate personal sketch of a
genuine Texan ranchman could be presented than that of
J. M. Choate;[205] a Tennesseean by birth but a Texan of
twenty-eight years' residence, [he] is perhaps as true a
specimen, both in appearance and manner of life, of the
patriarchal [18] ranchman and drover combined, as could
be presented. His broad, high forehead, open, frank countenance, full-grown untrimmed, and unshaven beard mark
him as a genuine frontiersman, one accustomed to untold
privations and hardships; yet one to whom no phase of
frontier life has either terror or trials that he would fear
to face or shrink from enduring. He is a close observer of
transpiring events, an unerring reader of human countenances and character. A man whose sincere aim is to do right
with his fellow man, one who suffers in heart when the
people of his state are outraged or are made to endure
unjust impositions. Although upon the shady side of life, yet
he is well preserved, hale and robust, and as fond of fun and
jollity, a good joke or a laughable story as are those many
years his junior. Such are, briefly, the characteristics of J. M.
Choate, of Helena, Texas, who has spent the entire time
that he has lived in Texas upon a farm and stock ranch.
Since the war he has devoted his time and energies to the
live stock business. He was a drover of 1866, and one of
those who wended their way into Iowa with their herds,
but he did not admire northern driving, regarding it as too

205 J. M. Choate was born in Tennessee, April 28, 1822, and moved to
Karnes county, Texas, about 1855. Four of his sons were trail drivers: J. H.
Choate, D. C. Choate, K. B. Choate, and W. M. Choate. He died at his
home in Karnes county, August 9, 1899. *Trail Drivers of Texas* (Hunter,
ed.), 736-738.

precarious — too uncertain, not to say dangerous, to life and limb; so in 1867 and 1868 he turned his herds toward New Orleans. But the following year a better report of the prospect north reached him, and hither he has annually driven from one to eight thousand head of cattle, and generally sold them upon the prairie in preference to shipping. There he feels at home and knows just what he is doing. Mr. Choate owns a ranch of about fifteen hundred acres, upon which and adjoining outlying government lands he keeps about three thousand cattle and five hundred horses. To his live stock interest he looks for his money, and when he can sell at home for satisfactory prices, prefers to do so; but when the home buyer fails to come, he does not hesitate to outfit one or more herds and drive them on his own account.

II. DRIVING CATTLE NORTH
IN 1866

For a quarter of a century or more the herds of Texas continued to increase much faster than the mature surplus was marketed. In fact, no market accessible existed sufficient to consume this surplus, so the excess grew greater and greater each year, and of course the stock less valuable in proportion as it became plentiful. [New] Orleans and Mobile were the only cities of size outside of the state [207] that consumed any considerable portion of Texan cattle, and those markets were controlled, in fact practically monopolized, by the Morgan line of steamers plying between the coast of Texas and those cities. To anyone outside of the ship company an enormous rate of freight was exacted, practically debarring the ordinary shipper.[208]

But few attempts were ever made before the war to drive cattle north, although it was done, but not largely or very successfully.[209] The outbreak of the Civil war was a disaster great and almost fatal to the stock interests of Texas, for as soon as the Mississippi river was occupied and patrolled by the gunboats of the Union forces, and Orleans captured, then Texas was, so far as a market for her live stock, complete walled out.[210] She could not drive north if she

[207] Between 1849 and 1860 many Texas cattle were sold at Kansas City and Independence, Missouri; during the latter part of the same period a limited number were also marketed in Chicago, St. Louis, and New York City.

[208] The *Galveston Commercial and Weekly Prices Current* (Sept. 1, 1856) gave the following statistics of the number of cattle shipped from that port to New Orleans: 1850, 2905; 1851, 5506; 1852, 3429; 1853, 2726; 1854, 5957; 1855, 4361; 1856, 4614. Some of these cattle were shipped originally from Indianola and merely stopped at Galveston on their way to New Orleans.

[209] This inaccurate statement has been corrected in the introduction to the present volume.

[210] A limited number of Texas cattle were driven overland to New Orleans after its capture by Farragut.

would; she would not if she could. A few droves were marketed by [20] surreptitiously swimming the Mississippi river below Vicksburg and thence were hurried east to the Confederate armies, but the vigilance of the Union gunboats rendered this an extra-hazardous business and but a small amount of it was done. Then dawned a time in Texas that a man's poverty was estimated by the number of cattle he possessed. Many ranchmen entirely neglected their stock, for they were regarded as not worth caring for. Stocks of cattle were, in certain sections, offered at prices ranging from one to two dollars per head, and that often without finding a purchaser.

The effect of the war on the cattle interest and supply in the North was the very reverse of what it was in Texas, for at its close the bullock — a select, mature animal, worth five or six dollars in Texas — was worth in the northern markets more than ten times that amount. This vast difference constituted a wide and tempting field to the cattle speculator — a field that he was not slow to attempt to occupy. During the winter and spring of 1865 and 1866 large herds of beeves were gathered in Texas preparatory to driving north the following summer. To give an idea of the value of cattle in Texas at this time, we will here state that an intimate friend, then in the trade, went to a herd of 3,500 head of beeves and purchased 600 head of his choice at $6 per head; then for the next 600 head, his choice, he paid $3 per head; making his purchase of 1,200 head cost on an average $4.50 per head, or something near forty cents per hundred pounds gross weight. At that price beef could hardly be called an expensive luxury, or its production a very profitable business.[211]

---

[211] The price of Texas cattle, both in Texas and in the northern states, depended upon their age, weight, condition, and place and time of purchase or sale. On March 20, 1866, George C. Duffield, of Iowa, contracted for 1000 beeves in San Sabá county, Texas, at $12 each. Early in 1867, according to the *Texas Almanac,* cattle could be obtained for "$3 to $5 per head in various parts of the state." During June, 1866, a small lot of Texas longhorns were disposed of in Kentucky at $88 each. Between July and September, 1866, Texas cattle fetched from $20 to $40 per head in the St. Louis market. About the middle of October, 1866, at Chicago, 130 head of "good Texas steers and oxen, averaging 1130 lbs.," sold for approximately $65 each. In Springfield,

We have heard the number of cattle that had crossed Red river during 1866 put down as high as 260,000 head.[212] We believe these figures approximate the number, if not exactly correct. We can readily believe that the bright visions of great profits and sudden wealth that had shimmered before the imagination of the drover, leading him on as the subtle mirage of the desert does the famishing traveler — nerving him to greater hardships, and buoying him up in many a [21] wild, stormy night, whilst he kept silent vigil over his herd — were shocked, if not blasted, by the unexpected reception given him in southern Kansas and Missouri by a determined, organized, armed mob, more lawless, insolent, and imperious than a band of wild savages. Under the pretext of a fear of disease being disseminated among the so-called native cattle, all manner of outrage, robbery, and murder were perpetrated. As is always the case, the men who were most likely to lose the least were the most forward in demonstrations of lawlessness; in short, the principal actors were outlaws and thieves, glad of an excuse to pillage, kill, and steal. The practice was to go in force and armed to the teeth, surround the drover, insult him by words such as a cowardly bully only knows how to use, spit in his face, snatch handfuls of beard out of the drover's face, tie him to a tree and whip him with anything they could lay their hands on, tie a rope around his neck and choke him; in short, provoke him to a demonstration of resistance or self-defense, then kill him, and straightway proceed to appropriate his herd. It was idle to talk about the protection of law; such a thing was utterly impossible. Anyone who is familiar with the quick, hot, impetuous temper of the southern drover will readily admit that he would brook but little of such treatment before he would shoot at his assailants. Many of them paid the forfeit of their lives, often, however, getting

Illinois, early in December, 1866, 94 longhorns, averaging about 1000 pounds apiece, sold at $25 per head; 58 others, "among whom were six yoke of work oxen," at $22. *Daily Missouri Republican,* June 12, July 17, Aug. 1, 3, 6, 18, Sept. 13, 1866; *Chicago Tribune,* Oct. 12, 1866; *Daily Illinois State Journal,* Dec. 8, 1866; *Texas Almanac for 1867,* p. 197; Duffield, *loc. cit.,* 248.

212 McCoy himself may have been responsible for this estimate, which is probably too high. *Kansas Daily Commonwealth,* Aug. 15, 1871.

in effective work before they were killed. Others took the unencumbered leisure of their return to balance accounts and avenge the wrongs of themselves or their friends, and often right thoroughly and to their full satisfaction did they do it. Southern Kansas and Missouri were the fields to which every rascal in either state annually rallied to cheat and swindle, by bogus checks, worthless notes, or any other villainous device, the southern drover out of his herds. In short, the tactics were to stop the drover by mob violence, then rob or swindle him out of his stock. Could the prairies of southeast Kansas [22] and southwest Missouri talk, they could tell many a thrilling, blood-curdling story of carnage, wrong, outrage, robbery, and revenge not excelled in the history of any banditti or the annals of the most bloody savages.

If the mob could not frighten the drover until he would abandon his stock, or if they failed to obtain a pretext for killing him outright, resort was had to stampeding the cattle. This was easily done by availing themselves of the cover of night and creeping stealthily until close to the herd, then suddenly rising up and flourishing a buffalo robe or blanket. Of course such sudden and unexpected demonstrations would frighten the cattle and cause them to dash off at full speed, pell mell, in the darkness. Before running far, the herd would be broken up into squads, and the farther they ran, the greater the fright, often rushing over rocks, cliffs, or high banks. The entire herd would be greatly injured and many of the cattle utterly ruined; some with limbs broken, others with horns broken off, and often weeks were required to regather them. Of course, many could never be found, for whilst the drover with all his available help was engaged in regathering the cattle, the members of the mob would be just as busy secreting all they could find; and knowing the country better than the drover, the mob usually got the lion's share. When the drover was exhausted, his horses worn out with hard service, and his case began to be deplorable, some member of the mob would come into the camp and offer to hunt up the lost cattle for a snug price, perhaps five dollars per head. So soon as a bargain was struck, the outlaw would mount his horse and in less than a day would return with many if not all the lost cattle. It would not require a Solomon to know that the cattle had been secreted in some out-of-the-way nook and carefully guarded until such time as it would be profitable for the thieves to return them to their owner or send them off to be sold for their own account.

The drover had no alternative; he must submit to be blackmailed or lose his cattle entirely. There was little use [23] in thinking about law or justice, much less enforcing the one or expecting the other. There are few occupations in life wherein a man will hold by so brittle a thread a large fortune as droving. In fact, the drover is nearly as helpless as a child, for but a single misstep or wrong move and he may lose his entire herd, representing and constituting all his earthly possessions. None understood this fact better than the mobs of outlaws that annually infested the cattle trail leading from Texas to Sedalia, Missouri. If the drover had ready money and could obtain an interview with the leader of the mob, it was not difficult to secure safe transit for his herd, but it was always expensive, and few drovers were disposed to buy a recognition of their legal rights. Many of them had not the money, for they had invested all their available cash in cattle before leaving Texas. Be it said to the credit of the law-abiding citizens of southeastern Kansas and southwestern Missouri that they neither aided nor abetted the mobs in their thieving and murdering schemes. The fear of Spanish fever was made the pretext for committing the grossest outrages, just as the late Civil war was a convenient pretext for lawless plundering, outraging, and murdering of civil, quiet citizens.[213]

Of the quarter of a million cattle that came up from Texas in 1866, but few found their way to a profitable market, for they were held back until the weather had become very cold and the grass long since dead and unnutritious, the cattle poor in flesh and weak from poverty and hard usage, and were finally put upon the market, unfit for any

[213] Statutes enacted by Missouri and Kansas in 1861 prohibited or restricted the driving of Texas cattle into those states—hence the opposition by the citizens. Besides, some Jayhawkers and lawless whites, survivals of the Civil war period and before, roamed through southwestern Missouri and southeastern Kansas, molesting the southern drovers or stealing their herds under the guise of preventing the introduction of Texas fever.

purpose.[214] Of course, they brought a small price per pound and weighed but little, netting the drover often less than first cost in Texas. In fact, many cases could be cited where the drover did not realize more than enough to pay freight and other expenses; whereas, had they been permitted to drive the stock direct to Sedalia, Missouri,[215] and there shipped over the Missouri Pacific Railroad to St. Louis, thence to other markets, fortunes would have been made instead of lost. That the reader may have a correct idea of what the southern drover endured, we [24] present a brief sketch of the treatment one or two of the drovers of 1866 received in southwestern Missouri.

James M. Daugherty, a young, enterprising drover, then of less than twenty years of age, crossed Red river near Rock Bluffs with a fine herd of cattle numbering over one thousand head, determined to place them upon the St. Louis market. Soon after entering the Indian Nation, he found, in order to avoid paying an arbitrary tax to the Cherokee Indians, he was compelled to turn his course more eastward and enter the state of Arkansas near Fort Smith. Then driving in a northern direction a short distance, he was compelled to turn northwest on account of the rough, rocky, barren character of the country. Soon after, entering the state of Missouri, he was aroused from the pleasant revery of beautiful prospects and snug fortune easily won, by the appearance of a yelling, armed, organized mob, which ordered him to halt. Never in his limited experience had he seen such bipeds as constituted that band of self-appointed guardian angels; dressed in coarsest homespun pantaloons and hunting shirts, with undershirts spun of coarsest tow, [and] a pair of rude, home-made cowhide shoes upon whose construction the broadax and jackplane had figured largely; all surmounted with a coonskin cap of great antiquity and unmistakably home manufacture. To this add a score of visages closely resembling the orang-outang, bearing evidence of the lowest order of humanity, with but one over-

---

214 Traveling over circuitous routes from southwest Missouri or southeast Kansas, many of the drovers of 1866 finally found a market for their cattle in Missouri, Kansas, Nebraska, Iowa, Illinois, Ohio, Indiana, and Kentucky.

215 No evidence has been found that any cattle were shipped from Sedalia in 1866.

J. M. CHOATE.

J. M. DOUGHERTY.

MOBBING DOUGHERTY IN SOUTHWEST MISSOURI.

powering passion – a love for unrectified whiskey of the
deadliest brand. Young Daugherty was told that "them
thar steers couldn't go an inch fudder. No sare." Daugherty
quietly began to reason with them, but it was like preaching
morality to an alligator. No sooner did they discover that
the drover was a young man and probably little experienced
in life, than they immediately surrounded him, and whilst
a part of the mob attacked his comrade and shamefully mal-
treated him, a half dozen coarse brutes dragged the drover
from his saddle, disarmed him, tied him fast to a tree with
his own picket rope, [26] then proceeded to whip him with
hickory withes in the most brutal manner.

Whilst these outrages were being perpetrated upon the
drover and his comrade, a preappointed Missourian dashed
into the herd of cattle at full speed, flourishing at arm's end
a striped blanket, all the while screeching and yelling as only
a semicivilized being can. Of course this had the intended
effect. The cattle took great fright at the, to them, unusual
demonstrations, and with a whirl and a snort were off at full
speed, rushing wildly over everything before them. Fortunately for the drover, one or two faithful cowboys were in
the rear of the herd, and quickly divining the trouble and
real situation, dashed ahead of the stampeded herd and led
it down a long hollow and around a rough high hill, which
was thickly covered with timber, into a smooth, open valley
of prairie, and there adroitly circled the leaders around and
kept them curving until the entire herd was running on a
small circle, which was gradually contracted until they were
rushing round and round in as small a space of ground as
it was possible for that number of cattle to occupy. In a
few minutes the cattle became quiet and the cowboys turned
their heads to the west and hurried them on for a distance
of five miles, leaving Daugherty and his comrade to the
tender mercies of the gentle, lamblike mob.

In the meantime, after each one of the Missourians had
sated his brutal instincts by whipping their bound victim,
they demanded of Daugherty that he would mount his horse
and leave the country instantly, not stopping to inquire or
look after his herd, but hasten away. His comrade had torn
himself loose from his persecutors, and putting spurs to his

mustang cow pony, was soon out of sight in the adjoining woods, where thick undergrowth and foliage afforded early seclusion. Daugherty staggered to where his faithful pony stood, and drawing his lacerated, bleeding body into his saddle, said to his assailants that they outnumbered him and were armed, whilst he was alone and disarmed, and that under these circumstances he would be [27] compelled to do as they directed. But there gleamed in the drover's dark, liquid eye a determination to balance accounts with as many of that mob as the future might afford opportunity.

Turning his horse's head at right angles from the direction in which his herd had retreated, the drover slowly rode away, feeling much more dead than alive. After riding a mile or more, his comrade hallooed to him from a cluster of underbrush not far distant and then rode out to meet him. Both were glad that they were not killed outright. After wandering slyly about for a few hours, they found the trail of the herd, and gladly discovered it was headed westward and that it was traveling at a quiet gait instead of running. Putting spurs to their ponies, they dashed ahead on the trail as fast as their steeds could carry them. A few hours after nightfall they beheld a small camp fire and approached cautiously until they were sure they were making no mistake. Once in camp, the drover soon had his bruised and lacerated body washed and dressed as well as could be under the circumstances. Before the earliest note of the vigil chanticleer the herd was again put upon the move, headed for the northeast corner of the Indian Territory near Baxter Springs, where it arrived without event of particular note. After Daugherty had halted on the prairies near Baxter Springs for a few weeks and had fully recovered from the severe trouncing he had received in Missouri, he started out with a few hundred head of cattle late one evening, and during the night ran the blockade; and after lying in a secluded spot during the day, made good his way to Fort Scott, Kansas, where he disposed of his cattle without trouble, and secured a buyer who returned to Baxter with him and purchased the balance of his herd. Having made a satisfactory profit, he returned to Texas and made necessary business arrangements in order to embark in the business of driving as a permanent occupation, which business he has steadily followed ever since, driving from one thousand to four thousand head of cattle to western Kansas market annually.[216]

Although now but a [28] young man in years, yet he is old in business experiences and in a knowledge of the ways of the world; always acting upon his own judgment in business matters, never having had a partner, but does his own thinking, lays his own plans, and personally attends to the smallest details, we need not add, is generally successful; of that quiet, unobtrusive turn, yet social and pleasant, fond of having a good time, but never rude or boisterous, always upright and honorable. Besides having a valuable property in Texas, he has established a fine ranch in Colorado, on which now are over one thousand head of cattle, besides horses and other necessary auxiliaries to success. It is easy to see that before many more years are numbered among the past, J. M. Daugherty will take position among the best and most substantial citizens of the Great New West.

During the summer of 1866 the whole country about Baxter Springs was alive with blockaded cattle, the owners of which were trying all manner of [29] expedients to get through southwest Missouri to some shipping point on the Missouri Pacific Railroad. The drover who was fortunate enough to have at his own command cash to the amount of two or three dollars for each head of cattle he wished to pass through to Sedalia, Missouri, had no trouble to arrange matters with the leader of the mob, to not only permit the herd to pass on, but give it safe conduct through the country to the railroad. But few of the drovers were so fortunately situated in financial matters as to be able to avail themselves of the opportunity of buying their way, or the permission to go to market. A strong prejudice existed in the minds of the mass of drovers to buying the privilege of exercising a plain, inalienable right, to wit: to take their stock unmolested to any market to which they might choose to go. But in that day and country a man's, especially southern

---

[216] McCoy's narrative of Daugherty's experiences is not entirely accurate, but it can be corrected by the latter's own account of his adventure in *Trail Drivers of Texas* (Hunter, ed.), 696-699. See also *Historical and Biographical Record of the Cattle Industry*, 352-353; *Prose and Poetry of the Live Stock Industry*, I, 284-285.

drover's, legal rights, without physical force sufficient to enforce them or secure respect thereof, were as useless as a piece of refuse paper.

A large number of the drovers of 1866, after learning fully the hopeless situation in southeastern Kansas and southwestern Missouri, turned their heads due west from Baxter Springs and drove them along or near the Kansas line near two hundred miles, then turned northwest through the state of Kansas just west of all settlement, until a point about due west of St. Joe, Missouri, was reached; then turning east or northeast, drove to St. Joe and shipped them to Chicago. Or, crossing the Missouri river near Nebraska City or Brownsville, Nebraska, pushed into central Iowa, and there sold to the cattle feeders of that state.[217] Those that took the latter course did very well, for they obtained good prices from the cattle feeders of Iowa, whose corn crops were very good, and millions of bushels thereof could only be profitably disposed of by feeding it to live stock, of which the supply was limited. But some of those who shipped their cattle to Chicago fared badly, either selling at low prices or packing on their own account, which latter operation was more [30] unprofitable than the former. The cattle had been driven so far and subjected to so much hardship that they had become poor in flesh, and were unfit for any purpose except to be fed during the winter and grazed until fat the following summer.

We might write a volume of sketches and personal experiences of drovers of 1866, but one more will suffice. R. D. Hunter, now a resident of Kansas City, Missouri, but of Ayrshire Scottish birth, came to this continent at the age of ten years with his father, who selected central Illinois, then a comparatively unsettled country, as his home, and devoted himself to farming and stock raising after the manner of that day and country; about which occupation the subject of this sketch was thoroughly instructed. Reared a farmer, it was but natural as well as wise for him to begin life for himself, following the footsteps of his father. But when Pike's Peak gold discoveries were heralded over the

217 George C. Duffield, of Iowa, who drove longhorns from San Sabá county, Texas, traveled this route into central Iowa. Duffield, *loc. cit.*, 257-262.

land, golden visions flitted before the imagination of the young farmer, too bright and persuasive for resistance. In the spring of 1859, R. D. Hunter, with his comrades, rigged for traveling overland, left "the States" for the gold fields of the Rocky mountains. Arriving at the mountain's base, but a brief stop was made, for each one was anxious to learn what fickle fortune had in store for him. In a short time they were numbered among the residents and miners of Gregory's Lode and Russell's Gulch. The first year Mr. Hunter did fairly and managed to wrest from mother earth's rugged bosom a snug sum of the glittering dust, but not an amount equal to his aspirations. The following year he embarked in a quartz milling enterprise, which proved unfortunate. About this time arose a great excitement among the miners, caused by reports of fabulously rich mines in Arizona, and hither R. D. Hunter turned his face. But the Indians, not liking the proposed inundation of pale faces, waxed hostile, and Mr. Hunter turned his course to the San Juan country, a valley of southwest Colorado. Whilst in that country he discovered what is now known as "Putnam's Lode," a gold-bearing [31] quartz vein of undoubted great richness; but owing to its peculiar location and the distance, the difficulty of access of the country, no more was done in the way of working it than enough to vest the title in the discoverer. This property he owns to this day, hoping for a railroad to go sufficiently near to make the working of it practicable.

The San Juan country proving a failure save for quartz mining, after spending two years in those regions, Mr. Hunter returned to Denver, and there, meeting his family, decided to make Denver his home, temporarily at least. But just then came the dark hour of life, the time that tries a man's soul. No sooner had he begun to feel that he might enjoy life and home, notwithstanding fortune's frown, than affliction marked him as a victim, prostrating him helpless upon his bed for near a year, unable to so much as raise his hand – all superinduced by hard labor and exposure in the mines, and that, too, without a fitting reward. When health was restored, he decided that gold diggings, with shovel and pick, was not his forte, and returned, after five years' absence, to Missouri, where he soon became engaged in a cattle trade, supplying oxen to freighters. At that date no railroads extended beyond the Missouri river.

At that business, success rewarded his efforts, and at the end of the Civil war he turned his face toward the Lone Star State in quest of cattle. Before reaching Red river, he met and purchased a herd of four hundred head, coming north, in the Indian Territory. Having paid twenty-five dollars per head for the cattle, a price which to him appeared very small, he felt that the day had come in which fortune for him was in reach, like a hanging apple just ready to be plucked. How delusive were these appearances and hopes, the sequel will show. The western line of Vernon county, Missouri, was passed but a few miles on the route to Sedalia, when a coonskin-capped biped calling himself the sheriff of Vernon county summarily took formal possession of his herd and at the same time placed the drover under arrest. About ten thousand head of cattle, with their owners or foremen in [32] charge, were seized and arrested at the same time. Here was a dilemma not expected, one not put down in their almanac of probabilities. How to get out with the least loss was the question that perplexed the drovers. During the first night, whilst under arrest, Mr. Hunter hit upon a plan to extricate himself and friends, which he disclosed to them privately and exacted their promise to perform the part assigned them. Early next morning he told the sheriff he did not want to go to jail, that he would prefer to make his own living and not burden the very good people of Vernon county with his support, and if the sheriff would accompany him to Lamar, the county seat, distant thirty-five miles, he thought some friends could be found who would go his bail. To this the sheriff assented, for it would then be convenient to put the drover in the lockup if bail was not obtained. No sooner were the sheriff and his prisoner well out of sight from the drover's camp than, according to previous arrangements, the herds were put upon the trail directly west toward the Indian neutral lands, distant thirty-five miles, and a brisk speed maintained without halting to graze or rest.

Upon the road to Lamar the drover had a chance to study

ROBERT D. HUNTER.

"THE VERNON SHERIFF TAKES BONDS."

the face of his captor, and came to the conclusion that he
was bacchanalian in his religious predilections, a persuasion
of large membership quite common among the denizens of
southwestern Missouri. Soon after arriving at the county
seat, they went to a Temple of Bacchus, of which there
were several in the village, to offer their devotions. As the
drover anticipated, the officer proved to be an enthusiastic
devotee, ready at all times to offer libations providing the
drover would pay the priest, which he was not loath to do.
But there is a limit to ordinary human capacity, and so there
was to the devotional capacity of that sheriff. When he had
passed that stage wherein everything was beautiful and
lovely, and the memory of his humble circumstances had fled
from his brain, and great wealth and joy inexpressible had
taken [33] possession of him – to the peculiar condition
when the ground will come right up and strike a fellow in
the face; when all these manifestations were visible upon the
county official, to the drover, he concluded that he had given
all necessary "bonds," and whilst the official was blubbering
and wallowing in the street, the drover mounted his steed
and, bidding Lamar and the sheriff good afternoon, turned
his steed westward. About daylight next morning Mr.
Hunter overtook his comrades and friends with their herds
in the Indian Nation. When he came up to them, he found
every cowboy not needed to care for the cattle, marshaled
in military style, guarding the rear of the last herd. It would
not have been altogether [34] healthy for a sheriff's posse
to have attempted a rearrest of those herds or the drovers;
but when they were sure they were out of the state of Missouri, all fear of disturbance ceased, and they soon halted,
rested, and grazed their herds.

After a few days spent recuperating, the herds were put
upon their travels, taking a westerly direction for the distance of about one hundred and fifty miles, then curving
northward; the Kaw river was crossed at St. Mary's. On
reaching the vicinity of Atchison, a German settlement felt
called upon to go upon the warpath after the drovers, and
would have caused them great trouble and, perhaps, loss but
for the kindness of a Mr. Joel Hyatt, a large landowner and
a good-hearted, sensible man of that section, who gave the

persecuted drovers an asylum upon his lands, where they rested for two weeks. Then they crossed the river at St. Joe and drove in a northerly direction to Bartlett Station on the Chicago and Rock Island Railroad, and there shipped their herds. Mr. Hunter decided to take his cattle off at Joliet, Illinois, and put them on blue-grass pasture, rather than to go direct on to the Chicago market as his comrades did. It proved a wise decision, for in a few weeks he was able to find a buyer at remunerative prices. The first year in the southern cattle trade closed, and Mr. Hunter stood six thousand dollars better off in cash, aside from experience, which was no small item, for a place and way had been found for future operations.

In 1867, R. D. Hunter went to Texas and bought twelve hundred head of cattle, which he drove to Omaha, Nebraska, and sold to government contractors at a snug profit. The summer of 1869 found him on the trail from Texas with a fine herd of twenty-five hundred head of cattle, which were sold in Chicago at paying figures. But in 1870 a herd of fourteen hundred head of select beeves was put upon the Chicago market, and four and one-half to six and one-quarter cents gross weight was realized, netting a profit of twenty dollars per head. [36] In every business there is bitter mingled with the sweet; this is strictly true in the cattle business, and the year 1871 was, from a multitude of causes, a bitter, bad year for the drover, and, although not a year of actual disaster to Mr. Hunter, yet it was without that desirable profit. Although he handled about five thousand, and did it to the best of his judgment, yet it was, as a year's transaction, "bad medicine." This was the last year of Mr. Hunter's driving. Since that time he has traded in cattle in the West and aided the Kansas Pacific Railway in the management of its live stock business.[218] In 1873 he established, in connection with Captain Evans and others, a live stock commission house with headquarters at Kansas City.[219] This house soon took rank among the leading ones

---

[218] Hunter may have been engaged in one of these activities when he was in Ellsworth, Kansas, in 1872 and 1873. In July of the latter year his residence was in Chillicothe, Missouri. *Ellsworth Reporter*, June 20, July 11, 1872, July 10, 1873.

[219] Hunter, Pattison & Evans. *Ibid.*, Apr. 17, 1873.

in the West and has handled many thousand head of cattle, almost invariably to the entire satisfaction of its numerous patrons, which includes many of the largest live stock operators in the West. Each member of the firm is a practical and successful stockman, and their combined capitals enables them to render ample aid to their patrons, besides rendering the firm entirely responsible and safe. As a man he is kind and courteous to all with whom he has business relations; but his manner is bluff and positive, bordering on the hauteur, and to one whom he dislikes, he is unmercifully severe. Indeed, it is little comfort his enemies receive at his hands. Language fails to express his intense contempt for a little mean action; and as for a dishonest transaction or its author, neither can receive other than his severest, outspoken condemnation. But for his friends, or for one whom he regards as worthy, he has a big heart, throbbing the warmest pulsations of sympathy. He is strictly honorable in his business transactions, dignified in his manner, courteous in his address, inflexible in will — self-reliant. Such is R. D. Hunter, and all right-feeling men freely yield him the palm of honorable, manly success.

Other drovers of 1866 turned their herds eastward from [37] Baxter Springs, and drove along or near the Arkansas line until they were able to flank the hostile regions and strike the railroad at a shipping point east of Sedalia.[220] But this route was mountainous, rocky, and much of the distance, heavily timbered and altogether unsuited for successful cattle driving. The cattle driven over it became footsore and miserably poor in flesh, and, of course, when put on the St. Louis market, sold for mean prices and weighed very light; so that when the drover had sold out and paid up expenses, but little cash remained to swell his impoverished pocketbook. But by far the larger half of the drovers remained near Baxter Springs, preferring to hope on and keep trying,

[220] Sedalia, founded in 1861, had a population estimated at 3500 by January, 1867. The Pacific Railroad of Missouri reached the place early in 1861, and the town remained the end of the track until May, 1863. The railroad was completed between St. Louis and Kansas City in September, 1865. Margaret Louise Fitzsimmons, Railroad Development in Missouri, 1860-1870, MS., M.A. thesis, Washington University; *Weekly Sedalia Times*, Jan. 3, 1867.

to risking any untried route with their herds.[221] Soon the frost came and killed the grass, which, after drying a few days, was set fire and the whole country burned over. This was a great calamity to the drovers.

All along the border a host of sharpers and thieves – men with good address and plausible pretensions – were anxious to buy cattle, but owing to the unsettled condition of affairs were afraid to bring the cash with them, but had what purported to be New York exchange, with which they bought cattle of such as they could induce to accept their drafts. Of course their drafts were worthless, but before the drover could find it out and secure himself, the rascal would have turned the stock into some secret confederate's hands and left for parts unknown to the drover. Others used worthless notes and such other devices as villainous ingenuity could invent, and each scheme or plan would surely catch some unwary, confiding drover. Other drovers, to save themselves from loss or financial ruin, placed their herds in winter quarters in southern Kansas and Missouri. Others found their way into the corn regions of central Illinois and there fed their stock until a purchaser was found.[222]

[221] Early in November, 1866, the *Nevada Times,* published in Nevada, Vernon county, Missouri, contained the following item: "At present there is about ten or twelve thousand head of Texas cattle en route across this county, for different points on the Pacific Railroad, to be shipped to St. Louis and Chicago. They are generally large cattle and in fine order, having been herded for the past summer in the southern part of this county, the northern part of Barton county and the Neutral lands. We understand there are upwards of thirty thousand head on the Neutral lands, moving up this way, destined for the same markets. It remains to be seen, whether or not, driving Texas and Indian stock through our country at this season of the year, will generate or commmunicate the disease commonly known as 'spanish fever,' to our native cattle. The general impression among the citizens seems to be that they ought not be permitted to come into or to pass through our county, as we have laws to prevent it." *Nevada Times* in *Independent Press,* Nov. 15, 1866.

[222] During the summer, fall, and early winter of 1866 thousands of Texas cattle were received at the stockyards of St. Louis, Missouri, and Quincy, Illinois, whence many were shipped or driven to central and northern Illinois for feeding. *Daily Missouri Republican,* July 17, 20, 28, Aug. 1, 2, 3, 6, 13, 18, Sept. 13, Dec. 24, 27, 1866; *Daily Quincy Herald,* Aug. 28, Sept. 13, 20, 25, Oct. 10, 16, 18, Nov. 14, 17, 22, 29, Dec. 6, 1866; *Daily Illinois State Journal,* Sept. 6, 8, 12, 26, 1866.

But the year 1866 was, taking all things into consideration, one of great disaster to southern drovers. All the
bright prospects of marketing profitably the immense surplus live stock of Texas faded away or, worse, [38] proved
to those who tried driving, a serious financial loss. So the last
great hope of the southern cattleman for an outlet and market for his live stock proved but bitter disappointment.
Never, perhaps, in the history of Texas was the business
of cattle ranching at so low estate as about the close of the
year 1866 and during the following year. The cattle-producing portions of the state were overrun with stock. The
ranges were becoming depastured, and, as a consequence,
the unprotected earth became parched by the hot sun, and
permanent drouth threatened. The stocks of cattle would
not yield sufficient revenue to pay the expenses of caring for
them — that is, branding, marking, etc. Strange as it may
seem, it is nevertheless true that within the bounds of that
great state no one came forward to open up an outlet for
the millions of her matured cattle. Over the business of
cattle ranching a deep gloom settled, crushing to earth the
hopes of many whose herds numbered multiplied thousands.
Such was the condition of affairs in Texas at the close of the
year 1866. But it is said that the darkest hour is that one
just before the break of day. And so it was in this case. Just
how and from whence came that brighter hour, that dawn of
day, will form the theme of a future chapter.

THE RAILROAD KING AND THE ILLINOISAN.

III. ESTABLISHING ABILENE
AS A SHIPPING DEPOT

The close of the year 1866 left the business of driving Texan cattle prostrate, and the entire driving fraternity, both North and South, in an utterly discouraged condition. And such was the effect of the experiences of 1866; but in 1867 events took a change for the better, and just how that change was brought about we propose to note.

At that time there lived in central Illinois three brothers doing a large live stock shipping business as one company or firm.[223] One thousand head of native cattle costing from $80 to $140 per head was not an unusual week's shipment. When it is remembered that three shipments were on the road at the same time during all the season, it will be seen that their resources, financially, were not limited. All three of the brothers were of that sanguine, impetuous, speculative temperament; just such dispositions as always look most upon the bright side of the picture, and never feel inclined to look at the dangers or hazards of a venture, but take it for granted that all will end well that looks well in the beginning. If the above could have been said of the brothers collectively, it could be said with particular truthfulness of the younger one of them. Ambitious, energetic, quick to scent out and [40] untiring to follow a speculation, fully possessed with an earnest desire to do something that would

---

[223] William K. McCoy & Brothers, of Springfield, Illinois. William, the senior member of the firm, was born in Sangamon county, April, 1829. About 1876 he was living in Bancroft, Daviess county, Missouri, but later moved to Oregon, where he died. James P. McCoy, the second member of the firm, was born in Sangamon county, July 3, 1832. He married Jane L. Seeley, of Springfield, and afterward moved to Topeka, Kansas, where he died. Joseph G. McCoy was the third member of the firm. Power, *History of the Early Settlers of Sangamon County, Illinois,* 488; Van Patten, "A Brief History of David McCoy and Family," *loc. cit.,* 125-127.

alike benefit humanity as well as himself — something that, when life's rugged battles were over, could be pointed to as an evidence that he had lived to some good purpose and that the world, or a portion thereof, was benefitted by his having lived.

This young man conceived the idea of opening up an outlet for Texan cattle.[224] Being impressed with a knowledge of the number of cattle in Texas and the difficulties of getting them to market by the routes and means then in use, and realizing the great disparity of Texas values and northern prices of cattle, he set himself to thinking and studying to hit upon some plan whereby these great extremes would be equalized. The plan was to establish at some accessible point a depot or market to which a Texan drover could bring his stock unmolested, and there, failing to find a buyer, he could go upon the public highways to any market in the country he wished. In short, it was to establish a market whereat the southern drover and northern buyer would meet upon an equal footing, and both be undisturbed by mobs or swindling thieves. The longer the idea of this enterprise was harbored by the young Illinois cattle shipper, the more determined he became and the more enthusiastic to carry it out. In fact, it became an inspiration almost irresistible, rising superior to all other aspirations of his life, and to which he gave unremitting attention and labor for years; indeed he is not now unmindful of the purposes which first impelled him forward.

It was not long after the project had taken crude shape in the mind of the projector, before he was casting his eye over the map of the western states, studying the situation and trying to determine whether the western prairies or the southern rivers would be the better place to establish the proposed depot. Before he had fully decided in his own mind, a trip to Kansas City was taken, and soon after ar-

[224] That McCoy was not the first person to conceive this idea has been demonstrated in the introduction to the present volume. It has also been shown that conversations with Charles F. Gross, of Springfield, Illinois, in 1866, and with W. W. Sugg, in Christian county, Illinois, during 1867, as well as information obtained from other sources, gave McCoy the idea of establishing a shipping point for Texas cattle.

riving there, he met with certain residents who were interested in a large herd of cattle coming up from Texas and expected to arrive somewhere in [41] Kansas, but just where was not known, as no particular place had been designated. After repeated conversations with these parties a trip up the Kansas Pacific, then called the Union Pacific, East Division, was determined upon.[225] The road was completed and operated at that time as far west as Salina, Kansas. Junction City was visited and a proposition made to one of the leading business men to purchase of him a tract of land sufficiently large to build a stockyard and such other facilities as were necessary for cattle shipping, but an exorbitant price was asked; in fact, a flat refusal to sell at any price was the final answer of the wide-awake Junctionite. So by that one act of donkey stupidity and avarice Junction City drove from her a trade which soon developed to many millions.[226]

Failing to obtain a location, but fully decided to select the prairies of the West instead of the banks of the southern rivers for a field to put his scheme on foot, the Illinoisan returned to St. Louis for the purpose of consulting the railroad magnates about rates of freight and other necessary facilities for the accommodation of live stock. Visiting the general offices of the Kansas Pacific [227] and introducing himself to the president [228] and executive committee there, stating fully his project and the reasons for the confident belief in him, giving a moderate estimate of the probable number of cars of live stock freight that would be sent over the road,

[225] Many years afterward McCoy wrote a more detailed account of his experiences in Kansas City in 1867. McCoy, "Historic and Biographic Sketch," *loc. cit.*, pp. 49-50.

[226] The *Junction City Weekly Union* published the following item on June 8, 1867: "A gentleman named McCoy proposes erecting all the sheds and buildings for a stock yard, on the railroad track, at Kansas Falls. Messrs. Streeter & Strickler gave him five acres for that purpose, and the railroad company tender him a side track a half mile long. He proposes making a large business of shipping all kinds of stock. His yard will be about five miles from town."

[227] Then called the Union Pacific Railroad, Eastern Division. On April 5, 1869, at a meeting of stockholders in Lawrence, Kansas, the name was changed to Kansas Pacific Railway. *Republican Daily Journal*, Apr. 6, 1869.

[228] John D. Perry.

offering as a reason the great number of cattle in Texas and the utter lack of an outlet and the urgent necessity of such a shipping depot. He closed with an appeal for such consideration as the importance of the proposed enterprise deserved. After hearing patiently the statement of the cattle shipper, the president, a pert, lively, courteous little gentleman, but evidently not a practical railroad man, and one that knew absolutely nothing about freighting live stock, replied, smiling incredulously, that they knew no reason why such a thing might not be done; that freight going east was just what they wanted, and if anyone would risk their money in the enterprise, the railroad company would stand by them [42] and afford such switches, cars, etc., as would be needed; and if it proved a success, the projector should be liberally paid, but they, having no faith in it, were not willing to risk a dollar in the enterprise.[229] How well the Kansas Pacific Company kept or did not keep this pledge, the sequel will show.[230] They evidently regarded the project as a wild, chimerical, visionary scheme, and so declared.

[229] On December 30, 1869, McCoy wrote a letter to the "executive board" of the Kansas Pacific Railway in which he recounted what happened at this interview with Perry. This letter was admitted as evidence in McCoy's subsequent suit against the railroad. It stated: "In 1867, we proposed to build up a cattle trade and the business of shipping live stock on your road. We were then told by President Perry the following: 'I do not believe that you can, to any extent, establish or build up a cattle trade on our road. It looks too visionary, too chimerical, too speculative, and it would be altogether too good a thing to ever happen to us, or to our road.' Then adding, 'But Mr. McCoy, if you think you can get cattle freighted over our road (it is just the thing we want) and are willing to risk your money in a stock yard and other necessary appendages, we will put in a switch and, if you succeed, I will pledge that you shall have full and fair recompense.'" McCoy vs. the Kansas Pacific Railway Company, 59, MS., Supreme Court of Kansas.

[230] McCoy's bitterness against the railroad, due to its violation of a contract with him in 1869, caused him to make misleading statements concerning their business relationship before that time. Sometime in 1867, according to his own admission in 1871, the Union Pacific Railroad, Eastern Division, made a verbal promise to pay him about five dollars per car for all cattle transported over its lines from Abilene during that year. Nearly a thousand carloads were shipped from that point in 1867. In 1870 he brought suit against the railroad for breaking its contract with him in 1869, but neither then nor at any previous time did he charge the company with breaking its agreement of 1867. *Ibid.*, 15, 60-61; *Brief of the Defendant in Error, Kansas Pacific Railway Company vs. McCoy*, 10.

After the above interview with the officers of the Kansas Pacific was ended, the office of the Missouri Pacific was visited to ascertain what rates of freight would be granted from the state line to St. Louis. Here was the first really great man engaged in the contemptible occupation of managing a railroad that the Illinoisan ever beheld. Entering the elegant office of the president and finding that dignitary arrayed in much "store clothes," quietly smoking a cigar while looking over some business papers, the Illinois "Bovine Puncher," dressed in a style that greatly contrasted with the [43] official's garb – rough, stogy, unblacked boots, a slouch hat, seedy coat, soiled shirt, and unmentionables that had seen better days twelve months previous when they had adorned the counter of the Jewish dealer – he timidly stated his business in modest terms and asked what rates of freight would be charged on the stock coming to St. Louis. When he had made his statement and propounded his question, the railroad official, tipping his cigar up at right angles with his nose, and striking the attitude of indescribable greatness when stooping to notice an infinitesimal object, and with an air bordering on immensity, said: "It occurs to me that you haven't any cattle to ship, and never did have any, and I, sir, have no evidence that you ever will have any, and I think you are talking about rates of freight for speculative purposes; therefore, you get out of this office, and let me not be troubled with any more of your style." If the heavens had fallen, the Illinoisan would not have been more surprised and nonplussed than he was by the answer and conduct of this very pompous railroad official. An attempt was made to explain, but not so much as a hearing would be accorded him; so the Illinoisan left the office, wondering what could have been the inscrutable purposes of Jehovah in creating and suffering such a great being to remain on earth instead of appointing him to manage the universe. But in less than twelve hours the general freight agent of the Hannibal and St. Joe Railroad had closed a contract, giving very satisfactory rates of freight from the Missouri river to Quincy, thence to Chicago. St. Louis never has, and perhaps never will, gain the prestige she might have had as a live stock market had she not blocked up the channels of access to her with egotistical pomposities. But in the events of this life it often occurs that inordinate pride and silly vanity meet their downfall, and such was the early fate of this great railroad man. His conduct became known in the city and finally was commented on by the press in very severe terms, [44] and when the directors next met for the annual election another man was found to fill his position. But just how an opportunity occurred to retaliate for insolent treatment, may be noted elsewhere.

But little time sufficed to arrange business matters temporarily, in Illinois, and as soon as accomplished, central Kansas was revisited for the purpose of selecting a point at which the facilities for holding, handling, and shipping cattle could be made. From Junction City the track of the Kansas Pacific Railway was closely followed, and various points inspected with regard to their adaptability to a cattle business, until Solomon City was reached, near which a fine site for stockyards was found; but after one or two conferences with some of the leading citizens, it became evident that they regarded such a thing as a cattle trade with stupid horror, and from all that could be learned upon thorough inquiry, the citizens of Salina were much in the same mood. The person making such propositions was apparently regarded as a monster threatening calamity and pestilence. After spending a few days investigating, Abilene (then as now the county seat of Dickinson county) was selected as the point of location for the coming enterprise.[231]

Abilene in 1867 was a very small, dead place, consisting of about one dozen log huts – low, small, rude affairs, four-fifths of which were covered with dirt for roofing; indeed, but one shingle roof could be seen in the whole city.[232] The business of the burg was conducted in two small rooms, mere log huts, and of course the inevitable saloon, also in

---

[231] McCoy selected Abilene as his cattle depot about the middle of June, 1867, for on June 18 of that year he made his first purchase of land there – two hundred and fifty acres north and east of the town – from Charles H. Thompson and Mary E. Thompson. Dickinson County, Deed Record A, 496, MS., Recorder of Deeds Office, Abilene.

[232] For a description of Abilene in 1867, see the introduction to the present volume.

a log hut, was to be found. The proprietor of the saloon [233] was a corpulent, jolly, good-souled, congenial old man of the backwoods pattern, who, in his younger days, loved to fish and hunt, and enjoyed the life of the frontiersman. For his amusement a colony of pet prairie dogs were located on his lots, and often the old gentleman might be seen feeding his pets. Tourists and others often purchased one or more of these dogs and took them east as curiosities.[234] [46] The principal owner of the town site [235] was living on a farm, and, alas for his virtue, had been a member of the legislature the previous winter.

One of the merchants doing business at Abilene, in an old abandoned cabin, was selling goods on commission, keeping a stock of about two wheelbarrow loads of second-class goods culled from a Manhattan country store, and as often as twice a year replenishing his stock with a small box of sundries; but he was a stunning fellow, with at least two-thirds of his small supply of brains located in that bump phrenologically called self-esteem.[236] You should have heard this great merchant talk, for, mind you, his subject was one (to him) of vast and overshadowing importance — it was himself. It was impossible for him to talk upon any subject without using the pronoun "I," often when it was not even proper or in anywise called for, much less in any kind of

[233] Josiah Jones, sometimes called "Old Man Jones," who purchased land in Abilene as early as November 8, 1861. Dickinson County, Deed Record A, 96, MS., Recorder of Deeds Office, Abilene; *Historical and Biographical Record of the Cattle Industry,* 494; "Recollections of John P. Simpson," *Dickinson County Clippings,* VI, Mrs. A. B. Seelye, Abilene.

[234] On June 6, 1867, a newspaper correspondent described Jones's prairie dogs at Abilene. *Daily Missouri Republican,* June 10, 1867.

[235] Charles H. Thompson.

[236] William S. Moon, proprietor of the Frontier Store, was born in Clinton county, Ohio, September 29, 1814. After studying medicine for a short time, he moved to Kokomo, Howard county, Indiana, in 1847, and ten years later came to Kansas. He settled at Abilene in 1864, when he bought the Frontier Store. Sometime afterward he moved to a farm southwest of the town, where he was living in the early eighties. He died about 1899. *History of the State of Kansas* (1883), 692; "Recollections of Melvina Moon Quinn," *Dickinson County Clippings,* IV, Mrs. A. B. Seelye, Abilene; "Lincoln Township," *Dickinson County Clippings,* X, *ibid.* The reasons for McCoy's antipathy to Moon have not been ascertained.

good taste. In short, he was an intolerable egotist, always extolling himself and pointing out how inferior someone was as compared with his very superior self. To hear him tell it, there was little intelligence, shrewdness, or even respectability in the universe outside of himself, and you would think that it was a sad mistake that he was not created before the "earth and the fullness thereof," so that Deity might have had the benefit of his wonderful wisdom in doing up that six days' job. As to wealth, as well as wisdom, Solomon was a fool and a pauper compared to himself; but, when "by ways that are dark and tricks that are vain" he managed to remove his petit business to a deserted saloon building, you should have seen him put on wealthy airs and talk about his assets, and tell how contemptible laboring people appeared to him as compared with himself, even going so far in his silly vanity as to say that "poor folks smelt like wet dogs," an odor that was peculiarly offensive to his aristocratic proboscis. This miserable being was not more afflicted with conscience than with good sense or decency. If, in after years, he ever contributed anything towards maintaining Abilene's [47] superiority in the cattle trade, it was usually charged up, in a covert manner, in some man's supply bill and collected. Never but once was he prevailed upon to put his name to a subscription list for public purposes, and that he repudiated, utterly refusing to pay a dollar. In short, he was by instinct much like a leech, always ready to suck substance from any arm of commerce that another had the sagacity and enterprise to bring before him or within his reach. To be sure, any other sordid, selfish man, by practicing only selfish arts, and by borrowing his neighbor's goods or chattels and never returning them, and if sued for their value plead the statute of limitations, could acquire a few hundred dollars' worth of property, however little sense he might have. But none other than an ingrate, cowardly wretch without honor or sense of shame could or would seek to obtain money or property in this way. But it was the favorite method of the great merchant.

Speaking about cowardice, you should have heard him tell of his great bravery, his wonderful deeds of valor and heroism. Why, the courage that met and slew [48] Goliath, or defended the pass of Thermopylae, or of Napoleon's last bodyguard, was contemptible, undiluted cowardice compared with his own bravery. Those he had met and vanquished in mortal combat were as the sands of the sea in number. In fact, where he had just come from (wherever that was), the country itself was too limited in which to bury his dead, and several hospitals were needed in which to care for his wounded. At last the surviving citizens came *en masse* on bended knees, begging him as they would a great Achilles, to depart from their country before their race became exterminated. In fact, you would suppose, to hear him talk, that every morning he breakfasted upon a man fricasseed or broiled on toast. But upon a certain day in later years, when there was an exciting local contest and election in Abilene, the great merchant took occasion to publicly speak in grossly slanderous terms of about two score of very respectable ladies. The good people of that, now very quiet, village could not stand this infamous outrage, much less let it go by unrebuked; so going in mass to the great merchant's office in the deserted saloon building, made him understand [49] in unmistakable terms their opinions and purposes. No sooner did he see that condign punishment was imminent than he fell upon his knees and, with a pallid countenance and frame quaking with guilty fear, begged and implored mercy. There was no end of his self-abnegation and self-reproach. To say that he "eat dirt" or "got down low" would be putting it mild. The sight of the trembling, jibbering coward disarmed the enraged citizens and they turned from him in loathing disgust. A desire that the world might know there was such a being as that great merchant of Abilene is the only apology we offer for devoting so much space to such a contemptible subject.

[50] A tract of land adjoining the town was purchased for the location of the stockyards, hotel, offices, etc. Abilene was selected because the country was entirely unsettled, well watered, excellent grass, and nearly the entire area of country was adapted to holding cattle. And it was the farthest point east at which a good depot for cattle business could have been made.[237] Although its selection was made by an

---

[237] As a matter of fact, according to the Kansas statute of February 26,

entire stranger to the country adjoining, and upon his practical judgment only, time has proved that no other so good point can be found in the state for the cattle trade. The advantages and requirements were all in its favor. After the point had been decided upon, the labor of getting material upon the ground began. From Hannibal, Missouri, came the pine lumber, and from Lenape, Kansas, came the hard wood, and work began in earnest and with energy. In sixty days from July 1st a shipping yard that would accommodate three thousand cattle, a large pair of Fairbanks scales, a barn, and an office were completed, and a good three-story hotel [238] well on the way toward completion. [239]

When it is remembered that this was accomplished in so short a time, notwithstanding the fact that every particle of material had to be brought from the east, and that, too, over a slow-moving railroad, it will be seen that energy and a determined will were at work.

We should have mentioned sooner that when the point at which to locate the shipping yards was determined upon, a

---

1867, trailing Texas cattle to Abilene was illegal; a mile west of Ellsworth was the most eastern point on the Union Pacific Railroad, Eastern Division, to which they could be driven. However, for some unaccountable reason this part of the law was not enforced. *Kansas Laws, 1867*, pp. 263-267.

[238] The following item is an early contemporary reference to the construction of the hotel: "McCoy & Bro., are building a frame hotel at Abilene, the main part of which is to be 30 x 46 feet, and three stories high, with a wing 16 x 30 feet in size. Matt Beckers, of this place [Junction City], has the job of painting. The building will therefore have a first class finish." *Junction City Weekly Union*, Aug. 31, 1867.

[239] Writing from Abilene on September 24, 1867, a correspondent of the *New York Daily Tribune* (Nov. 6, 1867) described the progress of McCoy's building operations there: "On the 1st day of September he [McCoy] had a stock and shipping yard built that would hold 800 head of cattle and load a train of 40 cars in two hours, had a ten-tun Fairbanks' scale in position that would weigh a carload at a time, and had Texas and all the South-West placarded with hand-bills. . . To-day is the 24th of September, and . . . [there] is a handsome three-story hotel, painted a delicate wood color, with green venetian blinds to the windows, and hard finished plaster on the walls, and handsome accomodations for 80 guests at bed and board, and possibility of feeding at a well-spread table three times that number. Opposite the hotel is a banking-house (the McCoys are bankers as well as buyers of cattle on a thousand hills), and behind the hotel is a vast livery stable for the horses of the drovers."

man [240] well versed in the geography of the country and accustomed to life on the prairie was sent into southern Kansas and the Indian Territory, with instructions to hunt up every straggling drove possible (and every drove was straggling, for they had not where to go) and tell them of Abilene and what was being done there toward making a market and outlet for Texan cattle. Mounting his pony at Junction City, a lonely ride of almost two hundred miles was taken in a southwesterly direction, crossing the Arkansas river [51] at the site of the present city of Wichita, thence far down into the Indian country; then turning east until trails of herds were found, which were followed until the drove was overtaken, and the owner fully posted in that, to him, all-absorbing topic, to wit: a good, safe place to drive to, where he could sell or ship his cattle unmolested to other markets. This was joyous news to the drover, for the fear of trouble and violence hung like an incubus over his waking thoughts alike with his sleeping moments. It was almost too good to be believed. Could it be possible that someone was about to afford a Texan drover any other reception than outrage and robbery? They were very suspicious that some trap was set, to be sprung on them; they were not ready to credit the proposition that the day of fair dealing had dawned for Texan drovers, and the era of mobs, brutal murder, and arbitrary proscription ended forever. Yet they turned their herds toward the point designated, and slowly and cautiously moved on northward, their minds constantly agitated with hope and fear alternately.

The first herd that arrived at Abilene was driven from Texas by a Mr. Thompson, but sold to Smith, McCord & Chandler, northern men, in the Indian Nation, and by them driven to Abilene. However, a herd owned by Colonel O. W. Wheeler, Wilson, and Hicks, all Californians en route for the Pacific states, were stopped about thirty miles from Abilene for rest and finally disposed of at Abilene, was really the first herd that came up from Texas and broke the trail, followed by the other herds.[241] About thirty-five thousand

240 W. W. Sugg, a native of Illinois.

241 An early contemporary reference to the arrival of Texas cattle at Abilene is found in the *Topeka Weekly Leader* (Aug. 15, 1867): "We are

head were driven in 1867.[242] It should be borne in mind that it was fully the first of July [243] before it was decided to attempt a cattle depot at Abilene or elsewhere, which, of course, was too late to increase the drive from Texas that year, but time enough only to gather together at that point such herds as were already on the road northward. Not until the cattle were nearly all at Abilene would the incredulous Kansas Pacific Railway Company build [52] the requisite switch, and then not until a written demand was made for it; after which an order was issued to put in a twenty-car switch, and particular direction was given to use "cull" ties, adding that they expected to take it up next year. It was with great difficulty that a hundred-car switch was obtained instead of the twenty-car one. Nor were the necessary transfer and feed yards at Leavenworth put in until plans were made and a man to superintend their construction furnished by the same parties that were laboring so hard to get their enterprise on foot at Abilene. But in a comparatively brief time all things were ready for the shipment of the first train.

As we have before stated, about 35,000 head of cattle arrived at Abilene in 1867. In 1860 we believe that the United States census gave Texas 3,500,000 head of cattle.[244] We are not sure that this is correct, but believe it is.

informed that there are several thousand head of Texas cattle at Abilene, Dickinson County, and that there is no sale for them. They will not bear transportation east, and the supply is far ahead of the demand for the army on the plains. These cattle were driven into the State by another route than that laid down by law."

242 Probably between 30,000 and 45,000 Texas and Indian cattle were trailed north into Kansas during 1867, most of which reached Abilene. About 18,000 or 20,000 longhorns were shipped from Abilene by railroad in the same year. Hazlett to Crawford, Nov. 19, 1867, Governors' Correspondence, MSS., K.S.H.S.; McCoy vs. the Kansas Pacific Railway Company, 60-61, MS., Supreme Court of Kansas; *Report of the Commissioner of Agriculture for the Year 1870*, p. 349; *Tenth Census of the United States*, III (*Agriculture*), 975; Kansas Pacific Railway Co., *Guide Map of the Great Texas Cattle Trail* (Kansas City, Mo., 1875), 8; *New York Daily Tribune*, Nov. 6, 1867; *Daily Illinois State Journal*, Oct. 29, 1867; *Daily Missouri Republican*, Sept. 26, Oct. 1, 1867; *Kansas Daily Commonwealth*, Aug. 15, 1871.

243 About the middle of June, 1867.

244 3,535,768 cattle, consisting of 601,540 milch cows, 172,492 working oxen, and 2,761,736 "other cattle." In addition, the census listed 861,646 neat cattle,

ABILENE IN 1867—CELEBRATING THE SHIPMENT OF THE FIRST TRAIN-LOAD OF CATTLE.

THE GREAT MERCHANT PLEADING STATUTES OF LIMITATION
AGAINST HONEST DEBTS.

THE GREAT MERCHANT SMELLING POOR FOLKS.

The drive of 1867 was about one per cent of the supply. Great hardships attended driving that year on account of Osage Indian troubles, excessive rainstorms, and flooded rivers. The cholera made sad havoc with many drovers, some of whom died with the malady and many suffered greatly. The heavy rains caused an immense growth of grass, too coarse and washy to be good food for cattle or horses, and but little of the first year's arrivals at Abilene were fit to go to market.

However, on the 5th of September, 1867, the first shipment of twenty cars was made to Chicago.[245] Several Illinois stockmen and others joined in an excursion from Springfield, Illinois, to Abilene, to celebrate by feast, wine, and song the auspicious event. Arriving at Abilene in the evening, several large tents, including one for dining purposes, were found ready for the reception of guests. A substantial repast was spread before the excursionists and devoured with a relish peculiar to camp life, after which wine, toasts, and speechifying were the order until a late hour at night. Before the sun had mounted high in the heavens on the [53] following day, the iron horse was darting down the Kaw valley with the first train load of cattle that ever passed over the Kansas Pacific Railroad, the precursor to many thousands destined to follow. This train of cattle sold in Chicago to a speculator at a small profit to the shipper. The second shipment was made in a short time afterward and was forwarded on to Albany, not finding a purchaser at Chicago.[246] This shipment, consisting of nearly 900 head costing about $17,500, was sold at Albany for $300 less than the freight

"the same not being returned on the schedules of agriculture." Hence the total number was 4,397,414. *Eighth Census of the United States, Agriculture*, 148, 192.

[245] Several days after leaving Abilene, this shipment reached Quincy, Illinois, whence, on September 10, it was forwarded to Chicago over the Chicago, Burlington and Quincy Railroad. *Daily Quincy Herald*, Sept. 11, 1867; *Daily Illinois State Journal*, Sept. 12, 1867.

[246] A live stock report from Quincy, Illinois, dated September 16, 1867, read as follows: "Fifty car loads, being the second installment of 25,000 head of Texan cattle to arrive at the stock yards here, were shipped to-day, forty-two cars by the C. B. & Q. R. R. to Chicago, and eight cars by T. W. & W. R. R. for the Eastern markets." *Daily Illinois State Journal*, Sept. 17, 1867.

bill, losing more than first cost. Indeed, Texan cattle beef then was not considered eatable, and was as unsalable in the eastern markets as would have been a shipment of prairie wolves.[247] Everything injurious that prejudice, ignorance, and envy could imagine was said against Texas cattle, and a concerted effort was made to prevent by any and every device that ingenuity could invent, to prevent them from going to market. Nevertheless, consumers soon learned that well-fatted Texan beef was as good as any other kind and much cheaper. The year 1867 was one of short corn crops and of low prices for thin-fleshed cattle, and the market continued to decline until midwinter. Notwithstanding all the impediments enumerated, the shipments of 1867 reached almost one thousand cars, all of which, except seventeen, went over the Hannibal and St. Joe Railroad to Chicago, and were there packed, largely on the owners' account.[248] The seventeen cars spoken of went to St. Louis over the Missouri Pacific.

Now, when the time arrived and shipments began to go forward at a lively rate, and any man, although a fool, could see the success of the enterprise, an agent of the Missouri Pacific Railroad put in an appearance at Abilene and was very solicitous for business for his road. But the memory of the insulting conduct of his official superior was still fresh in the mind of that Illinoisan, and he told the agent that it just occurred to him that he had no cattle for his road,

---

[247] This statement is misleading. Texas cattle sold at good prices in Chicago, St. Louis, and New York during the later fifties, as well as in 1866 and the spring and summer of 1867, and many of them were slaughtered or packed for beef. But the large and unexpected shipment of longhorns from Abilene to the middle western and eastern markets during the late summer and fall of 1867, together with other factors, resulted in a surplus of live stock for sale, thus depressing prices and arousing antagonism to the Texans. Besides, Texas cattle could be sold at cheaper rates than other stock. *Daily Illinois State Register* (Springfield), Sept. 18, Oct. 2, 9, 1867; *Daily Illinois State Journal*, June 1, July 16, 30, Aug. 2, 1867; *Daily Quincy Herald*, Sept. 15, Oct. 16, 20, 29, 1867; *Chicago Tribune*, July 13, 26, Aug. 14, 16, 23, Sept. 20, Oct. 2, 11, 12, 16, 17, 19, 21, 24, 25, 1867; *Daily Missouri Republican*, Apr. 1, 5, 13, June 10, Sept. 21, 1867. See also footnote 268.

[248] The *Chicago Live Stock Reporter* estimated that "little short of 25,000 head of Texas cattle, either wild or fed," were sold in Chicago during 1867. *Daily Herald* (San Antonio), Feb. 25, 1868.

never had, and there was no evidence then that he ever would have, and [54] to please say so to his president. The agent seemed to relish the force of such language and departed forthwith to deliver the message.

It was amusing to observe with what mingled joy and suspicion the drover of 1867 contemplated the arrangements completed and under way at Abilene for his accommodation. He could hardly believe that there was not some swindle in it somewhere. He there beheld more done and doing for him than he had ever seen before in his life. In his own state, great as the wealth of some of its citizens were, no one had manifested public spirit and enterprise sufficient to establish an outlet for her millions of cattle; and to this day we know of no other state which has so few public-spirited citizens, so few that are willing to do an act or develop an enterprise which has for its object the benefit of the whole people. They are all mindful of individual, selfish undertakings, but are stolidly indifferent to public ones. For instance, why should the business men of any northern point, at great expense, advertise the Texan cattle as being for sale upon the prairie adjacent to their villages, and how seldom a Texan will pay a dollar willingly to advertise up a given point as being a good market for his cattle. They do not hesitate to squander tens, fifties, and hundreds for the gratification of their appetites or passions, yet to pay a few dollars to help on some legtimate enterprise for the benefit of the whole, is generally esteemed a great hardship, and often they refuse entirely. This is not because they are penurious, for they are not, but because they lack that public spirit so necessary for the accomplishment of any great public good. Talk to them about advertising the point as a cattle market at which they are stopping their herds, and they will regard it as money thrown away. More advertising has been done for them gratuitously than for the people of any other state. An appreciation of the benefits of advertising is something of which the majority of Texans are destitute.

They are, as a class, not liberally educated, and but [55] few of them are extensive readers, but they are possessed of strong natural sense, well skilled in judging human nature,

close observers of all events passing before them, thoroughly
drilled in the customs of frontier life, more clannish than
the Scotch, more suspicious than need be, yet often easily
gulled by promises of large prices for their stock; very prone
to put an erroneous construction upon the acts and words
of a northern man, inclined to sympathize with one from
their own state as against another from the North, no matter what the southern man may have been guilty of. To beat
a northern man in a business transaction was perfectly legitimate, and regarded all such as their natural enemies, of
whom nothing good was to be expected. Nothing could
arouse their suspicions to a greater extent than a disinterested act of kindness. Fond of a practical joke, always
pleased with a good story, and not offended if it was of an
immoral character; universal tipplers, but seldom drunk-
ards; cosmopolitan in their loves; in practice, if not in
theory, apostles of Victoria Woodhull, but always chival-
rously courteous to a modest lady; possessing a strong, innate sense of right and wrong; a quick, impulsive temper;
great lovers of a horse and always good riders and good
horsemen; always free to spend their money lavishly for
such objects or purposes as best please them; very quick to
detect an injury or insult, and not slow to avenge it nor
quick to forget it; always ready to help a comrade out of
a scrape; full of life and fun; would illy brook rules of restraint; free and easy.[249]

Such were some of the traits of character often met with
in the early days of Abilene's glory, but there were good
reasons for all these phases and eccentricities of character.
Their home and early life was in a wild frontier country,
where schools were few and far between, their facilities for
attaining news by the daily press exceedingly limited. They
had just passed through a bitter civil war, which graduated

---

[249] On September 24, 1867, a correspondent of the *New York Daily Tribune*
(Nov. 6, 1867) at Abilene described the Texas cowboys there: "And here are
the drovers, the identical chaps I first saw at Fair Oaks, and last saw at
Gettysburg. Every man of them unquestionably was in the Rebel army. Some
of them have not yet worn out all of their distinctive gray clothing—keen-
looking men, full of reserved force, shaggy with hair, undoubtedly terrible
in a fight, yet peaceably great at cattle-driving, and not demonstrative in
their style of wearing six-shooters."

their former education of hatred and suspicion of northern men, and above all, the long and bitter experiences they had [56] endured in southern Kansas and Missouri — swindling, outrage, robbery, rapine, and murder — were full sufficient to embitter beings more than human. But we are not disposed to do the character of Texan drovers injustice, for the most of them are honorable men, and regard their pledged word of honor or their verbal contract as inviolable, sacred, and not to be broken under any circumstances whatever. Often transactions involving many thousands of dollars are made verbally only and complied with to the letter. Indeed, if this were not so, they would often experience great hardships in transacting their business, as well as getting through the country with their stock. We remember but few instances where a Texan, after selling his herd, went off home without paying all his business obligations. But one occurs to us now which we relate. A certain young drover, more youthful than honest, after selling off his herd, slipped off to Texas, leaving his supply bills and banker unpaid. A number of leading drovers met together and, after counseling about the effect of such conduct upon the credit of drovers as a class, decided to send one of their own number to Texas after the young rascal; which was done, and in a few weeks he was brought back and compelled to settle his outstanding indebtedness, also the expense in full of his own arrest and return. It is true that the western cattle trade has been no feeble means of bringing about an era of better feeling between northern and Texas men by bringing them in contact with each other in commercial transactions. The feeling today existing in the breasts of all men from both sections are far different and better than they were six years ago.

Strange as it may appear, there were a few Texan drovers who were from the beginning opposed to making a market, a general center, a drovers' headquarters for cattle sale and shipment at Abilene, and were always for driving on north or somewhere else, and never let an opportunity slip to speak and work against the enterprise; but it was made a success in spite of their opposition. Most of those who [57] opposed it were not of the open, bold, outspoken class of men, but of that class who would make loud professions of friendship to your face but slander you to your back, and manufacture out of what you may have said in friendly conversation, perverted and false stories, and privately retail them to such as would listen, whilst they would distort every word and act into some hideous offense; such men as had no good, clean motives themselves and could not impute such to anyone else — men who were as lank and scrofulous in soul as they were in physical appearance. Be it said to the credit of Texan drovers as a class, that but few, very few, of those scrubby ones ever put in an appearance among the many hundreds who visited western Kansas, and their influence was as limited as their dispositions were devilish.

Among certain Kansans there developed an opposition as malignant as it was detestable. Certain old, broken-down political bummers and played-out adventurers got up and secured the passage through the Kansas legislature of a certain "Texas Cattle Prohibitory Law," so drawn as to make Ellsworth the only point at which such cattle could be legally driven.[250] When Abilene began to develop as a shipping depot, their hostility knew no bounds. Utterly unscrupulous as to means employed, destitute of honorable manhood, and incapable of doing a legitimate business in an honest manner, full of low cunning and despicable motives, these ghouls resorted to every device their fertile brain could conceive to defeat the efforts of the parties who were at work at Abilene. After visiting threats of law and bodily harm upon all concerned, they finally traveled overland a distance of one hundred miles in a buggy, and spent a week trying to get the settlers of Dickinson county to mob such drovers as were stopping their cattle within the county limits. But all their efforts were unavailing and they were compelled to leave, infinitely more chagrined than language can express. It never was their intention to make a shipping point at Ellsworth, but to force the cattle to go there and then swindle [58] their owners out of them by such means as those same tricksters, in connection with other thieves, had often done in other years on the southern border of Kansas.[251]

---

250 The act of February 26, 1867. *Kansas Laws, 1867*, pp. 263-267.

251 The accuracy of this diatribe has not been ascertained by the editor.

Of the adventurous drover of 1867, but few are still found in the cattle trade. Some have retired from business, others changed their occupations, and not a few have become bankrupt by some adverse turn of fortune's wheel. Perhaps no one has more persistently and quietly kept on the even tenor of his way than J. L. Driskill, of Texas.[252] A Tennesseean by birth and education, he tried Missouri for four years, but hearing such glowing accounts of the land baptized to freedom at Alamo, he decided to go and see the state for himself. The year 1848 found him trying his skill at agriculture in Texas, but not liking the results, turned his attention to merchandising until the outbreak of the Civil war. For three years Mr. Driskill furnished beef to the Confederate army, and many Texas Rangers fared sumptuously upon fat roasts from [59] Driskill's droves. Notwithstanding fine profits were realized in the army trade, and large amounts of money was made, yet, owing to the Confederate currency becoming valueless, he found himself bankrupt with a cord of "money." When the "cruel war" was over and peace established, after taking a calm view of the actual situation, he determined to turn his entire attention to the cattle trade, and after one year spent in driving to New Orleans, he turned his droves toward western Kansas. From that day to this, each year has witnessed his herds of from one to six thousand head cross Red river, bound northward. There are few ways of disposing of cattle, after having driven them north, that he has not tried, and usually with at least moderate success. One year he will pack on his own account; another he will sell on the prairie; another finds him shipping; and still another, as in 1873, finds him sending four thousand head to Cheyenne to the territorial market; whilst as an experiment he tanks out a couple of thousand cows, and sends one thousand fine beeves to be slaughtered and packed on his own account, whilst the train goes forward to Chicago freighted with his cattle. All of

---

[252] "J. L. Driskill, than whom no shrewder cattle man ever put brand to yearling." *Fort Worth Democrat*, Mar. 18, 1876. Between 1873 and 1886, Driskill drove cattle to Ellsworth, Dodge City, Ellis, and the western states and territories. *Ellsworth Reporter*, June 26, 1873; *Dodge City Times*, June 2, 1877; *Kansas Daily Commonwealth*, June 15, 1876; *Dallas Morning News*, June 4, 1886.

which business is so quietly dispatched, no one would scarce know that he was in the country, much less doing anything. During his six years' driving, fortune has dealt kindly with him and gave unto his charge a comfortable amount of this world's goods. And few more worthy custodians could be found in the western cattle trade than the subject of this sketch — a kind, quiet, unassuming gentleman, with whom it is only necessary to become acquainted in order to appreciate his courteous, dignified manhood. Those who know him best are his warmest friends. Those who once have business transactions with him are always glad to meet him again and to know that it is his purpose to continue driving to western Kansas.

There are few more widely known and persistent drovers that H. M. Childress, a native-born Texan. For the last seven years he has been on one trail or another leading northward, with a herd varying in size from one to ten [60] thousand head of cattle. Born and reared to the stock business, he took to it on his own account just as natural as a duck to water, beginning at fifteen years of age, and has never changed his occupation — that of live stock — and claims justly, we think, to be "to the manor born." In 1866 he pushed his herd into central Iowa and sold it at thirty-five dollars per head, which was quite satisfactory. He was among the drovers of 1867 who arrived at Abilene, but failing to meet a purchaser, he sent his herd to Junction City and there disposed of it to an amateur packing company.[253] This packing operation was not a financial success, and the final wind-up was as unsatisfactory to the drover as to the packing company. However, Childress got his money, but not without great delay and vexatious wrangling. Each year for four years Childress drove fully twenty-five hundred head, mostly beeves, to the Abilene market, but the last year, [61] that of 1871, was one fraught with misfortune to him. He not only lost heavily in business but recklessly squandered many thousands of dollars, so that his finances were not in such shape as to enable him to drive again during the year 1872.

253 E. W. Pattison & Company, which commenced operations on October 9, 1867. *Junction City Weekly Union*, Oct. 12, 1867.

H. M. CHILDRESS.

J. L. DRISKILL.

But, being a man of indomitable energy, he would not long be idle. Meeting with a Texan who had secured necessary authority from the governor of Texas, and many ranchmen who had suffered great loss by theft committed by banditti and cattle thieves from New Mexico, they set out on a raid into that territory to recapture the stolen cattle. This was an undertaking fraught with hardship and danger, for those in whose possession the stolen cattle were found would not give them up without a struggle; and sometimes quite a pitched battle occurred, in which more than one Mexican bit the dirt, before Childress and his party could accomplish their aim. Although they went in a lawful manner after that that they had a lawful right to take, yet they were compelled to have a detachment of United States cavalry as an escort and to aid them in retaking the stolen property wherever found. The adventure resulted in recapturing eleven thousand cattle and three hundred horses, which were driven to Colorado and there disposed of to good advantage. Childress wound up his year's work with a snug fortune as a reward for his daring and labor. Although on the trip he was in seven fights, yet he lost no men nor received an injury himself. After closing up his business in Colorado, he returned to western Kansas and from there to Texas, after an absence of two years, to renew his old business occupation of droving. The year of 1873 found his familiar face among the cattlemen at Kansas City. There are few drovers, or for that matter few men, of the peculiar type of Childress. A convivial, jolly fellow, always full of fun and frolic, with a heart as large as that of an ox. He will walk boldly into death's jaws to relieve or avenge a friend; has a nerve of iron, cool and collected under fire; is a deadly pistol shot, and does not hesitate to use one effectively when occasion requires; yet [62] would always rather avoid a quarrel than seek one, but will not shrink from facing the most desperate characters. Nevertheless, there are few more kind-hearted men more true to friends than Childress. But to his enemies he presents, in anger, that peculiar characteristic of smiling demoniacally whilst he is plainly and openly maneuvering to shoot them through the heart. However, the reader will be in error if he concludes that Childress is a desperado, for he is not. Upon the other hand, many of the finest traits of the true gentleman are his. Generous, scrupulously honorable and honest, chivalric and impulsive, in his heart he wishes everyone well, and is never so happy himself as when he can make his friends happy by performing generous acts of kindness.

IV. THE CATTLE TRADE
ON THE FRONTIER

We have stated previously that there were but few settlers near Abilene; but in the eastern portion of the county there were quite a thick settlement of farmers, all comparatively poor, struggling hard to make a home and a competence, but with the usual privations, hardships, and misfortunes that attend the pioneer settlers of every new country. A full and comprehensive statement of all an average new settler endures before himself and family are comfortable, is a theme that few have done justice, and a theme for a better article than many that find prominent places in the public press of the day.

But the few settlers that were near Abilene became greatly excited about the proposed introduction of Texas cattle in the county,[254] and after talking the matter over privately among themselves, they determined to organize

[254] William H. Lamb, Henry Whitley, and Newton Blair wrote letters of protest to the governor. Lamb asserted: "If I mistake not there is a State law prohibiting any person or persons driving Texas cattle inside the limits of civilization on the frontier. If there is such a law why not enforce it; for there is now, and will be still coming, several thousand head of Texas cattle in the immediate vicinity; they have built a stockade and intend to ship them east. As a mass the settlers are against it. There are some very fine herds of cattle in this part of Kansas, and now to have Texas cattle fever break out among them, would indeed be too bad. We are all afraid and ask your advice in regard to the matter; hoping to hear from you soon." Lamb to Crawford, Aug. 31, 1867, Governors' Correspondence, MSS., K.S.H.S. Blair wrote: "I gathered up some of the facts and went before a Justice of the Peace to enter complaint but found him averse to doing any thing in the matter. . . He showed so much aversion to the matter that I enquired around for another magistrate and found but one not bought and the legality of his election is very doubtful. We have no Prosecuting Attorney for this Co. and the prosecuting Attorney for Saline as well as Davis Counties are bought up. In fact all the officers from whom those cattle men thought they had anything to fear are bought up." Blair to Crawford, Oct. 7, 1867, ibid.

a company to stampede every drove of cattle that came into the county; and to this end elected one of the most intelligent of their number to be their captain, and bound themselves in a solemn pledge to stand by each other and to keep up their organization until the proposed introduction of Texas cattle was abandoned. We think certain old seedy politicians whom we have before mentioned were at the bottom of this organization. However, to conciliate this resistance and dissolve this hostile organization was the work of a day. Word was sent to the captain (a determined fellow, but withal a man of [64] good practical sense, with a sharp eye for the main chance) to call as many of his company as possible to a meeting at his cabin on a designated evening, whereat the matter of Texan cattle would be discussed pro and con in a friendly manner by parties representing both sides in interest. When the appointed afternoon came, several Texan drovers who had lately arrived in advance of their herds to inspect the prospects of Abilene as a cattle market, accompanied the party who was building the shipping facilities at Abilene, to the captain's cabin where a few settlers had gathered, feeling that a fight was quite as likely to be the result of the meeting as anything else. By a previous arrangement made, on the way to the captain's domicile by the cattlemen, the Illinoisan took the stump and proceeded to talk to the settlers in a calm, friendly spirit and in a manner that impressed every hearer with his sincerity. He told the settlers that he came among them to do them good, not harm, to build them up and not tear them down, to enrich and not impoverish them, to give unto them a home cash market for their farm products, and to make their county burg a head center of a great commerce that would justly excite the envy of every rival town in the valley. Then the speaker pointed out how the immense influx of men camping on the adjacent prairies would need every aliment of life, and told them that if they taxed their little farms to their utmost in raising grain and vegetables, yet they could not furnish a tithe of the amount that would be needed; and of course if the supply was small and the demand great, the prices must and would be exorbitantly high, and that the only trouble would be that they could or would not furnish one-half the amount needed, no matter what the price might be. In addition to the above-named advantages, there was that of an opportunity to invest their savings in cheap, young cattle, which would pay one hundred per cent in ten months and consume only the hay, straw, and cornstalks, and such unmarketable farm products.

Whilst this little talk was being made, nearly every drover [65] present, by previous arrangement, went to bartering with the Kansans for butter, eggs, potatoes, onions, oats, corn, and such other produce as they might be able to use at camp, and always paying from one-fourth to double the price asked by the settlers. At the conclusion of the meeting the captain said he had got a "sight" of the cattle trade that was new and convincing to him. "And, gentlemen," said he, "if I can make any money out of this cattle trade, I am not afraid of 'Spanish fever;' but if I can't make any money out of this cattle trade, then I am d—d fraid of 'Spanish fever.' " The entire hostile organization dissolved without any further trouble, and before a single steer was stampeded. The captain of the company was accused by his comrades of turning traitor and selling out, but the fact is that his good sense dictated the course he finally took; and but few years elapsed before a substantial frame house and miles of good fencing, with other comforts and substantial improvements, aside from a fine herd of wintered, fat Texan cattle, were among the fruits that he enjoyed by following the course marked out and suggested to him at that meeting. Many others who, at the time the cattle trade was first established at Abilene, were living in dug outs, or mere hovels constructed of poles and dirt, and whose poverty was extreme, were soon enabled to build themselves beautiful houses, and provide other comforts that they could not have afforded for years later had it not been for the money expended annually by the stockmen in their midst. All these things soon dawned on the minds of many of the settlers, and there was soon a strong cattle trade party among them — men friendly to the trade and powerful enough to neutralize the efforts and influence of the few who remained hostile.

An incident occurred during the fall of 1867 that illustrates the enormous profits, not to say swindles, of contractors for the supply of beef for the Indians under the old system of feeding Poor Lo and family. As it illustrates more than one phase of the western way of doing things, we venture [66] to relate it. A Texan drover, whose herd consisted largely of young stock cattle, arrived at Abilene, and shortly obtained an offer of $11 per head for his stock, which offer he refused, but borrowed $1,000 and went to Leavenworth and got on a spree, which lasted until the cattle season was over and the grass was killed by the frost, and his cattle began to die of poverty and cold. Then he returned, bringing a government contractor with him, who bought his herd at $6 per head; and straightway, after getting from some settlers a half dozen of large rough oxen which he turned in with the herd, proceeded to drive them 140 miles southwest to Fort Larned, where upon arrival he turned the entire herd over to an Indian agent at an estimated average net weight of 600 pounds gross. The price was 6¼ cents per pound net weight, or $37.50 per head, or a profit of fully $30 per head. When it is remembered that the entire herd would not have averaged four hundred pounds gross, the financial brilliancy, not to say villainy, of the transaction is apparent.

But in those days an Indian contract was only another name for a big steal and swindle. Not one contract in each hundred made was ever filled in letter and spirit. Often the cattle would be delivered at an agreed average of net weight greater than the actual gross weight, and when delivered on one day would be stolen from the government agent at night and redelivered the next day. Of course the government agent was entirely innocent and was not conniving with the contractor. Oh, no! It is someone else that is on the make, not Indian agents. They are pure, self-sacrificing patriots, and are notorious for their abhorrence of money, for don't they always get poor in a year, when taking care of some little starving remnant of a tribe, and are compelled to remove their families from a sumptuous log cabin to an abhorred brick mansion abounding with lawns, drives, arbors, statuary, and other afflictions peculiar to that class of poverty. It would take volumes to chronicle the unalloyed benevolence and disinterested virtues [67] of that army of noble men who rush to the front of civilization and offer themselves for immolation upon the altar of some Indian agency. The immortal Washington's deeds of love performed for his enslaved countrymen pale into the mellow glow of phosphorus or the jack-o'-lantern of the marsh when compared with the brilliant, heroic, self-abnegation of an Indian agent. We doubt not but that the battalions set to guard the commissary stores of the pearly eternal city, seen by none of earth save the wandering peri, will be chosen from the ranks of the Indian agents of the West.

We are glad to note that under the present system of managing the Indians of the plains, much of the wholesale plundering of the government has been prevented. But we yet see a greater desire among those who strive to obtain government contracts for furnishing the Indians with beef, to obtain the supplying of such agencies as are farthest out from civilization, and where superior officials will trouble the contractor with their presence least, and where the facilities for obtaining correct weights are the most limited. Of course, this arises from a desire existing in the breasts of the contractors to feed full-blood Los instead of halfbreeds and mongrels — such as are on the border of civilization and at semisavage agencies — and in no wise arises from any desire to have an opportunity to perpetrate, in collusion with the Indian agent, a stupendous swindle on the government. Oh, no! Perish the thought, and blistered be the tongue that says so! By far the larger portion of the cattle consumed by the northern Indians are bought on the western plains of Kansas after their arrival from Texas. A lively struggle is witnessed every spring among the drovers who try to get their cattle into the Indian contracts. It now takes between thirty and forty thousand head of cattle annually to feed the Indians of the upper Missouri country. After purchasing them in western Kansas, they are put upon the road or trail and driven northward from four to eight hundred miles and [69] delivered in installments to the various agencies, and as soon as delivered, are slain and devoured by the hungry redskins. The regulations require full-grown beeves for the Indian supply, but often cows and stock cattle are put in and are, in fact, preferred by the

Indians to older cattle. A cow forward with calf is a delicious morsel to their palate, especially the unborn calf, which, "from its mother's womb is untimely ripped," is devoured with a relish peculiar to the fastidious epicurean tastes of the "noble red man." In the winter that portion of the herd which is held for the last installments during February and March, get very poor, in fact often reel as they walk with poverty and starvation. For they have been held without sufficient food for months, in a most rigorous climate. Indeed, it is not uncommon for the poor brutes to freeze stiff and dead during the bitter cold nights incident to those regions. If they could have a sufficiency of good, nourishing food, they would be able to withstand far greater degrees of cold than that under which they perish miserably. It is not difficult to imagine about what grade of beef — about how fat and juicy — Mr. Lo is permitted to gorge himself with, semioccasionally, during the winter and early spring months.

If there are no facilities for weighing provided by [the] government, it is usual for the contractor and Indian agent to estimate the weight, or "guess off" the herd or lot of cattle about being turned over. Just here is where great frauds upon the miserable Indians as well as the government are perpetrated. It once was not uncommon to get an estimated average weight fully fifty per cent greater than the real weight. This sometimes arose from the lack of correct judgment in the agent, but much oftener it was the result of his corrupt villainy. What "arguments" a contractor would be most likely to use in dealing with an agent, both out on the wilds of the Great West, can be easier imagined than described. It is not infrequent that one-half of the number of cattle only that are contracted to be furnished, are taken to the vicinity of the agency. How a fellow can fill a [70] contract for ten thousand head of cattle with only five thousand head is a proposition that most any Indian contractor can solve and explain if he will. But whatever numbers and whatever weights agreed upon by the agent and contractor, are set forth in a voucher, wherein Uncle Samuel is made the debtor. Upon presentation of these vouchers properly certified, the Bureau of Indian Affairs

in the Interior Department pays the sum therein called for
or draws a check against the appropriation previously made
by Congress for feeding the Indians. Could our readers
see those untutored redskins go for the bullock, once it is
turned over to them and shot down, it would perhaps go
far towards dispelling that halo of sentimentality with
which certain dreamy poets and maudlin writers have
clothed the degraded, miserable beings. The very parts of
the animal that a civilized being rejects as unfit to be eaten
in any shape whatever, are the very richest and first-to-be-
devoured dainties, according to Mr. Lo's notion of good
things.

Northern men usually obtain the contracts to furnish the
Indians with beef, and they contract with southern drovers
to furnish the cattle delivered at or near the various agencies, at which the government turns over other supplies,
such as flour, meal, bacon, blankets, etc. It requires no small
amount of determined will and stamina, as well as practical
knowledge of handling cattle on the plains, to be a successful
northern drover. Their hardships and privations are four-
fold greater than are endured by the average driver from
Texas to Kansas. The trail is through an unsettled country.
The weather stormy, and soon bitter cold winter sets in,
and there are few comfortable days before the opening of
the following spring, which occurs much later than in more
southern latitudes.

For several years in succession Captain E. B. Millett,[255]
of Texas, has furnished cattle to Indian contractors for the
upper Missouri river agencies. He began driving north in
1866, and was one of the drovers who turned their herds
east from Baxter Springs [71] along the Arkansas line
around or past the blockaded districts of Missouri. On
reaching the Mississippi river, his cattle were too poor in
flesh to put upon the market, and not meeting a northern
feeder to whom he could dispose of his herd, he wended his

[255] Eugene B. Millett, of Seguin, Guadalupe county, Texas. Starting in
1868, he drove cattle to Abilene, Ellsworth, Dodge City, and other points,
some of the time in partnership with Seth Mabry. Millett was living in
Kansas City, Missouri, in 1881. *Abilene Chronicle*, Apr. 6, 1871; *Ellsworth
Reporter*, May 1, 1873; *Dodge City Times*, Oct. 14, 1876; *Daily Democrat*
(Fort Worth, Tex.), Jan. 11, 1881; *Trail Drivers of Texas* (Hunter, ed.), 489.

way into east central Illinois and there went into winter quarters. Buying feed for his cattle until after the lapse of a few months, he was able to sell them, but not at such figures as sufficiently paid him for his labor, risk, and hardship endured. When he returned to Texas in the latter part of the winter of 1866 and 1867, it was with the fixed opinion that driving Texan cattle north was unprofitable and, in fact, next thing to impracticable. So the following summer of 1867 he was not among the few drovers who ventured to start herds northward, for of that he felt he had had enough. But when the drovers of 1867 returned to Texas and told of Abilene, the captain was among the first to gather a very choice herd of eight hundred beeves [256] and put [72] them upon the trail to western Kansas. After carefully driving his herd for about sixty days after crossing Red river, he found himself and herd in the immediate vicinity of Abilene. Selecting excellent herding grounds convenient to the village, the captain took up his quarters at the Drover's Cottage and awaited further developments, hoping for the appearance of a buyer. He did not wait long, for he had one of the most carefully selected and driven herds that could be found on the market, and it was of this herd that a certain Illinoisan selected two hundred and twenty-four choice beeves, mentioned elsewhere, upon which he essayed to get back some of his losses of the previous year; but with what results suffice it to say that the Illinoisan's returns from that drove of cattle, good and fat though they were, were fully six thousand dollars less than his investment. The balance of the captain's herd was sold at remunerative figures to a packer later in the fall. So the first year's operation was highly satisfactory and the determination was formed to continue the business. He could fully appreciate the benefits of a shipping depot to which he could bring his herds unmolested by mobs and thieves, where he would stand a good chance of meeting a buyer, or, if he chose, could go unmolested direct to any desired market in the North.

---

[256] In a statement made at Abilene, August 22, 1868, Millett asserted: "I have this season driven 950 head of cattle to Kansas." *Transactions of the Illinois State Agricultural Society*, VII, 144.

THE GREAT MERCHANT UPON HIS MARROW BONES.

CAPT. E. B. MILLETT.

COL. J. J. MYERS.

The captain obtained his military title in the Confederate army, where he won honorable distinction and made innumerable friends. Indeed, it would be difficult to find a superior example of a high-minded, dignified southern gentleman than he; quiet in turn of mind and manner, is never heard talking loud and coarsely, not even to his inferiors or subordinates. Perhaps the entire droving fraternity could not furnish a better student or one who loves to pass so many of his leisure hours in reading, and there is not in the western cattle trade a better-informed or better-read man than Captain Millett. In his various business undertakings he has been at least moderately successful. He has driven from one thousand to eight thousand cattle annually, but seldom, if ever, ships or packs on [73] his own account, always preferring to sell on the plains and, if need be, drive to any desired point in the territories to accomplish the desired object. He has spent several winters in the upper Missouri river country and furnished thousands of cattle to government contractors for Indian supplies. To Nevada and Idaho he has sent one or more herds and, after wintering and fattening, sold them to the mining villages of those regions. He is a man of great energy and integrity of character, with clear, solid business ideas.

The demand for cheap cattle in the territories at the close of the war was very great, and the supplying thereof aided materially in making Abilene a success. For each year there were large numbers of stock cattle brought there from Texas, many more than could have possibly found purchasers if there had been no territorial demand. Almost every territory in the Union is well adapted to raising cattle, and in each there is and has been more or less demand for beef from those engaged in mining and other vocations. The markets thus created always afforded good prices, and that in gold. Besides, just at that time the Union and Central Pacific Railroads were in process of construction, employing many thousands of men, who, of course, had to be fed. All of these circumstances conspired to make an active demand for all grades of cattle, and when it is remembered that a succession of drouthy seasons had destroyed nearly all the cattle in California, it will be seen that the supply must needs come principally from east of the Rocky mountains.

As we have remarked, the demand for cattle to supply the territories was great, and the turning of attention of territorial operators to Abilene as a place to buy, greatly aided that point in becoming a complete market – one in which any kind, sort, or sized cattle could either be bought or sold; and the driving of herds purchased at Abilene, to the territories, became quite as common as driving from Texas to Abilene. There were certain Texan drovers who looked almost exclusively to the territorial operators for buyers for their stock. [74] In case they succeeded in meeting a purchaser, the drovers would often deliver their herds at some agreed point in whichever territory the buyer might desire. In such cases the same outfit and the same cowboys that came from Texas with the stock would go on to its territorial destination.

Perhaps the most prominent drover engaged in supplying the territorial demand is Colonel J. J. Myers, of Lockhart, Texas.[257] In June, 1867, during the first visit of the Illinoisan to the West, and whilst his project of a cattle shipping depot was not yet fully determined upon, and whilst stopping temporarily at the Hale House in Junction City, he was introduced to a small-sized, quiet gentleman, who was evidently entering that class upon whose head Time had begun to sprinkle her silver frosts. The gentleman was introduced as being late from Texas; and here, thought the Illinoisan, was just the man before whom to lay the plan of the contemplated project and thus secure the Texan's judgment upon it – whether or not it was plausible or advisable, and if such a shipping depot was created, would the Texan drovers bring their herds to it. So, inviting the venerable gentleman to take a walk, they strolled off to a lumber pile on a vacant lot and there sat down, deeply engaged in conversation for two or more hours, in which time the Illinoisan explained his contemplated project fully and noted

257 John J. Myers (or Meyers) drove cattle to Abilene between 1867 and 1871, to Ellsworth in 1872 and 1873, and to Omaha in 1874. He died at his home in Lockhart, Caldwell county, Texas, December, 1874. *Abilene Chronicle,* Apr. 6, 1871; *Junction City Weekly Union,* July 3, 1869; *Ellsworth Reporter,* June 20, 1872, June 26, 1873; *Trail Drivers of Texas* (Hunter, ed.), 489, 591, 637, 734-735.

closely the comment and opinions of the Texan drover, for
such he proved to be. He there told that young Illinoisan
that such a depot for cattle sale and shipment was the greatest need of Texan stockmen, and that whoever would establish and conduct such an enterprise upon legitimate business principles would be a benefactor to the entire Texan
live stock interest and would undoubtedly receive all the
patronage that could reasonably be desired. From the hour
of that informal interview between the Texan drover and
the Illinoisan, the project, such as was soon developed at
Abilene, became a fixed fact or purpose in the mind of its
projector. There are moments in one's existence when a
decision or a purpose arrived at, shapes future actions and
[75] events — even changes the whole tenor of one's life
and labor. Such was the effect of the two brief hours spent
in conversation by the Texan drover and the Illinoisan.
When they shook hands and parted, there existed in the
breast of the Illinoisan an impression that he had been talking to a sincere, honest man, who spoke his convictions without deceit or without any desire whatever to mislead anyone,
but with a firmly fixed determination to give only correct
information. The decisions and determinations formed at
that interview fixed the life and labor of the Illinoisan.

That Texan drover was Colonel J. J. Myers, a man of
that peculiar build and stature that can endure untold physical hardships without fatigue. There are few men in the
West or Northwest who have so thorough a knowledge,
gathered from actual travel and observation, of all the
territories of the Union as Colonel Myers. One of his early
tours over the West was made across the continent [76]
with John C. Frémont on his famous exploring expedition.
This occurred almost forty years ago, when the colonel was
but a youth just entering into vigorous manhood. Such a
strong desire to roam became implanted in his bosom that
he did not give himself rest until he had traversed almost
every foot of territory between the Mississippi river and
the Pacific ocean. And when he had seen all that Dame
Nature had to show, he turned his attention to stock ranching in Texas, making his home at Lockhart. He too was a
drover in 1866 and endured all kinds of outrages before he

was able to sell his herd. But in 1867 he decided to drive into western Kansas and so flank all settlements, and take his chances to find a purchaser somewhere on the frontier, but just where he could sell, he did not know.[258] The colonel was among Abilene's first patrons and warmest friends, and so long as it was a market, he annually made his appearance with from four thousand to sixteen thousand head of cattle, which, of course, were driven in several herds, never more than three thousand head in one herd.

The class of cattle the colonel usually drove was just suited for the territorial demand; therefore, he never shipped but few carloads. For four years he sold his herds to parties living in Salt Lake, genuine Mormons of the true polygamist faith, and delivered his stock to them in Utah. The Mormons, as all well know, are very clannish people and, especially the lay members, are little disposed to trade with or buy anything of a Gentile. Therefore, to avoid this religious prejudice, and in order to get into and through the territory without trouble or having to pay exorbitant damage bills to the Latter Day Saints, it was his practice to instruct his men to tell every resident of Utah they met that the cattle belonged to Heber Kimball, one of the elders or high priests in Mormondom. No matter whose farm the cattle ran over nor how much damage they done to crops, it was all settled amicably by telling the residents that the cattle were Elder Kimball's. No charge or complaint was ever made after that [77] statement was heard; and it did appear that if Heber Kimball's cattle should run over the saints bodily and tread them into the earth, it would have been all right, and not a murmur would have been heard to escape their lips. When the cattle reached their destination, the colonel never went near them, but allowed Elder Kimball to dispose of them always as if they were his own, which he

---

[258] In 1867, Myers drove cattle to Junction City, near which a large number of Texas longhorns had arrived by July of that year. The *Junction City Weekly Union* (July 20, 1867) stated: "There are some five thousand head of cattle within twenty miles of town, waiting for buyers from the east. The stock corrall, five miles above town, we understand is being built for their shipment. Hale & Rice advertise two thousand head. We heard a man say that the country is lined with them from this place south, and that there will be fully twenty thousand drovers here this season."

could do at a rapid rate. The Mormons appeared to consider it a great privilege to buy of the sainted elder, although they were paying from one to three dollars in gold more per head for the cattle than they would have had to pay to the Gentile drover. Indeed, they would not have bought the same stock of the Gentile at any price. When it is known that this people are such complete dupes of cunning, smart men, is it any wonder that they submit to be plucked like a goose for the benefit of their quondam keepers? Or is it anything strange that their leaders manage to get immensely rich? But Utah, notwithstanding her great city and her immense mining population, has now more than a supply of cattle for her own consumption and is beginning to export cattle to Chicago and the East. Several thousand head of fat beeves were driven from Utah over the mountains to Cheyenne and there shipped to Chicago during the year 1873. So there is no longer a demand for stock cattle in that territory.

There are few Texan drovers who handle or drive more cattle from Texas than Colonel Myers – few are more widely or favorably known than he. He is a man of great experience and solid judgment, and one that has few enemies, but wherever he is known, his name is spoken with respect akin to love and admiration. He is a man true to his pledges, and one who would not reap advantage from or oppress a fellow man simply because he had the power or the legal right to do so. When he is given the title of "a father in Israel" among the drovers, there will [be] found few, if any, who will dispute his right or his worthiness of the appellation.

UNCLE SAM FEEDING "POOR LO" AND FAMILY.

V. LIFE AND LABOR OF
THE DROVER

We have seen something of the production of live stock in Texas. Let us now, before going farther into the history of the cattle trade, look briefly at the life and labor of a drover, or one who markets cattle. Many owners of large ranches and stocks of cattle are drovers also, not only of their own production but buy of others and drive them also; however, the lines of business are regarded as distinct, and as is the case in other differing vocations, most men are not adapted by nature to both occupations. The life of the ranchman is commonplace and routine in duties and labors, whilst that of the drover is ever subject to changes, new combinations of circumstances, as well as new acquaintances and new scenery, always attended with more or less excitement arising, if not in the events that do actually occur, then in the hope of good markets, large profits, and sudden fortune.

Let us trace the footsteps of the drover who has determined to drive to the northern markets. Early in the year he determines to drive, and straightway goes into the section from which he has decided to bring his herd; and riding from one ranch to another, contracts with the owner or his agent at the ranch for the delivery at a given place, usually at the corral, of a certain number of cattle of whatever age he may have decided to drive. Droves are usually largely [79] composed of what are termed "beeves," that is, a steer four years old or older; and it matters not whether he weighs seven hundred pounds gross or seven tons gross, so [long as] he is the proper age he is a "beef" and counts one and only one; and it matters not whether he be lean or fat, thrifty or scrubby, if he is four years or fourteen years old, he is "beef"; and a drove thereof is styled a drove of "beeves." Our drover pays but one price to all ranchmen; and when he has completed his contracts and whilst the ranchman is gathering the stock to fill them, the drover rides to some horse ranch and buys the necessary saddle horses, *i.e.,* gets up a caviyard, also a wagon for hauling camp supplies; and then secures the necessary number of cowboys to aid him in driving, not forgetting to obtain a cook, whose duties on the road in addition to cooking is to drive the camp wagon and to take care of the usual regulation supplies. When the day for receiving his purchases arrives, the drover, with his outfit of hands and camp equipage, puts in an appearance at the designated place, and all such cattle as will fill the contract are received; and often many that do not fill the contract are taken simply because a custom has obtained to take almost everything the ranchman has gathered, and a drover who will not do so is termed very particular and illiberal, a reputation that they abhor — so thus, often, the drover is pulled into taking animals that he never bought and that his business sense tells him he should not take. And this is the reason, more than anything else, why so few really select droves of Texan cattle reach the western market. It is no lack of judgment, but because it is the custom to take almost everything that is gathered by the ranchman. Again, these contracts are usually verbal only, and to be particular would lead to wrangles and differences of memory and understanding which are not pleasant to the drover. The ranchman, in gathering the stock to fill his contract, drives together, or, in drover parlance, "rounds-up," a large number of cattle of all ages and sexes, and whilst from six to ten cowboys hold the herd together, the ranchman with [81] one or two assistants separate such as are suitable. This process is termed "cutting out."

The process of cutting out is one that requires skill and expert horsemanship, both of which the experienced cowboy invariably possesses in a high degree, especially the latter; for it is indeed a desperately bad cow pony that he cannot ride. The reputation of Texas for horsemanship is national and needs no eulogiums in this place. To accomplish the greatest amount of labor with the least effort and the least amount of hard riding, two cowboys work together. When a beef is selected to be cut out, he is adroitly and quietly maneuvered to the outskirts of the round-up, and when the opportune moment occurs, the cowboys dash at him, and, before he is aware of it, is on the outside of, and separated from, the herd; but no sooner does he discover the situation than he makes a desperate effort to regain his comrades, and just here is where the skill of the cowboy is put in requisition. Whilst one rides beside the steer, the other rides just behind him, to prevent or check any sudden change of direction that the frantically excited bovine may choose to make in his efforts to get back with the herd, which he tries desperately to do and persists in trying so long as there is a shadow of a chance to outrun his pursuers. Often the race is close and the contest exciting, and sometimes the outer circle of the round-up will be run more than once, before the beef will be induced to abandon the effort to get back into the herd. But when he finds himself outrun and outgeneraled, he will toss up his head and look for the comrades which have been previously cut out and are being held a few hundred feet distant. In the beginning of the cut-out, a few gentle cows or working oxen are driven a short space from the round-up and held, to form a nucleus to which those cut out gather.

Cutting out is always done on an open, smooth spot of prairie, and never done inside a corral as a northern man handles or separates his cattle. When north with their herds, a Texan drover always prefers the prairie to any enclosure to handle his stock, [82] for there, mounted on his pony, he feels at home and knows just how to manage; besides, he has a fixed, constitutional prejudice against doing anything on foot that can possibly be done on horseback, not to speak of the almost universal fear they entertain of being among their stock on foot. They are justified, to some extent at least, in indulging this wholesome fear, for but few Texan bullocks will hesitate, when enclosed alone in a strong corral, to show decided belligerent proclivities or to furiously charge the venturesome wight who dares to show himself on foot within the enclosure. Occasionally, whilst loading a herd upon cars, a bullock will become detached from his comrades, and almost invariably, so soon as he finds himself alone, without ability to escape, will manifest a disposition to fight anything or anybody that may chance to be in sight. Often considerable difficulty is experienced in getting him to any desired place. A northern man, unaccustomed to handling Texan cattle, will often rush into the corral wherein is a single bullock. He will have scarcely got cleverly in the corral before the bullock, with arched back, down-set head, extended nostrils, and glaring, fiery eyes, darts toward his supposed adversary, who, suddenly taking in his dangerous situation, but too late to retreat by the way of his entree, rushes posthaste to the nearest fence, which is usually so high he cannot spring to the top of it; but reaching the top with only his finger tips, draws his body as high as possible, and clinging to his hold with frantic grip, yells lustily for help. In the meantime the bullock, failing to pin the body of the man to the wall, puts in vicious strokes with his horns at the dangling coat-tails and posterior of the thoroughly alarmed man. When the frightened fellow is relieved from his perilous attitude, he finds, on casual examination his coat-tails in shreds and the seat of his unmentionables ripped in a shocking manner, much resembling a railroad map of a western commercial metropolis. He does not want to either sit down or lay down on his back. This excites his profound disgust, and he is an immediate applicant to borrow or buy a [83] new suit of clothes. At all events he is fully decided that driving Texan critters on foot is not his best forte, and he has a modified opinion of his own prowess as a live stock driver. At another time, when he attempts to drive or cut out a Texan bullock, he decidedly prefers the horseback mode. But to return to the main subject.

Those cut out are held under herd until others are added from other quarters; and when finally the required number is got together they are taken to the corral, herded in daytime and corralled at night until the day of delivery to the drover comes, when, as I have before stated, he is expected to take all gathered for him. As fast as the drover receives the various detachments of his drove, they are by his own men driven to some previously secured corral, and when all are in and the herd is complete, then the job of road branding begins, which, by the aid of plenty of help, is soon completed. All things being ready, [84] a start is made, but not

RECEIVING A RAILROAD MAP.

J. H. STEVENS.

J. W. TUCKER.

before the drover has secured and recorded a bill of sale from each ranchman or his lawful agent from whom the stock was purchased. The bill of sale sets forth not only the ranch brands but all the earmarks. The appearance of a bill of sale is much like Egyptian hieroglyphics. The more a northern man looks at one, the less he knows about it. But it is necessary for the drover to have it, for without it the officers of the law would regard him as a thief and, of course, arrest him.

Now that a start is once made, hard driving for the first few days is the custom. For several reasons this is done: first, in order to get the stock off of their accustomed range, whereon they feel at home and know all the country and are much harder to keep under control than when on strange ground; second, it is done to break or accustom them to being driven, at the same time to tire them by hard traveling so they will feel at nightfall like lying down and resting instead of running off, as they would be sure to do if they were not fatigued. We have heard drovers say that they traveled the first three or four days at the rate of twenty-five or thirty miles per day; but as soon as the cattle are driven off of their usual range and are got onto the regular trail, the distance of a day's drive is reduced to ten to fifteen miles each day. They are permitted to go out on the range in the morning early and to feed, care being taken that they be kept headed in the direction the drover is desirous of going. They will feed along for two or three miles, then turn into the trail and travel three or four miles, when, after drinking their fill of water, they will lie down and rest from two to four hours in the middle of the day. Getting up from their beds, they soon turn from the trail upon the grass and take their afternoon feed preparatory to being rounded up for the night. When upon the bed ground, one or more men remain with them during the silent hours of the night, being relieved by regular relays from the camp, much as the soldier upon guard is relieved. With each herd are about two men to every three hundred cattle; and each man [86] should have at least two saddle horses, which he rides alternately, they living exclusively upon the grass. The extra horses not under the saddle are called the caviyard, and are driven behind the camp wagon; which is drawn by one or more yokes of oxen, and is often a cumbersome, rude cart made with an eye to strength rather than beauty, and is made the receptacle of the provisions and camp outfit.

To drive a drove of cattle properly more patience and perseverance than labor is required. The cattle are often shamefully abused on the road. Especially is this the case when Mexican help is employed, for they will not drive any other way than in a rush, and have no more feeling or care for dumb brutes, either cattle or horses, than they have for a stone. Their heartless cruelty is proverbial, and we have yet to see a drove of cattle driven by them or a cavi-yard used by them that was not as poor as wood. They are the dearest help in a long run that a drover can employ, although they will work for considerable less wages than white boys. But unless their boss keeps them under strict surveillance, they are intolerably impudent and mean. An Indian would not be more treacherous than are some of the Mexican cowboys. Several instances of brutal murders of the men in charge of herds have been perpetrated by the Mexican cowboys employed to drive to western Kansas. Nothing but gold will pay them for their services. The idea that greenbacks are of value does not and cannot be made to enter their understanding, and they will accept one-third or one-half wages if it is only paid in gold. But we would not do them injustice, for many of them are good, faithful help and true to the interests of their employers. But as a rule they are unprofitable as well as unreliable help.

Many traders of moderate capital do a profitable business in Texas in getting together herds ready for the trail, then selling out to some regular drover. Quite a number of young, energetic men have thus made considerable sums of money; in fact, laid the foundation of future fortunes in this manner.[259] [87] Perhaps no better specimen of a local Texan trader could be presented than J. W. Tucker, of Trio City [Frio Town], Texas. Born in Georgia but reared to young manhood in Alabama, he turned his steps toward Texas at nineteen and spent several years in traveling over the state,

[259] For descriptions of the cowboy and his activities, see Rollins, *The Cowboy;* Douglas Branch, *The Cowboy and his Interpreters* (New York, 1926).

"CUTTING OUT."

CAMP WAGON ON THE TRAIL.

running upon first one stage route, then upon another, thus getting a complete knowledge of the geography of Texas, as well as of the ways of the world. Becoming dissatisfied with the precarious life of the stage driver, he turned his attention to the local cattle trade, and for five years did little else than furnish herds to drovers, who forwarded them to market. Having thus obtained a thorough, practical knowledge of the cattle business and acquired sufficient means, in the year 1872, Mr. Tucker determined to try the trail with a herd on his own account, and we need only add that such were the results of his first effort that the succeeding year found him again upon the market with another herd of eighteen hundred head of fine [88] cattle, for which he soon found a buyer at satisfactory prices. But the spirit of speculation was abroad in his breast, and but little time elapsed, after selling out, before he purchased about two thousand head of superior cattle in western Kansas, which in consequence of the widespread financial panic of 1873 he was not able to dispose of at prices that would justify him in selling. Fortunately an opportunity presented itself, and he put them to feed in large distilleries at Peoria, Illinois. Mr. Tucker is a remarkable quiet drover, seldom having anything to say, and never heard talking in a boisterous manner. But his quiet turn and affable manners mark him as a young man of generous impulses and manly aspirations, and one who will make good impressions and enduring friendship wherever he goes.

Wherever you meet a man who in his childhood was trained to business and labor as a cattle drover, you find a being whose second nature and greatest delight is to be with live stock. No endearments of home or profits of a more quiet or routine business can retain or allure him from persistently following his favorite pursuit, no matter if it is not half so profitable, really, as are other more quiet, unexciting employments. He loves the drove and the trail, the risk, excitement, and ever-changing scenes and circumstances incident to the drover's life.

Willis McCutcheon, of Austin, Texas, is a native of the Lone Star State and was reared to the business of farming and stock ranching. He accompanied his father with a herd

of cattle, which was one among the few driven north as
early as the year 1857. At that time Willis was but a boy,
but his memory of events occurring on that trip, then the
greatest one of his life, is as distinct as though they had
transpired but yesterday. They crossed the Missouri river
near Independence, and met a purchaser for the herd at
Quincy, Illinois, at the remunerative price of twenty-five
dollars per head, in gold, which afforded a snug profit. This
early induction [89] into the life of the drover had a marked
effect in shaping McCutcheon's future, for no sooner had
he arrived at the years of maturity than he selected a location in the stock regions of Texas and went largely into stock
raising; always selling at home when an opportunity presented itself, but driving to other markets when the home
purchaser failed to put in an appearance. In connection with
his associates in business he has gathered and marketed many
tens of thousands of cattle. During the Civil war he furnished the Confederate army with thousands of beeves, and
at its close began driving cattle. In 1866, when he learned
of the blockade in southeast Kansas and southwest Missouri,
he had his herd turned westward and drove around the
settlements of western Kansas and landed it in Iowa, where
good prices were obtained. During the year 1865 he drove
several herds to Mexico; also made several trips to New
Orleans with cattle. Not liking [90] his experiences in 1866,
he stayed upon his ranch the following year, but in 1868
engaged with his associates in driving about twelve thousand
head of cattle to the mouth of Red river, where they were
delivered to certain Chicago gentlemen to whom they had
been previously contracted. The cattle were put upon river
steamers, in crowded, hot quarters, without room to feed,
water, or lay down to rest, and shipped to Cairo, Illinois,
and there carried up into the central and eastern portion of
that state. This importation of cattle into Illinois was a sad
misfortune to the sections of country that received them,
and a calamity in its effects to the state of Texas. Just how
this was, will appear elsewhere. However, McCutcheon
did well and returned to his home satisfied with his summer's
work. But the habit of driving cattle, much like that of shipping them, once formed, is hard to break up. Home and life

on the ranch seems too quiet, and the excitement of a trip off is longed for, to break the dull monotony of existence. So the years of 1869, 1870, 1871, 1872, and 1873 found Mc-Cutcheon's herds en route for the western Kansas market, in which he has disposed of about two thousand head annually.[260] Willis McCutcheon is one of those substantial, matter-of-fact, everyday kind of men that you feel instinctively will do to tie to, and when you look into his frank, open countenance, a sense of his straightforward manner of life and business integrity impresses you. You feel that in him – a true, big-hearted man, who could not have pleasure in a mean, dishonorable transaction – you can rely with safety.

The Civil war was, in its effects upon the agricultural interests of the South, a complete revolutionizer and bankrupter. Many whose lands were valuable for purposes of cultivation and whose wealth consisted in agricultural lands and slaves, suddenly found themselves without laborers, and their lands so depreciated in market value as to be almost worthless. The owners of these departed fortunes in many cases became vagabond loafers, spending their [91] despairing hours lounging in barrooms, hotels, and other public places, never tiring of the story of their calamity, and ever trying to maintain the semblance, at least, of that genteel dignity once the pride of a southern slave owner; although the effort generally results in but a seedy appearance and frequent loud declarations of their "high tone." Other planters who became bankrupt, or nearly so, by the war, were able to rise superior to their misfortunes and, after fully taking in the situation, turn their energies and efforts to some promising field of industry, and therein put forth noble efforts to retrieve their damaged fortunes.

To this latter class belongs J. H. Stevens, whose magnificent plantation or farm of fifteen hundred acres, once in high state of cultivation, became, to him, worthless; nor can it be sold for anything now, although before the war

---

[260] Willis McCutcheon trailed longhorns to Abilene in 1870, to Ellsworth in 1873 and 1874, and to Dodge City in 1878. *Abilene Chronicle*, May 12, 1870; *Ellsworth Reporter*, June 26, 1873; *Denison Daily News* (Denison, Tex.), May 16, 1874; *Dodge City Times*, May 11, 1878.

twenty dollars per acre in gold was its market value. It is not profitable to hire laborers and cultivate it; [92] so it is allowed to lay awaste whilst its owner has turned his face to stock driving; sometimes horses are driven exclusively and sold in Missouri or Illinois. In later years cattle have received his undivided attention, of which he annually drives about four thousand head; first to western Kansas; then, if no buyer is found there, he goes on to some one of the more northerly territories, or delivers them to some government contractor to be turned over to the Indians. Mr. Stevens has been a constant driver since 1868, and has each year driven larger herds, or more of them, than the previous year.[261] He is a substantial, solid man, of good practical sense and fine judgment, and one that has a large list of friends. His quiet, affable manner, and air of genuine courtesy attract the attention of observing men, who are always able to discern in him the true North Carolina gentleman.

[261] J. H. Stevens drove cattle to Ellsworth in 1873. *Ellsworth Reporter,* May 29, 1873.

WILLIS McCUTCHEON.

VI. ON THE TRAIL AND IN THE STOCKYARDS

We left the herd fairly started upon the trail for the northern market. Of these trails there are several: one leading to Baxter Springs and Chetopa; another called the "Old Shawnee trail," leaving Red river and running eastward, crossing the Arkansas not far above Fort Gibson, thence bending westward up the Arkansas river. But the principal trail now traveled is more direct and is known as "Chisholm trail," so named from a semicivilized Indian who is said to have traveled it first.[262] It is more direct, has more prairie,

[262] The Chisholm trail, strictly speaking, was the route running south from Wichita, Kansas, to some point or points on or near the North Canadian river in the Indian Territory; but soon after it was extended north into central Kansas and south into northern Texas, the entire length of the expanded route began to be popularly known as the Chisholm trail. Although the trail was named after the half-breed Cherokee Indian, Jesse Chisholm, it was traveled by others, at least in part, before he used it. Buffaloes and Indians probably first traversed the region later followed by the trail. On August 27, 1855, Major Enoch Steen, of the Second dragoons, in command of six companies of his regiment, left Fort Belknap, Texas, and, proceeding "about ten degrees east of north," marched to Fort Riley, Kansas, where he arrived on September 28; his detachment included 213 men, 232 horses, 468 mules, and 76 wagons. He reported that there was plenty of water along the route, that the country traversed was "a rolling prairie the whole distance," that the crossings of the streams were good, and that the course was "an easy and perfectly practicable one for wagons." Steen appears to have marched a short distance west of the later Chisholm trail in the Indian Territory and along or near it in southern Kansas. On May 9, 1861, Lieutenant-colonel William H. Emory, leading the retreat of eleven companies of United States troops from the Indian Territory, left a point about thirty-five miles northeast of Fort Cobb and proceeded north, taking "the most direct course to Leavenworth that the nature of the ground would permit." His command, which included "750 fighting men, 150 women, children, teamsters, and other non-combatants," was guided by Delaware Indians, among whom was Black Beaver. Part of the route he followed was very similar to the one subsequently known as the Chisholm trail. Late in 1863 or early in 1864 some

less timber, more small streams and less large ones, and altogether better grass and fewer flies (no civilized Indian tax or wild Indian disturbances) than any other route yet driven over, and is also much shorter in distance because direct from Red river to Kansas. Twenty-five to thirty-five days is the usual time required to bring a drove from Red river to the southern line of Kansas, a distance of between two hundred and fifty and three hundred miles, and an excellent country to drive over. So many cattle have been driven over the trail in the last few years that a broad highway is tread out, looking much like a national highway; so plain, a fool could not fail to keep in it.

One remarkable feature is observable as being worthy of note, and that is how completely the herd becomes broken [95] to follow the trail. Certain cattle will take the lead, and others will select certain places in the line, and certain

Wichita Indians, refugees from the Indian Territory, settled at the junction of the Arkansas and Little Arkansas rivers, the site of the present city of Wichita, and at least as early as the summer of 1864 began to journey south into the Indian Territory and bring back horses, cattle, buffalo robes, and furs. Starting in the same year, some Wichita, as well as a few other refugee Indians in the immediate vicinity of the mouth of the Little Arkansas, made trips to the south, probably over the same route, to steal cattle in the Indian Territory and drive them north into Kansas to sell to lawless whites. Jesse Chisholm, a half-breed Cherokee who had become widely known as a guide, interpreter, and Indian trader before the Civil war, resided with the Wichita at the mouth of the Little Arkansas. Probably as early as the fall of 1864 he loaded some wagons with goods and, following at least in part the trail or trails already marked, traveled south to the North Canadian river, returning in the spring of 1865 with buffalo robes, furs, and cattle. Thereafter Chisholm, as well as other Indians (and some whites) at or near the junction of the Arkansas and Little Arkansas rivers, continued to travel down this trail into the Indian Territory. Chisholm died on the North Canadian, March 4, 1868; the refugee Indians moved south to their old homes during 1867 and 1868. Cattle drovers coming north from Texas may have used this trail as early as 1867, striking it at or some distance north of the North Canadian river. Between 1869 and 1871 newspaper correspondents at or near Wichita referred to the route extending south from that place as the Great Texas Cattle trail, Great Cattle trail, Texas Cattle trail, or Old Wichita trail. In 1870 a correspondent of a Dallas newspaper called the trail from Red river to Abilene, the Abilene trail. The earliest printed use of the name Chisholm trail that the editor found in a contemporary newspaper was in a letter written at Eldorado, Kansas, on May 18, 1870. On October 7 of the same year James Richards Mead, writing from

COL. O. W. WHEELER'S HERD, EN ROUTE FOR KANSAS PACIFIC RAILWAY, IN 1867.

SWIMMING A RIVER.

ones bring up the rear; and the same cattle can be seen at
their post, marching along like a column of soldiers, every
day during the entire journey, unless they become lame,
when they will fall back to the rear. A herd of one thousand
cattle will stretch out from one to two miles whilst traveling
on the trail, and is a very beautiful sight, inspiring the
drover with enthusiasm akin to that enkindled in the breast
of the military hero by the sight of marching columns of
men. Certain cowboys are appointed to ride beside the
leaders and so control the herd, whilst others ride beside
and behind, keeping everything in its place and moving on,
the camp wagon and caviyard bringing up the rear.

When an ordinary creek or small river is reached, the
leaders are usually easily induced to go in; and although it
may be swimming, yet they scarce hesitate, but plunge
through to the northern shore and continue the journey, the

Wichita, also employed the term. Thereafter the name was used with in-
creasing frequency, together with such variations as Chisholm Cattle trail
and Old Chisholm trail. However, some maps published by the United
State government during the seventies and eighties called it the Abilene
Cattle trail. *House Ex. Docs.*, 38 cong., 2 sess., no. 1, pp. 463-464; *ibid.*, 39
cong., 1 sess., no. 1, pp. 472-473; *ibid.*, 40 cong., 3 sess., no. 1, pp. 747-748;
Official Records of the Rebellion, ser. 1, vol. 1, pp. 648, 667; *ibid.*, ser. 1, vol.
XLVIII, pt. 1, pp. 309, 936, 1097, pt. 11, pp. 869, 1009, 1021, 1042, 1164, 1176;
ibid., Atlas, plate CXIX; *New York Daily Tribune*, May 6, 1858, Nov. 6, 1867;
Kansas Daily Tribune, Aug. 8, 1869; *Junction City Weekly Union*, Sept. 4,
1869; *Kansas Daily Commonwealth*, May 27, Oct. 11, 1870, Jan. 21, July 16,
Aug. 10, 1871; *Leavenworth Daily Times*, July 29, 1870; *Wichita Vidette*,
Aug. 13, 25, 1870; *Dallas Herald*, Aug. 27, 1870; *Kansas City Journal of
Commerce*, Aug. 16, 25, 1871; *Wichita City Eagle*, Aug. 2, 1872; *Denison
Daily News*, Apr. 28, 1874; *Wichita Daily Eagle*, Mar. 1, 1890; *Wichita
Weekly Eagle*, Mar. 30, 1900; William H. Emory and N. Michler, *Map of
the United States and their Territories between the Mississippi and the
Pacific Ocean and Part of Mexico, 1857-8;* John H. Oberly and C. A. Max-
well, *Map of the Indian Territory, 1889; From Everglade to Cañon with the
Second Dragoons* (Theo. F. Rodenbough, compiler, New York, 1875), 171;
Joseph Stroud, *Memories of Old Western Trails in Texas Longhorn Days*
(1932), 4, 6; Joseph B. Thoburn and Muriel H. Wright, *Oklahoma. A
History of the State and its People* (New York, 1929), 1, 309, 409, 11, 861;
J. R. Mead, "Trails in Southern Kansas," Kansas State Historical Society,
Transactions, v, 92-93; John Rossel, "The Chisholm Trail," *Kansas His-
torical Quarterly*, v, 3-14; *Portrait and Biographical Album of Sedgwick
County, Kan.*, 156, 159-160; *History of the State of Kansas* (1883), 1385;
Henry, *op. cit.*, 37; Ridings, *op. cit.*, 15-41, 570-585.

balance of the herd following as fast as they arrive. Often, however, at large rivers, when swollen by floods, difficulty is experienced in getting over; especially is this the case when the herd gets massed together. Then they become unwieldy and are hard to induce to take the water. Sometimes days are spent, and much damage to the condition of the herd done, in getting across a single stream. But if the herd is well broken and properly managed, this difficulty is not often experienced. As soon as the leaders can be induced to take to the water and strike out for the opposite shore, the balance will follow with but little trouble. Often the drover can induce the leaders to follow him into and across the river by riding ahead of them into the water and, if need be, swimming his horse in the lead to the opposite shore, whilst the entire herd follow much in the same order that it travels on the trail. It sometimes occurs that the herd will become unmanageable and frightened after entering the water and refuse to strike out to either shore, but gather around their leaders and swim in a [97] circle round and round, very similar to milling on the ground when frightened. The aspect is that of a mass of heads and horns, the bodies being out of sight in the water, and it is not uncommon to lose numbers by drowning. When the herd gets to milling in the water, to break this mill and induce the leaders to launch out for the shore, the drover swims his cow pony into the center of the mill and, if possible, frightens the mass of struggling, whirling cattle into separation. Not infrequently the drover is unhorsed and compelled to swim for his life, often taking a swimming steer by the tail and thus be safely and speedily towed to the shore. Swimming herds of cattle across swollen rivers is not listed as one of the pleasurable events in the drover's trip to the northern market. It is the scarcity of large rivers that constitutes one of the most powerful arguments in favor of the Chisholm trail. Nevertheless it is not entirely free from this objection, especially during rainy seasons. When the herd is over the stream the next job is to get the camp wagon over. This is done by drawing it near the water's edge and, after detaching the oxen and swimming them over, a number of picket ropes are tied together (sufficient to reach across the river) and attached to the wagon, which is then pushed into the water and drawn to the opposite shore; whereupon the team is attached and the wagon drawn onto solid ground.

Few occupations are more cheerful, lively, and pleasant than that of the cowboy on a fine day or night; but when the storm comes, then is his manhood and often his skill and bravery put to test. When the night is inky dark and the lurid lightning flashes its zigzag course athwart the heavens, and the coarse thunder jars the earth, the winds moan fresh and lively over the prairie, the electric balls dance from tip to tip of the cattle's horns — then the position of the cowboy on duty is trying, far more than romantic. When the storm breaks over his head, the least occurrence unusual, such as the breaking of a dry weed or stick, or a sudden and near flash of lightning, will start the herd [99] as if by magic, all at an instant, upon a wild rush, and woe to the horse or man or camp that may be in their path. The only possible show for safety is to mount and ride with them until you can get outside the stampeding column. It is customary to train cattle to listen to the noise of the herder, who sings in a voice more sonorous than musical a lullaby consisting of a few short monosyllables. A stranger to the business of stock driving will scarce credit the statement that the wildest herd will not run, so long as they can hear distinctly the voice of the herder above the din of the storm.

But if by any mishap the herd gets off on a real stampede, it is by bold, dashing, reckless riding in the darkest of nights, and by adroit, skillful management that it is checked and brought under control. The moment the herd is off, the cowboy turns his horse at full speed down the retreating column and seeks to get up beside the leaders, which he does not attempt to stop suddenly, for such an effort would be futile, but turns them to the left or right hand and gradually curves them into a circle, the circumference of which is narrowed down as fast as possible until the whole herd is rushing wildly round and round on as small a piece of ground as possible for them to occupy. Then the cowboy begins his lullaby note in a loud voice, which has a great effect in quieting the herd. When all is still and the herd well over its scare, they are returned to their bed ground, or held where stopped until daylight.[263] Often a herd becomes scattered and run in different directions, in which case the labor is great to collect them; some will run a distance of twenty or thirty miles before stopping and turning out to rest, after which they will travel on at a rapid rate. Many times great loss in numbers and condition is sustained by a single stampede; and a herd, when once the habit of running is formed, will do but little good in thrift – if they do not become poor and bony and get the appearance of greyhounds. And the habit, once contracted, is next to impossible to break up and get the cattle to be quiet and thrifty, save by putting them in small herds or fenced [100] pastures, and this will not always remedy the evil or break up the habit.

During rainy, stormy seasons herds of cattle are apt to form the habit of stampeding every cloudy or stormy night. And although they may have long been off of the trail, held on good grazing ground, yet they are very liable to form the habit of running. It is generally the case that less than a score, often less than a half dozen, of old, wild, long-legged beeves do the mischief by getting a chronic fright, from which they never do recover; nor are they ever afterwards satisfied unless they are on the run. They would rather run than eat, any time, no matter how empty of food they may be. Stampeding becomes a mania with them, and day or night they seem to be looking for or studying up a pretext to set off on a forty-mile jaunt. How well one stampeder gets to know every other stampeder in the herd is astonishing, and they may be seen close together at all times, as if counselling how to raise Cain and get off on a burst of speed. The moment anything happens that may startle the herd, no matter how little, every chronic stampeder in the herd

---

[263] One writer described the actions of the cowboy during a stampede: "Having obtained the lead of the herd, he does not attempt to stop the now frantic horde of cattle, but rides steadily in the lead, singing a hymn or a song or perhaps yelling at the highest pitch of his voice. Having attracted the attention of the leaders, he gradually veers off to right or left—the herd following—and in a short time leads the rushing herd into a circle, which he gradually contracts until all are rushing around in a compact body." *Kansas City Journal of Commerce,* June 19, 1873.

sets off at full speed, hooking and goring every steer before or upon either side of him. It does seem as if they had become possessed of several such devils as stampeded the swine into the sea in ancient Judea. It is actual economy to shoot down, if you cannot otherwise dispose of, a squad of these vicious stampeders. And often the prudent herder will order a single car cut out, and ship off every stampeder he may have in his herd; not that he expects to get anything of much account for them, for they are generally very poor and lean, but simply to abate them and their pernicious example and influence on the balance of the herd. The way the cowboy takes sublime pleasure in prodding a lot of stampeders into a car and sending them off, he cares not where, is beyond expression and beggars description. You should hear him pronounce his parting blessing on the brutes as the engine moves off with the car in which they are confined. The [101] expression would not create an exalted opinion of the cowboy's piety. For he could tell you of the unnumbered sleepless hours they have cost him, and how many times they have caused him to leave his couch of sweet slumber, mount his horse, and ride through darkness and storm to overtake and bring back the herd from following the racy stampeders; and now that they are gone, words fail to tell his joyous delight.

Drovers consider that the cattle do themselves great injury by running round in a circle, which is termed, in cowboy parlance, "milling," and it can only be stayed by standing at a distance and hallooing or singing to them. The writer has many times sat upon the fence of a shipping yard and sang to an enclosed herd whilst a train would be rushing by. And it is surprising how quiet the herd will be so long as they can hear the human voice; but if they fail to hear it above the din of the train, a rush is made, and the yards bursted asunder unless very strong. Singing hymns to Texan steers is the peculiar forte of a genuine cowboy, but the spirit of true piety does not abound in the sentiment. We have read of singing psalms to dead horses, but singing to a lot of Texan steers is an act of piety that few beside a western drover are capable of. But 'tis said that "music hath charms that soothe the savage breast," or words to that effect, and why not "soothe" a stampeding Texan steer? We pause, repeating, "Why not?" [264]

After a drive of twenty-five to one hundred days the herd arrives in western Kansas, whither, in advance, its owner has come, and decided what point at which he will make his headquarters. Straightway a good herding place is sought out, and the herd, upon its arrival, placed thereon, to remain until a buyer is found, who is dilligently sought after; but if not found as soon as the cattle are fat, they are shipped to market. But the drover has a decided preference for selling on the prairie, for there he feels at home and self-possessed; but when he goes on the cars he is out of his element and doing something he doesn't understand much about and doesn't [102] wish to learn, especially at the price it has cost many cattle shippers.

Before going further into the history of the development of the western cattle trade, simple justice demands that we mention some of the very few who did have an appreciative conception of the Abilene enterprise. First on the list is Ex-Governor Crawford, then governor of Kansas, who seemed to comprehend in the fullest sense the magnitude and importance of the undertaking, and freely gave a letter commending the point selected and the parties engaged thereat.[265] This action of the governor brought down upon his

---

264 "Each cowboy as he rides around the herd sings or shouts a sort of lullaby, old Methodist hymns being the most popular, although good, old fashioned negro minstrel songs have been found equally effective in soothing the breast of the wild Texas steer." *Ibid.*

265 Early in March, 1913, Governor Samuel J. Crawford wrote the following recollections of his aid to McCoy in 1867: "Let me reflect upon my first interview with Mr. McCoy, which occurred about the first of June, 1867, in my little garret office as governor of the state at that time. Mr. McCoy came into my office, introduced himself, and stated that he had a problem in his mind, that he was out west seeing if he could find a solution for it. . . The problem in McCoy's mind was to go somewhere in the west and put in a cattle shipping depot and other needed facilities and locate a trail directly south to Texas that would be west and beyond all settlements and not be interfered with and have that trail open by sending herds over it to a shipping point at Abilene. . . After hearing Mr. McCoy's statement of his proposition, I believed in it. . . So, I wrote a plain, vigorous letter, commending Mr. McCoy's scheme and the location that he selected and approved the undertaking in a semi-official manner. . . Later, I sent a commission of

head the bitter maledictions of certain pothouse politicians, whose pet schemes, shaped by the famous "Texas Cattle Law" of Kansas, passed by the legislature during the previous winter, were ruined by the success of Abilene, and all the bright visions of wholesale plunder dissipated, as is the mist by the sunshine. Others thought the governor had made a grave error in encouraging Texan drovers to bring their stock to Kansas. But to such he said: "I regard the opening of that cattle trail into and across western Kansas of as much value to the state as is the Missouri river." But sound and sensible as this statement now appears, it was then regarded as heretical to the best interests of Kansas. Few now will maintain that his words were not prophetic and true. Governor Crawford is one of the few pure and patriotic statesmen of which Kansas can boast and deserves the highest confidence of her citizens.

Among the editorial fraternity, M. W. Reynolds, then of the Lawrence *Journal,* now of the Parsons *Sun,* was a staunch, true friend of Abilene. Unpaid and unsolicited, he was ever ready to write up in kind, truthful words the steady progress and development of the Abilene cattle trade. And justice forbids that we should fail to remember Mr. Prescott, of the Leavenworth *Commercial,* who often spoke effective words in behalf of Abilene. Other editors casually noticed it, but generally in an unappreciative manner, often showing [103] how incredulous they were of the ultimate success of the enterprise. A correspondent of the *New York Tribune,* Mr. Samuel Wilkison, took notes in August, 1867, of the enterprise and what was proposed to be accomplished, and wrote it up in a highly sensational style in a column-and-a-half article under the title of "The Story of a Cattle Speculator." [266] Nothing was more evident to the

citizens of Kansas down over that trail [from Abilene to Caldwell] and helped line it up across the Indian Territory to persuade the Indians that were in that country . . . not to interfere with the upcoming herds. My commission looked the proposition over and accomplished its purpose, returned and so reported and I publicly reported the trail to be established and sanctioned from Abilene, Kansas, to Red River Crossing, in Texas, in a semi-official manner." *Cattle Industry Clippings,* I, 148, K.S.H.S.

[266] This article, entitled "Beef from Texas," was published in the *New York Daily Tribune* on November 6, 1867, and was reprinted in the St. Louis

readers of that effusion than the patent fact that its author had more stupid incredulity than brains. He regarded the whole affair as a visionary farce of which nothing tangible could be realized.

We have in a former paper said that Texan drovers, as a class, were clannish, and easily gulled by promises of high prices for their stock. As an illustration of these statements we cite a certain secret meeting of the drovers held at one of the camps in 1867, whereat they all, after talking the matter over, pledged themselves to hold their cattle for 3 cents per pound gross and to sell none for less. One of the principal arguments used was that their cattle must be worth that price or those Illinoisans would not be expending so much money and labor in preparing facilities for shipping them. To this resolution they adhered persistently, refusing $2.75 per 100 pounds for fully 10,000 head; and afterwards, failing to get their 3 cents on the prairie for their cattle, shipped them to Chicago on their own account and sold them there at $2.25 to $2.50 per 100 pounds; and out of that paid a freight of $150 per car, realizing from $10 to $15 per head less than they had haughtily refused upon the prairie. Some of them refused to accept these prices and packed their cattle upon their own account. Their disappointment and chagrin at their failure to force a buyer to pay 3 cents per pound for their cattle was great and bitter, but their refusal to accept the offer of 2¾ cents per pound was great good fortune to the would-be buyers, for at that price $100,000 would have been lost on 10,000 head of cattle. An attempt was made the following year to form a combination to put up prices; but a burnt child dreads the [104] fire, and the attempted combination failed, and every drover looked out sharply for himself.

Now one instance touching their susceptibility to being gulled by fine promises. In the fall of 1867, when Texan cattle were selling at from $24 to $28 per head in Chicago, a well-dressed, smooth-tongued individual put in an appear-

Daily Missouri Republican (Nov. 19, 1867) under the headlines, "Cheap Beef from Texas – the Story of a Cattle Speculator." Although written in a lively style, the article appears, on the whole, fairly accurate. It characterized McCoy as "a young cattle-dealer, with Scotch blood in his veins, and the shrewdness, courage, and enterprise of his race in his head."

ance at Abilene and claimed to be the representative of a
certain (bogus) packing company of Chicago, and was desirous of purchasing several thousand head of cattle. He
would pay Chicago prices at Abilene or, rather than be
particular, $5 or $10 per head more than the same cattle
would sell for in Chicago. It was astonishing to see how
eagerly certain drovers fell into his trap and bargained their
cattle off to him at $35 per head at Abilene, fully $15 more
than they would pay out. But, mark you, the buyer, so "childlike and bland," could only pay the little sum of $25 down
on 400 to 800 head, but would pay the balance when he got
to Leavenworth with the cattle, he being afraid to bring
his wealth up in that wild country. In the meantime they
would load the cattle on the cars, bill them in the name of
the buyer, and of course everything would be all right.
Strange as it may appear, several of the hitherto most suspicious drovers of 1867 fell in with this swindler's scheme;
and were actually about to let him ship their herds off on a
mere verbal promise, when the parties in charge of the
yards, seeing that the drovers were about to be defrauded
out of their stock, posted them to have the cattle billed in
their own name, and then, if the pay was not forthcoming,
they would have possession of their own stock without
troublesome litigation, as every man of sense anticipated
they would have. When the swindler, after various excuses
for his failures to pay at Leavenworth, Quincy, and Chicago
(all the while trying to get the cattle into his own hands)
found that he must come down with the cash, he very
plainly told the Texan to go to Hades with his cattle. Instead of obeying this warm parting injunction of his new-
found, high-priced buyer, he turned his [105] cattle over to
a regular commission man and received about $26 per head
at Chicago less freight charges, or almost $18 per head at
Abilene instead of $35 per head.

But we did not think the drovers who were saved from
the loss of their entire herds by a disinterested friend were
grateful to him for his kindness. They were too mad at their
own stupidity to be conscious of feelings of gratitude. And
now whilst speaking on the subject of swindlers and ingrati-
tude, we will mention another instance occurring two years

later. A certain man (if it be proper to call a rascal a man) who flourished in central Illinois ten years before the particular incident we are about to relate occurred, put in an appearance at Abilene during the fall of 1869 and, after spending money lavishly at the saloons, proceeded to purchase several droves of cattle at more liberal figures than others were able to pay or the markets east would justify. The time was quite brief before he became the most popular man that ever came to Abilene. Among his purchases was a large drove of 900 beeves, for which he agreed to pay $30 per head, but actually only paid $2,000 on the purchase; and [he] was about to ship the stock off in his own name when the party in charge of the yards gave the seller a confidential hint to be careful and to be safe, which he acted upon, but not until he had told the would-be purchaser who had put him on his guard; at the same time repeating what had been told him by the yardman in confidence at his own solicitation, adding that he (the seller) did not believe the statement of the yardman. Of course, the would-be shipper got mad and drunk, and swore he was persecuted maliciously without just cause, and wanted to shoot the fellow who dared say he was a proper subject to be watched in business transactions. Several Texans espoused his cause, and one gave him over twelve thousand dollars' worth of cattle on short credit; another gave him $5,000 in cash as a loan of honor; another $2,000 in cash to repay at his leisure. Now mark the sequel — not one single dollar [106] of this snug sum of $17,000 did one of the Texans ever see again, and we suppose they regard it now as a permanent investment. Their pet buyer is at this writing languishing in a county jail not one thousand miles from Kansas City, awaiting his trial on the charge of stealing, of which charge we have no doubt of his guilt, and only hope justice may get its dues after being cheated so long. Many more similar cases to the above could be given, but we will not tax patience further, only adding that not in one single instance of the many that occurred did the Texan ever show a spark of gratitude for being saved from a swindling scheme, but were more generally sour and suspicious of the motive that prompted their real friend to forewarn them.

Of the 35,000 cattle that arrived in 1867 at Abilene, about 3,000 head were bought and shipped to Chicago by the parties owning the stockyards; of the balance, much the larger portion was sent to Chicago and either sold on the market or packed for the account of the drovers. The latter proved more [un]fortunate for the drover. The cattle were thin in flesh and made only the lower grades of beef, for which there was but little demand at ruinously low figures. Those who sold on the market did better than those who packed, yet they lost money heavily. Another portion of the drive of 1867 went into winter quarters. A few were taken north to the Platte country for the Indians, but quite a large number were packed at Junction City, where an enterprising firm of citizens, headed by a now well-known cattleman, but then late of Indianapolis, Indiana, had erected a temporary packing house, in which several thousand cattle were slaughtered, the product thereof being shipped direct to New York. But this experiment resulted unsatisfactorily to both packers and drovers. The cattle were not as good or fat as both parties had anticipated, and it proved a disastrous loss to all concerned. A few cattle were packed at the same place the following season, but the establishment was soon abandoned and finally torn down.[267] Had the drovers of 1867 gone into [107] winter quarters and kept their stock until the following season, a fine profit instead of a loss would have been realized.[268] But it was upon the tongue of

[267] E. W. Pattison & Company, the pioneer packing firm in the Great Plains region, moved to Kansas City, Missouri, in 1868 and established the first packing plant in that city. Writing from Junction City on November 13, 1867, a correspondent of the *Chicago Republican* stated: "Junction City now boasts of a large beef-packing house, where two hundred Texas cattle are killed daily. At present the markets for this beef are in Baltimore, Philadelphia, and New York; and so increasing are the demands upon the establishment that its proprietor, Mr. Patterson [Pattison], is about to enlarge it so that two hundred and fifty or three hundred head can be disposed of daily." *Junction City Weekly Union*, Nov. 30, 1867. See also Miller, *op. cit.*, 169.

[268] "The failure of the corn crops in Ohio, Indiana and Illinois has thrown thousands of head of cattle into the Chicago market, which has put a quietus partially, upon the Texas branch of the business. To a man who is prepared to winter them, an investment in these cattle will by spring prove the most profitable in the country." *Junction City Weekly Union*, Nov. 16, 1867.

nearly everyone that the cattle would not stand the rigors
of a northern winter, and inasmuch as there was no prece-
dent by which to be governed, it was thought best to sell and
pack them as before described.[269]

The summer season of 1867 was one of extreme sultry
weather, and [of] great rainfall flooding the country and
producing an immense growth of grass, which was soft and
washy, utterly failing to produce any tallow in the animal
consuming it; and when the hot weather set in, the grass
became hard and uneatable; and when the first frosts
touched it, not a single bit of nutriment was left in it – but
little better than dry shavings for food. In addition to poor
grass, the rainstorms by day, the bellowing thunder and
vivid lightning of the often-recurring storms at night, got
all the cattle on the prairie in the way of stampeding. When
this habit becomes chronic, it is impossible to fatten the
herd, often impossible to keep them together. All these
causes, and others not enumerated, combined to make the
final wind-up of the cattle market of 1867 at Abilene unsatisfactory, and to none more so than the parties who expended
so much money in creating the necessary facilities for conducting a cattle market. Their losses were very severe – far
more so than if they had had a criterion by which to be
governed. Shipping cattle at the rate of one thousand each
shipment, costing nearly a score of thousands of dollars, and
then having them sold for a considerable sum less than the
freight bill, is a lively way to do business but a poor way to
get rich quick.

Although the business of shipping did not begin until the
fall – the first train being shipped on the 5th of September –
nearly one thousand cars were loaded. Yet the enterprise
was considered a failure, and everyone, save the parties
directly interested, freely expressed themselves that no cattle
would be driven there the next year; and many people
seemed to rejoice over the misfortune that they supposed
had befallen [108] the enterprise, offering hypocritical
words of condolence to the projector of the enterprise.
Others there were who became suddenly endowed with pro-

---

269 Texas cattle had been wintered in the North during the fifties and
afterward. See the introduction to the present volume.

found wisdom and sagely ejaculated, "I told you so." Notwithstanding the practical demonstration of the feasibility of cattle shipping over their road, yet the managers of the Kansas Pacific Railway in St. Louis were still incredulous and freely jested at the whole project, regarding it as the big joke of the season; but there was one young and worthy man in the office of purchaser of supplies who was firm in the belief that there was yet something to be expected of the undertaking at Abilene. He was jeered at by every other officer, both great and small — and the most of them were small in more senses than one — and ridiculed him as one championing a self-evident failure.

A few incidents of a personal nature and we leave the year 1867 in tracing the early developments of the cattle trade. On the occasion of the shipment of the first trainload of cattle, about which we have before given some items, a certain managing director of the Kansas Pacific approached the parties in interest at Abilene and proposed to enter privately into a partnership, and as an inducement to the acceptance of his proposition said that he would work secretly in the executive committee in St. Louis for the special advantage of the firm. After consulting over the matter, the parties concluded that a man who would be willing to "sell" a railroad company would be equally as willing to "sell" another company. So they rejected his proposition, which excited the managing director's ire and indignation to a high pitch. But not long after this occurred, a certain subordinate railroad official appeared at Abilene and expressed a deep desire to make some money out of the cattle trade; or, in other words, asked the party who was building the yards if he would not give him a certain amount on each car loaded. After a few moments' reflection, in which the many courtesies and the kind aid that had been extended to him by this official were mentally reviewed, the official was told that at the end of the season he might [109] expect a present of an amount of cash equal to one-half the sum for which he had asked. This proved to be an unfortunate step and was the only one of the kind ever made by that cattle trader; for no sooner had the next season opened than this same official reappeared at Abilene, demanding one-half the gross amount which the parties were to receive from the railroad company for their services and expenditures during the year 1868. And when this modest request was declined, the official left, muttering threats of vengeance, and did actually go to a point twenty-five miles west of Abilene and give a lower rate of freight from that point than was given from Abilene. After several unavailing remonstrances with the official about his conduct, which he knew to be in violation of the provisions of a written contract existing between the railroad company and the parties at Abilene,[270] the general officers of the company at St. Louis were visited and the matter placed before the executive committee. It eventuated in the official receiving a polite invitation to tender his resignation, which, of course, under the peculiar circumstances, he did.

But we will close this chapter with brief sketches of two widely known and universally liked drovers and traders, one of whom is J. D. Reed, a resident of Texas for twenty-three years but an Alabamian by birth.[271] Upon entering Texas, he went straightway on a stock ranch of his own selection on the frontier of his adopted state. Notwithstanding he devotes much of his time and attention to driving and trading in cattle, he keeps up his stocks in Texas. Of cattle he has about ten thousand head, and of horses a stock sufficiently large to keep good the supply of saddle ponies with which to care for his cattle stocks. Although his ranch consists of fully one thousand acres of land, his stock ranges over an immense area of country, mostly belonging to the state of Texas. Mr. Reed contented himself for many years upon his ranch, where his family now, as then, reside; but in 1861 he decided to try the project of driving to Louisiana,

270 McCoy's contract, or agreement, with the railroad in 1867 was a verbal one. See footnote 230.

271 James D. Reed, born in Alabama in 1830, came to Texas as a boy. He enlisted in the Confederate forces during the Civil war, in which he was wounded and lost an arm. From 1871 to about 1882 he trailed cattle and horses to the northern plains, disposing of them at Abilene, Wichita, Ellsworth, Dodge City, and other places. He died in New Mexico in 1891. *Wichita City Eagle*, May 24, 1872; *Ellsworth Reporter*, May 1, 1873; *Daily Fort Worth Democrat*, Apr. 28, 1877; *Dodge City Times*, Mar. 9, 1878; *San Antonio Daily Express*, Apr. 27, 1881; *Trail Drivers of Texas* (Hunter ed.), 690-691.

MIDNIGHT STORM AND STAMPEDE.

J. D. REED.

MAJOR SETH MABRY.

which [110] proved moderately satisfactory, and would perhaps have been repeated in future years but for the outbreak of the Civil war. In this, Reed, in common with almost every other southern man, took part; but was not long in the service before he received a severe wound which disabled him for military duty, and he soon found himself back upon his ranch, fully satisfied with military life and its fruits. Having imbibed the spirit of trading and roaming away from home, Reed was soon off with a herd of beeves for Mexico, which trade he continued in until the close of the war, when he abandoned it and turned his herds toward New Orleans, to which market he continued to ship and drive for five consecutive years. But in 1871 he changed his plans of operation and turned his herds toward western Kansas. Each year since has witnessed on an average fully thirty-five hundred head of beeves en route for western Kansas driven by Mr. Reed's [111] cowboys. Whatever frontier cattle town can secure his patronage and influence, regards him a host in its behalf. He drives none but good beeves, and is, upon arrival, ready to sell out all or in part; or if prices do not suit him to sell, he will turn about and buy. He is not particular which he does, so he is doing something, for he is a man of fine energy and great perseverance; a man who is familiar with all phases of life and is always in to see, know, and learn everything that may be going on, among the highest to the lowest, where he may be stopping. He is one of that type of men that make friends in all spheres of life, and few there are who have a larger list of warm admirers than J. D. Reed, of Goliad, Texas. During the year 1872 he handled fully eight thousand head of beeves and put fourteen hundred head into winter quarters the same fall. During the year 1873 he drove about three thousand head, and selling out soon after arriving in western Kansas, was in good shape to join his friend, A. H. Pierce, in buying seven thousand head at panic prices to put into winter quarters. Certainly money in large amounts was made upon the cattle bought during the months of October and November, 1873. In 1871, Mr. Reed wintered about sixteen hundred head of cattle in western Kansas. It matters little in what country he comes in contact with the cattle trade, so thorough is his practical knowledge of the business and so unerring his judgment that he seldom fails to meet with success in all his live stock operations.

Austin, the capital city of Texas, is the home of Major Seth Mabry, a popular drover whose cheerful presence in any company or place is always welcome; one of the most appreciative, affable drovers; among the most chivalric, courteous cattlemen the Lone Star State sends to the North annually with his thousands of beeves.[272] Everybody in anywise connected with the live stock trade knows the major and feels the right to call him their friend; for he knows everyone and has a pleasant word for each; is ever ready to do some one a favor or perform a kind office; is well read and [112] has traveled extensively; is a close observer of human faces and conduct; is very fond of social companions and quite conversational; always entertaining; loves a good story and has an inexhaustible fund thereof, from which one just pat to the occasion is always ready at his tongue's end, to be told in his own inimitable manner. This extensive drover went with his father from Tennessee to Texas in 1837, and under the paternal tuition learned practically the business of ranching; was, in fact, brought up on a stock ranch and thoroughly drilled in all the mysteries of successful stock growing. Very wisely did he decide when he determined to be a ranchman on his own account. When he had arrived at the age of manhood and started in the business world for himself, for fifteen years he studiously, and we need not add successfully, followed his early and well-chosen occupation. Fully twenty thousand cattle bore his brand, and annually from three to five thousand calves felt his hot branding iron cauterizing their [113] tender hides and stamping indelibly the badge of ownership to be seen and read by all men.

---

[272] Seth Mabry, a Confederate veteran, drove cattle to Abilene, Ellsworth, Dodge City, and other places between about 1869 and 1886, some of the time in partnership with Eugene B. Millett. Later he moved to Kansas City, Missouri, where he died. *Abilene Chronicle,* Apr. 6, 1871; *Ellsworth Reporter,* May 14, 1874; *Fort Worth Democrat,* Apr. 24, 1875; *Dodge City Times,* Mar. 8, 1879; *Fort Worth Daily Gazette,* June 23, 1883; *Dallas Morning News,* May 23, 1886; *Trail Drivers of Texas* (Hunter, ed.), 718; Pelzer, *op. cit.,* 64.

In 1867 and 1868 the major tried the rocks of the New Orleans market, but upon the following year he put in his first appearance in western Kansas with large herds; and annually has he made his pilgrimage to western Kansas with about five thousand head of cattle. The major would always rather sell than buy, but would rather buy than do nothing; would rather sell on the prairie, but does not hesitate to ship east or drive to some more northerly territory; or go to the frigid upper Missouri country and furnish the government contractor with a few thousand bovines to nourish the inner man of Poor Lo and family. In 1872 the major became tired of furnishing the Indians of western Texas with cow ponies without pay, and therefore sold out his ranch in Llano county, Texas. But about the same time he and his business associate established a permanent cattle ranch in Idaho, upon which they placed four thousand cattle, mostly cows and heifers, and the year following branded about two thousand calves. But this enterprise received but a small part of their attention; so little of it that in 1873 they found time to drive from Texas about fifteen thousand head of cattle, and were fortunate enough to get the supplying of the Indian contractors to the extent of their herds. The major has been at least moderately successful in all his business undertakings and ranks with the more influential class of Texan stockmen.

INDIAN SCARE.

VII. DROVER'S COTTAGE

Notwithstanding the disastrous experiences of the fall of 1867, and the maudlin gibberings of many who took such a deep (?) interest in the result of the first experiments in creating a cattle market at Abilene, the founders of that enterprise determined to make a systematic effort to secure a large drive of cattle from Texas in 1868. To this end a systematic scheme of advertising in Texas was prosecuted with energy and without regard to expense.[273] To every Texas man whose address had been obtained previously, and to all whose address was subsequently obtained by reference to commercial agencies, directors of cities and county officials, including every newspaper in the state – to all these were addressed a circular setting forth the contemplated purpose of the Abilene enterprise, and inviting the drovers and stockmen of Texas to bring their herds of marketable cattle to that point; assuring all who would do so, of a cordial reception, fair dealing, protection from mob violence, perfect equality upon the market and in the use of shipping facilities; a concerted, joint effort to get buyers for their stock; in short, to give to the stockman of Texas what he did not before have, to wit, a market in which he could sell any and all the live stock which he might bring thereto, and, if failing to find a purchaser on the prairie for his stock, he could ship them unmolested to any point or market he might choose. The [115] papers throughout the state of Texas copied into their columns the circular letter, and

---

[273] A Texas drover, writing from Dallas on January 18, 1869, asserted: "Last summer there was but one firm engaged in the cattle commission business at Abilene, and that firm in the early part of the spring of 1868, sent their circulars to the different parts of the stock region, inviting the drover to come with his cattle, rather holding out inducements to him. The consequence was that there were a great many cattle driven from Texas to Abilene." *Dallas Herald,* Jan. 23, 1869.

many of them gave the subject favorable editorial notices. Every office, business house, and hamlet in the state was the recipient of one or more of the letters. So all Texas was reading and talking of the new star of hope that had arisen in the north to light and buoy up the hitherto dark and desponding heart of the ranchman.

In addition to the circular letters above mentioned, two gentlemen [274] of tact and address were sent into and traversed the state for no other purpose than to inform, so far versed the state for no other purpose than to inform, so far as possible by word of mouth, the Texan drovers, of Abilene and the inducements there held out to stockmen. Inasmuch as a drover or seller of stock is only one of the parties necessary to make a complete cattle market, the buyer being just as indispensable a personage as the seller, therefore it was necessary to do an equal amount of advertising throughout the northern states and territories, proclaiming to the northern cattle world the expected concentration of Texas cattle at Abilene. In order to accomplish this result, access was had to the advertising columns of every newspaper widely read by northern cattlemen.[275] Fully five thousand dollars were expended in this advertising scheme during the winter of 1867 and 1868.[276] In the communications sent into Texas, definite advisory instructions were urged upon the Texan

[274] Charles F. Gross and Samuel N. Hitt, both of Springfield, Illinois. *Abilene Weekly Reflector,* Apr. 30, 1925; Henry, *op. cit.,* 34, 44.

[275] The following advertisement appeared in a St. Louis newspaper: "Cattle. The best grazing cattle in the United States can be had in any number, on and after 15th May, 1868, at Abilene, Kansas, weighing from 1000 to 1200 lbs. live weight. They reach Abilene from the Southwest, and will take on from 50 to 150 lbs. more than native cattle, and cost less than half as much. Until 1st of May we may be conferred with personally at Springfield, Illinois, and thereafter at Abilene, Kansas. W. K. McCoy & Bros." *Daily Missouri Republican,* Mar. 27, 1868. See also *Daily Illinois State Journal,* Mar. 16, 1868.

[276] In 1871, McCoy testified as follows: "In the Spring of 1868 we spent $5000 in advertising throughout Texas, and sending men there to recommend Abilene as a good place to bring cattle to, and in advertising in the north west for buyers to come there to trade during 1868. In the summer we labored persistently to get men to come there, and run a livery stable and Hotel on dead head plan, at an expense of $5000. I also paid $3300 out of my own pocket to settlers around Abilene to appease the settlers who had suffered losses through this trade." McCoy vs. the Kansas Pacific Railway Company, 16-17, MS., Supreme Court of Kansas.

drover to bring only good, choice, select cattle. But the habit of taking everything that was gathered by the ranchman was generally persisted in, and the instructions to bring select cattle only, were disregarded by all drovers – save a few who heeded the advice given, and such received a satisfactory reward for the pains taken in getting up their herd, in the ready sale and fine prices obtained soon after their arrival at Abilene.

Thirty days before the cattle began to arrive at Abilene, in the spring of 1868,[277] quite a delegation of buyers were at the Drover's Cottage, a hotel erected for the special accommodation of cattlemen awaiting the advent of the cattle, when [116] trade would open. To while away the tedious hours till the cattle came, resort was had to divers expedients, such as reading newspapers, talking over business projects and prospects, telling stories, perpetrating jokes, etc. During the spring of 1868 the Indians made a hostile raid upon the frontier settlers of northwestern Kansas. It was a determined effort on their part to prevent the settlement of the Solomon and Salina river country, their favorite hunting ground. They made a sudden descent upon the sparse settlements, and such whites as did not make a hasty retreat from the country were brutally massacred and their women taken captive. The redskins extended their raid within fifty or sixty miles of Abilene. Of course, there was considerable excitement, and all sorts of rumors afloat among the sparse settlements near and west of Abilene. The Indians and their barbarous atrocities, and the probable point east to which they were likely to extend their raid, were the absorbing topics of the day, and pallid cheeks and nervous twitchings were observable on every hand among the timid, such as had no particular anxiety to form the acquaintance of Mr. Lo and his coadjutors, especially whilst their appetites for scalps seemed so insatiable.

Several eastern live stock men who had come to Abilene to purchase cattle were among the guests of the Cottage, and it was among that class that the greatest uneasiness was manifested. Especially was this the case with a certain

---

277 "Two herds of Texas cattle arrived at Abilene during the past week. This is the first of the season." *Junction City Weekly Union*, Apr. 25, 1868.

young man from Green or Jersey county, Illinois, who had, against the advice of his young and newly married wife, come out to invest his first venture in Texan cattle. It was soon observed by the old, experienced frontiersmen and drovers present that this young man "had the Injun scare bad." Whenever a story was told about Indian fighting, scalping, and massacring, this young cattleman's cheek would blanch, his frame tremble, and groaning sighs escaped his lips. The boys thought him a fit subject to perpetrate a joke upon. So they posted the landlord of the Cottage, also the telegraph operator, of the respective parts they were [117] desired to play. Just before the appointed hour, the guests gathered in a cluster and began telling the most horrible Indian stories they ever heard or could imagine, always winding up with the confident prediction that the Indians, then so near, would never stop short of cleaning out every white man in that portion of Kansas, and that a bloody encounter was to be expected soon. All unanimously agreed that it was every man's duty to burnish and load up every weapon that could be found. Expectations of the Indians that afternoon or night were expressed on all sides. This was all told and acted in the most serious manner and had the effect of almost overwhelming the young cattle dealer with fear. Then the telegraph operator came rushing from the office toward the landlord and in an agitated manner handed him a (bogus) dispatch. The landlord glanced at it, then made one of those excited exclamations expressive of sudden alarm, and jumping upon a chair, proceeded to read a general warning to the [118] citizens of Abilene and vicinity of the near approach of the Indians in great numbers with bloody war clubs and gory scalping knives; also bidding the citizens to arm for their own defense and to prepare for "war to the knife, the knife to the hilt." Of course the excitement arose to fever heat during the reading of the message, which purported to be dated at a station forty miles west of Abilene.

The young drover was horror personified, transfixed with fear, each particular hair standing erect, knees knocked together in true Belshazzar style, his hand yielded its grip upon his hat, the tears trickled down his pallid cheeks, his

before the young stockman came in sight, belaboring his old rack of bones in desperate earnest, making a moderate-sized stick of cordwood bounce off of the poor old horse's ribs every jump. If ever an old horse suffered grief in unbroken doses, that old charger was the one. This paper is blackness compared with the cattle dealer's face. But when he arrived at the hotel, the joke had gone far enough, and all took a hearty laugh at the young man; and then for the first time dawned upon his mind the fact that he was the subject of a cruel hoax. The first train going east bore away the young cattleman, without Texan cattle, to the bosom of his "poor wife."

The buyers were in every instance brought to Abilene by the advertising and other efforts of the parties who founded the enterprise.

Although the Drover's Cottage was completed and furnished in the fall of 1867, yet it was not formally opened as a hotel until the following spring, no competent landlord being found or wanted until that time. But when the hotel began to fill up and first-class entertainment was demanded, the proprietor decided to go east and procure a good, experienced landlord to take charge of the house. Before reaching St. Louis, an old acquaintance was met and the subject of the trip made known to him; the result [120] of which was a call at the St. Nicholas Hotel in St. Louis.[278] Entering the reception room and quietly taking a seat, a servant was sent into the dining room to request an interview with the steward, who was reported to be anxious to take charge of a hotel upon his own account. In a few minutes the steward, his wife, and the rough-clad Illinoisan were chatting earnestly upon the proposed business transaction, which conversation resulted in the steward and his wife going to Abilene to be the first landlord and landlady (afterwards proprietors) of the Drover's Cottage — a name still perpetuated on more than one hotel in the West. In less than one hundred hours from the time the start was

278 The St. Nicholas Hotel, of which Enos Jennings was manager, was located at 817 N. Fourth street. It was a very good hotel, ranking just below the Planters' and the Southern. *Daily Missouri Republican,* June 26, 1867; *Edwards' St. Louis Directory, 1868,* p. 637.

made, the hotel domiciled its future proprietor, Mrs. Lou Gore.[279]

In a brief time it was apparent that in the person of the new landlady of the Cottage, the drovers had a true, sympathizing friend, and in their sickness a true guardian and

[279] The hotel called the Drover's Cottage, which became the headquarters for cattle buyers and Texas drovers, was built by McCoy during the summer and fall of 1867 at an estimated total cost (including furnishings and a barn) of $15,000. It was a three-story frame structure which measured about 40 by 60 feet, had green venetian blinds at the windows, was painted "a delicate wood color," had hard-finished plaster walls, contained about forty or fifty rooms, could accommodate about eighty guests, had a billiard room and saloon, and was "neatly and elegantly furnished in all its apartments." The first manager of the hotel was Jonathan B. Warfield, whose wife was a sister of Theodore C. Henry. But in the spring of 1868, McCoy made a trip to St. Louis and employed a new manager – James W. Gore, steward of the St. Nicholas Hotel. Gore and his wife, Louisa M., both of whom were natives of the state of New York, came to Abilene shortly afterward and took charge of Drover's Cottage at a stipulated salary. The Gores had two children, Mollie and Maggie, aged about eight and four, respectively. On April 29, 1869, Gore rented the hotel from McCoy until September 1, 1870, promising to pay $15,000 for the period of the lease; but on July 26, 1869, McCoy and Gore agreed to cancel this agreement. On the latter date McCoy, desirous of placing himself in a more advantageous position when negotiating with the railroad, disposed of Drover's Cottage to Samuel N. Hitt, of Springfield, Illinois, who, in turn, also on July 26, 1869, leased the hotel to Gore until September 1, 1870, for $8,000. Business was so good that Gore purchased the property from Hitt on February 26, 1870, for $8,000. During the fall of 1869 or early in 1870 some additions were made to the hotel. By the latter year Drover's Cottage had acquired a wide reputation in Texas and the West for its excellent food, fine appointments, and good management, and its rooms were always "flooded with guests" during the spring and summer months. On October 28, 1870, Gore sold the hotel to Moses B. George, of Kansas City, Missouri, who at the same time became manager of the property. The purchase price was $12,000. Early in 1871, George made extensive additions to the establishment, running the total cost of its construction up to about $40,000. In July of the same year, according to an eyewitness, Drover's Cottage measured 70 by 90 feet, contained nearly 100 rooms, could accommodate about 175 guests, had an iron roof, possessed an ice house and a laundry, and had an additional barn with space for 50 carriages and 100 horses. The rooms were described as "large, airy, clean, and well furnished." Early in 1872, after the Texas cattle drives had ceased to come to Abilene, George moved to Ellsworth and erected a hotel there, calling it Drover's Cottage. Part of the building at Abilene was taken down and moved to the new location. On January 8, 1873, George sold the Drover's Cottage at Abilene to Louisa M. Gore for $10,000. Renaming it the Cottage

nurse; [121] one whose kind, motherly heart was ever ready to provide for their every proper want, be they hungry, tired, thirsty, or sick, it mattered not; she was the Florence Nightingale to relieve them. From her earliest memory her home has been in a hotel, her father being to this day the proprietor of a large one at Niagara Falls, at which drovers en route to New York or Boston, going via the Falls, delight to stop. Many a sick and wearied drover has she nursed and tenderly cared for until health was restored; or in the event of death, soothed their dying moments with all the kind offices that a true sister only so well understands how to perform. Many western drovers — rough, uncouth men, such as nature and the wild frontier produces — will ever hear the name of Mrs. Lou Gore mentioned only with emotions of kindest respect and tenderest memory, and feelings near akin to the holy passion that binds earth to Heaven.

The cattle trail broken and driven over in 1867 from the crossing of the Arkansas river (which was at the mouth of the Little Arkansas river and on the present site of the city of Wichita) to Abilene was not direct but circuitous. In order to straighten up this trail and bring the cattle direct to Abilene, and, by shortening the distance, to counteract the exertions of western would-be competing points for the cattle trade, an engineer corps was sent out under the charge of Civil Engineer T. F. Hersey — a noble, true man, whose

House, Mr. and Mrs. Gore still owned and managed the hotel during the early eighties, when it contained only thirty rooms and accommodations for the same number of guests. Drover's Cottage stood on or near the spot now occupied by the offices of the Belle Springs Creamery. Dickinson County, Deed Record B, 401-402, 485, 521, MS., Recorder of Deeds Office, Abilene; ibid., Deed Record C, 103-106, 313; ibid., Deed Record E, 402; Ninth Census of the United States, Dickinson and Doniphan Counties, Kansas, MS., K.S.H.S.; Abilene Chronicle, Mar. 3, Nov. 3, 1870, May 25, July 6, 1871; Junction City Weekly Union, Aug. 31, Nov. 2, 1867, July 17, 1869, Aug. 19, 1871; Republican Daily Journal, Oct. 19, 1869, Jan. 31, 1871; Kansas Daily Commonwealth, May 19, July 2, 1870, Mar. 9, 1872; Ellsworth Reporter, Feb. 29, Apr. 11, June 13, 27, Aug. 8, 1872, June 12, 1873; Kansas Daily Tribune, June 23, 1868; Leavenworth Times & Conservative, June 25, 1869; New York Daily Tribune, Nov. 6, 1867; Abilene Weekly Reflector, Apr. 30, 1925; History of the State of Kansas (1883), 688, 690; Trail Drivers of Texas (Hunter, ed.), 454-455; Edwards' St. Louis Directory, 1868, p. 340; McCoy, "Historic and Biographic Sketch," loc. cit., p. 52.

heart was always found in the right place and full of warm blood for his friends; an early settler of the extreme frontier, at whose cabin Bayard Taylor got his last square meal as he went out on his famous overland trip to the Pacific coast many years before the projection of the Pacific Railroad. Mr. Hersey, with compass and flagman and detail of laborers with spades and shovels for throwing up mounds of dirt to mark the route located by the engineers, started out and run almost due south from Abilene until the crossing of the Arkansas river was reached, finding good water and abundant grass with suitable camping points the entire distance. Meeting at the [122] Arkansas river the first drove of cattle of the season, the party returned, piloting the herd over the new trail, and thus, by use, opening it to the many thousand herds of cattle that followed in months and years afterward.[280]

Notwithstanding the jeers of rival towns both east and west of Abilene at her ridiculous (to them) presumption in assuming to be a cattle market, seeing the immense commerce that was about centering at Abilene, when they heard the news of the many herds that were on the trail bound northward, became greatly exercised upon the subject, and determined to erect shipping yards at one town east [281] and at three towns west [282] of Abilene. In order to make amend

[280] Timothy Fletcher Hersey was born in Sumner, Oxford county, Maine, August 17, 1827. When he was still a boy, his family moved west to the Rock river region in northern Illinois and a few years afterward to Beloit, Wisconsin. Later Timothy migrated to Jo Daviess county, Illinois, where, on January 18, 1852, he married Eliza R. Johnson, a native of Ohio. He was the first settler in the immediate vicinity of the later town site of Abilene, locating a farm on the west bank of Mud creek in July, 1857. In 1860 he was elected county clerk, and in 1862 and 1864 a representative to the state legislature. He was appointed a member of the first board of trustees of the town of Abilene in September, 1869. During the early seventies he helped to found the town of Beloit, Kansas, naming it after his former home in Wisconsin. He died at Castlerock, Cowlitz county, Washington, May 5, 1905. "Tim Hersey's Own Story," *Dickinson County Clippings*, III, Mrs. A. B. Seelye, Abilene; Hersey to Edwards, Feb. 27, 1905, *ibid.*; Sylvia Hersey Barger, "Timothy F. Hersey," *ibid.*; *History of the State of Kansas* (1883), 685, 1023.

[281] Junction City.

[282] Salina, Ellsworth, and Brookville (or Solomon City).

for their failure to systematically advertise their respective point during the past winter, as had been done for Abilene, each town sent to the crossing of the Arkansas river from two to ten drummers, or runners, for their respective points, to induce the drovers to turn to the right or left and go to other towns instead of Abilene.[283] To counteract this choir of solicitors, Abilene sent one young man to represent and to protect her interests, not to say rights, for by her enterprise in working and advertising she did have a semblance, at least, of right to claim the cattle trade as hers. But the young man sent out by Abilene was the same one who was sent alone in July, 1867, to proclaim the good tidings of Abilene to the wandering and mob-fearing drovers; a man upon whose countenance truth and honesty sat enthroned supreme, which could be readily discerned by the most casual observer and readily detected by the close-scrutinizing drover.

He deserves more than a passing mention. Few young men connected with the western cattle trade is wider and better known than W. W. Sugg, and none will outrank him in quiet, persistent, unvarying friendship to the southern cattle trade. He is an Illinoisan by birth and education, but early in life was thrown upon his own resources and upon the frontier, to seek the glittering wealth every adventurer believes Dame Fortune has in store for him. Although but a [123] young man, there are few townships of land which he has not roamed over in Missouri, Arkansas, Nebraska, Kansas, Colorado, New Mexico, and Texas, having soldiered during the war in the frontier service. He, too, is a drover of 1866 and to this day bears the scars — results of gashes made by well laid on hickory withes in the hands of southern mobs. After enduring untold outrages, he finally succeeded in getting his herd through to Christian county, Illinois, and there went into winter quarters. Early in the following spring he sold out to the Illinoisan with whom he afterwards became so intimately acquainted at Abilene. Indeed it was

283 The *Junction City Weekly Union* (July 25, 1868) published the following item: "A cattle meeting was held at Brown's Hall [Junction City] last Monday forenoon. Mr. Booth who was sent to the Little Arkansas to influence drovers this way, made a report. The meeting made all sorts of guarantees."

E. H. GAYLARD.

GAYLARD'S AFFECTIONATE PONY.

MRS. LOU. GORE.

J. M. DAY.

from his lips that the story of Texas's great supply of cattle and the insurmountable barrier in southwestern Missouri and southeastern Kansas was attentively listened to by the Illinoisan but a few weeks before he sought out and undertook the development of Abilene's famous enterprise. We need scarcely add that Mr. Sugg and the Illinoisan became fast and true friends, and that in him the Illinoisan found a genuine, unflinching, warm friend; one who was as unwavering in the hour of adversity and need as in the hours of prosperity; one whose heart was as true and whose friendship as sincere (where every other one had passed but a cold recognition, if not words full of bitter calumny, for the Illinoisan) as is the heart of him who cares for us when our kindred forsake us. Such is the real character of this humble, unpretentious man. Every western drover knows him and believes in him; and his name would be put near the head, if not at the very head, of the list of those whom they believe, in western parlance, "it will do to tie to."

But a few words, a single sentence, from him in his own quiet, modest way was sufficient to outweigh in the mind of the drover all the multiplicity of words and loud declarations of the score of verbose solicitors who opposed him and attempted to obtain trade for their respective towns. Aside from his manner, the magic, winning words that caught the listening ear of the drover was that "at Abilene buyers for their cattle are awaiting their arrival." Now, by the by, a [124] cash purchaser for his herd is just the man a Texan drover is very anxious to see, and he is more interested in knowing just where he (the buyer) can be seen than in all the railroad towns in the state of Kansas. We drop this hint, a key which will unlock the Pandora box of success to every town that is desirous of making itself a successful cattle market. One (at least) of Abilene's competitors for the cattle trade in 1868 became so desperate when it found all its efforts [failed] to induce drovers to go its way that, as a final resort, [it] actually hired a drover (paying him six hundred dollars) to leave the Abilene trail and bear off east toward another city.[284] But such inducements could not

[284] Junction City. On March 20, 1868, a resident of Junction City wrote to the *Dallas Herald* (May 16, 1868): "I would advise persons to avoid

be extended to many drovers, and soon the attempt to divert the trade in that direction was abandoned. The western competing points were even more unsuccessful and soon withdrew their unavailing solicitors.[285]

As has been stated, the Cottage at Abilene was full of cattle buyers awaiting the arrival of the cattle from Texas long before the first herd had passed the southern line of Kansas. No sooner did the cattle begin to arrive than trade opened lively and at good prices. Many thousand were taken by Illinois grazers and Indian contractors, also [by] ranchmen from Colorado, Montana, Utah, and other northern territories. Speculators from Nebraska, Iowa, and other northern states all put in an appearance on the Abilene market and made purchases. Thus Abilene as a cattle market was at last established beyond cavil or doubt. The demand for cars for eastern shipment reached over one thousand during the month of June, and the hitherto incredulous Kansas Pacific Railroad Company was taxed to its utmost capacity to furnish needed cars.[286] It was compelled to transform many of its flat cars into cattle cars by putting a framework on them. The bridge over the Missouri river was not

driving to Abilene, as the people are opposed to it in a measure. Those of this section are anxious for them as they can see the advantages derived from it. (Abilene is a small place west, on the railroad)."

285 McCoy was forced to meet the competition of these places, as well as of towns on the Union Pacific Railroad in Nebraska. Testifying in court in 1871, he asserted: "[In 1868] we had 10 men in our employ to keep the cattle from being driven north and to have them shipped through and from our yard at $50. per month per man." McCoy vs. the Kansas Pacific Railway Company, 17, MS., Supreme Court of Kansas.

286 The *Junction City Weekly Union* (June 27, 1868) published the following account: "We met Mr. McCoy, of Abilene, a few days ago, and from him received much information regarding the cattle trade in and about Abilene. During the past two weeks two hundred and seventy-seven car loads were shipped by them, or five thousand five hundred head. These cattle were mostly shipped to Illinois for grazing purposes preparatory to being slaughtered and packed in the fall, while a few are shipped to the Chicago market. They are generally in excellent condition, well-fitted for the butcher's market of St. Louis and Chicago, and not a few for that of New York. The Texas men are realizing satisfactory prices. . . There are about twelve Illinois cattle buyers at Abilene, besides McCoy & Bros., among whom are the agents of John T. Alexander, the largest cattle shipper in the world."

completed at that time and the chance to hire foreign cars was very limited.

Every effort was made in good faith to so arrange and [125] conduct the cattle trade as not to work a hardship upon the few settlers then in the county, and to this end a man was employed to locate on eligible herding grounds the herds as fast as they arrived. This man, W. F. Tomkins, detailed to this duty, was a venerable gentleman whose head was whitened by the cold blasts of many frigid Wisconsin winters, where he had seen better days and a fine heritage of his own selection and improvement. But political, ambition and surety debts made him a wiser but a poorer man, a wanderer seeking a retrieved fortune. This old gentleman had fine energy and unswerving honesty of purpose, and until the day of his death a firm hope that fortune would favor him. He received the sobriquet of "Almighty Dollar" from an impromptu and witty, yet withal sensible speech, made on the occasion of the shipment of the first train of cattle in 1867. He was respected and loved by all who knew him for his sterling honesty, his energy, and good practical sense, and his memory is and always will be sweet and green to more than one heart that knew him. And many true, sad friends who followed his bier to its last resting place just north of the village of Abilene, upon a prairie mound overlooking the scene of his last labors, felt that they were paying a merited tribute of respect – the last office of love to one of earth's few really good men, one who deserved better fortune than was given him.

But there was one character that Texan drovers and for that matter everybody else that ever visited Abilene during its palmy days will remember, and will laugh while they recall to mind the phiz, the actions, the gestures and above all the talk – that irresistible, unanswerable avalanche of words that was always heard when near the immense Twin Barn – flowing from the lips of the irrepressible Ed Gaylord, the natural-born liveryman.[287] For a succession of

287 Edward H. Gaylord and his wife, Sarah M., of Junction City, owned property in Abilene. Gaylord operated the Twin Livery Stables in Abilene, as well as a livery stable in Junction City. Many years afterward J. B. Case, who was employed by Gaylord from June to September, 1870, wrote the

years the opening of each cattle season would find Gaylord
making all necessary arrangements to conduct a first-class
cattleman's livery stable. A half dozen ponies, a couple of
second-hand buggies, two or three second-hand saddles and
riding bridles, [126] with about one ten-dollar note bor-
rowed of some confiding friend, was all the capital and stock
he required to begin business with. It would be but a few
short weeks after the opening of the cattle trade before
every stall, fully one hundred or more, would be full of
cow ponies. Some he had traded for, others boarding only.
It was a rare instance that an applicant for livery accommodation was turned away unaccommodated; no matter
what he thought he wanted, Gaylord always could give
him just what he called for, or convince him that some other
available outfit was what the customer really ought to want.
Should the applicant happen to be an overfastidious or a
"fine-haired" specimen of the *genus homo*, Gaylord would
certainly manage to get him upon some inveterate, desperate
Spanish pony, whose first and last impulse would be to buck
as long as it had strength. Of course, Gaylord would, at
first, extol the pony to the skies as the best of saddle ponies –
gentle, kind, amiable, affectionate, and in every way de-
lightful to ride. Of course, as soon as the man was mounted,
the vicious brute would set off bucking at a furious rate – as
nearly all western ponies do when first [127] mounted – and
never let up until the amateur horseman was sent sprawling
through the air, only to land roughly on the ground in an
utterly demoralized condition. Then Gaylord would swear
that he bought the pony of a preacher, who recommended

following description of the stables: "The Twin Livery Stables which were
the headquarters of the Texas cattlemen, with accomodations for about
one hundred horses, were located where the Henry-Hodge block is now
[1932] situated, and occupied all the ground between Spruce Street and
Buckeye and Second Street and Third with the exception of about fifty feet
at the east end used for a corral. These Twin Stables faced south and the
space between them was roofed over." J. B. Case, "Early Days in Abilene,"
Dickinson County Clippings, I, Mrs. A. B. Seelye, Abilene. See also Dickinson
County, Deed Record C, 157, MS., Recorder of Deeds Office, Abilene; M.
Hoffman, "Abilene's Early History," *Dickinson County Clippings,* VIII, Mrs.
A. B. Seelye, Abilene; *Junction City Weekly Union,* Sept. 5, 1868, Aug. 19,
1871.

the animal as being a lady's horse, and declare he believed the pony perfectly gentle, and that its conduct was only play and nothing vicious intended. But all this was poor comfort to the dirt-begrimed customer, who invariably concluded to wait for an opportunity to walk, or decided he did not really care to go out into the country at all.

In a few weeks the incurred bills on the boarding ponies would be sufficient to buy every pony in the barn – aside from the odd, nice cash sums that the enterprising liveryman had accumulated by letting his boarding ponies. And such bills as he could manage to make out and present with the *sang-froid* of a pettifogger, was astonishing to his patrons. It was no use to complain, or dispute his bills, or grumble, or [128] swear at what you might call extortion, or declare you would not pay it. The instant a murmuring breath would escape your lips, he would open such a battery of slang and abuse, highly seasoned with impious expressions, to which would be added all sorts of hints about the penurious man who did not want to pay for first-class accommodations, that you would gladly pay your bill and run. It was idle to attempt a stay of his speech or answer his torrent of good-natured abuse. You could not think, much less speak, one-half so fast as the liveryman could talk; and such expressions, such tongue lashings as a complaining patron would receive, would induce him to pay his bill no matter how exorbitant and rush away, glad to escape. Often a patron would be indignant and want to fight; but Gaylord never got mad, but talked so incessantly that anger could neither do or say anything but submit and retreat. Nevertheless, Gaylord had innumerable friends; in fact no one was his enemy. He was a shrewd horse trader, a very jockey by nature, and loved a horse better than all other things combined. Each cattle season he would acquire from four to five thousand dollars' worth of ponies, buggies, and accouterments; but during the winter, when but little business was doing, he would become reckless, and by the opening of spring would have recklessly spent his previous summer's profits and be ready to take his place and make another raise off of the cattle trade. He was a man of good impulses, undaunted energy, of excellent judgment on all matters pertaining to a horse, and had a big, true heart full of sympathy for the unfortunate.

J. M. Day, of Austin, Texas, is a Missourian by birth, but at the early age of ten years emigrated to Texas with his father, who went at once into stock ranching and adhered closely thereto during the remainder of his life, thus thoroughly and practically educating his son in the business of live stock raising. As soon as Mr. Day had attained the years of manhood, he engaged in live stock driving on his own account, having a few years previously went as assistant [129] driver with a herd to Kansas City; also one or more trips to Tipton, Missouri, where the herds were shipped to St. Louis. This was among the first shipments of Texas cattle brought to the St. Louis market and was as early as 1857. But before the trade was fairly opened, the Civil war began, and further efforts to drive northward was abandoned. At the close of the war Mr. Day turned his attention to his old occupation and was a drover of 1866, but one of the fortunate few who had sagacity sufficient to enable them to see that a route west of all settlement in western Kansas was practicable; and so it proved in his case. In Iowa he found cash purchasers for his cattle at figures that afforded a fine profit. The opening of a cattle market at Abilene induced him to put several herds upon the trail for western Kansas. From the years 1868 to 1871, inclusive, Mr. Day annually drove from three to seven thousand head of cattle, and his [130] herds were generally of good quality, well-selected beeves. He was recognized as one of the most substantial, straightforward, honorable drovers that engaged in the western cattle trade. Seeing so many engaged in driving, Mr. Day decided to abandon it and devote his time and capital to buying and selling in Kansas — a kind of local trader or speculator — and for two years has handled fully ten thousand head each year, never failing to make a reasonable profit on each transaction.[288] Whilst he has been looking after the cattle in western

---

[288] Texas cattle owned by J. M. Day were driven to Ellsworth in 1873 and to Dodge City in 1877 and 1879. *Dodge City Times*, June 2, 1877, Mar. 8, 1879; *Ellsworth Reporter*, June 26, 1873.

Kansas for a few months annually, he has devoted the balance of his time in establishing and opening up a large wheat farm and a thoroughbred stock ranch in Denton county, northern Texas, which enterprise he expects to make his permanent business, and there expects to make his home. Mr. Day is one of those quiet, affable gentlemen that makes good impressions and warm friends wherever he goes. Texas has few better, truer men than he; kind-hearted and honorable, straightforward in all his business transactions, he has much good will and hearty cheer for everyone.

DRUNKEN COW-BOY ON THE "WAR-PATH."

VIII. COWBOYS ON THE TRAIL
AND OFF

No sooner had it become a conceded fact that Abilene as a cattle depot was a success, than tradespeople from all points came to the village and, after putting up temporary houses, went into business. Of course, the saloon, the billiard table, the tenpin alley, the gambling table — in short, every possible device for obtaining money in both an honest and dishonest manner — were abundant. Fully seventy-five thousand cattle [289] arrived at Abilene during the summer of 1868; and at the opening of the market in the spring, fine prices were realized and snug fortunes were made by such drovers as were able to effect a sale of their herds.

It was the custom to locate herds as near the village as good water and plenty of grass could be found. As soon as the herd is located upon its summer grounds, a part of the help is discharged, as it requires less labor to hold than to travel. The camp was usually located near some living water or spring where sufficient wood for camp purposes could be easily obtained. After selecting the spot for the camp, the wagon would be drawn up; then a hole dug in the ground, in which to build a fire of limbs of trees or driftwood gathered to the spot; and a permanent camp instituted [132] by unloading the contents of the wagon upon the ground. And

---

[289] This estimate is identical with the one made by McCoy to a newspaper correspondent at Newton, Kansas, in August, 1871. The same figure appears in the United States Census of 1880, for which McCoy was also responsible. The editor has located no additional reliable data with which to check McCoy's estimate. Probably between 45,000 and 50,000 cattle were shipped from Abilene by railroad during 1868. McCoy vs. the Kansas Pacific Railway Company, 61, MS., Supreme Court of Kansas; *Report of the Commissioner of Agriculture for the Year 1870*, p. 349; *Tenth Census of the United States*, III (*Agriculture*), 975; Kansas Pacific Railway Co., *Guide Map of the Great Texas Cattle Trail*, 8; *Junction City Weekly Union*, Feb. 13, 1869; *Republican Daily Journal*, Sept. 7, 1869; *Kansas Daily Commonwealth*, Aug. 15, 1871.

such a motley lot of assets as come out of one of those camp carts would astonish one and beggar minute description: a lot of saddles and horse blankets, a camp kettle, coffeepot, bread pan, battered tin cups, a greasy mess chest, dirty, soiled blankets, an ox yoke, a log chain, spurs and quirts, a coffee mill, a broken-helved ax, bridles, picket ropes, and last, but not least, a side or two of fat, mastfed bacon; to which add divers pieces of rawhide in various stages of dryness. A score of other articles not to be thought of will come out of that exhaustless camp cart. But one naturally inquires what use would a drover have for a rawhide, dry or fresh? Uses infinite; nothing breaks about a drover's outfit that he cannot mend with strips or thongs of rawhide. He mends his bridle or saddle or picket rope, or sews his ripping pants or shirt, or lashes a broken wagon tongue, or binds on a loose tire with rawhide. In short, a rawhide is a concentrated and combined carpenter and blacksmith shop, not to say saddler's and tailor's shop, to the drover. Indeed, it is said that what a Texan cannot make or mend with a rawhide is not worth having or is irretrievably broken into undistinguishable fragments. It is asserted that the agricultural classes of that state fasten their plow points on with rawhide, but we do not claim to be [an] authority on Texan agriculture [and] therefore cannot vouch for this statement.

The herd is brought upon its herd ground and carefully watched during the day, but allowed to scatter out over sufficient territory to feed. At nightfall it is gathered to a spot selected near the tent, and there rounded up and held during the night. One or more cowboys are on duty all the while, being relieved at regular hours by relays fresh aroused from slumber and mounted on rested ponies; and for a given number of hours they ride slowly and quietly around the herd, which, soon as it is dusk, lies down to rest and ruminate. About midnight every animal will arise, turn about for a few moments, and then lie down again near where it arose, only [133] changing sides so as to rest. But if no one should be watching to prevent straggling, it would be but a short time before the entire herd would be up and following off the leader or some uneasy one that would rather travel than sleep or rest. All this is easily checked by the cowboy on duty. But when storm is imminent, every man is required to have his horse saddled, ready for an emergency. The ponies desired for use are picketed out, which is done by tying one end of a half-inch rope sixty or seventy feet long around the neck of the pony, and fastening the other end to a pointed iron or wooden stake twelve or more inches long, which is driven in the firm ground. As all the strain is laterally and none upward, the picket pin will hold the strongest horse. The length of the rope is such as to permit the animal to graze over considerable space, and when he has all the grass eaten off within his reach, it is only necessary to move the picket pin to give him fresh and abundant pasture. Such surplus ponies as are not in immediate use are permitted to run with the cattle or herded to themselves, and when one becomes jaded by hard usage he is turned loose and a rested one caught with the lasso and put to service. Nearly all cowboys can throw the lasso well enough to capture a pony or a beef when they desire so to do.

Day after day the cattle are held under herd and cared for by the cowboys, whilst the drover is looking out for a purchaser for his herd, or a part thereof; especially if it be a mixed herd, which is a drove composed of beeves, three-, two-, and one-year-old steers, heifers, and cows. To those desiring any one or more classes of such stock as he may have, the drover seeks to sell, and if successful, has the herd rounded up and cuts out the class sold; and after counting carefully until all parties are satisfied, straightway delivers them to the purchaser. The counting of the cattle, like the separating or cutting out, is invariably done on horseback. Those who do the counting, take positions a score of paces apart, whilst the cowboys cut off small detachments of cattle and force them between those counting; and when the bunch, or cut, is [134] counted satisfactorily, the operation is repeated until all are counted. Another method is to start the herd off, and when it is well drawn out, to begin at the head and count back until the last are numbered. As a rule stock cattle are sold by the herd, and often beeves are sold in the same manner; but in many instances sale is made by the pound gross weight. The latter manner is much the safest for the inexperienced, for he then pays only for what he gets; but the Texan prefers to sell just as he buys at home – always by the head. However, in late years it is becoming nearly the universal custom to weigh all beeves sold in northern markets.

Whilst the herd is being held upon the same grazing grounds, often one or more of the cowboys not on duty will mount their ponies and go to the village nearest camp and spend a few hours, [and] learn all the items of news or gossip concerning other herds and the cowboys belonging thereto. Besides seeing the sights, he gets such little articles as may be wanted by himself and comrades at camp; of these, a supply of tobacco, both chewing and smoking, forms one of the principal and often-recurring wants. The cowboy almost invariably smokes or chews tobacco – generally both, for the time drags dull at camp or herd ground. There is nothing new or exciting occurring to break the monotony of daily routine events. Sometimes the cowboys off duty will go to town late in the evening and there join with some party of cowboys whose herd is sold (and they preparing to start home), in having a jolly time. Often one or more of them will imbibe too much poison whiskey and straightway go on the warpath. Then mounting his pony, he is ready to shoot anybody or anything; or rather than not shoot at all, would fire up into the air, all the while yelling as only a semicivilized being can. At such times it is not safe to be on the streets, or for that matter within a house, for the drunk cowboy would as soon shoot into a house as at anything else.

Many incidents could be told of their crazy freaks, and freaks more villainous than crazy, but space forbids, save one only. [135] In 1868 a party of young men, mostly residents of Abilene, numbering six or seven, were returning from a walk at a late hour, when all of a sudden they heard the footsteps of a running pony, each moment coming nearer. Before they could scarce divine the meaning thereof, a mounted, crazy, drunk cowboy was upon them, yelling in demoniacal voice to halt, adding horrible oaths, abuse, and insult. Before the young men fully comprehended the situation, the cowboy was rushing around them at a furious rate of speed, firing both his revolvers over their heads in the darkness, demanding an immediate contribution from each one of a ten-dollar note, swearing instant death to every one who refused to comply at once with his request. The party of young men were entirely unarmed and in imminent danger of being shot. But no time was to be lost. As a sub-terfuge, one of the young men, a drover, began talking in the kindest tone of voice, saying to the cowboy: "Now hold on; we are all cowboys just off of trail and have been out to see a little fun. We have no money with us, but if you will just go with me to the Cottage, you shall have all the ten-dollar notes you want. Certainly, certainly, sir! anything you want you can have, if you will only go with me to the hotel. Certainly, certainly, sir!" Whilst this was being played, each of the other boys betook himself to his hands and knees and crawled away in the darkness until a few paces were gained, [and] then tried his utmost capacity in running to a place of safety. In the meantime the cowboy followed the spokesman, swearing instant death to everyone if the money was not forthcoming. No sooner did they reach the Cottage than the young drover, after reassuring the cowboy of his intention to get him the money, passed inside the hotel and at once rushed for his pistols. But friends who compre-hended his intent, and seeing "shoot" in his eye, prevented him from going outside again. The cowboy, having his sus-picions aroused by the delay, whirled his pony and dashed off for the village, screeching and [137] yelling in genuine Indian style as he went. Coming to a large, open-fronted tent, he dashed toward it, emptying the last loaded chamber of his revolver into it; then drawing his huge knife, cut the tent from end to end; and when it had fallen to the ground at his feet, rushed his pony over it and was off for a bagnio, where he robbed every inmate of their money, jewelry, and other valuables; then turned his pony's head toward the cattle trail and was off for Texas.

Such hard cases made it necessary to institute corporate government in the village. It was a hard struggle before law and order was established, and to maintain it cost the utmost firmness and perpetual vigilance. It was often necessary to disarm drunken cowboys and such roughs as inevitably congregate at frontier commercial centers, which could be done only by force and terror. No quiet-turned man could or would care to take the office of marshal, which jeopardized his life; hence the necessity of employing a desperado – one who feared nothing and would as soon shoot an offending subject as to look at him.

The life of the cowboy in camp is routine and dull. His food is largely of the regulation order, but a feast of vegetables he wants and must have, or scurvy would ensue. Onions and potatoes are his favorites, but any kind of vegetables will disappear in haste when put within his reach. In camp, on the trail, on the ranch in Texas, with their countless thousands of cattle, milk and butter are almost unknown; not even milk or cream for the coffee is had. Pure shiftlessness and the lack of energy are the only reasons for this privation, and to the same reasons can be assigned much of the privations and hardships incident to ranching. It would cost but little effort or expense to add a hundred comforts, not to say luxuries, to the life of a drover and his cowboys. They sleep on the ground, with a pair of blankets for bed and cover. No tent is used, scarcely any cooking utensils, and such a thing as a camp cook stove is unknown. The warm water of the branch or the standing pool is drunk; [138] often it is yellow with alkali and other poisons. No wonder the cowboy gets sallow and unhealthy, and deteriorates in manhood until often he becomes capable of any contemptible thing; no wonder he should become half civilized only, and take to whiskey with a love excelled scarcely by the barbarous Indian.

When the herd is sold and delivered to the purchaser, a day of rejoicing to the cowboy has come, for then he can go free and have a jolly time; and it is a jolly time they have. Straightway after settling with their employers, the barber shop is visited, and three to six months' growth of hair is shorn off, their long-grown sunburnt beard "set" in due shape and properly blacked. Next a clothing store of the Israelitish style is "gone through," and the cowboy emerges a new man in outward appearance, everything being new, not excepting the hat, and boots with star decorations about the tops; also a new —,[290] well, in short, everything new.

---

290 This line appears in the book.

Then for fun and frolic! The barroom, the theater, the gambling room, the bawdy house, the dance house, each and all come in for their full share of attention.[291] In any of these places an affront or a slight, real or imaginary, is cause sufficient for him to unlimber one of more "mountain howitzers" invariably found strapped to his person, and proceed to deal out death in unbroken doses to such as may be in range of his pistols, whether real friends or enemies, no matter; his anger and bad whiskey urge him on to deeds of blood and death.

At frontier towns where are centered many cattle, and, as a natural result, considerable business is transacted and many strangers congregate, there are always to be found a number of bad characters, both male and female, of the very worst class in the universe, such as have fallen below the level of the lowest type of the brute creation — men who live a soulless, aimless life, dependent upon the turn of a card for the means of living. They wear out a purposeless life, ever looking blear-eyed and dissipated; to whom life, from various causes, has long since become worse than a total blank; [139] beings in the form of man, whose outward appearance would betoken gentlemen, but whose heartstrings are but a wisp of base-sounding chords, upon which the touch of the higher and purer life have long since ceased to be felt; beings without whom the world would be better, richer, and more desirable. And with them are always found their counterparts in the opposite sex; those who have fallen

---

[291] For the names of Abilene's principal saloons in 1871, see the introduction to the present volume. The Alamo, the most popular saloon and gambling resort, was described by a contemporary as follows: "At night everything is 'full up.' The 'Alamo' especially being a center of attraction. Here, in a well lighted room opening on the street, the 'boys' gather in crowds around the tables, to play or to watch others; a bartender, with a countenance like a youthful divinity student, fabricates wonderful drinks, while the music of a piano and a violin from a raised recess, enlivens the scene, and 'sooths the savage breasts' of those who retire torn and lacerated from an unfortunate combat with the 'tiger.' The games most affected are faro and monte, the latter being greatly patronized by the Mexicans of Abilene, who sit with perfectly unmoved countenances and play for hours at a stretch, for your Mexican loses with entire indifference two things somewhat valued by other men, viz: his money and his life." *Daily Kansas State Record*, Aug. 5, 1871.

low — alas, how low! They, too, are found in the frontier cattle town;[292] and that institution known in the West as a dance house is there found also. When the darkness of the night is come to shroud their orgies from public gaze, these miserable beings gather into the halls of the dance house and "trip the fantastic toe" to wretched music, ground out of dilapidated instruments by beings fully as degraded as the most vile. In this vortex of dissipation the average cowboy plunges with great delight. Few more wild, reckless

[292] Abilene, like all cow towns, was visited by prostitutes during the cattle trading season. As a result of an ordinance of May 20, 1870, which authorized the court to eject from the corporate limits all individuals who had been convicted of being owners or inmates of brothels, the lewd women moved to the banks of Mud creek about a mile northwest of town, where they occupied a number of shanties until September. Early in the latter month Chief of Police Thomas J. Smith, acting in the capacity of a deputy sheriff, "served notice on the vile characters, ordering them to close their dens — or suffer the consequences." On September 7 they left Abilene by train, decamping, according to the *Abilene Chronicle,* for Baxter Springs and Wichita. But the prostitutes returned to Abilene in greater numbers than ever during the spring of 1871 and established their resorts in various parts of the city itself. Outraged by this invasion, over a hundred women residents of Abilene, on May 27, presented a petition to the city council, asking it to take "active measures for the suppression of brothels." On June 16 that body passed a resolution appointing Mayor McCoy and Councilman Gauthie a committee "to cause the removal from the limits of the city proper of all bawdy houses or houses of ill fame and relocate the same upon some uninhabited portion of the city commons." The committee located the prostitutes on a plot of ground southeast of Abilene, where they did a flourishing business until the following September; then they left the city permanently, since Abilene ceased to be a cow town after 1871. Theophilus Little, who established a lumberyard in Abilene during March, 1871, later described the section occupied by the lewd women southeast of the city: "These women built houses on this ground and it was literally covered with them. Some of them were over 100 feet long. Beer gardens, dance halls and dancing platforms and saloons galore were there. It was called 'The Devil's Addition to Abilene,' rightly named, for Hell reigned there — Supreme. Hacks were run day and night to this addition. Money and whiskey flowed like water down hill and youth and beauty and womanhood and manhood were wrecked and damned in that Valley of Perdition." Theophilus Little, "Early Days of Abilene and Dickinson County," in Roenigk, *Pioneer History of Kansas,* 38. See also Abilene, Minute Book of the City Council, 67, 68, 70, 71, MS., Mayor's Office; Abilene, Ordinance Book, 56, MS., *ibid.; Abilene Chronicle,* May 12, Sept. 8, 1870, June 1, July 6, Sept. 14, 1871; *Junction City Weekly Union,* Sept. 30, 1871; *Daily Kansas State Record,* Aug. 5, 1871.

"DANCE-HOUSE."

A. H. PIERCE.

scenes of abandoned debauchery can be seen on the civilized earth than a dance house in full blast in one of the many frontier towns. To say they dance wildly or in an abandoned manner is putting it mild. Their manner of practicing the terpsichorean art would put the French cancan to shame.

The cowboy enters the dance with a peculiar zest, not stopping to divest himself of his sombrero, spurs, or pistols; but just as he dismounts off of his cow pony, so he goes into the dance. A more odd, not to say comical, sight is not often seen than the dancing cowboy. With the front of his sombrero lifted at an angle of fully forty-five degrees, his huge spurs jingling at every step or motion, his revolvers flapping up and down like a retreating sheep's tail, his eyes lit up with excitement, liquor, and lust, he plunges in and "hoes it down" at a terrible rate in the most approved yet awkward country style, often swinging his partner clear off of the floor for an entire circle, then "balance all," with an occasional demoniacal yell near akin to the war whoop of the savage Indian. All this he does, entirely oblivious to the whole world and the balance of mankind. After dancing furiously, the entire [141] "set" is called to "waltz to the bar," where the boy is required to treat his partner and, of course, himself also; which he does not hesitate to do time and again, although it costs him fifty cents each time. Yet if it cost ten times that amount he would not hesitate; but the more he dances and drinks, the less common sense he will have, and the more completely his animal passions will control him. Such is the manner in which the cowboy spends his hard-earned dollars. And such is the entertainment that many young men — from the North and the South, of superior parentage and youthful advantages in life — give themselves up to; and often more, their lives are made to pay the forfeit of their sinful foolishness.

After a few days of frolic and debauchery the cowboy is ready, in company with his comrades, to start back to Texas, often not having one dollar left of his summer's wages.[293] To this rather hard-drawn picture of the cowboy

[293] A contemporary wrote: "Cut loose from all the refining influences and enjoyments of life, these herdsmen toil for tedious months behind their slow herds, seeing scarcely a house, garden, woman or child for near 1000 miles,

there are many creditable exceptions – young men who respect themselves and save their money, and are worthy young gentlemen. But it is idle to deny the fact that the wild, reckless conduct of the cowboys while drunk, in connection with that of the worthless northern renegades, have brought the personnel of the Texan cattle trade into great disrepute, and filled many graves with victims – bad men and good men – at Abilene, Newton, Wichita, and Ellsworth. But by far the larger portion of those killed are of that class that can be spared without detriment to the good morals and respectability of humanity. It often occurs when the cowboys fail to get up a mêlée and kill each other by the half dozen, that the keepers of those "hell's half acres" find some pretext arising from business jealousies or other causes, to suddenly become belligerent, and stop not to declare war but begin hostilities at once. It is generally effective work they do with their revolvers and shotguns, for they are the most desperate men on earth. Either some of the principals or their subordinates are generally "done for" in a thorough manner, or wounded [142] so as to be miserable cripples for life. On such occasions there are few tears shed, or even inquiries made, by the respectable people, but an expression of sorrow is common that active hostilities did not continue until every rough was stone dead.

We will present in this chapter a sketch of the widely known A. H. Pierce, familiarly called "Shanghai" Pierce, a nickname given him in Texas to distinguish him from one of lesser stature and shorter legs but bearing the same name and engaged in the same business.[294] Born in Rhode Island, Pierce went to the state of Virginia at the early age of thir-

and like a cargo of sea worn sailors coming into port, they must have – when released – some kind of entertainment. In the absence of something better, they at once fall into liquor and gambling saloons at hand." *Junction City Weekly Union*, Oct. 29, 1870.

294 Abel H. Pierce was employed by the Atchison, Topeka and Santa Fé Railroad in 1872 to induce Texas drovers to trail their herds to Wichita. In 1873 he drove longhorns to Ellsworth, whose citizens, in the following year, hired him to attract Texas cattlemen to that place. He trailed stock to Dodge City in 1879. *Wichita City Eagle*, Apr. 19, May 24, 1872; *Ellsworth Reporter*, May 29, June 26, 1873, Apr. 30, May 14, June 18, 1874; *Dodge City Times*, Mar. 8, 1879; Streeter, *Prairie Trails & Cow Towns*, 110; *Trail Drivers of Texas* (Hunter, ed.), 923-924.

teen, where he remained for five years and then turned his
wandering steps toward Texas. The lapse of time was brief
after landing in his chosen state, before he took a situation
at fifteen dollars per month with a stock raiser, aiding him
to establish a new ranch; mauling rails, breaking oxen, and
bucking ponies, were among the refining services that young
Pierce first engaged in. For eight years he continued on a
salary to serve the same man. The latter part of his term of
service was devoted to driving beeves to New Orleans and
other markets. But when the Civil war began, he went into
the ranks of the Confederate army and for four years did
duty as a soldier. At the close of the war and the collapse of
the Confederate cause, Pierce returned to his former haunts
and devoted his energetic attention to stock driving on his
own account to the New Orleans market. It is claimed that
he drove one among the first herds, if not the first herd,
that was taken to New Orleans after the close of the war.
Having driven for several years before the war, he was
not without friends and acquaintances in New Orleans. But
in a few years he changed his occupation and, in connection
with other parties, founded a ranch now somewhat famous
and named it "Rancho Grande"; where in a few years he
so increased his stock of cattle that in the year 1871 he
branded fifteen thousand eight hundred head of calves and
mavericks. Indeed, it was ominously hinted that Pierce's
New England [143] energy was too great for his competitors and other neighboring ranchers, and that they became
jealous of his success and did not stop at calling him names
more expressive than complimentary, but inaugurated a
semibelligerent state of affairs, in which both parties took an
active part. From time to time various cowboys on both
sides were missed, but afterward found dead with their
boots on. Finally this state of affairs began to take the
dimensions of a small war; but upon one fine morning seven
or eight Mexican and other cowboys belonging to the ranks
of Pierce's mortal enemies were seen hanging to the limbs
of a dead tree as human fruit. Pierce says: "Had that tree
been green and alive, he doesn't know how much larger
crop it would have borne." That vexatious and ever-med-
dling institution called a grand jury was more officious about

this and other similar occurrences than was comfortable or pleasing to Pierce; so he sold out his interest [144] in the fine large stock he had become part owner of, for a snug sum of money, and went into Kansas to trade in cattle, where he has since occupied his attention and capital in various large transactions in live stock.

Of late, everyone who visits the western cattle market sees or hears of Shanghai Pierce. And if they ever get within cannon shot of where he is, they hear his ear-splitting voice, more piercing than a locomotive whistle, more noisy than a steam calliope. It is idle to try to dispute or debate with him, for he will overwhelm you with indescribable noise, however little sense it may convey. Nevertheless Pierce is an energetic, shrewd trader, a good and successful business man of great experience; knows how to make money and full well how to keep it; is fond of large operations; and is ambitious to be looked up to and quoted as authority on cattle matters. This, perhaps, is his greatest vanity or weakness. He loves a good story and knows quite well how to tell one. Each year since his arrival in Kansas he and associates have handled from eight to ten thousand head of cattle. During the year 1873 the great financial panic found him in good shape to join with his friend, J. D. Reed, in buying at panic prices seven thousand head of cattle and put them in winter quarters in central Kansas. Mr. Pierce is interested with his brother in establishing a large ranch in southwestern Texas; and recognizing the necessity of improving their stock in blood, they are fencing an immense tract of land for pastoral purposes and placing graded bulls with their herds. He is in the fullest sense a self-made man, which is not to be construed as relieving his Creator of great responsibility. There are few cattle dealers better calculated for, or more determined on, taking care of themselves than A. H. Pierce.

In concluding the numerous sketches of Texan ranchmen and drovers, we offer a few reflections on the general character of southwestern cattlemen. In doing so we are not animated by other motives than a desire to convey a [145] correct impression of that numerous class as a whole — reflections and impressions based upon close observation and a varied experience of seven or eight years spent in business contact and relation with them. They are, as a class, not public spirited in matters pertaining to the general good, but may justly be called selfish, or at least indifferent to the public welfare. They are prodigal to a fault with their money when opportunity offers to gratify their appetites or passions, but it is extremely difficult to induce them to expend even a small sum in forwarding a project or enterprise that has other than a purely selfish end in view. In general they entertain strong suspicions of northern men and do not have the profoundest confidence in each other. They are disposed to measure every man's action and prompting motives by the rule of selfishness, and they are slow indeed to believe that other than purely selfish motives could or ever do prompt a man to do an act or develop an enterprise. If anything happens [to] a man, especially a northern man, so that he cannot do or perform all that they expect or require of him, no explanation or reasons are sufficient to dispel the deep and instant conviction formed in their breasts that he is deliberately trying to swindle them, and they can suddenly see a thousand evidences of his villainy — in short, instantly vote such an one a double-dyed villain. Their reputation is widespread for honorably abiding [by] their verbal contracts, for the very nature of their business and the circumstances under which it is conducted, renders an honorable course imperative; and, as a rule, where agreements or contracts are put into writing, they will stand to them unflinchingly, no matter how great the sacrifice. But when the contract or understanding is verbal only and not of the most definite nature, their consciences are fully as pliant as are those of any other section. A promise made as to some future transaction is kept or broken as their future interests may dictate. Nor are they any more brave, or more fond of facing [146] death's cold pellets on an equal footing with their adversaries, than are men in general from other sections of the country. True, their habits of life and the necessities and exposed nature of their business renders the daily use and carrying of firearms imperative; hence their habitual use of the pistol renders them fair to good shots. Besides, the habit of settling their disputes, often very trifling, with the revolver (which, with some, is considered the first and only legitimate law, argument, or reason) has given to the denizens of the Lone Star State a name and reputation abroad for universal, genuine bravery, not warranted by the facts. They are just as brave, but no more so, than are the men of other sections.

They are almost invariably convivial in habit, preferring as a rule the strongest liquors, and take them "straight." Nevertheless, it is rare indeed that a drover is a confirmed drunkard or sot. They think, act, and conduct their business in an independent, self-reliant manner, seldom seeking or following the advice of others. Each man seems to feel himself an independent sovereign and as such capable of conducting his affairs in his own way, subject to nobody or nothing save the wishes, tastes, and necessities of himself. They are, in common with all stockmen, universal lovers of the ladies, and as a class present a discouraging field for a Shaker missionary. Indeed, they are specially noteworthy as being obedient to the first commandment. Sanguine and speculative in temperament, impulsively generous in free sentiment, warm and cordial in their friendships, hot and hasty in anger, with a strong innate sense of right and wrong, with a keen sense for the ridiculous and a general intention to do that that is right and honorable in their dealings, they are, as would naturally be supposed when the manner of their life is considered, a hardy, self-reliant, free, and independent class, acknowledging no superior or master in the wide universe.

IX. THE SPANISH FEVER
EXCITEMENT

Among the many fine herds of cattle that arrived at Abilene [295] in the spring of 1868, there was one of 800 head, a very choice selection. Great pains had been taken in the best cattle regions of Texas in selecting choice, fat cattle, and equally as great caution had been exercised in driving them to Kansas. After arriving at Abilene, they were put on the best herd grounds in the county, where they added greatly to their already fine condition. The eye of a certain Illinoisan had been upon this herd for some time, fully determined, when the opportune day arrived, to retrieve some of his severe losses sustained the previous year. When the proper time came, he purchased 224 head, his choice of the 800 head; and after selecting them carefully, one by one, drove them four miles to the shipping yards, and after standing them therein for twelve hours, weighed them. They made the remarkable average of 1,238 pounds each, and amounted to $7,468. They were placed upon the cars and sent forward to Chicago, thence forwarded to Buffalo, New York, where they were sold and due account of sale made to shipper; but, alas, the net returns was only $1,468, six [148] thousand being lost and not since found or heard of. The shipper has come to regard it as a permanent contribution, of a benevolent nature he hopes, toward feeding the

295 Writing from Abilene on June 17, 1868, a newspaper correspondent described the town as follows: "It has nearly all been built in less than a year, and consists of a hotel, known by the romantic name of Planters' Cottage [Drover's Cottage], a boarding house, two or three stores, two saloons, a school house, and a church nearly completed, besides several dwelling houses. The hotel is 40 x 60, three stories high, and is finished and furnished in good style. The school house is of stone, 24 x 30, and cost $2700. The church, which is Baptist, is a frame building, and will cost about $22,000." *Kansas Daily Tribune,* June 23, 1868.

oppressed laborers of New England's manufactories. So let it be, but not any more in the same way. The charity of that cattle shipper is nearly exhausted, and bread for himself and family much in the same fix. This great loss was not because the cattle were not good and fat, for they were, but arose in part from the prejudice of the people against Texas cattle; and the farther east, the greater the prejudice and the less they actually knew about the cattle. But the main cause of great sacrifice was the outbreak of the so-called "Spanish fever," which caused a tremendous excitement throughout the North.[296] A disastrous panic occurred among holders of shorthorn cattle, resulting in severe losses and often ruin to many northern cattlemen.

But before we go further into the discussion of the subject of the disease, its primal cause, preventives, etc., we will notice another enterprise that took practical shape in the spring of 1868. A certain firm of cattlemen in Chicago went to Texas and contracted with certain large cattle drovers to deliver about forty thousand head of cattle on the Mississippi river at the mouth of Red river, where, upon delivery, the cattle were crowded in large numbers on the

[296] In 1898, after many years of study by the bureau of animal industry of the United States Department of Agriculture, Texas fever was described by the chief of the pathological division of that bureau as follows: "Southern, or splenetic, fever (usually called Texas fever) is an infectious disease caused by a microparasite. This parasite, when it enters the system of susceptible animals (those animals which have been reared in sections of the country where the tick is not indigenous), destroys the red corpuscles of the blood to such an extent that the blood becomes thin and watery. The disease is always accompanied by high fever, and the course is, as a rule, acute, reaching the climax on the fifteenth or sixteenth day after infection, when death generally results. Considered as a parasite, the Texas fever tick, so long as it is confined to cattle which are reared in sections of the country where the tick is native, is less injurious than those which are the cause of itch, mange, and other cutaneous diseases. But when by any means, natural or artificial, the tick come in contact with cattle from other parts of the country, they produce the fatal disease commonly known as Texas fever. Therefore, when cattle from a territory infected with these ticks are to be taken into a noninfected territory, it is of the greatest importance that they first be freed of all ticks. So far as known at this time, the only remedy is to dip the cattle in a strong disinfecting solution." *Yearbook of the United States Department of Agriculture, 1898*, p. 453.

hot, unventilated decks of large steamboats. After six to twelve days of perpetual standing upon the hard deck without room to lay down, or drink, or feed, suffering with heat and overcrowding, they were landed at Cairo, Illinois, in great poverty of flesh and famishing with hunger, and so near dead from exhaustion that in many instances they had to be helped up the levee to the shipping yards of the Illinois Central Railroad, upon which road they were shipped to Tolono, Illinois, and there unloaded and turned upon the prairies, whereon all the domestic cattle of the county were grazing.[297] Many of the Texas cattle were sold to feeders

[297] During the spring of 1868 the firm of Gregory & Hastings, of Chicago, made arrangements to ship large numbers of Texas cattle by boat up the Mississippi and Ohio rivers to Cairo, Illinois, and thence by railroad to Tolono, Illinois, the junction of the Illinois Central and Toledo, Wabash and Western railroads. The longhorns were taken from Texas to Cairo over two different routes: one by way of the Mississippi and Ohio rivers, and the other by way of the Gulf of Mexico and the Mississippi and Ohio rivers. Those which traveled the former route were driven from various ranches in Texas to the mouth of the Red river in Louisiana, where they were loaded on steamboats and taken up the Mississippi and Ohio to Cairo. Those which came the latter route were shipped on barges from Lavaca, Texas, to New Orleans, and thence on river steamers to Cairo. On both routes the cattle suffered severely from heat, confinement, lack of water, and improper and inadequate feeding, and as a result many died on reaching Cairo or Tolono. The first longhorns arrived in Cairo on April 23, and the initial shipment came to Tolono over the Illinois Central Railroad sometime in May. Between 15,000 and 18,000 Texas cattle were unloaded at Tolono, where they were kept in a large stockyard built by the Illinois Central or grazed on the prairie. Most of them were sold to the cattle feeders of Illinois and adjacent states at prices ranging from $20 to $40 a head. The *Cairo Democrat* commented: "As a general thing they are the ugliest brutes we ever saw of the bovine species. With horns so long that they can scarcely pass the car door, which they must enter for shipment, and hoof corresponding, they are, as the boy said, 'bully chaps for glue.' But a few months on pasture will remove from sight many of their acute angles, and render them quite presentable." *Daily Illinois State Journal*, May 23, 1868. The Champaign *Gazette and Union* (July 15, 1868) observed: "We are glad to see them come, it makes a home market for our corn, and will lessen the price of beef." See also *Transactions of the Illinois State Agricultural Society*, VII, 138, 143; *Yearbook of the United States Department of Agriculture, 1899*, p. 126; *Daily Illinois State Journal*, May 1, 23, June 9, July 6, Oct. 30, 1868; *Gazette and Union*, July 15, Aug. 5, 1868; *Chicago Tribune*, Aug. 7, 1868; *Daily Missouri Republican*, July 5, 1868; Dale, *op. cit.*, 55; Cole, *op. cit.*, 377.

and grazers in that portion of Illinois, and some went into Indiana and were put in pastures, often mixed with the [149] domestic cattle, no danger being apprehended. But before thirty days of hot weather had elapsed, the domestic cattle on the prairies and in the pastures began to sicken and die at a frightful rate. Many grazers became alarmed and rushed their cattle off to market, fearing if they kept them that they would lose the entire herd by the dreaded disease. Several herds of domestic cattle which had been exposed were shipped east, and upon the way developed the disease and speedily died, causing great losses to their owners and a feeling of indignant fear and excitement among all eastern as well as western cattlemen, resulting, as before stated, in a crash and panic throughout the entire northern cattle market and a feeling of intense hostility toward southwestern cattle. Upon the prairie about Tolono, Illinois, nearly every cow of domestic blood died. In one township every milk cow except one died. This was a great and serious loss to many poor farmers of that region, and they became perfectly enraged at Texan cattle and would have mobbed a man unto death who would have dared to talk in favor of Texan cattle, much less shipped a carload of them. The trade via mouth of Red river was thoroughly broken up, with disaster to those engaged in it from the North. It was just at the outbreak of the excitement in the East that shipment of the two hundred and twenty-four head of fine Texan cattle from Abilene arrived at Buffalo. Hence the great loss.

About the same time that the disease appeared near Tolono, it also appeared in a much less fatal and less malignant form in other portions of Illinois, among domestic cattle which had been grazed with Texan cattle that had been introduced via Abilene, Kansas. But it is a fact well authenticated that but few cases of disease actually occurred after exposure to Texan cattle coming via western Kansas, and those that did occur were of a milder type and not sufficiently alarming to have created more than a local excitement; but, coupled with the disaster that arose from the introduction of cattle via mouth of Red river, it was sufficient to put an entire stop to the eastern demand, and [150] consequent shipment of Texan cattle from all points to the East or anywhere into the Northwest.[298]

At the same time the disease appeared in Illinois, a few cattle died near Abilene, which were all, or nearly all, paid for by voluntary contributions of the cattle drovers and parties interested at Abilene; and thus the verbal pledges made to the farmers more than a year before (at a public meeting called to effect the dissolution of a hostile organization, the particulars of which have already been given) were made good to the letter. The total loss of domestic cattle in Dickinson county was about forty-five hundred dollars in value. However, the prices at which the animals were appraised were often grossly exorbitant, and in one or two cases fraudulent claims were made, a few of which were paid before detection. Of the fund necessary to liquidate

[298] Texas fever broke out in Illinois during the latter part of July and began to subside in September. Among the counties affected were: Alexander, Champaign, Clinton, Cook, Douglas, Dupage, Effingham, Ford, Grundy, Iroquois, Macon, Massac, Morgan, Pope, Pulaski, St. Clair, Sangamon, Vermilion, and others. The greatest damage was done in Champaign county, where, it was estimated, the loss was $150,000. Meetings were held in various places and resolutions were adopted condemning the importation of longhorns into the state. A number of these assemblies appointed vigilance, or investigating, committees, to prevent the unloading of Texas cattle in the county, to stop the driving of longhorns along the principal highways, to urge the local owners of Texas stock to keep them separate from the rest of their cattle, or to collect damages from the possessors of longhorns. A meeting in Champaign passed a resolution asserting that the members present would be "justified in making personal efforts by forcible means if necessary to prevent any further admission of such cattle into our county." A correspondent at Sadorus, Champaign county, wrote: "The citizens are fully aroused, and I dont think it would be safety for a Texas steer to be seen in these parts nor would I vouch for a man having them in possession." The city of Champaign secured a plot of ground northeast of the corporate limits, which was called the "cow cemetery," where the cattle were buried. Texas fever also raged about the same time in parts of Indiana, Ohio, Missouri, and Kansas, and to a lesser extent in New York, New Jersey, and Pennsylvania. *Report of the Commissioner of Agriculture for the Year 1868*, pp. 38-40; *Yearbook of the United States Department of Agriculture, 1899*, p. 126; *Transactions of the Illinois State Agricultural Society*, VII, 134, 136; *Gazette and Union*, July 15, Aug. 5, 12, 19, 26, Sept. 9, Oct. 7, 1868; *Daily Illinois State Journal*, Aug. 5, 6, 13, 14, 17, 25, Sept. 1, 1868; *Chicago Tribune*, July 30, 1868.

these claims, about twelve hundred dollars was contributed by the drovers then at Abilene; the balance was paid by the parties who owned the shipping yards.[299] The Kansas Pacific Railway Company, by its general superintendent, agreed to contribute five hundred dollars; but after the claims were all settled and the Texan cattle shipped, the railway company repudiated its agreement and refused to pay anything. Such conduct became quite fashionable with the Kansas Pacific Railway Company in after days; indeed, they soon became notorious for their bad faith in regard to contracts. It seemed to be their policy to repudiate every contract made. But we will speak of this more definitely in its proper place.

Throughout the entire western states an unprecedented excitement arose about Spanish fever, a name given by common consent to the malady or disease disseminated by Texan cattle. It was the subject of gossip by everybody and formed the topic of innumerable newspaper articles, as well as associated press dispatches. A panic seized upon owners of domestic herds everywhere, and many rushed their cattle off to market, only to meet panic-stricken operators from other sections and ruinously low prices for their stock.[151] The butchers, venders, and consumers were alike alarmed and afraid to buy, sell, or consume beef of any kind. The Agricultural Society of Illinois appointed of its members a committee of three to investigate the cause of the disease, the remedies, and the preventive, if any could be found. This investigation was conducted in all the districts in Illinois where the disease had made its appearance, also at Abilene, Kansas .We believe it was as thorough in character and as conscientiously made as circumstances would admit. But no satisfactory cause of the disease was discovered, and of the various theories maintained, none seemed to be entirely satisfactory or conclusive.[300]

299 In 1871, McCoy testified that during 1868 he paid $3300 "to settlers around Abilene to appease the settlers who had suffered losses through this trade." McCoy vs. the Kansas Pacific Railway Company, 17, MS., Supreme Court of Kansas. McCoy's attorneys claimed that in 1868 he paid "over $5000 to settlers around Abilene, in order to avoid trouble." *Brief of the Defendant in Error, Kansas Pacific Railway Company vs. McCoy,* 10.

300 On August 6, 1868, Doctor H. C. Johns, of Decatur, and James N.

Soon after the outbreak of the disease the governor of New York appointed inspectors and attempted to quarantine all cattle from the West or Northwest. This soon began to work a hardship on the cattle shippers from Illinois, and the governor of that state appointed two commissioners to look after the interests of the Sucker State cattle boys. This diplomatic choir of ministers plenipotentiary in all matters pertaining to bulls of Suckerdom, were heavy weights, intellectually and otherwise. We doubt not the state of New York was awed into respectfully considerate conduct by the magnetic presence of the mighty geniuses sent into her borders by the governor of Illinois. Under the old Quaker rule they must have made splendid envoys.[301]

Brown, of Island Grove, received a request from John P. Reynolds, secretary of the Illinois State Agricultural Society, to investigate the Texas cattle fever then prevalent in Illinois and other states. Leaving Springfield on August 18, they visited the following places: Groves' Farm at Williamsville, Sangamon county; Broadlands Farm of John T. Alexander near Homer, Champaign county; Twin Grove Farm of J. L. Sullivant in Champaign county; Abilene, Kansas; Kansas City, Sedalia, and St. Louis, Missouri; and Chicago, Illinois. After making preliminary reports on August 19 and August 29, they submitted a final report on September 21. On the latter date, at a meeting of the executive board of the society in the club house of the Quincy Fairgrounds, the appointment of Johns and Brown was approved and their final report presented and accepted, about $1000 being allowed for their expenses. Their final report is printed in the *Transactions of the Illinois State Agricultural Society*, VII, 134-157. See also *ibid.*, VII, 61-63; *Daily Illinois State Journal*, Aug. 8, 19, 20, 31, Oct. 30, 1868.

[301] Shortly after the outbreak of Texas fever in the Middle West, New York adopted certain quarantine regulations that affected the stock interests of Illinois adversely. On August 31, 1868, an "informal meeting" of some cattlemen was held at Springfield, Illinois, at which a committee of three was selected which requested Governor Richard J. Oglesby to appoint Harvey N. Edwards and Edmund H. Piper special commissioners to proceed to New York and urge the officials to remove the restrictions on the importation of cattle from Illinois. Complying with this request on September 1, Oglesby at the same time wrote a letter to Governor Reuben E. Fenton of New York in which he introduced the commissioners and stated the purpose of their visit. Edwards and Piper journeyed to Buffalo, Albany, and New York City, returning to Springfield on September 30. On the following day they reported to Oglesby that they had "frankly but courteously" informed the New York officials how their quarantine regulations had affected "the free trade in and shipment of western cattle to the eastern markets." Claiming that their mission had been a success, the commissioners asserted: "A regulation was instantly made allowing all healthy cattle to pass on to the

This immortalizing act of the governor of Illinois was followed by another — the calling of a convention of experts to assemble in the Sucker Capitol. This convention, as a collection of quondam quacks and impractical theorists and imbecile ignoramuses, was without an equal. There were in attendance delegates from most of the northern states; also two or more from the Canadas. A portion of the delegates were esculapians of the most deadly type (others mere political bummers), sent to that [152] convention by their respective governors to relieve the community, for a short time at least, of a pestilential crew. Others were so prejudiced as to be utterly unfit to deliberate on or investigate anything. A portion were of that class who will enjoy especial immunity on the final day, if it be true that "unto whom little is given, little will be required." There were a few earnest seekers after truth and information upon the vexed subject of Spanish fever, and the importation of Texas cattle and "what to do about it." The convention, as a body, was a prejudiced, impractical one, filled with a burning hatred of long-horned kine.

The object of the convention was to determine upon a practical mode of protecting domestic cattle from disease and to recommend a practical basis of legislation against the introduction of Texan cattle. Upon the organization of the convention it was patent to the most casual observer that recommendations of absolute prohibition for at least eight or ten months in the year was the only policy that could or would be adopted, and such was the case.[302] There was but

great eastern market. Only sick ones were detained in quarantine." The *Daily Illinois State Journal* (Oct. 1, 1868) commented: "Their visit has been quite successful." *Daily Illinois State Journal,* Aug. 19, Sept. 2, Oct. 1, 2, 1868.

302 On October 13, 1868, the cattle commissioners of the state of New York, following suggestions from similar officials in other states and the Dominion of Canada, wrote a circular letter calling a cattle convention. The communication was endorsed by Governor Fenton on the following day and then sent to the governors of the states. It recommended that a convention be held at Springfield, Illinois, on December 1, 1868, in order to "consider the pathology, symptomatology and history of the Texas cattle fever and other infectious and contagious diseases to which cattle and stock are subject," discuss "the best methods of preventing the spread of such diseases, with reference to the interests of the producer and consumer," and "prepare a draft of a law which shall provide for the accomplishment of these objects,

one man upon that floor, and he an honorary member from
Kansas, that dare raise his voice in behalf of Texan cattle;
and his speech brought forth a storm of indignation from
the members of the convention, for it was exceedingly unpalatable to hear Texan cattle spoken of in any other terms
than those of the strongest condemnation. And it was idle
for the speaker to point out that an attempt to prohibit
absolutely the products of one state from passing through
or into another state, or to the common markets of the
country, by the legislative enactment of a state, was clearly
in violation of the Federal constitution, wherein is delegated
to congress only, the power to regulate commerce between
the states. It was futile to urge the equal rights of the owners of cattle, no matter whether the cattle's horns were long
or short, although the owner of the former might be a citizen of Texas. It was useless to point out the utter [153]
failure of prohibitory legislation, as exemplified in the case
of several of the western states, to accomplish the design
sought, to wit: To protect the shorthorn cattle from disease.
It were words spent in vain to point out legitimate and legal
quarantine measures or methods of attaining the end desired. There were few who would heed whilst the arrangement of nature was pointed out, in that, that the West and
Southwest must produce, the Northwest fatten, and the
East consume the beef product of the United States, and

---

to be submitted to the Legislatures of the States represented therein for
adoption." On October 26, Governor Oglesby issued a circular announcing
the appointment of the Illinois commissioners to the convention and inviting
commissioners from the other states to meet with them in the hall of the
house of representatives in Springfield on the following December 1. The
meeting was opened at the appointed time and place, with commissioners
present from the following states: Illinois, Indiana, Maryland, Massachusetts, Michigan, Missouri, New York, Ohio, Pennsylvania, Rhode Island,
Wisconsin, Ontario (Dominion of Canada). Besides, at the invitation of the
convention, seven other persons attended the sessions, including Joseph G.
McCoy. The assembly, which called itself the American Convention of Cattle
Commissioners, held meetings on December 1, 2, and 3. The condensed
proceedings were published in the *Transactions of the Illinois State Agri-
cultural Society*, VII, 173-273; briefer accounts appeared in the newspapers.
See also Missouri, *House Journal*, 25 Gen. Assem., regular sess., pp. 277-280;
Daily Illinois State Journal, Oct. 2, 19, 27, Nov. 21, Dec. 1, 2, 3, 4, 1868, Jan.
5, 1869; *Chicago Tribune*, Dec. 2, 3, 4, 1868; *Daily Missouri Republican*,
Dec. 4, 1868; Cole, *op. cit.*, 377.

that one section was dependent on the other for its ultimate prosperity. All these and other weighty considerations were urged upon the attention of the convention; but their announcement fell as soft water upon the flinty stone, for it had predetermined on prohibition.

Of the various theories advanced concerning the primal cause of Spanish fever, three only had any considerable number of adherents. The first, called the natural, or "Sporule" theory, was advocated, if not invented, by the scientists and doctors who composed, in part at least, nearly every commission sent out to investigate the disease and its causes. This theory is that the primal cause of the disease is found to be [154] a small egg, or sporule, deposited upon the blades of grass in Texas, which, being eaten by the animal, finds its way into the blood and grows to be microscopic monsters. Disorganization of the blood, disease (the symptoms of which is fever), and death follows as a kind of natural result. But it was worth enduring the evils of a perverse generation to have heard those sage theorists dilate upon the devilish character and proclivities of those horrible sporules – how their discovery had cost them so much profound scientific research; how they had dived in the carcass of the defunct bovine, searched his utmost intestine, torn to atoms and inspected his paunch, and subjected his stomach to the most rigid scrutiny; bursted asunder his liver and looked into its innermost recess; pried into the secrets of his kidneys; subjected his bladder to the severest chemical tests; looked through powerful telescopes into his dying eye and discerned the anguish of his departing spirit. But it was in his gore that their indominitable energy and profound research was rewarded by the discovery of the inexpressably horrible sporule. They well knew that in the very nature of things he must be somewhere, for it was plain to them that [155] the symmetry and perfection of the universe would have been incomplete without him; the elements of material nature would have long since resolved themselves back into original chaos if there had been such an omission in creation as the sporule. They justly felt that the discovery of him was the crowning glory and most momentous event of the nineteenth century, if not of all modern times. It was plain

"EXPERTS IN COUNCIL."

"THE SOWER OF SPORULES.

EXPERTS HUNTING SPORULES.

"ANCIENT SCIENTISTS INVESTIGATING."

that none since the days of the ancient mathematician en-
gulfed in his ablutions had so good a reason to cry out,
"Eureka! Eureka!"

But the advocators of this theory failed to inform the
waiting world what villain put those sporules upon the grass
blades in Texas, or from whence he got them, or why he
wanted to make short-horned cattle sick unto death, or
whether he had been told to desist, or warned that drawing
back pay for services once paid for would not be tolerated,
or that he was not "putting things where they would [156]
do him the most good." That fellow, whoever he is and
whatever his malicious intent may be, must be a diabolical
monster and worthy of immediate extermination. His body
should be embalmed in carbolic acid and placed in the cabi-
net of those scientists, there to remain as a trophy of the
most profound scientific research of the nineteenth century.
But in this case it is questionable whether all the investigating conventions, commissions, doctors, and scientists ever
did the cause of truth one iota of practical good. Their
learned and beautifully arranged theories were enunciated
and elaborated with all manner of profound erudite detail,
although in practice and for all practical good they were
valueless, unless it be as a curious specimen of what great
profound thinkers can do for the relief of their country in
distress. Indeed, their bulky disquisitions clothed in high-
sounding words, when shorn of their verbiage and com-
pressed into intrinsic truth and practical common sense,
would remind matter-of-fact cattlemen of the fabled mountain bringing forth the mouse. In fact, the results of the
various commissions for the investigation of Spanish fever
reminds one of the ancient royal commission of sage scientists who spent many days and weeks investigating and
profoundly debating the all-absorbing question of natural
history, to wit: "Which is the butt end of a billy goat?" [303]

[303] That McCoy's contempt for the accomplishments of the cattle convention was shared by others is apparent from the following comment of the
Champaign *Gazette and Union* (Dec. 23, 1868): "Texas Cattle Fever Convention. A new doctor wanted. There was a meeting of Doctors, stock feeders,
and Texas cattle men, held at Springfield, Dec. 1st, 1868... There was much
discussion relative to the introduction of the disease, symptoms, cures, manner
of communicating it, &c., &c., nothing new being advanced, and no new

Aside from the honorary member from Kansas, who was the party in interest at Abilene, the convention was as eager to deal a death blow to the new opening stock trade of the Southwest as are a pack of ravenous wolves to devour the powerless lamb. It was a noticeable fact that Texas, as a state, was without a single representative upon the floor of that convention, although the subject had been brought to the attention of a large number of drovers sojourning at Abilene, who did appoint a certain ex-governor of their state to be a delegate, but failed as usual to provide funds for defraying necessary expenses; so he failed to put in an appearance. So Texas, the state above all others the most [157] interested, was entirely unrepresented where her most valuable product was the subject of discussion, and measures adopted recommending a basis of legislation which effected her for weal or woe to the amount of many millions of dollars in value; and all for the lack of public spirit and public enterprise of her citizens.

The recommendation of that convention formed the basis of legislation enacted by many of the northern states during the following winter.[304] During the summer of 1868 the

light given on the part most desirable to know, viz: how to cure it. Farmers, as a class, care little for fine spun theories, and it matters little to them whether a disease is communicated by eating ticks, fungii, or rubbing noses together, those questions are only interesting to science, but we do like to know how to prevent and cure diseases, no matter what their origin, so long as we have them among our cattle and other domestic animals."

[304] The following states passed such laws on the dates indicated: Indiana, February 9, 10, 1869; Nebraska, February 15, 1869; Missouri, February 26, 1869; Wisconsin, March 10, 1869; Kentucky, March 16, 1869, March 21, 1870; Michigan, April 5, 1869; Illinois, April 16, 1869; Territory of Washington, December 1, 1869. The statutes varied in content, a few absolutely prohibiting the introduction of Texas or Cherokee cattle but most restricting their importation to certain months of the year. *Indiana Laws, 1869*, pp. 28-30; *Nebraska Laws, 1869*, pp. 249-250; *Missouri Laws, 1869*, pp. 89-90; *General Laws of Wisconsin, 1869*, pp. 145-146; *Kentucky Acts, Adjourned Session, 1869*, p. 656; *ibid., Regular Session, 1869-1870*, I, 135; *Michigan Acts, Regular Session, 1869*, I, 319-320; *Public Laws of Illinois, 1869*, pp. 402-405; *Statutes of the Territory of Washington, 1869*, pp. 404-406. The state of Louisiana objected to the proposed passage of some of these laws, and on January 29, 1869, when a number of Texas cattle bills were being discussed in the state legislatures, the governor approved the following joint resolution passed by its general assembly: "That the enactment of laws, by any State

Federal government employed, to thoroughly investigate the subject of Spanish fever and its prime causes, manner of contraction, and prevention, Professor John Gamgee, an English veterinary surgeon who had won distinction in England during the time when rinderpest made such sad havoc among the herds of England. This capable gentleman visited all portions of the United States where Spanish fever had raged, and also the state of Texas, and made a thorough and [158] practical investigation of the disease, endeavoring to trace its primal cause, origin, and nature. But we have never seen his report in print; and we are not sure that the government had it printed, for the excitement soon abated and Texan cattle began to appear on market both east and west.[305] Indeed, we have often thought that the outbreak of Spanish fever and the consequent excitement really served to draw toward Texan cattle the attention of stockmen from every quarter of the country, and eventuated in their becoming recognized as a staple commodity upon the markets.

It is the opinion of others that the doctors and scientists had caught up one of the effects or symptoms of the disease and manufactured a finespun theory which looks plausible

of the Union, prohibiting the introduction therein of Southern cattle during the season when no disease can be communicated, will be deemed an unjust discrimination against a large and growing interest of this State and a direct interference with commerce between the States, as guaranteed by the Constitution of the United States." *Louisiana Acts, 1869,* pp. 8-9.

[305] Horace Capron, United States Commissioner of Agriculture, made the following report to President Andrew Johnson on November 30, 1868: "On the breaking out of the splenic fever at the halting places of Texas cattle during the past summer, I commissioned Professor John Gamgee, of the Albert Veterinary College of London, to investigate its character and causes and the means for its prevention. The labor was undertaken at once and continued with zeal and activity in several western States, including the Texas cattle stations of Western Kansas. Post mortem examinations, not only of diseased native stock but of the cattle from Texas, were repeatedly made, and their results carefully recorded, all tending to connect the migrating herds of the Gulf coast unmistakably with the existence and spread of the disease." *Report of the Commissioner of Agriculture for the Year 1868,* p. 5. Gamgee's investigation was published during 1870 in an *Extra Report* of the Commissioner of Agriculture for that year. On August 4, 1868, Gamgee spoke to the Pork Packers Association of Chicago, outlining the results of his study of Texas fever in Illinois. *Chicago Tribune,* Aug. 6, 1868.

on paper, but has not one ounce of truth or fact in it. In Spanish fever, like pneumonia in horses, the blood, we opine, becomes totally disorganized (in fact might be called rotten), and upon examining it with the microscope, a very unnatural appearance is detected. But the actual cause of the disease can only be conjectured from this standpoint. Another, the second, theory is that the disease is solely and entirely caused by the ticks peculiar to the climate and country of the Southwest. It is argued that only ticky cattle will disseminate disease, that every native that dies of Spanish fever will always be found to have almost one tick for every hair on his hide, [and] that his stomach will be found often to contain ticks, although small, yet numerous, mingled with the food. It is held, truthfully too, that the large ticks seen in great numbers on almost all cattle fresh from Texas that have been shipped direct north, soon yield their hold on the animal and fall to the ground, where they, by a process peculiar to their nature, become as an egg, from each one of which a thousand or more little ticks will be hatched in a short space of time and crawl upon the blades of grass, wherefrom they get on the legs of the grazing animal, and when it lays down to rest, get onto its body; also the ticks, whilst in this diminutive state, are eaten by the domestic [159] animal in great quantities. Whether on the outside of his body digging into his skin or within his stomach, they are to the domestic cattle rank poison, which, when a sufficient amount has been absorbed by the animal's system, acts in such a manner as to create fever and death. It is urged in support of the tick theory that the advent of frost, as is well known to be the case, puts a stop to the spread of the disease by killing the young ticks. It is also a well-known fact that in every case wherein a ticky herd of cattle came upon the pasture in contact with natives, that disease was sure to follow. The cattle that were introduced into Illinois via the Red river route were always very ticky, often having so many that the actual color of the animal would be hid by the large, distended, grayish-white bodies of the million of ticks which were clinging to his hide and sucking blood from him. Wherever on the pasture fields or prairies these cattle came in contact and grazed with the domestic stock, pestilential disease and death followed with infallible certainty. The tick theory had for its advocates some able, practical cattlemen, some of whom had lost heavily by Spanish fever, and had made close observations and tests to ascertain the real cause of the disease and its manner of contraction.

The third theory is that the Spanish fever is superinduced by much the same causes as ship fever aboard emigrant steamships, to wit: by hard usage and privation of the usual and necessary rest, food, and water. The cattle of Texas being wild and free, almost as much so as the buffalo of the plains in the West, are fretful and worried by restraint and handling, much as is the full-grown wild animal when caged. It is not uncommon to overdrive and starve the Texan cattle en route for market. Often in dry seasons, water being scarce, herds do not get sufficient for a week at a time, and often the haste of the drover or his indolence allows [160] his cattle to be overdriven, and that, too, without sufficient food to prevent his stock from suffering.

We leave the reader to form his own opinion which of the theories stated is the correct one, only adding that a carefully driven herd of Texan cattle coming via western Kansas into the northern states seldom if ever disseminate disease. If permitted to rest for thirty to sixty days on good range abounding with plenty of water and grass, they will not infect the domestic cattle. This we know to be correct. But whether during this rest from travel and hardship the fever becomes extinct by the recuperative power of the animals, or whether the losing of the ticks, as they invariably do, rids them of the seeds of disease, we leave the reader to form his own opinion, only adding that after the closest observation of many cases and often trying to seek out the real causes of Spanish fever, we are unable to say whether the tick theory or the ship fever theory is the correct one; for both theories have almost unanswerable arguments in their favor. Of one thing we feel certain, that is, that the cattle in Texas upon their accustomed range are as healthy as any cattle in the world.

There is one peculiar characteristic of Spanish fever among Texan cattle, that is, its presence is scarcely perceptible to the casual observer; for it never kills a Texan animal, and effects them so slightly that it requires an experienced eye to detect its presence in a herd of Texan cattle. Nevertheless, they do have the disease, and occasionally one of them will be sick near unto death with it; especially is this the case with Texan cattle that have been wintered in the northern states. It is a well-settled fact settled by every investigation yet instituted, as well as by the unanimous testimony of the closest-observing, practical cattleman, that the disease is communicated to the domestic stock only by grazing and laying upon the same grounds or pasture lands which have been previously grazed over by Texan cattle; [161] that to travel upon the same road, to drink at the same pond of water, to pass through the same shipping yards or in the same cars, will not furnish the necessary conditions for contraction of the disease; but, we repeat, the domestic stock must eat of the same grass that has just previously been depastured by the Texan cattle. Whether the seeds of disease left on the grass are in the shape of ticks, or is a poison left in and with their saliva or slobbers, or in and with the urine or residuum deposited upon the grass, or whether they are the veritable sporules of the scientists, is an undetermined question and one about which practical cattlemen as well as doctors disagree.

We propose to deal with facts or practical effects rather than with theories. One thing, there is little use to deny or gainsay that there is such a malady as is commonly called Spanish fever, or that it is under certain circumstances disseminated by Texan cattle. It is in ninety-nine cases in one hundred fatal in its effects upon the shorthorn cattle. While it is an unsettled question just how the shorthorn contracts, or the Texan disseminates, the disease, none other than an obdurate man, one who would not or could not be convinced by evidence, will longer dispute or disbelieve the actual existence, at certain seasons of the year, of the disease among certain classes of cattle. In about two to four weeks after the shorthorn has been exposed to the necessary conditions — that is, grazed over and rested upon the same pastures upon which certain herds of Texan cattle have previously been pastured — he may be observed to become stupid; refuse to eat or drink; inclined to stand or lie in the fence corners; his head will droop below its natural position; his ears will lop down beside his head; his eyes will become nearly fixed, and a wild, glaring stare will be observed; whilst from his nostrils or mouth will constantly drool a whitish ropy slobber resembling excessive salivary secretion. The animal's coat of hair will stand up on end or turn forward, presenting a rough, unthrifty [162] appearance, whilst his back will become arched. Frequent urinary discharges will occur, presenting the appearance, to the casual observer, of pure blood; but rare evacuations of the bowels will occur, and those will be very hard and dry. The animal will become intensely hot and suffer great pain, and when near dissolution, will often bellow piercing shrieks expressive of the racking pain endured. Sometimes they will plunge about wildly for a few moments and then suddenly fall down and expire instantly. If the subject is milch stock, one of the first symptoms of approaching disease will be the diminution of the supply of milk, which in one or two days will cease altogether. Milch cows are more liable, for some unknown reason, to contract the disease than are other cattle.

A sucking calf never takes Spanish fever, no matter if it sucks its dying or dead mother, as they have been seen do, without contracting the disease. One shorthorn will not contract the fever from another shorthorn; nor will a herd of shorthorns contract Spanish fever from the worst-infected herd of Texans, if they are separated by so much as a partition fence. Although the water the shorthorns drink may have come first through the pasture whereon are grazing infected Texans, it will not convey the seeds of disease to the shorthorns. We repeat, it is the necessary conditions for the native cattle to graze over and lie upon pastures which have just previously been grazed over by Texans, in order to contract Spanish fever. No well-authenticated instance of the contraction of the disease in any other manner or under other circumstances has yet been produced.

It is not difficult generally for an experienced western cattleman to detect the Spanish fever existing in a herd of Texan cattle, but it requires close scrutiny and experience, for the evidences of its presence are not discernible to the casual observer or inexperienced cattleman. No specific, in-fallible remedy has yet been found for Spanish fever; but enough is known or established as the result of experiments [163] to warrant the assertion that if the animal is thor-oughly drenched with any powerful purgatives, so as to re-lieve the system of all food while the animal is in the earlier stages of the disease, it is quite likely to recover. But inas-much as the animal's stomach, or manifold, becomes as dry as a gunny sack, and the contents as dry and hard as a pine board, looking much like a hard sponge, in the latter stages of the disease, it is plain that physics or any other remedy cannot afford relief. It has been found very beneficial as a preventive and cure to feed green corn to exposed animals or those taking the disease. It is found that corn will in this case, as in milk sickness, neutralize the poison, much as the essence of corn, familiarly called "whiskey," will neutralize the poison of the rattlesnake. Many cattlemen are fond of neutralizing snake bites; in fact, some of them neutralize so often that they dream of snakes being in many disgustingly familiar attitudes, especially about their boots.

Perhaps no one man sustained greater losses, both direct and indirect, from Spanish fever, than John T. Alexander, of Morgan county, Illinois.[306] Certainly no man in that state or any other has handled more Texan cattle on his own ac-count than has he. Indeed, there are few, if any, who have handled more cattle of all classes than has Mr. Alexander. Beginning when he was a lad of thirteen years to assist his father, then an extensive drover from Ohio to the eastern markets, he gradually grew to the business for which he had a natural taste and great, good judgment – two indis-

---

[306] John T. Alexander was born in Virginia about 1822. After living for a time in Ohio, he moved to the eastern part of Morgan county, Illinois, about 1848, where he purchased a farm. In 1866 he also bought the Broad-lands Farm of about 26,000 acres near Homer, Champaign county. On account of his extensive dealings in live stock, he was known as the "Great Cattle King of the Mississippi Valley." Out of a total of 165,663 cattle shipped from Illinois to New York City during 1868, Alexander shipped 36,028. He died at his home in Morgan county, August 21, 1876, and was buried in the Diamond Grove Cemetery, Jacksonville. *Champaign County Gazette*, Aug. 18, 1869; *Daily Illinois State Journal*, Jan. 16, 1869; *Daily Inter-Ocean*, Aug. 25, 1876; Paxson, "The Cow Country," *loc. cit.*, 67; Cole, *op. cit.*, 376-377, 382-383.

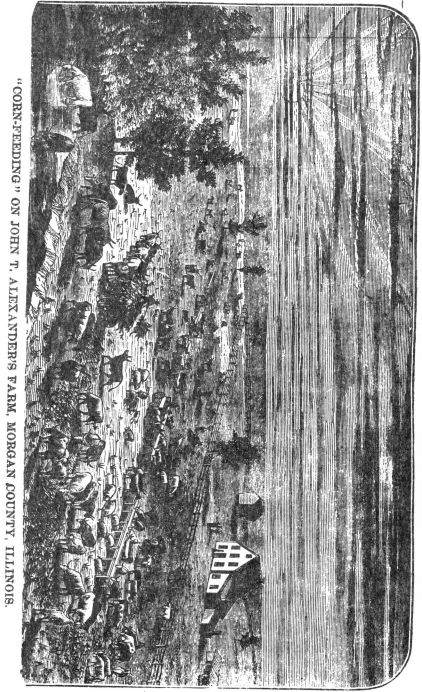

"CORN-FEEDING" ON JOHN T. ALEXANDER'S FARM, MORGAN COUNTY, ILLINOIS.

A "PINCKNEYVILLE" PIG VENDER.

pensable qualifications for the successful cattleman. Although a Virginian by birth, he was reared in Ohio, spending his youthful days in aiding his father drive cattle from that state over the Allegheny mountains to the Philadelphia, Baltimore, New York, and Boston markets. At the age of twenty years, his father having met one of those severe reverses so common to the life of the drover or cattle shipper, young Alexander determined to try the West on his own account. Accordingly, but [164] a few short weeks elapsed before he might have been seen in St. Louis, looking for something to do in the line of his chosen business, without capital other than his abilities and energy. He was not afraid of work, and gladly accepted a situation upon a moderate salary, to aid Christian Hays, then one of St. Louis's heaviest operators, in his live stock transactions. At that early day such a convenience as live stock scales for weighing animals alive was unknown, or if known, unused so far west as St. Louis. It was the custom to select an average bullock, slaughter him, weigh the carcass, and then from that compute the average weight of the entire herd. It was the custom then in vogue for the drover and the purchaser to select, or arrive at, the average steer by choosing alternately, one the best and heaviest steer, the other the lightest and meanest steer, until all but one steer was chosen. This, of course, was taken for the average. It is easy to see that much depended upon the judgment of the parties who did the selecting. If the drover was a better judge than the buyer, he was sure to get the better of him, and *vice versa*. Young Alexander was soon detailed to average a drove for his employer, and the manner in which he did that duty, the mature judgment, the "cattle sense" which he evinced, was noticed by Mr. Hays; and he concluded that young Alexander possessed abilities fitting him for superior duties, and at once put him into commission and sent him to central Illinois to buy fat cattle for the St. Louis market. Mr. Hays made no error in sending the young cattleman out with instructions to buy upon his own judgment, for it was more and more apparent from day to day that young Alexander well understood his business. In a few months, after several trips to central Illinois, he determined to feed a moderate-sized drove on his own account. His friend Hays was quite willing to aid him to accomplish the undertaking by loaning any needed funds.

After spending two or three years in operating in live stock in connection with Mr. Hays, young Alexander [165] determined to drive a herd of two hundred and thirty head of fat cattle of his own feeding to the eastern market. In those days there were no railroads extending into Illinois. Sending western cattle direct to the Atlantic coast markets was an experiment never before extensively tried, and it required a man of will and energy to undertake and execute the effort, for it was not only a great hazard, but required the entire summer to accomplish it. Great care had to be exercised and the herd prudently managed and carefully driven, to prevent a ruinous shrinkage in flesh and condition. The cattle had been fullfed during the previous six months and were well fatted. Upon the skill of the drover in handling his herd depended the retaining or losing of this flesh or condition. No one understood how to handle a drove of fat cattle better than Mr. Alexander, and it is needless to add that he was successful. After driving over the broad prairies of Illinois and western Indiana, feeding the cattle upon the natural grasses while upon the prairies (through the timbered portion of the remainder of his journey), turning them upon the fenced pastures of the farmers, he arrived in Albany, New York state, just in time to meet a purchaser, at thirty-one dollars per head, delivered in Boston, Massachusetts. This price was considered very satisfactory, although it looks to a cattleman of the present day to be a very low figure. But everything was proportionately lower then, and one dollar would buy as much land or other valuables as will ten dollars at this time. As a proof that Mr. Alexander made a good sale, we add that his purchaser lost money on the cattle, not because they were not good, but because the Boston markets were too low.

After operating for three or four years longer as a trader, Mr. Alexander decided to purchase land and embark in farming and cattle feeding exclusively. Accordingly, in 1848 he made his first investment in real estate, selecting lands in Morgan county, central Illinois, as being the best in the

state. The first purchase was made at three dollars per acre
for a large tract of land; still owned by Mr. Alexander
[166] and now worth not less than seventy-five dollars per
acre; and is located upon the Toledo, Wabash and Western
Railway near a station named after the extensive cattle
shipper. Indeed, there are few, if any, superior lands for
agricultural or pastoral purposes within the limits of the
United States than are found in central Illinois, and in that
district there is no better lands than are those selected by
Mr. Alexander. Central Illinois has become universally
wealthy by corn raising, and hog and cattle feeding, or, in
other words, making the live stock product of other regions
fit for eastern markets and consumption.

The manner of cornfeeding cattle is familiar to most
northwestern men. But as it is a business of great importance
and magnitude, one in which millions of dollars are annually invested, one that engages the attention and efforts
of thousands of enterprising, energetic men, and one that
doubles the value of every head of cattle fed, of which
there are many thousands, it is deemed worthy of more than
a passing notice. The best inland corn-growing regions
where corn can be produced or bought cheaply are the cattle-
feeding centers. The farmer, who is often a feeder also,
devotes his whole attention during the spring and summer
months to planting and cultivating a large crop of corn.
When the fall season arrives and the corn begins to mature,
it is cut and shocked, which process consists in cutting and
placing in the center all the corn on a space of ground equal
to fourteen or sixteen corn hills square. The cornstalks are
cut off near the ground and are set up snugly together, forming a compact shock, which is allowed to stand in the field
until it is fed.

A few weeks before the grass in the pasture fails, the
feeder begins to give his cattle corn, at first but little, gradually increasing the amount until the cattle become thoroughly
accustomed to it, without gorging or foundering. When the
pasture becomes bare of grass, the cattle are brought into
the feed yards and there daily fed for from four to six
months. The feeder's outfit is usually an ox team of [167]
one or more pairs of cattle, which are attached to a wagon,

upon which is placed a long, rude, strong rack, much like a hay frame; upon which the shock corn is thrown, then drawn from the field to the feed yard. Entering the yard with his team, the feeder mounts the load, and with a stake or standard from the rack, throws the corn to the ground, first upon one side then upon the other, while the team moves around a beaten circuit; which they soon become accustomed to follow, and which is soon marked by a high ridge of cornstalks, which in muddy, rainy times forms a dry spot or circle, as well as an excellent bed in cold weather. The ground is literally floored or paved with cornstalks in the feed yard, and the cattle are allowed to eat as much as they desire, and that too of the best ears of corn. An average-sized bullock will eat and waste one-half bushel of corn each day and will become in time very fat. The usual gain in four to six months' feeding is from two to three hundred pounds. Extra good feeding of extra good cattle will often make greater gains. Many feeders prefer to feed husked or snapped corn, which is fed in boxes or troughs. There is less waste of corn, but this method requires feeding hay or straw for roughness.

When shock corn is fed, two yards are provided, in which the cattle are fed alternate days. Whilst they are being fed in one, a herd of swine are eating up the waste and offal in the other. One to two hogs to each bullock are thus made fat. The profits on the hogs fatted is no inconsiderable item in the feeding operation.

To secure the hogs to follow the feeding cattle, sometimes the whole country is scoured, and occasionally resort is had to distant counties. This branch of trade, like all others, develops characteristics peculiar to itself. In central Illinois, a noted cattle-feeding district, resort is sometimes had to southern counties for stock hogs to follow cattle; those counties less adapted to corn production, but abounding in heavy forests of oak, hickory, and walnut, which furnish [168] mast, upon which the industrious long-nosed, cat-hammed porcines indigenous to those regions subsist. When the local trader becomes aware of their value, he will industriously seek them out, gather them into small squads, and ship them to central portions of the state, where, with a manner the most bland, he will seek to sell them to some cattle feeder. These itinerant pig-peddlers are of very doubtful morals or virtue, and usually reside upon a state road or public thoroughfare in a hilly district where the yellow clay soil is uppermost, usually a few miles east of some pleasant plains. These pig-venders are genuine heroes, and often hail from Pinckneyville or other mellifluous regions. Should the reader ever journey in those regions, he will not fail to hear of or meet one of those "heroes," and will know at once that he is in the presence of unappreciated greatness, of which he will be aware.

[169] There is quite a diversity of opinion among feeders as to the most profitable manner of feeding, as well as to kinds or classes of cattle to feed. Many hold and practice a system of fullfeeding, and selling off of the grain feed; whilst others feed less grain during the winter and finish fatting on the pasture the following spring and summer; others simply "rough through" and fatten exclusively on the grass. Many feeders will not feed other than graded Durhams, or natives, whilst just as respectable and successful a class prefer the Texan, or southern, cattle. Of course, the whole matter hinges upon the question of profit. The native to begin with cost fully twice as much as the southern bullock, and when fat sells for a better price per pound than Texan. But when both are fat, the difference in price per pound is not so great as the difference in first cost; but the native feeds better, eats corn to better advantage, takes on more fat on cornfeed than does the Texan; but the southern bullock excels the native in fatting on grass – makes great gains in less time than the native. It may be truthfully stated that for fatting on corn the native excels and is therefore preferable, whilst for "roughing through" and fatting on grass, the Texan is superior. The feeder who reverses this order, in handling either class, rarely does it to his profit. Nevertheless, a herd of Texan cattle which has been delivered in the North during the early part of summer, and has become thoroughly rested and climated before winter, can be made really fat on corn. In various experiments made in feeding Texan cattle, it has been demonstrated that to shell the corn is of great advantage. It has been found that

the cob, being hard and unnutritious, is unpalatable to them and is a great obstacle to successfully feeding them. But as a rule, to "rough through" and fatten on the grass is the most profitable manner to handle Texan cattle in the northwestern states. In central Illinois many of the most successful dealers in southern cattle feed them upon the blue-grass pastures [171] and never lot them up, but aim only to bring them to grass the following spring in strong, thrifty condition, upon which they will soon become fit for the shambles of New York. This is the manner in which Mr. Alexander handles his large purchases of Texan cattle.

For many years all the suitable cattle of the Missouri valley region were driven to central Illinois, and there, by six months' cornfeeding, made fat and doubled in value. Thus, by combining the products of those rich corn lands, as much money or value was created in six months as the producer of the unfatted steer had made in three years handling or rearing the same animal. This fact soon became patent to the thinking agriculturists, and it was not long before the corn-growing portions of Illinois became either a cornfield or feed yard, annually sending to eastern markets thousands of fatted cattle. In this business Mr. Alexander saw and realized great profit and was fast becoming princely wealthy. But there occurred a year of severe drouth, something uncommon to that country, cutting off the corn crops upon the uplands, so that corn in sufficient quantities for cattle-feeding purposes could be found only on the river bottoms; and to those sections Mr. Alexander took his herds and fullfed them during the winter of 1854 and 1855. When spring came, no buyer offered him such prices as he thought he ought to have; so he determined to drive and ship on his own account. At that date the nearest railroad terminus, or shipping point, was at Logansport, Indiana, a distance of three or four hundred miles, and hither he turned his droves, carring them to Toledo, Ohio; thence to Dunkirk by lake steamer; then recarring them to New York City; from whence a part was sent to Boston. In this transaction Mr. Alexander did not realize so much by several thousand dollars as he had had offered him for his cattle in the West.

JOHN T. ALEXANDER.

Instead of discouraging him from future shipments, it only excited his energy and determination to retrieve his losses in the same place and business wherein he had [172] sustained them. Many readers would suppose that no man would leave a business in which he had in a few years acquired four thousand acres of fine, valuable land and ten thousand dollars in cash, to engage in another, especially one that was uncertain and had already lost the snug sum of five thousand dollars. But if they do so think, they do not understand the peculiar turn of mind and temperament necessary to constitute a cattle shipper. Nothing arouses his will and determination more surely and drives him to greater ventures than losses on the first shipments. Like the devotee of the card table, he determines to get even and more. This determination has ruined many good men and turned them out of house and home. Mr. Alexander's loss only seemed to make him determined, and contrary to the advice of his financial friends, he engaged in shipping cattle via Chicago to the eastern markets during the year 1856, but without making or losing to speak of. But during the following year, in connection with his partner, he shipped via the Toledo, Wabash and Western Railway, then just completed, ten thousand head of cattle, and at the end of the season divided the snug sum of sixty thousand dollars. But success only stimulated him to greater undertakings, and the following year, his partner having been killed in a railroad accident, Mr. Alexander shipped eleven thousand head of cattle, but with more loss than profit. The succeeding year (that of 1859) fifteen thousand head of fat cattle went east as the contribution or business of Mr. Alexander. To say that this year's operation was a losing one, is putting it mild; it was "a ripper," as a cattleman would style it. Mr. Alexander's losses were equal to, or greater than, the value of his entire estate, but the public did not know it and still had the greatest confidence in his ability. During the two succeeding years but little money was made or lost, although an immense business was done.

Then the Civil war broke out. There were many thousands of cattle and mules in the state of Missouri, one of the states [173] deeply involved in the struggle, in fact was largely the battle ground. This turn of affairs made the tenure of personal property very insecure in that state, and most owners were willing to sell at any price, no matter how low. This offered a good opportunity to venturesome cattlemen, and Mr. Alexander's financial condition was such that he was prepared to take any manner or kind of risks to retrieve his financial losses. Accordingly, he put several energetic buyers in Missouri, with instructions to penetrate the disturbed districts and, where war's dreaded cloud hung darkest and most threateningly, there buy every steer or mule they could (of course, as cheap as possible) and send them to his farm in Illinois. Two years, affording such opportunities for good investments, were sufficient to make good all previous losses of Mr. Alexander. At the close of the war an inventory of his assets would have shown seventy-two hundred acres of land worth seventy-five dollars per acre, one hundred thousand dollars in bank, his pastures full of cattle, and not one dollar of debt. One would think that such an exhibit would satisfy anyone's greatest desires for wealth, so far, at least, as to prevent him from engaging in any operations in which there was great hazard. But such was not the case with Mr. Alexander; he, like the ancient conqueror of the same name, looked and longed for other and greater conquests. But, different to his ancient namesake, he soon found a "New World" which he essayed to conquer — it was the purchasing and improving of what was then called the "Sullivan," but afterwards the "Broad Lands," Farm, a tract of twenty-six thousand acres of land near the Toledo, Wabash and Western Railway in Champaign county, Illinois. This purchase, in connection with heavy losses by cattle shipping, also a loss of fully seventy-five thousand dollars by Spanish fever (to this may be added the repudiation of a contract by certain railroads, whereby he was made to sustain a loss of near two hundred and fifty thousand dollars), produced a crisis in his affairs of the gravest nature. As is usual in such cases, every effort [175] put forth to prevent impending disaster only brings additional distress. So in his case. Finally, he took a survey of his affairs and concluded to sell his Broad Lands Farm; accordingly hunted up a purchaser in the person of the agent of a

Canadian company and contracted to sell him the entire tract for six hundred and seventy-five thousand dollars. Of this transaction he hastened to inform his most pressing creditors. But alas for him, when the time came to ratify the contract, the Canadian company refused to abide the contract of its agent, and the land trade failed. This precipitated the impending crisis. In compliance with the advice of his friends, he turned his entire estates and immense personal property — in short, all his assets — into the hands of three assignees for the benefit of his creditors.

This was perhaps the darkest, bitterest year of his existence — a year of crushing disappointment and pungent humiliation such as a high, ambitious, sensitive soul could scarce endure. It was crushing and overwhelming to Mr. Alexander, for he had ever been a man of the keenest sensibilities, of the most exalted honor in all his business transactions, above petty spites or contemptible actions. The word "failed," which was bandied about from mouth to mouth, grated harshly upon his ears and wounded deeply his inmost soul and rendered life itself almost an undesirable burthen. Such were the results of a few years of persistent cattle shipping in connection with incidental disastrous business transactions; a fortune of colossal proportions, riven to shreds, as is the oak by the lightning's hot bolt; scattered as if by a cyclone, as are the fragments of a rock-riven ocean steamer. Notwithstanding the liabilities reached the enormous figures of twelve hundred thousand dollars, the estate was ample to pay every creditor, dollar for dollar, and leave Mr. Alexander about two thousand acres of the best of his Morgan county lands, without a single legitimate unpaid claim [176] outstanding. With an energy peculiar only to men of real ability — but never found in the fungus brains of the maudlin goslings who flash like a meteor athwart the business horizon and die out never to be seen or heard of again, save as some abandoned loafer or drunken saloon ornament — Mr. Alexander set himself about retrieving his lost fortunes; and if his success during the last two years can be taken as a harbinger of the future, the time will be quite brief before his Morgan county estate will be as large as ever. His greatest losses occurred in 1868, during the great excitement about Spanish fever, and were carried until 1870, in which a desperate effort was made to cover, and fully seventy thousand head of cattle were shipped to the eastern markets. This is the largest year or season's business ever done by a single individual in marketing cattle in the United States, or perhaps in the world. Mr. Alexander regards himself as taking his third start in the world — one at St. Louis, one at the beginning of the war, and one now.

His first financial friend was Christian Hays, of St. Louis; his second was Thomas Condell, for many years president of a strong banking institution of Springfield, Illinois, and a man who had almost unerring judgment in business matters, especially those pertaining to cattle transactions — one who stood by and aided with money and council, his friends and business patrons in the darkest hours, as well as in the brightest. More than one cattleman remembers the name and fidelity of Thomas Condell with feelings of the deepest gratitude, if not of love and veneration. He has some years since retired from active business, greatly to the regret of many cattlemen of central Illinois. It seems strange that of the many bankers who in former years were more than willing to loan their money to Mr. Alexander, not one was willing, after he had met his great reverses, to aid him in his effort to recuperate his shattered fortune, although he had paid in full every legitimate claim against him. Yet [177] it is said, "Where there is a will there is a way," and Mr. Alexander certainly had the will, and a good vigorous one at that. Finally, to him came George Wilson, a banker of Geneseo, Illinois, a man of considerably ready means and a shrewd operator; one who has made his money largely out of cattle and with cattlemen; one who is blessed with that rare quality called "cattle sense" (an article quite rare among bankers) ; and proposed to furnish all cash needed to stock up Mr. Alexander's lands. This he did for two years, besides paying for three thousand fine cattle at panic prices during the fall of 1873 for the pastures and feed yards of Mr. Alexander. These cattle will be grazed on blue-grass pastures until February, and then be fed corn on the pastures until spring. Then they will be grazed on the blue-grass pastures and fatted, which requires but few months to accomplish.

But we cannot close this imperfect sketch without offering a few thoughts upon the life and labors of such men as Mr. Alexander. No right-thinking man can regard them other than public benefactors, and as such are of much greater consequence and benefit in a substantial way than many think. They take from the feeder's yards his fatted stock, and four times out of five pay him more than it is worth, and that in cash without delay or serious inconvenience. By their perseverance and business tact they are able to get the lowest rate of freight possible, which the local feeder, nine times in ten, gets the benefit of, in the increased price obtained for his fat stock. We do not hesitate to assert that the cattlemen of the Northwest, and especially those of central Illinois, owe to John T. Alexander a debt of gratitude for many hundreds of thousands, yes, millions of dollars distributed among them by his liberal hand. We confidently affirm that for more than ten years he added from three to ten dollars per head to the value of the cattle fatted in central Illinois, which were and are many thousands of head annually. Mr. [178] Alexander is not above fifty-three years of age, is tall and of commanding appearance, looks hale, fresh, and youthful, is of sanguine mental temperament and naturally impulsive. He is very quiet and unassuming in manners; speaks but little, and never in a loud or boisterous tone; is affable, social, warm hearted; appreciates true manhood; is upright, honorable, and high-minded in his business transactions. No superior has gone before him, and there are none to follow after him.

CAPTURING AND LOADING BUFFALO.

X. PROHIBITORY LEGISLATION AND OTHER DIFFICULTIES

Fully seventy-five thousand cattle arrived at Abilene during 1868, one-fourth of which were taken by Illinois grazers and shipped to pastures during the month of June. Several thousand were taken by territorial operators. But when the Spanish fever excitement broke out, all trade and demand ceased, and a dullness amounting to distress ensued. Finally, great uneasiness began to be manifested by the drovers who had not sold, lest there would be no more demand, and many began to talk of driving off to other points. Especially was this the case with those who had driven mixed or stock herds, for which there was little or no demand. As it had proved futile to try to prevent Texans from bringing stock cattle to market, the next thing was to find buyers for such as were there. The parties interested in Abilene were anxious to make it a complete market for everything in the line of live stock that was brought to it. Finally, the plan of advertising a large semimonthly public sale of stock cattle to take place at the shipping yards was hit upon, and a large number of handbills, dodgers, etc., announcing the auction sale were provided, and young men were sent by train all [180] over western Missouri and Iowa, eastern Nebraska and Kansas, to distribute them. The first sale was largely attended and one thousand head of stock was sold at satisfactory prices.[307] Before the day

---

[307] The first auction of longhorns at Abilene was advertised to take place on July 22, 1868, when, it was claimed, a thousand head would be offered for sale. The *Junction City Weekly Union* (July 25, 1868) gave the following account of this auction: "At the stock sale at Abilene a few days ago, five hundred head were disposed of. The large sized work cattle averaged thirty dollars per head, 2-year olds ten dollars per head. A large number of bidders were present from four States. The sales will hereafter occur semi-monthly, E. H. Gaylord, salesman. The next one comes off on the 5th of August." See also *ibid.*, July 11, 1868; *Daily Illinois State Journal*, July 13, 1868.

arrived for the second sale, every herd of stock cattle on the range was sold. Such was the result of the advertising done.

But no buyers for the grown cattle, or beeves, arrived, and it was thought best to do something to call public attention to the fact that there were twenty-five thousand or more grown cattle for sale at Abilene. The plan adopted was to send east a carload of wild buffaloes, covering the side of the car with advertisements of the cattle. But how to get the buffaloes — that was the question. The frame or slats of an ordinary stock car were greatly strengthened by bolting strong, thick plank parallel with the floor and about three feet above it, to the sides of the car. Putting in a camp outfit and supplies abundant in one car, and a half dozen horses well trained to the lasso in another car, a party of half a dozen departed for the buffalo regions, out into which the Kansas Pacific Railway was then being operated. Arriving at Fossil creek siding, the cars were put upon the sidetrack and camp pitched. The horses were unloaded by means of an inclined plane or platform temporarily improvised for that purpose. In the party were three or four Texan cowboys, also three California Spaniards, all experts with the lasso.

After partaking of a hearty dinner, the party saddled up the ponies and started out in quest of the buffaloes. Although they were not plenty upon that portion of the plains at that date, yet the time was brief before a huge old bull was spied, and immediately preparations to chase and lasso him were made. Circling around, he was started in the direction of the railroad, and when within a few hundred yards thereof, a sudden dash was made upon him by two Spaniards, and in the twinkling of an eye their lariats were around his neck. So soon as the old monarch found himself entangled and his speed checked, he became furiously enraged, and alternately charged first at one and then [181] the other of his pursuers. It was noticeable how intensely angry he became; he would drop his head and stiffen his neck, set his tail erect over his back, and with eyes green with pent-up wrath, await the near approach of his tormentors. So soon as one came near, he would plunge at him and pursue at his utmost speed so long as there was the least hope of overtaking him; then stop and whirl about, and attack his nearest pursuer. After getting him quite close to the railroad track by stratagem, the third lasso was adroitly thrown around his hind legs, and in a jiffy the great behemoth was lying stretched, helpless, upon the ground. It was vain for him to struggle; the well-trained horses watched his every motion and kept the lariats as tight as fiddle strings, shifting their positions dexterously to check or counterbalance his every motion. When he ceased to struggle, his legs were securely tied together with short splashes of rope or thongs previously prepared for the pur- pose; then the lassos were taken off, and after adjusting the inclined plane, a block and tackle were brought into requisi- tion, one end of which was attached to his head, the other to the top of the opposite car door; and before the hot panting bison was aware of what was being done, he was aboard the car, his head securely bound to a post of the car frame, and his feet relieved. He would not bound up and show fight, but lay and sulk for hours. In two days ten full-grown bull buffaloes were lassoed, but the weather being very hot, four of them died from the heat and the anger excited by capture. Three became sullen and laid down before they could be got near the cars; so but three were got aboard in good condition.

It was very exciting to witness the feat of lassoing one of those powerful monsters, to see how skillful those Span- iards could throw the lariat, and, above all, how well trained were the horses. From the moment the lasso was thrown, they seemed to know just what motion or maneuver was necessary to counteract whatever motions the captured animal might make. It is astonishing what strength they develop; [182] how much they can draw forward or hold back by the horn of the saddle — fully twice their own weight. It is impossible to divert their attention from the captured animal or entangle them in the lasso. They know by experience the consequences.

After hanging upon each side of the car a large canvas, upon which a flaming advertisement was painted in striking colors of the cattle at or near Abilene, it was sent through to Chicago via St. Louis, eliciting a great amount of attention and newspaper comment. Upon arrival at Chicago, the buffaloes were turned upon the enclosed commons of the stockyards, and afterwards presented to Professor Gamgee, an English veterinary surgeon, who sent their stuffed hides to London.[308] This advertising feat was followed by an excursion of Illinois cattlemen to the West. The party was taken to the end of the railway track, and upon returning to Abilene, was taken upon the prairies and shown the many fine herds of cattle. Several excursionists were induced to invest, and in a few days the market assumed its wonted life and activity.[309] Indeed it seemed to rebound from the depressing effects of the Spanish fever excitement, and long before the cold weather set in, the last bullock was sold.

The year of 1868 closed with Abilene's success as a cattle market of no mean proportions assured beyond cavil or

[308] On August 27, 1868, McCoy loaded three buffaloes, three wild horses, and two elk on a railroad car at Abilene and, accompanied by two Mexicans from California, a Kansan named Thompson, and other attendants, took the animals east to give exhibitions in various cities. A buffalo killed one of the elk en route. Arriving in St. Louis early in the following month, McCoy gave performances to large and enthusiastic audiences at Laclede Park on September 5 and 8. Among the acts of skill displayed were throwing wild steers with and without a lariat; capturing the elk, wild horses, and buffaloes with a lariat; and other feats of horsemanship. The Mexicans were dressed in black velvet pants, red sashes, and colored shirts, carried rawhide lariats about sixty feet long, and rode "spirited ponies." A St. Louis newspaper commented: "The whole affair was a great success." On September 9, McCoy passed through Springfield, Illinois, on the way to Chicago. *Junction City Weekly Union*, Sept. 5, 1868; *Daily Missouri Republican*, Sept. 4, 6, 1868; *Daily Illinois State Journal*, Sept. 1, 5, 10, 1868; *Trail Drivers of Texas* (Hunter, ed.), 99-101.

[309] McCoy advertised this "buffalo hunt" in various newspapers. One of the advertisements read in part: "Grand Excursion to the Far West! A Wild and Exciting Chase after the Buffalo, on his Native Plain. . . This Excursion is gotten up expressly for those directly interested and engaged in the Live Stock Trade (other parties invited expected). Every provision for luxury and comfort will be found provided for a large number of sportsmen. A number of horses and equipments will be provided. Parties must bring their own firearms. . . Parties wishing to bring ladies with them . . . will find at Abilene . . . a commodious, first-class Hotel. . . Every effort will be made to make this *The Grand Excursion Hunt* of the Season, if not of the West. . . *Kansas State Record*, Sept. 3, 1868. See also *Daily Illinois State Journal*, Sept. 1, 1868.

doubt. Indeed, Texan cattle became suddenly very popular and in great demand for packing purposes, and those of suitable size and quality outsold the shorthorns of the same weights. It was held that a fat Texan was better for packing purposes than a native; that their meat was marbled, that is, the fat distributed in alternate layers with the lean fiber, and when cut presents the appearance of variegated marble. The fall of 1868 afforded the first brief season in which a dollar could be made by shipping Texan cattle to market, during which time the parties who had expended so much labor and money at Abilene and had sustained such great losses were able to cover a small portion thereof.

[184] The speculation in buying and shipping cattle was not their chief source of profit, but there existed a written contract between the Kansas Pacific Railway and themselves, wherein the railway company agreed to pay them one-eighth of the gross amount of freights that they would procure to be shipped over the railway east from Abilene. It was upon, or in consideration of, the guarantees of this contract that they had made such lavish expenditures of money and labor to establish a permanent cattle market and shipping depot at Abilene. The contract was not limited as to time, but was, by its terms, as perpetual and binding as the charter upon which the road was built.[310] The Illinoisans very naturally

---

310 McCoy is writing about the agreement of 1868. In that year a written contract was drawn up between William K. McCoy & Brothers and the Union Pacific Railroad, Eastern Division (later called the Kansas Pacific Railway), which was probably signed for the railroad by Adna Anderson, of Lawrence, Kansas, its general superintendent. Neither Joseph G. McCoy nor the company introduced this agreement as evidence in the former's suit against the latter during 1870 and 1871, although both parties then admitted that such a document had been signed. The contract provided that the railroad was to pay the McCoy Brothers some money for each carload of cattle shipped from Abilene in 1868. Joseph's attorneys claimed that the amount was five dollars a carload and that he had been paid that sum for 1868; Anderson asserted that it was "a certain sum for each car load of cattle shipped"; and Perry, the president, said that "there was an arrangement by which the McCoys received a sum of money as a drawback upon the amount of shipments of cattle made from Abilene in 1868." The railroad officials and McCoy had different opinions about the duration of this contract, the former claiming that it terminated with the year 1868 and the latter that it was for an indefinite length of time. Besides, an agreement existed, which was not a part of the written contract, that the railroad was to com-

thought that if they could but establish, beyond competition, Abilene as the place to sell and ship cattle, no matter at what cost in 1868, that in future years they would have but an easy time and but little effort to reap great profit; not dreaming for a moment but what the railway company would stand up manly and honorably to its part of the contract. But in this they soon found they were in great error. When the railway offices at St. Louis were visited for the purpose of settling up for the first season's work,[311] in which about twenty-five hundred cars of cattle had been loaded at Abilene, they were blandly informed by the executive committee of the railway company that the committee had concluded that it had made a mistake in making such a contract and had determined to demand the cancellation thereof; and until that demand was complied with, the railway company would pay no part of the amount or sum already earned, and in future years would not furnish a single car to any parties desiring to load at Abilene. This was the style and character of honor, the recompense, the honorable treatment (?) the little piping president had assured in the beginning would be accorded to such parties as would load their trains with eastward-bound freight. It was honesty and honor indeed (?) with a vengeance. It was idle to remonstrate, or point out the labors, losses, and expenditures which had been incurred [185] to open up and establish the cattle trade. It was futile to show them wherein they were acting in mean, bad faith, or how their proposed course would bring financial ruin on the heads of their best friends and servants. To all such appeals the committee was as deaf and callous, as mean, dishonest, avaricious men could be.

Rather than to cancel that contract, the Illinoisans offered all the establishments for the convenience of cattle trade at Abilene, for one-fourth of their cost; but this the com-

pensate the McCoy Brothers for yarding and loading the cattle – charges which the McCoys made but which the railroad collected for them from the individual shippers. McCoy vs. the Kansas Pacific Railway Company, 17, 40-41, 43, 52, 54, MS., Supreme Court of Kansas; *Brief of the Defendant in Error, Kansas Pacific Railway Company vs. McCoy*, 10, 13-14.

311 The shipping season of 1868, which was the first under the contract of that year.

mittee would not accept – nothing but cancellation would it have. To obtain this, it proposed to make a contract at a lower rate, such as it claimed the railway company could afford to give and the Illinoisans afford to work for; but without cancellation of the original contract it would do nothing but fight and seek to ruin the very men that in the beginning it so cordially pledged itself to uphold and sustain. After several ineffectual efforts to adjust matters and obtain the money so dearly earned, the Illinoisans decided, rather than to enter into a legal contest, to accede to the committee's unjust demand for cancellation, and then for two of the three brothers to withdraw from any connection with the Abilene enterprise and leave the younger one (who had first conceived the project) to continue its operation. When this was done (the contract canceled), the money was paid – an amount not equal to one-third of the expenditures incurred by the Illinoisans previously in establishing the cattle market and shipping depot at Abilene.[312]

---

[312] The contract of 1868 was annulled in February, 1869. McCoy testified in 1871: "In February, 1869, at the time of cancelling the contract made the year before, he [Perry] agreed if we would agree to cancel this contract he would make another contract with us at a lower rate." At no time during the court proceedings did McCoy claim that the railroad refused to pay him for 1868 unless he consented to void the agreement of that year. Perry, in a deposition made on September 17, 1870, asserted: "When the interview was had at the time the contract was cancelled, the McCoys claimed that it was for an indefinite period, and not for a year. The reason why the contract was cancelled was that the company wished for no outstanding paper although we thought it terminated itself at the end of the year." In the same document Perry made an evasive answer to a question whether he had promised to make another agreement with McCoy if the latter consented to void the contract of 1868. Both parties admitted that the official paper annulling the agreement of 1868 contained no provisions for renewing that instrument at a lower rate. As for McCoy's compensation, he testified: "I received in 1868 about $13,000 from the Rail Road Co." Whether this sum was for 1868, or for 1867 and 1868, he did not state. Perry's deposition in 1870 claimed that the railroad had paid the McCoy Brothers "from fifteen to eighteen thousand dollars," but for what period of time and for what specific services he failed to make clear. Whatever amount the McCoy Brothers received from the railroad for their services in 1868, it is certain that some of the compensation was for yarding and loading longhorns, and the rest was a bonus of a certain sum for each carload of cattle shipped from Abilene. The editor has not ascertained whether the McCoys were paid in full for their services in 1868. The railroad's gross receipts from

During the pending of the controversy between the railroad company and the Illinoisans, the legislature of Illinois met in regular session. From the Danville senatorial district, which included Tolono and most all that portion of country which had suffered losses by the introduction of Texan cattle via the Mississippi river, came a state senator elected and specially deputed to secure the passage of an act totally prohibiting the introduction of Texan cattle into the state of Illinois. And in pursuance of this purpose he introduced a bill, [186] the provisions of which were absolute prohibition of longhorn kine, no matter where raised, wintered, or fatted. It was impossible for language to convey or express stronger proscriptive provisions than those found in that bill. It was not only sweeping in its provisions as to southern cattle, but at all times of the year and under all circumstances, even proposing to debar southern cattle from passing through the state by rail or otherwise to the eastern markets. In short, its provisions could not have been made more prohibitory, nor its penalties for violation scarce more severe. Inasmuch as the state of Illinois extends from Lake Michigan to the Ohio river, every car of freight from the West, whether dead or alive, must pass through it in order to reach the eastern markets, there being no available practical routes either south or north of it to the eastern cities. Therefore the success of that measure as introduced would have been not only ruin to the southern cattle trade and all those engaged in it, but absolute ruin to the Abilene enterprise.[313]

To defeat the measure, or at least modify it, absorbed the undivided attention of the younger Illinoisan, who held the Abilene enterprise so near his heart. During a session

Abilene in 1868 were about $123,000. McCoy vs. the Kansas Pacific Railway Company, 13-15, 17, 20, 44-45, MS., Supreme Court of Kansas; *Brief of the Defendant in Error, Kansas Pacific Railway Company vs. McCoy*, 10-11, 14.

[313] Senator John L. Tincher, a banker from Danville, was born in Indiana about 1821. On January 7, 1869, he introduced a bill prohibiting the introduction of Texas or Cherokee cattle into Illinois between February 1 and November 1 of each year. Illinois, *Senate Journal*, 26 Gen. Assem., regular sess., vol. I, p. 162; *Manual of the Twenty-Sixth General Assembly of the State of Illinois* (Jos. R. Howlett, compiler, Lanark, Ill., 1869), 59; *Gazette and Union*, Jan. 27, 1869.

of seventy-two days he could have been seen watching and resisting that bill in all its various stages of passage. In the senate, where the principal fight was made, the bill had some active enemies, and often could the young Illinoisan have been seen in earnest consultation with them, discussing or devising plans to defeat or modify the measure or so amend it that wholesale ruin would not be entailed upon him. It was plain that unless there was some place where Texan cattle could be unloaded, no one would care to load or ship any of them, and if none were shipped, nothing could be made out of the Abilene enterprise. That measure did not go before a committee that he did not there meet and fight it direct, or by delaying action upon it. It was perfectly unaccountable how the clerk of the committee would forget the manuscript of the bill at his room, always too far off to permit him to [187] go and get it in time for that session of the committee. Then the next meeting a part of the committee would be unavoidably absent, attending the sessions of some other committee, or off on a big drunk, if nothing else. No quorum being present, an adjournment would occur. When its consideration was had, a great effort was made to secure the adoption of a substitute, which provided ample guarantees and provisions a thousand times better calculated to be regarded and enforced to protect the shorthorn cattle from disease than all absolute prohibitory measures ever enacted by legislatures. But the famous convention of experts had recommended prohibition, and no other idea or principle could be successfully presented. It was found impossible to defeat the measure outright, but upon its final passage in the senate, an amendment permitting wintered Texan or southern cattle to come at any time, was adopted. The evidence that the cattle had been so wintered should be the certificate of any officer "bearing seal." This amendment was adopted by one majority only, but that was enough. The Illinoisan was satisfied to have the bill (with the amendment) enacted; and to guard it and prevent the amendment from being stricken off by the author of the bill, became his daily care.

The senator from Danville swore terribly, charging that the very vitals of his pet measure were cut out by the amend-

ment and that he should see that the bill was restored to its
pristine provisions. To prevent this, resort was made to the
tactics of delay. It was astonishing how long it took the
public printer to print the bill, and then it took the public
binder at least a week to accomplish what he might have
done in a few hours.[314] When the bill went before the lower
house of the legislature, it was, after an inexplicable delay,
referred to the proper committee. It seemed next thing to an
impossibility for that committee to get a quorum at the
sittings at which that bill was to be considered, and then
when it finally got together, the clerk thereof, who had in
custody the bill, was reported at his room fully a mile
away, [188] too sick to attend; so another series of adjourn-
ments were had. Finally, near the end of the legislative
session the committee hastily considered the measure, and
unanimously decided to report it just as it was, without
alteration. It was feared that if the senate amendment was
stricken off, the time would be too short to pass it. Then the
amended bill (although it was plain, so far as its prohibition
clauses were concerned, would be a dead letter on the statute
books) would perhaps satisfy the enraged populace of the
Danville district. So it was passed on the last day of the
session, just as it came from the senate, and was signed,
although reluctantly, by the governor, and thus became a
law.[315]

[314] On January 7, 1869, Tincher's bill, called senate bill 98, was referred
to the committee on agriculture. He reported it out of the committee on
January 26 "by a substitute, and recommended the passage of the substitute";
on the same day the substitute was laid on the table and ordered to be
printed. On February 9 it was engrossed. The substitute bill passed the
senate on February 24 by a vote of 16 to 8, Tincher casting his ballot in the
affirmative. Illinois, *Senate Journal*, 26 Gen. Assem., regular sess., vol. I,
pp. 162, 348, 563, 822-823.

[315] On February 24 the house received the senate bill and two days later
referred it to the committee on manufactures and agriculture. On March 6,
by a vote of 67 to 5, the house passed the bill, with amendments. The amendments were concurred in by the senate on April 16, and the governor signed
the bill on the same day. *Ibid.*, vol. II, pp. 317, 961; Illinois, *House Journal*,
26 Gen. Assem., regular sess., vol. II, pp. 282, 408, 793, 804, vol. III, pp. 718,
749. The portion of the act which McCoy was responsible for was found in
section 9: "PROVIDED, it shall not apply to section one of this act, when such
Texas or Cherokee cattle shall have been introduced into either the states

Perhaps no severer struggle against overwhelming numbers was ever witnessed in the history of the legislation of Illinois, where one man, an inexperienced lobbyist, a mere cattleman without means and almost unaided, successfully combated a measure of which nine-tenths of the lower house and a majority of the senate were in favor; he practically defeated it by securing the adoption of such amendments as made its principal and objectionable clauses entirely inoperative and worthless.[316] For it was astonishing the following summer how many "wintered cattle" arrived at Abilene. In fact, it was found difficult to get a steer or cow four or five years old without it having been "wintered" somewhere. And as to those "certificates under seal," there was no trouble to procure them in abundance of a hatchet-faced, black-headed limb of the law, a veritable notary public, at Abilene. He was one of those unprincipled, petty demagogues whose highest idea of professional honor was to disclose the secrets of his client's business to anyone who would give him a pittance therefor; one who never failed to betray his employer, or engage in any low scavenger work for which he could get pay, no matter how small the sum; who to this day is more widely known for his infamy than his ability. He had been for months oscillating between beggary and starvation, [189] and was only too glad of the opportunity to "manufacture" certificates by the dozen or the cartload for a small consideration. Thus he became a convenience to enable cattle shippers to evade Illinois' high sounding prohibitory legislation.

of Kansas, Missouri, Nebraska, Iowa or Wisconsin prior to the first of January, before being brought into this state; but the burthen of alleging and proving that such cattle were introduced in either of the states above mentioned prior to January first and wintered there the remainder of the winter, shall be upon the defendant: PROVIDED, FURTHER, that the official certificate of the county clerk of the county where such cattle have been wintered shall be *prima facie* evidence thereof." *Public Laws of Illinois, 1869*, p. 405.

[316] In 1871, McCoy testified: "I was at great expense in Springfield that winter [1868-1869]. I spent $2000 in paying board of self and wife, and in various other ways there. It was spent directly and indirectly in shaping legislation so as to allow Texas cattle to come into and go through the State of Illinois." McCoy vs. the Kansas Pacific Railway Company, 16, MS., Supreme Court of Kansas.

Indeed, the long-protracted effort of the legislature of Illinois in bringing forth that great abortion, only served to again advertise Abilene and Texan cattle, much as did the convention of experts, and create an increased feeling in favor of Texan cattle and a widespread desire to handle them; so that when the season of 1869 opened, more buyers than ever before put in an appearance at Abilene, and trade was decidedly lively at astonishingly good prices. Many herds of good beeves were taken at from twenty-five to thirty-five dollars per head. A brisk demand sprang up for Texan stock cattle for ranching purposes in the West.

Before the opening of the cattle season, the young Illinoisan visited the railway general offices at St. Louis and made a contract with the executive committee of the Kansas Pacific Railway, and then proceeded to Kansas and put all things in readiness for a good season's business.[317] However, since the executive committee had acted in such bad faith, not to say dishonorable and mean, concerning the previous

[317] In February, 1869, according to McCoy, when the agreement of the previous year was annulled, Perry promised to make another one with him at a lower rate and asked him to come to St. Louis to interview the executive committee of the board of directors. McCoy saw the president and the committee in St. Louis about March 1, again in Lawrence, Kansas, about April 1, and at least once subsequently, but each time Perry gave some excuse to defer completing the contract. When McCoy was in St. Louis on business sometime in March, he met Adna Anderson, general superintendent, who assured him that the railroad would continue to collect his yarding and loading charges from the individual shippers during 1869. Finally, on or about April 10, 1869, at Perry's invitation, Joseph McCoy, accompanied by his brother, James, interviewed the president and executive committee in Perry's office opposite the Southern Hotel in St. Louis. Joseph asked for a payment of five dollars for each carload of cattle shipped from Abilene in 1869, and, in addition, special freight rates for his own longhorns during the same time. Perry, after consultation with the committee, refused to grant McCoy any special freight rates, but said: "[We] have determined to give you $2.50 per car, for each and every car load of live stock, that you obtain and load on our cars at Abilene, during the year 1869." Although Joseph complained that the offer was too low, he finally accepted it. Perry, however, refused to put this agreement in writing. When McCoy asked the president how he would get his money, Perry replied: "At the end of the cattle shipping season, come down here and bring with you a certificate of the number of car loads shipped during the season, and I will see that the money is paid to you here." Perry also confirmed the verbal promise made by Anderson to McCoy in March. *Ibid.*, 7-10, 13-16, 19-22, 27, 40-42, 45, 48, 52-53, 56, 63, 67.

contract, the Illinoisan decided to dispose of the Drover's Cottage and such other real property, except the shipping yards, as he held at Abilene, so that he would not be so completely at the mercy of the unprincipled, avaricious executive committee. For it had already been seen that so long as much money was invested in large buildings which, without a cattle trade, would not be worth three per cent of their cost, the railway company had a great advantage with which to work oppression. No one would care to own a hotel with capacity to accommodate one or two hundred guests, located in the midst of an unsettled plain, where, without a foreign commerce, it could have no adequate paying custom. This state of affairs constituted the advantage that the railway executive [190] committee held of the Illinoisans; and the committee well understood it and did not hesitate or scruple to take advantage of it, and thus compel the cancellation of the original contract made with the Illinoisans. It was plain that without a cattle trade the thirty-five thousand dollars invested at Abilene in necessary accommodations for doing a large cattle business would have been almost a total loss.

Before the first of May, 1869, the advance herds of a drive of one hundred and fifty thousand head began to arrive, and soon many buyers were in attendance from every northern and western territory; even California, Nevada, and Washington Territory buyers were in attendance. Cattle changed hands at very satisfactory prices to the Texan drovers. The lately passed prohibitory law deterred for a few months the usual quota of Illinois buyers, for they did not know, and it took a little time for them to learn, that so many "wintered cattle" were at Abilene. But they, too, soon became initiated, and were out in full force to swell the number of buyers. Indeed, it seemed that Abilene was destined to survive in spite of the Spanish fever, conventions of experts, and hostile legislation.[318]

[318] During July, 1869, the *Junction City Weekly Union* published two reports of cattle sales at Abilene. The first, which appeared on July 17, read as follows: "We are indebted to G. A. Wills, Esq., for the following partial report of transactions for the first four days of last week, and this we are informed, is only about one quarter of the transactions of the previous week: 580 second class steers at $23.00 each; 360 second class at $24.00

If it did not fail, it was not the fault of the Kansas Pacific Railway's executive committee and their superintendent, who was a cold, calculating man, not overscrupulous, and one in whom it was absolutely impossible to inspire or awaken the smallest particle of warmth or enthusiasm. Indeed, he well merited the appellation of "Old Frigidity," from his near resemblance to an iceberg. But he was, like his employers, not overscrupulous about repudiating contracts. It was a day of general rejoicing among the attachés and employees of the railway when he took his departure and gave place to another, in whom a little blood and the "milk of human kindness" could be found. Instead of the railway company coöperating with Abilene, as they had engaged to do, and as anyone would naturally suppose they would have done to make it the shipping depot, the cattle point, and by [191] such concentrated effort build up a permanent cattle market on the line of the road — instead of this, they began to intrigue and devise plans to divert as much of the cattle trade to other points on the road as possible. In pursuance of this plan they repudiated every former engagement made, and spent many thousands of dollars in building shipping yards at Brookville (a town laid out and owned by the railway company or the managers thereof) and at other points west of Abilene, and gave lower rates of freight per car per mile than was given from Abilene.

each; one drove 700 head at 2½ gross; 700 head mixed cattle – average – at $25.00; 20 yoke work cattle, poor, at $70.00 per yoke; 3000 head beef steers, second class, at $22.50; 360 do. average at $24. Several lots of wintered Texas cattle, from one to four years old, sold at three cents gross. 6000 head left during the week for Salt Lake; 400 for Montana; 1000 for Omaha; and 300 for Idaho. There are now remaining for sale in the Abilene market 12,000 steers and 10,000 mixed cattle which are expected to be wintered here." The second report was published on July 31: "We have received the following transactions in cattle at Abilene, to date, including sales of last week: 4000 head @ $23.00; 5000 head at $24.00; 800 head stock cattle @ $12.50; 300 extra @ $26.00; 600 extra @ $26.00; 200 average @ $25.00; 150 extra good @ $28.00; 400 head @ 3¼ cts. per lb. gross; 1000 stock cattle @ $12.00. In addition to the above about 1000 head of stock cattle were sold for the western market – Colorado, Montana and Idaho – eight hundred were sold for the Montana market alone. The number of cattle at present is rather slim, but large herds are expected daily. In the course of a few weeks the prairies will be literally black with herds."

Great efforts were made to induce the company to withdraw such lands from market as they owned in the west half of Dickinson county and hold them as a reserve for grazing purposes; and to secure such congressional legislation as would have established a national highway on or about the sixth principal meridian, over which the cattle commerce of Texas could and would have flowed on to the line of their road for many years undisturbed by state legislation. But no such enlightened and intelligent policy found favor with the railway company. Theirs was one of narrow selfishness, such as induced them to hazard the loss of the cattle trade by dividing and diverting it to points where they owned a part, at least, of the town site. Indeed, it was the custom of the junta who built and first operated the Kansas Pacific Railway to compel the owner of any town site along their line to give them one-fourth to one-half the town site. In penalty for refusing to comply with the demands, no depot accommodations would be furnished, no matter how much business was done at the station. Thus, the proprietors of Abilene gave the railway company the right of way – a strip of land one hundred feet wide, through a section of land a distance of one mile, and for the distance of one-fourth of a mile gave an additional strip of two hundred feet – all in consideration that a good depot should at once be erected. The deed conveying the land was made and recorded; but what was the surprise and [192] chagrin of the proprietors of the town when they saw, after tedious delay, a shabby clapboard shanty, twelve by fourteen feet in dimensions, put up on blocks with a pent-up platform, as "the ample depot accommodations." The whole structure could not have cost over one hundred and fifty dollars, and was not as good as a humane man would provide for a donkey stable. In it was to be found accommodations (?) for freight arriving and departing, a freight office, a telegraph office, a ticket office, a baggage room, a gentlemen and ladies' waiting room. The balance of the enclosed space we suppose was devoted to the agent, in which to practice the art of gentility and politeness; at any rate he was a rare gem illustrative of all those graces. When the railway company was remonstrated with, it coolly demanded one-half

the town site, both of the land laid off in lots and the balance outlying. This modest (?) request was declined; but
as a punishment no better depot was built for four or five
years. This may be taken as an index of character of the
junta and its manner of treating other towns along its line.
In fact, its tactics and practice were to induce men of energy
and means, by fair promises and advantageous contracts,
to locate and invest their money and labor at some point on
the line, and then remorselessly crush and financially ruin
them. It did not scruple to repudiate contracts or act in any
manner that would accomplish its mercenary purpose. It is
as fortunate for the welfare of the public as it is for the
interests of the stockholders of the railway that the administration and management of that line have been changed,
and men installed in power who respect the rights of private
individuals, and who, by pursuing an honorable course, have
and are making friends for the railway as fast as its former
management made enemies, which is at a rapid rate.

The cattle season of 1869 brought to Abilene many local
traders and shippers – men who bought and sold on the
prairie, and men who bought and shipped to the eastern
markets. The latter class are commonly called "cattle shippers," and such as [193] appeared on the western markets
were usually young men of energy and more or less good
judgment, who made it their special business to keep posted
on the condition of the eastern markets and (especially)
just where they could profitably place a carload or two of fat
cows or butcher's steers. The local dealers and shippers
were ever wide-awake, looking for chances to invest their
usually small capital in a little herd or bunch of cattle such
as they would know just where to place. Of this class of
shippers, perhaps no better type could be found than Charley
Strausenbach, a veritable Dutch boy, as his name would
indicate; one who came to America in his extreme youth
and has spent many years roaming over the North American
continent, and has tried every clime and business, from sailing as ship's butcher on a Pacific mail steamer, to driving
goats from Lower into Upper California and even into
British America and retailing their carcasses [194] to the
miners, as mutton, antelope, or venison, just as suited the

JOHN B. HUNTER OF ILLINOIS.

THOMAS J. ALLEN.

CHARLEY STRAUSENBACH.

whim or taste of his customer. If there is any corner on the continent he has not been in, it is not now known. He is one of those "stubby, pluggy," irrepressible Dutchmen who is always doing something, be it much or little; always ready to have a good time, to go anywhere, to see anything. In business he is shrewd and honorable, loves very well to make money, and full as well to spend it. He would as soon buy a thousand cattle as a dozen, but never takes the blues if he can't buy one. He is full of energy and get up, always looking for a chance to make a good speculation. Annually he is found on the frontier market, and there are but few drovers who do not know Charley and have for him a hearty welcome. Perhaps the entire list of local cattle shippers of the West could not produce a more eccentric character than he, and certainly none has wider acquaintance with the drovers and cowboys.

But there is another class of shippers who do business on a different scale – those who buy of the largest, fattest herds of fresh-driven cattle, or such as have been wintered in the northern states and are maturely fatted. Usually this class of shippers send their consignments to eastern markets, often to the Atlantic cities. This class of operators require a much larger capital than the local shipper or he who sells his stock in the first market he reaches.

There are many good young men engaged in the perilous, or hazardous, business of cattle shipping. It requires a man of more than ordinary good cattle sense and business judgment and prudence, besides considerable capital, to be able to continue the business of cattle shipping for any great length of time without becoming bankrupt. Every western cattle market annually ruins a full score of young, ambitious, energetic cattle shippers, who begin with a few thousands, or perhaps only hundreds, of dollars, and essay to take the city of good fortune and great wealth by storm; or attempt to climb the slippery pole of speculation, and thus [195] avoid the slow and long plodding way of constant labor and small annual profits. But, "alas, poor Yorick!" they are numbered soon among the operators that were; and moodily meditating upon the mutability of things earthly, feeling very much like joining some church, teaching Sunday school, or going as missionary to some far-off isle, drop out of sight and give place to their successors, who are crowding close upon their heels, more than overanxious to plunge into the inviting waters of speculation, only in turn to be swallowed up in the inevitable maelstrom of ruin. Strychnine is not more certain death when swallowed into the physical system than is persistent cattle shipping to the financial body. It has been truly said that whatever Deity may have made or ordained, He has not yet created the man who can persistently ship cattle upon the system the business is usually done in the West for a term of ten years without an aggregate loss greater than his gains. Usually in half that time, or less, the losses are greater than the gains and capital combined. One of the principal reasons for this is that the cattle shipper becomes reckless, loses his wonted caution, and buys to receive in the future, by which time the markets are often much lower than the one upon the basis of which he made the purchase. Again, the market is quite liable to decline between the time of shipment and arrival at destination. The cattle market is one of frequent violent and sudden fluctuations, and shippers generally meet more downward fluctuations than any other kind.

But we introduce our reader to Thomas J. Allen, a cattle shipper who is fast becoming well and extensively known throughout the West. He is of that florid complexion and impulsive temperament well calculated, if not necessary, to constitute a cattle speculator and shipper. Born in Illinois on a farm, and closely drilled in that staid vocation, from which he gradually deviated by feeding live stock for four or five years; annually shipping it to market, and just taking along "a few of his neighbor's to pay expenses," which, of [196] course, they do. The first ventures were nearly always successful; and the money seemed so easily made that he finally decided to leave the slow-plodding ploughman's life, and go west and try his hand exclusively in the great faro game of cattle shipping. Not content to stop at Kansas City or the near West, he entered the very recesses of the Rocky mountains and brought from the far-famed valleys of San Louis, Wet mountain, and South Park fully five thousand head of fatted cattle, climbing with his herds over the snow-clad peaks in mid-August's hottest day. A more inspiring, beautifully picturesque scene was never beheld than the long-drawn-out line of fat bovines following their leader up the mountain gorges, over vast snowdrifts, up among the ancient peaks where Old Boreas and Hoary Winter hold perpetual sway over loftiest realms. But Mr. Allen is not the man to be daunted by obstacles or serious difficulties, and more than one herd of [197] cattle listened to the echo of his voice of command among the granite peaks and yawning canyons of the snowy range. He had the distinguished privilege of shipping the first trainload of cattle from Denver, Colorado. He is a young man of fine energy, affable address, and one who has many friends in the West. It matters little whether Dame Fortune smiles or frowns, he is ever up and doing. His persistent perseverance will always lead him into business, and the great, broad, new West affords ample opportunities and facilities for men of his type to lay well the foundations and build strong and high the superstructure of great wealth; and Mr. Allen is just the man to improve well his great opportunities.

Few men gain national reputation as cattle shippers, for but few men's money will last long enough; or, in other words, few can manage to weather adverse markets, bad purchases, and occasional mismanagement for any considerable length of time. Perhaps there is not a better specimen of a persistent live stock shipper in the United States, if in the world, than John B. Hunter, of Illinois, which is the state of his nativity.[319] [He is] a man of near threescore years, and since his earliest manhood, has been engaged marketing live stock. At first, his capital being quite limited, he was able to buy not above twenty-five head of cattle at one time. These he would drive to the St. Louis market, then the principal, if not the only, one in the West, there being no such thing in the West as a railroad. In this small way did he begin his trading life, and by diligence, energy, and

---

[319] John B. Hunter inserted the following advertisement in McCoy's book: "Jno. B. Hunter & Co., Live Stock, Commission, and Forwarding Merchants. Office, No. 2 Exchange Building, Saint Louis National Stock Yards, East St. Louis, Ill. Particular Attention given to Forwarding Stock." For a brief sketch of John B. Hunter, partly based on McCoy's book, see Powell, *op. cit.*, 176-177.

persistent application to business, never shrinking from doing the most irksome portions of the necessary labor with
his own hands, lay the foundation of a substantial fortune.
Indeed, there has been times in the last twenty years that
he could have retired from business with a handsome competence, if not actual great wealth. As year by year passed
away, his business steadily increased, his droves became
larger and larger, until he became to be recognized as the
largest operator in the St. Louis live stock market. [199]
In his early business years, when the season arrived for
moving the hog crop of the country, he was among the most
active, often driving thousands, and sending numbers of
teams loaded with hogs such as were too fat to travel on
foot, not hesitating if need be to drive a team with his own
hands. In later years, when the live stock trade of the Mississippi valley developed into larger proportions, his growth
in business was commensurate therewith. All the while he
was devoting his attention to the live stock traffic, he was
not unmindful of his farming interests. His first purchase
was a small tract of scarce more than forty acres of tillable
land, to which he added such other tracts as time and his improved circumstances would permit. Finally, after a series
of successful operations, he purchased a fine large farm
near Greenville, the finest tract of land in the county. Upon
this he made his permanent home. During the war he furnished many thousands of cattle to the Union armies. At its
close he returned to cattle shipping, generally to the Philadelphia market, but lately to New York.

There are few departments or phases of the live stock
business of the Northwest or West that he is not familiar
with, and of which he has not a practical knowledge obtained by actual experience therein. From his earliest manhood he has been a feeder of live stock, often on a very large
scale and in every known manner of feeding; in yards upon
corn, and in pastures, hay or cornstalks, and in the stillhouse,
he has been an extensive and successful cattle feeder. He
was among the first to full and successfully cornfeed large
lots of Texan cattle, at which he has had extraordinary success. By an extensive and liberal series of experiments he
demonstrated the superiority of shelled corn as being the

best food upon which to fatten Texan cattle, and by that manner of feeding has produced extraordinary good fat cattle in short periods of time. A small herd of Texan cattle fed by him were successfully exhibited at Kansas City during the Exposition of 1873, [200] and were pronounced the fattest ever seen. The herd averaged near two thousand pounds. During 1870 he extended his operations west, and was among the heaviest operators and shippers from Abilene and other western points. But few Texan drovers do not know his familiar name, and but few have not had business transactions with him. His cattle shipments reached the enormous aggregate of from forty to sixty thousand head annually. The capital to conduct so large a business must necessarily be very large, and the men in his employ – clerks, shippers, drivers, and assistants – were little less than a formidable army.

Of course, in a business of such magnitude the losses or profits must be large, for so large a game is never an even draw. Previous to the great panic of 1873 he was the only man in the United States who had managed to ship live stock constantly for a score or more of years without meeting such [201] severe losses as to compel a suspension of business. But when that great panic came, the men who were doing the most business – consequently were the most extended – were the ones that suffered most. Indeed, it was safe and correct to conclude when a man, firm, or bank boasted that they did not feel the effects of the crisis, that they were doing little or no business. John B. Hunter stood at the head of a firm, or house, which, at the beginning of the panic, was in the midst of handling a large number of cattle, amounting to many thousands of head, which had been bought at a previous time, when no human foresight could have seen the impending financial storm which wrecked so many of the strongest men and business institutions of the United States. His losses were very severe; this, coupled with the persistent continuance of the financial stringency, compelled a suspension of the house, which many hundred friends sincerely hope and believe will be but temporary. The event cast a deep gloom over the entire cattle business of the West, and precipitated events of a disastrous nature from which it will require years for Kansas City and the western cattle trade to recuperate. Mr. J. B. Hunter is a man of quiet turn and but few words; a solid, substantial man, and one who has ever borne a high reputation for honorable, liberal dealing; one who commands the highest respect of those who know him best; a man of steady, temperate business habits, and one of indefatigable energy and fine, sound judgment in all matters pertaining to live stock; a good financier; in short, a genuine upright, self-made man, who has done great good to his fellow man and deserves to be entitled a benefactor.

PREMIUM TEXAS CATTLE FED BY JOHN B. HUNTER.

XI. THE RAILROAD REPUDIATES
ITS CONTRACT

When the cattle trade at Abilene had withstood so much bitter and powerful opposition, and still continued to increase, everyone conceded its success, and most of its opponents and competitors abandoned the contest. Abilene had become a synonym for Texan cattle, and as a great cattle market, as widely known as any other one in the United States. The receipts of cattle each year doubled those of the previous one. Thus in 1867 thirty-five thousand cattle arrived, in 1868 seventy-five thousand, and in 1869 fully one hundred and fifty thousand.[320] Throughout the stock regions of Texas it was recognized as the only cattle market in which any considerable number of stock could be sold. It certainly was the first depot or shipping market Texan drovers ever had to which they could come unmolested by mobs or hostile legislation. Perhaps no point or

---

[320] This estimate is identical with the one made by McCoy to a newspaper correspondent at Newton, Kansas, in August, 1871. But the number given in the United States Census of 1880, for which McCoy was also responsible, is 350,000. Although the latter figure is an obvious typographical error for 150,000, it has been used as an authentic estimate by all writers on the cattle trade. The *Abilene Chronicle* (Mar. 3, 1870) asserted: "During the season of 1869, about 160,000 head of cattle were sold in this market." Approximately 40,000 longhorns were shipped from Abilene by railroad during 1869, according to the official records of the Kansas Pacific Railway. David R. Gorden, the railway's agent at Abilene in 1869, gave the following statistics of the carloads of cattle shipped from McCoy's Great Western Stockyards during each month of that year: January, 2; March, 21; May, 11; June, 7; July, 149; August, 221; September, 391; October, 999; November, 210; December, 6; total, 2017. McCoy vs. the Kansas Pacific Railway Company, 24, 61, MS., Supreme Court of Kansas; *Tenth Census of the United States,* III (*Agriculture*), 975; Kansas Pacific Railway Co., *Guide Map of the Great Texas Cattle Trail,* 8; *Republican Daily Journal,* Aug. 6, Sept. 7, 1869; *Abilene Chronicle,* Mar. 3, 1870; *Kansas Daily Commonwealth,* Aug. 15, 1871.

village of its size ever had been so thoroughly advertised or had acquired such widespread fame.

One at a distance would suppose from the many reports that it was a large town or city of many thousand inhabitants, instead of a small village of a few hundred denizens. One morning a newly arrived southern drover appeared in the midst of the village, and reigning up his cow pony, inquired how far and what direction it was to Abilene. He was told that he was then in the place. He could scarce [204] believe his informer, and broke forth, saying, "Now, look here, stranger, you don't mean this here little scatterin' trick is Abilene!" He was assured that it was. "Well I'll swar I never seed such a little town have such a mighty big name."

No point in the West of five times its resident population did one-half the amount of business that was done at Abilene. And in the days of its full tide in cattle business, its streets were crowded from early morning to a late hour in the night by a busy throng of merchants, traders, and other business men, besides a host of that floating population which perpetually drift from point to point wherever business centers, just as the eagles gather to the carcass. And in the eastern portion of the village, where were located the stockyards and the Drover's Cottage, which was the headquarters of the cattlemen, could have constantly been seen great numbers of cattlemen and the busiest scenes of activity: cattle arriving from the prairie for shipment; others just being yarded; others being weighed; and a full choir of men busy loading trains; empty cars arriving and others heavily loaded departing; while in every direction could be seen the cowboy hastening his pony at full speed to perform some duty. From the shipping yards to the front of the Cottage, a concourse of footmen could have been seen hurrying to and fro.[321]

Abilene's cattle commerce amounted to more than three millions of dollars yearly, and was annually increasing; aside from an immense lucrative trade in camp supplies and outfitting, from a pair of huge spurs or star-spangled top-boots

---

[321] For a description of Abilene in 1869, see *Leavenworth Times & Conservative*, June 25, 1869.

ABILENE IN ITS GLORY.

ABILENE IN ITS GLORY.

to a thimble-skein wagon. The farmers of the county had a home demand at high cash prices for every bushel of grain, peck of vegetables, pound of butter, or dozen eggs that they could possibly produce; and still it was necessary to import many carloads of these articles to supply the demand. In every direction over the county the farmers could be seen merging from their dugouts, mere hovels of dirt built in the bank of some ravine, into substantial frame houses, with other outdoor [206] improvements of a substantial character — all betokening the greatest comfort and prosperity, such as their brightest hopes had not anticipated.

During the shipping season of 1869 the Illinoisan exerted himself to his utmost to increase the shipment of cattle and to otherwise accommodate the trade, and spent no small amount of time in securing buyers for cattle who would ship them to eastern points. Indeed, it would be difficult for a man to exert himself more, or devote nearer all his time, night and day, to work and business than did he. Often, two hours' sleep would suffice him; and scarce a week passed in which he did not spend one or more nights without sleep, so determined was he to repair his damaged fortunes and to make the Abilene enterprise a complete success. For it was the undertaking of his life, and upon its success or failure he felt that not only his fortune depended, but his manhood and the respect of his relatives and friends. Perhaps there never was a project so bitterly assailed, misrepresented, and made the scapegoat of so much caloric misery and misfortune as was that at Abilene. In all this, its projector was made to share, having first conceived the project and put it into execution. Therefore its success was nearer and dearer to him than life itself, and no more cruelly withering and heart-crushing day ever dawned in its history than that upon which, by a combination of adverse circumstances coupled with bad faith, he lost the shipping yards and cattle business of Abilene.

At the close of the season he invested every dollar that he could command in a herd of nine hundred head of cattle, intending to winter them on hay and fat them on grass the following summer. The cattle were put into winter quarters along the Smoky Hill river and its tributaries. For the means to pay feed bills and other expenses during the winter, the Illinoisan expected to use the sum due him from the railway company, as per the contract made the previous spring. Over two thousand cars had been bedded, and loaded [207] with cattle at Abilene during the season of 1869, for which there was due a sum exceeding five thousand dollars.[322]

After his cattle had been placed in winter quarters, he went to the general offices of the railway company in St. Louis to effect a settlement and to get the sum due him for his services. Entering the office of the executive committee, he found all the members present except the president, who was absent in Europe, and straightway presented his business. To his dismay the vice president,[323] a burly biped of Teutonic extraction, and the treasurer,[324] a soulless, conscienceless money-lover, after scratching their pates and looking dubiously at each other, as if hesitating between acting out their honest convictions by paying the amount due or repudiating the contract, piped out in dishonest tones that they did not then know of any contract existing wherein the railway company had agreed to pay for having cattle loaded at Abilene. With such men the impulse to keep all they get is generally stronger than that to do as agreed, no matter how dearly the party to whom they may be debtor has earned the pittance claimed, or how much profit they may have received from his labors in their behalf. Such, at least, seemed to be the case with that vice president and treasurer. After one or two more urgent applications for settlement, the Illinoisan was finally insolently told by that model treasurer that he had as well leave the office, for they had decided not to pay him a cent.[325] That Shylock may make a very good railway treasurer, but were we deputed to select an honest man, he would stand as little chance of being chosen as of being struck by lightning. His conduct might have been fun and congenial pastime for him, but it was financial ruin to the Illinoisan. If that treasurer's action was

[322] 2017 carloads, at $2.50 each, amounted to $5042.50.

[323] Adolphus Meier.

[324] Carlos S. Greeley.

[325] McCoy's interview with Meier and Greeley probably took place in December, 1869.

honest or honorable, not to mention decent, it was not appreciated.

However, the Illinoisan did not desire rupture with the company, and still hoped to obtain justice without trouble [208] or having to resort to legal measures. Accordingly, he departed from the railway offices, where they would not listen to his verbal appeals, and going to his room, wrote and caused to be printed a circular letter setting forth the basis, the equity, and the justice of his claim, and making a fervid appeal to the railway management to act in good faith with him. To each one of the directors a copy of that circular letter was mailed, also one to the president to New York, in care of his banker, where it would reach him upon his landing from Europe, which event was soon expected to occur.[326] During the time expiring between those interviews, the winter passed away.

Finally, when the Illinoisan learned that the president had arrived home, he went to St. Louis to see him, for he entertained the conviction that the president would not permit so mean an outrage as his associates were disposed to perpetrate.[327] On entering the president's room, that *petite* functionary was found alone, apparently meditating upon what a queer thing it was to be a president of a railway and yet be so small a man. Arising, with a bland smile, he greeted the Illinoisan in a friendly manner, inviting him to be seated and make known his desires. This was done in a plain, moderate manner, to which the president replied that he remembered that some arrangement or contract had been

[326] McCoy's circular letter, or address, to the "executive board" of the railway was dated at Abilene, Kansas, December 30, 1869. It was introduced as evidence by the railway during the court proceedings in 1871. It read in part: "The claim is just – has been dearly earned – and we do and shall insist on its payment. We have been in all things loth to appeal to law, and greatly prefer not to do it, but unless the pittance is paid, we shall try to collect it. It so happened that at the time the agreement was made, two persons were present, by whom we can prove the contract and establish our claim." In 1871, McCoy testified that the "two persons" he had in mind were James P. McCoy, his brother, and Mr. McPherson, one of the directors of the railway. McCoy vs. the Kansas Pacific Railway Company, 59-67, MS., Supreme Court of Kansas.

[327] McCoy saw Perry in St. Louis in March or April, 1870. *Ibid.*, 12.

made, but owing to the great lapse of time and the vast number of other business matters that had occupied his attention, he could not tell just what the arrangement was, but that he would give the matter close investigation and try to do justice in the premises, and – just then the immense corporeal proportions of the Teutonic vice president hove in view at the doorway. The little president, apparently remembering the circular letter he had received at New York, suddenly jumped up on his feet and affected to have been terribly insulted forsooth, because the Illinoisan had dared say in that printed letter "that if no other means would be effectual in obtaining a settlement, he would resort to law, [and] although greatly preferring friendship to antagonism, he could not and would not purchase peace at the cost of all [209] his rights." The memory of those unpalatable, straightforward statements seemed to grate harshly upon the *petite* president and to throw him into paroxysms of rage. He assured the Illinoisan that he felt himself highly insulted, and that he did not read the circular letter but cast it with contempt under the car seat. This assurance was repeated so often that the Illinoisan felt quite certain that the irate president not only had read the whole of the letter but reread it a time or two, and then perhaps chewed it into quids and spit them out through the car window. The interview ended by the president telling the Illinoisan to "go and sue the railway company as soon as he chose," in a voice indicating that to sue a corporation over which he presided with all his might and weight would be something no insignificant mortal like a cattleman would dare have the temerity to do.[328]

At the termination of the interview the Illinoisan re-

---

[328] In March, 1871, McCoy, under oath, gave the following account of this interview with Perry: "He [Perry] asked me on what foundation I based my claim. I answered him, for obtaining and loading stock at my yard in accordance with the contract made with them in April [1869]. He said he remembered of a meeting, and we being then present, but could not remember what action was taken at the meeting. He said he couldn't remember what was said or agreed upon, but would consult his notes and letters, and if he could find any indications of any contract having been made, he would write me at Abilene and let me know. The President then got into quite a pet about my having written and printed a letter and sent him a copy." *Ibid.*

turned to Kansas, where he had spent the most of the previous winter in a terrific struggle to keep his nose above the troubled financial waters which threatened to engulf him. The constantly accruing expense and feed bills on his herd of cattle were becoming enormously large and numerous. In fact, the winter had been but a prolongation of the previous summer's struggle, only that it daily intensified, until whole weeks were spent by him without adequate rest or sleep. An iron man could not have scarce withstood such constant strain and labor, much less a man of flesh and blood. And it soon began to tell fearfully on the health of the Illinoisan.

No sooner did it become known that the railway company had repudiated its contract again with him [329] than some of his most unprincipled creditors, men who he had been the means of raising out of poverty's lowest ditch, became uneasy, [and], thinking other people were like themselves, ungrateful and dishonest, began suit for the amount of their bills. This occurred in the spring, when every resource had been exhausted by the Illinoisan to raise means, and the action of the railway company had become known. [210] Everyone has heard, and many know from sad experience, the inevitable fate of the man who is embarrassed when some uneasy, malicious creditor begins legal action against the debtor. It serves only to frighten other creditors, and then they rush onto him, bringing sudden and irretrievable ruin; whereas, often, had a little patience or decency been exercised, a brief time would have made all things good and much loss saved to the debtor. Such was the case with the Illinoisan. So soon as he saw that no longer time would be accorded him in which to shape his own affairs, he surrendered all his assets to certain creditors, even placing a mortgage upon his little cottage home and gave the proceeds thereof to his creditors. [330] Then with only a single ten-dollar note, he

---

[329] The railway paid McCoy $5872 for his yarding and loading charges in 1869, thus carrying out a part of the agreement of that year. *Ibid.*, 15.

[330] McCoy disposed of much of his property in July and August, 1869, and in February and March, 1870, indicating that he was in financial trouble before the railway repudiated its contract with him. He purchased land in Abilene during April and May, 1870. Dickinson County, Deed Record B,

withdrew from business, compelled by adversity and sickness, induced by overwork and anxiety, causing complete nervous exhaustion. The entire succeeding summer he was nearer a dead than a live man. It would tax language to tell the bitter despair, the intense physical and mental weakness and anguish, the pain and exhaustion endured that summer, as day by day dragged its hopeless, cheerless length along, only to bring a slumberless night.

But then it was refreshing to witness the action of certain quondam friends, who were in the days of prosperity all smiles, ready to laud and defend every action. So soon as adversity's day dawned, they were distant, and as cool as an iceberg, and would meet and pass their former benefactor with their backbones as rigid as if they were cast iron, and head as elevated as though they were engaged in surveying the planetary system. It was condescension, a most gracious thing, if they deigned to nod their head in cold recognition. And as to showing they had a spark of true generous manhood by lending a helping hand, or speaking a kind word of comfort or good cheer, they never thought of such a thing. Nor did they seem to be conscious that their late conduct had added greatly to the distress of the situation and had rendered themselves detestable. But they were content to daily manifest their actual [211] flunkyism and manly dignity (?) by bending the supple knee to some one whom they supposed had money. Then it was so consoling to see how "childlike and bland," not to say piously serene, the countenance of an old family friend could be whilst he modestly charged enormous commissions for trivial services, and how complacently he could pocket the gross proceeds and retire to his Sucker home and leave a wronged and outraged man to starve and be sold out of house and home. Indeed, a man in adversity has an opportunity to see how many real friends he has, and he will find but little trouble in distinguishing between the real and the spurious ones; and he will have no trouble to count the real ones upon his finger ends, and ten to one he will not need more than

485, MS., Recorder of Deeds Office, Abilene; *ibid.,* Deed Record C, 241-242, 306, 311, 336, 340, 443, 451-452, 620; *ibid.,* Deed Record J, 173.

the fingers on one hand, and perchance not more than half of those.

But a firm consciousness of rectitude of purpose and an inward sense of honorable manhood will raise a real man above any and all adverse circumstances, and lead him to pity, while he despises, the weak and heartless creatures who snap and snarl beneath his feet. Then nothing will so speedily and thoroughly develop real manhood, sterling integrity, and an intensely keen appreciation of the real, the good, and the true, as downright persistent adversity. True, at first, human nature being weak, opportunity and inducement being great, one is sorely tempted to act dishonorably, if not dishonestly. But genuine integrity and noble manhood will reassert itself in time to command, to prevent, to save. The experience of the year of 1870 will long be remembered by the Illinoisan as affording a full insight into the hollowness of human nature and the frivolous flunkyism of the majority of mankind. Besides, it taught him valuable lessons that sank deep into his heart, that would perhaps have never been learned under any other circumstances. Perhaps in life's final make-up it will be found that what was endured then has [212] had much to do in creating a correct estimate of the really meritorious and true, and, if so, will not have been in vain. Besides, had events been different, life might have been passed without having learned the intrinsic value of real, true friends and the hollow worthlessness of spurious ones. Therefore his future may be of more worth to himself and humanity than a dozen such lives as his would otherwise have been. Who can tell what an empty blank, life might have been without adversity's trenchant drilling? Indeed, this book might not have been written, and all the wondrous and important events related therein, remained undisclosed in the bosom of its author; and many of the faces herein gazed upon by the reader would have slept in oblivious graves, and the story of their life, with their names, never been rescued from obscurity and oblivion. Who can contemplate without a shudder of horror the terrible hiatus that would have occurred in the literary world had not this book been written and published!

But a serious survey of the situation would not have been uninstructive, and a retrospective view would not have been uninteresting. When that young Illinoisan left his beautiful home near the capital of the Sucker State, his heart was full of ambition to do something that would be of benefit to his fellow men as well as to himself, and he chose the enterprise developed at Abilene as the one in which he could best work. He was heard to say in a brief talk on the occasion of the shipment of the first train of cattle from Abilene that: "Whether this enterprise ultimately proves to be to our financial weal or woe, as individuals, it has been begun and will be prosecuted to the end, with the confident hope that it will be of great benefit to the people of the Southwest and the Northwest, as well as to the laboring millions of the Northeast." Such were the aims and desires that animated the projector of that enterprise. And it need not be added that the undertaking was a success, although the parties at whose expense it was made such, were repaid with [213] repudiation and financial ruin for their labors, and from a position of substantial comfort brought to one of penury. The railway company, which reaped the greatest profit from the enterprise, did perhaps the least towards making it a success, but upon the other hand acted throughout in the most ungrateful and perfidious manner. But the company has the benefit of the profit, and it also has the benefit of being placed upon record as a dishonest repudiator. If the managers' consciences twinge not at the means to which they resorted in order to acquire what they gained, and at what they did to crush and ruin the man who gave it to them, then indeed are they callous in soul. An honest man or company would not have money or commerce obtained at the expense of honor or at the cost of ruin to others.

Inasmuch as all peaceful appeals had been made in vain, and every effort to get a settlement with the railway company had proved ineffectual, there was no other alternative left for the Illinoisan than to appeal to the courts of justice. Accordingly, a suit was begun in the district court at Junction City, which, after tedious continuances, came up for hearing, and a verdict was rendered in favor of him for every dollar claimed. But with the usual perverseness of railway corporations, the case was appealed to the supreme court, where, after a moderate delay only, it was again decided in favor of the Illinoisan.[331]

So after a two years' struggle the railway company paid the amount originally claimed, and for the lack of which the Illinoisan had been bankrupted. All the bright promises and assurances given him in the beginning by the railway executive committee through its president, thus terminated, and poverty in abundance was given where emoluments had been promised. True, he obtained the amount of the judgment less expenses and attorney's fees, but it lacked only twelve days of being two years after it was due; in which time his business [214] had gone to ruin, and losses were

[331] On May 1, 1870, at Junction City, Kansas, Joseph G. McCoy filed a suit against the Kansas Pacific Railway in the district court for Davis county, alleging that it had broken its agreement of April, 1869, and asking for damages to the amount of $5127.50. This sum represented the promised compensation of $2.50 for each carload of cattle (2017 carloads) shipped from Abilene during that year ($5042.50), in addition to the costs of the suit ($85). McCoy's attorneys were Martin, White, and Austin. The case (Joseph G. McCoy, plaintiff, vs. the Kansas Pacific Railway Company, defendant) was tried during the March (1871) term of court, William H. Canfield, of Junction City, presiding judge. Joseph G. McCoy, James P. McCoy, and E. H. Osborne appeared in court to testify, whereas John D. Perry, Adolphus Meier, Carlos S. Greeley, Adna Anderson, and David R. Gorden gave testimony through depositions. On March 28, 1871, the jury returned a verdict against the railway, allowing McCoy $5042.50 damages and $80 costs. The company immediately filed a motion for a new trial, but this motion was overruled by Canfield. On April 3 it appealed the case to the supreme court of the state, where it filed a petition in error on May 17. McCoy's attorneys before the supreme court were Martin, Burns, and Case. The court then consisted of Samuel A. Kingman, of Atchison, chief justice, and D. M. Valentine, of Ottawa, and David Josiah Brewer, of Leavenworth, associate justices. The case (Kansas Pacific Railway Company, plaintiff in error, vs. Joseph G. McCoy, defendant in error) was reviewed during the July (1871) term. The opinion, written by Justice Brewer, was delivered on November 16, 1871, and affirmed the decision of the district court. In 1889, Brewer was appointed by President Harrison to the Supreme Court of the United States, where he served with distinction until his death in 1910. McCoy vs. the Kansas Pacific Railway Company, 1-83, MS., Supreme Court of Kansas; Supreme Court of Kansas, Appearance Docket C, no. 602, case no. 704, p. 104, MS., ibid.; Kansas Reports, VIII, 538-545; Brief of the Defendant in Error, Kansas Pacific Railway Company vs. McCoy, 1-18; Junction City Weekly Union, May 7, 1870, Apr. 1, 1871.

entailed upon him of many thousands of dollars. His shipping yards had passed into the hands of an inexperienced
cattleman, a stranger, for a trifle, who, in the brief space
of five months, cleared over thirteen thousand dollars, and
sold out and went home.[332] Indeed, the amount of the judgment was to the Illinoisan like giving a loaf of bread to a
man already dead from starvation – a very good thing to receive, but entirely too late. Nevertheless, he did not mourn
for his lost fortune. It was regarded as being hazarded upon
a legitimate enterprise which had been carried to a successful
issue – one that was of vast, almost incalculable benefit to
southern drovers and ranchmen, to the northwestern cattle
feeders and grazers, as well as to the laborers of the Northeast; in that it gave the first a reliable market or outlet for
their live stock; and to the second it opened up a source from
which they could fill their feed lots and pastures with unfatted cattle at reasonable prices; and to the latter it gave
good, wholesome beef at prices within the reach of the poor
and laboring man. These being among the fruits or results
of the Abilene enterprise, its projector, although bankrupted, felt quite differently from what he would had he
gambled off at cards, or spent in riotous living, his fortune.
He felt that he had lost his money in an honorable effort
to develop a worthy, legitimate enterprise; one which had
as its results, great good to the beef producing and consuming world; and to that extent he was a benefactor to his
fellow man.

The Abilene enterprise opened up, or was the precursor
to, many lucrative vocations, one of which was the business
of buying late in the fall, the thin unmarketable cattle, and
holding them over winter and fattening them during the
following summer upon the native grasses. This operation

332 E. H. Osborne, of Quincy, Illinois, who purchased the Great Western
Stockyards in Abilene from McCoy, owned and operated them from May
28 to November 22, 1870. John Freeland, formerly of Leavenworth, owned
and operated them in 1871. A second stockyard was built in Abilene during
1870, and maybe a third in the following year, but the Great Western Stockyards did most of the business. McCoy vs. the Kansas Pacific Railway
Company, 18, MS., Supreme Court of Kansas; *Abilene Chronicle*, Mar. 23,
Apr. 6, 1871; *Junction City Weekly Union*, July 30, 1870; *Leavenworth Times
and Bulletin*, May 4, 1871.

MAJ. J S. SMITHS' HERD—WINTERING ON HAY IN CENTRAL KANSAS.

was found to be very profitable and in due time many engaged in it. Among the first, if not the first, was Major J. S. Smith, of Springfield, Illinois, who was the first northern cattleman or [215] buyer that came to Abilene in 1867 and bought cattle for his Illinois pastures and feed lots; and whilst at Abilene, was induced to buy a small lot of scalawag cattle and to put them into winter quarters in Kansas as an experiment.[333] Everyone was astonished the following spring to see how well the cattle had wintered. They had actually gained in flesh and general condition during the winter. In a few months after spring opened and grass was abundant, the small herd was in sufficiently good condition to go to the eastern market. This experiment was sufficient to demonstrate the practicability as well as the profit of wintering Texan cattle in Kansas. The following fall many engaged in it. This, of course, created a demand for hay.

The wild grasses of the valleys of Kansas, when mowed and properly cured in the months of July and August, makes hay of equally good quality to the best timothy and clover hay of the middle states. Many young men of energy found lucrative employment in putting up hay to sell to cattlemen desirous of wintering stock. No eastern meadow has so smooth a surface as the valleys of western Kansas. In many places the mowing machine can be driven for miles without meeting an obstruction or running over a single rod of rough or uneven ground. The major was not slow to see the prospective profit in the operation of wintering cattle, and to engage in it extensively. Besides sending to his Illinois farm about five hundred cattle annually to depasture his bluegrass fields and consume his corn crops (after which but a few months' grazing upon tame grass pastures would fit them for the New York markets), he has for five successive winters held from one thousand to two thousand head in Kansas over winter.

Wintering Texan cattle in Kansas has some peculiar features worthy, perhaps, of definite description, more from

[333] Jay S. Smith trailed longhorns to Wichita in 1872 and to Ellsworth in 1873. He also drove cattle into Kansas during the early eighties. *Wichita City Eagle,* May 24, 1872; *Ellsworth Reporter,* June 5, 1873; *Fort Worth Daily Gazette,* June 23, 1883.

the magnitude of the business, the great numbers annually
wintered, rather than from the scientific manner in which
it is done. [217] The cattleman who undertakes to winter
a herd of cattle secures about one ton of hay to each head he
desires to winter. This he provides at his permanent ranch,
if he has any, sometimes cutting the grass, curing, and putting it up in long ricks from forty to one hundred feet in
length and from ten to twenty feet in breadth — on his own
account. At other times he secures his hay by contracting
with hay-making parties, or buys it of those who have put
it up on purpose to sell it. Often in the latter case he will
establish a temporary ranch in the immediate vicinity of
the hay, by improvising temporary camps; sometimes mere
tents, other times rude dugouts in the banks of some ravine,
will be constructed for the comfort and convenience of the
men.

A large adjacent tract of land, embracing many thousands
of acres, will be fireguarded, in order to secure a winter
range from the ravages of prairie fires so common and often
so destructive in prairie countries. To guard against such
contingencies, two or more plow furrows about four rods
apart are run around the tract of land desired to be fireguarded, and then upon some quiet, breezeless evening, the
intervening strip is set fire and closely watched until it is
consumed. Thus it will be seen that an impassable barrier
would be created between the unburned grass within the
encircled tract and that upon the outside of the fireguard.
Unless the fireguard is perfect and of ample width, it is
worthless as a protection against the great fires, fanned
and driven by high winds which invariably sweep over large
prairie countries. Sometimes the fireguard is made during
the summer, when the grasses are green and inflamable,
by mowing two swaths a few rods apart instead of plowing,
and after the mown grass has lain in the hot sun a few days,
it will burn without igniting the adjoining standing grass.
Then, when frost has come and the prairie grass is dead-
ened, the intervening strip of grass between the two burned
swaths is [218] burned off much in the same manner as in
the case of the plow furrows. It is customary with cautious

RANCH BRANDING—ROAD BRANDING.

MAJOR JAY S. SMITH OF SPRINGFIELD, ILLINOIS.

operators to burn circumscribed fireguards around their ricks of hay and camp as a precaution against accidents.

So long as there is no snow and the weather is fine, the cattle will get ample food on the range upon which they are allowed to graze in the daytime, but are usually corralled or rounded up near the camp at night much in the same fashion as in summer herding. But when stormy weather occurs, or there is much snow or ice upon the ground, the cattle are held near camp and hay given them to eat. One or two yoke of oxen attached to a wagon upon which is a rude hayrack or frame, usually constitutes a feeder's outfit, upon which the hay is loaded, and then scattered off in a circle upon the ground to be eagerly devoured by the hungry Texans. Hay made from wild grass such as is found in the valleys of central and western Kansas in great abundance, is very good and contains a great amount of nutriment. Texan cattle eat it with avidity, and without any trouble learning them to take hold of it. It will keep in good heart and flesh any Texan bovine that can get enough of it, and will in many cases increase their weight and condition during the winter. The experienced cattleman usually chooses or prefers a wintering situation which has good running water, with considerable timber and underbrush; or one that has, near the location of the hay, a tract of rough, broken country in the gulches, and behind the hills of which the cattle can find shelter from the piercing winds and driving storms to which western Kansas, in common with other prairie countries, is subject.

Many cattlemen prefer to winter in eastern Kansas, where they turn their herds upon fields of cornstalks from which the corn has been previously gathered, and in February and March give them a few bushels of corn to strengthen them up, so they will take the new grasses and improve [220] rapidly; whilst in extreme western Kansas many herds are put through the winter with little or no other feed than the buffalo grass, which, cured up during the previous summer, contains a great amount of nutriment. So long as the cattle can get a sufficient amount of the dry buffalo grass they will thrive finely. Many thousands are wintered in that manner annually. But it is liable to serious objection as a method of wintering, inasmuch as when the snow or sleet falls deep, as it sometimes does, the cattle are compelled to fast longer than is profitable to the owner or consistent with the laws of life, and the poor brutes starve to death or stray away in quest of food. When the cattle are wintered upon the range, it is customary to place them in some suitable district, and then herd or outride the country daily, turning back any that may be found going beyond the prescribed limits. In all styles of wintering, the inevitable and necessary cow ponies are used, which, in addition to the grass or hay they get whilst picketed out, are fed corn, oats, or other grain. This is done to give them strength requisite for riding service and to enable them to withstand the rigors of the climate, for the Texan cow pony cannot withstand the cold of northern winters hardly so well as Texan cattle; besides, he is daily ridden more or less.

But we have digressed from the personal sketch of Major Smith. He was not only the first but a persistent winterer of cattle until within the last year or two; since which he has withdrawn from the business altogether, except upon his Illinois farms, where, in the fall of 1873, he sent near six hundred head of smooth Texan cattle, besides over one thousand head which he placed in the stables of a still-house near Springfield, Illinois. The manner of fattening cattle at a stillhouse is one differing altogether from all other methods of feeding in the Northwest. Each particular bullock is tied up by a chain around the neck, in a separate stall, the front of which is a manger or platform for hay. A box to receive the allowance of swill is also provided and placed where the bullock can [221] reach it easily; into which the slop is conducted by pipes running from an immense tank or cooler, which is kept constantly full of slop fresh from the stillhouse, which stands at some distance from the cattle stables. Behind the stall is a trench or gutter provided to receive all the filth and offal from the cattle, and is daily cleaned out. The slop is the refuse arising from distilling or manufacturing grain into liquors, and would, without something to eat it, become an entire loss. The stalls are arranged in long rows, and the platform in front serves to place hay on, daily to be consumed by the stalled ox, which, by the economy of his nature, must have some rough, coarse food, or else he would soon lose his appetite after becoming gorged upon rich, concentrated food. Cattle are usually stillfed for from six months to two hundred days, and in that time become very fat, and are considered as good beef as if fatted in any other manner. Being long tied up, they become clumsy and almost lose the use of their limbs; so it is common to let them out in an enclosure once or twice during the two or three weeks previous to shipping them to market, and let them run about and recover the proper use of themselves. It is amusing then to see the dumb brute rejoice at regaining his liberty and to get once more into the sunshine. He attempts to kick up his heels, which usually results in falling headlong on his nose; then he will look foolish, and walk about the yard carefully but awkwardly until he regains self-confidence; when he will spurt off at some tangent, only to be again hopelessly discomfited by tumbling down.

Little trouble is experienced in getting every bullock to learn to eat the slop, and they usually get very fat. Inasmuch as they become mature before grass-fatted cattle can be had, and at a time when the supply of cornfed cattle is almost exhausted, they invariably command good prices, and generally make large profits to the feeder. It is the cheapest way to fatten cattle on feed during the winter, from the fact that the slop would be a waste if stock [223] was not provided. This the still operator does not care or have time to do. Hence he sells the slop at low figures, say from three to eight cents per diem per bullock, which is much cheaper than the animal could be fed on corn. In no one year, perhaps, were there so many cattle put upon stillfeed as that of 1873, and perhaps never before were the prospects so encouraging for handsome profits. No one discerned this state of probabilities earlier than did Major Smith, and straightway he made needful arrangements to put one thousand head, bought at low prices, upon slops in central Illinois.

The major is a Kentuckian by birth, although at a very early period he removed with his father to Illinois, in which state he was reared and educated. However, he frequently went to his native and other southern states, to which he has taken many Illinois and Missouri raised mules to market. When the war broke out, he was South with a drove of mules which he, unfortunately, sold on credit. Soon after returning home, he went into the military service, with the expectation and understanding that his regiment would be detailed to duty on the western plains, which, proving to be incorrect, the major resigned his commission. He then started a number of mule teams across the plains to California, taking out from the Missouri river full loads of corn, which he freighted to various stage stations along the overland mail route; then went over the mountains into California, where, after wintering and recruiting his animals, he made sale of them. After spending a few months looking at the various sections of the Pacific slope, he again returned to his Illinois home, which he had purchased years before, and which lies west of Springfield, at Bates' Station. Directly after returning from California, he was induced to go to Abilene and look over the prospect for business operations there — with what results has already been stated. The major is a quiet, affable, dignified gentleman; a man of few words and little noise; one who makes but few business transactions during the year, but every one is made [224] upon the strictest business basis; a man of almost unerring judgment; and in all his affairs a high sense of honor and manhood is always manifested; one who has many friends, all of whom rightly repose the greatest confidence in his business integrity and abilities.

XII. EXPANSION OF THE CATTLE TRADE IN KANSAS

The year of 1870 witnessed a drive of fully three hundred thousand head of cattle from Texas to western Kansas.[334] From all points north the buyers came flocking to Abilene. As if to help out and complete the climax of success, all the railroad companies east of the Mississippi river engaged in a fierce war of competition for the carrying of live stock freights. The price of freight per car from Chicago to Buffalo, Albany, and New York was but a trifle, sometimes as low as one dollar only per car. Indeed, it is alleged that in several instances whole trains of cattle were carried from Chicago to New York for nothing. Rather than miss doing the business, they would pay the shipper something as an inducement to permit his stock to be shipped free of charge. Of course, this state of affairs had the effect to put up prices of cattle at Chicago and correspondingly at other western points. It was practically bringing ordinary New York prices to Chicago, and better than Chicago prices to Abilene. Hence it was not uncommon for a drover to realize a profit of fifteen to twenty-five dollars per head on his herd. The greatest possible activity prevailed, and there was a multi-

---

[334] The estimate is identical with the one given by McCoy in August, 1871, and in the United States Census of 1880, but in both instances he stated inaccurately that all these cattle were driven to Abilene. The *Junction City Weekly Union* (Oct. 29, 1870) asserted: "It is estimated that 150,000 head of cattle have been driven from Texas into Abilene and vicinity this season." In April, 1871, John Freeland, then proprietor of the Great Western Stock-yards, claimed that 110,000 Texas cattle had been shipped and driven from those yards during 1870. About the middle of August, 1871, McCoy estimated that 120,000 longhorns had been shipped from Abilene in 1870. *Tenth Census of the United States*, III (*Agriculture*), 975; *Kansas Daily Commonwealth*, June 15, Aug. 15, 1871; *Leavenworth Times and Bulletin*, May 4, 1871.

tude of live stock operators in the field. Heavy trainloads
of cattle were shipped daily, mostly going direct to Chicago.
[226] No drover whose stock was good for anything had
any trouble to find a buyer at good prices, and the season
closed with the most satisfactory results to all interested.[335]
Many "through," or fresh-driven, herds sold at thirty to
forty dollars per head; and from fifty to sixty dollars were
realized for wintered herds, of which there were quite a
large number.[336] The season was dry, the grass was rich, and
the cattle became very fat.

The following year, that of 1871, the largest drive occurred ever known in the history of the trade. Fully six
hundred thousand head of cattle arrived in western Kansas.[337] Indeed, for miles north, south and west of Abilene
you could scarce be out of sight of a herd; and when upon
a commanding hillock overlooking any considerable amount
of territory, often thirty, forty, or fifty thousand head of
cattle could be seen at one view, grazing, herding, and
driving about like large columns of human beings.[338]

[335] "Every man who has dealt in cattle at Abilene, during the season just
closed, has made money." *Abilene Chronicle*, Nov. 3, 1870.

[336] The *Abilene Chronicle* (Oct. 13, 1870) listed the following prices of
cattle: "BEEVES – Common $20 to $25. First class cattle $3 to $4 [a hundred
pounds]. STOCK CATTLE – Yearlings $7 to $8; 2 year olds $12 to $15; three
year olds and cows $14 to $20."

[337] In the United States Census of 1880, McCoy gave an estimate of
700,000, but stated inaccurately that all of them were driven to Abilene.
Tenth Census of the United States, III (*Agriculture*), 975. The Topeka
Kansas Daily Commonwealth (Nov. 19, 1871) asserted: "An estimate has
been made this season as to the number of beeves driven during the year
into Kansas, Nebraska, and the western states and territories from Texas,
and they find that the number reaches about 600,000."

[338] On February 1, 1872, the *Abilene Chronicle* published the following
statistics of the cattle trade: "Cattle Shipments. We are indebted to Mr.
W. T. Davidson, of the Great Western Stock Yards at Abilene, for the
following facts and figures: The monthly shipments of Texas cattle at these
yards the past season beginning May 18th and closing November 30th, are
as follows: CARS – May, 18; June, 83; July, 201; August, 272; September,
294; October, 837; November, 329; total, 2034. HEAD – May, 350; June, 1450;
July, 4400; August, 5300; September, 6300; October, 15,700; November,
6300; total, 40,000. The shipments at points west as far as Ellsworth, are as
follows: CARS – Solomon, 900; Salina, 448; Brookville, 343; Ellsworth, 1500;
Abilene, 2034. HEAD – Solomon, 17,100; Salina, 8500; Brookville, 6520; Ells-

But the season was a rainy, stormy one, and the cattle stampeded badly; besides, the grass was coarse, washy, and spongy, and would not make tallow. Again, the railroads had adjusted their differences, or exhausted their belligerent proclivities, and had agreed upon a high freight tariff on live stock from Chicago east. There seemed to be an entire change of feeling in regard to cattle – a complete reverse of those existing during the previous year. There seemed to be but comparatively few buyers. The cattle daily grew poorer in flesh instead of fatter; so when any were put upon eastern markets, they brought low prices and weighed very light, thus discouraging further shipments. A great number of the herds were held until fall, hoping the later markets would be better, but when fall came there was but little better demand. Multiplied thousands were sent forward. In consequence of the number and poor condition of the cattle, the markets were oversupplied, and many shippers met disaster and not a few financial ruin. Finally, shipping had to be entirely abandoned and other sources of disposal looked up. [227] It has been estimated that fully three hundred thousand head of cattle were put into winter quarters during the fall of 1871, mostly on the drover's own account. Of course, there could not be found a sufficient amount of hay for so many cattle, and most of them were driven west onto the plains, where abounded plenty of buffalo grass. In regions where the tall bluestem grass covered the ground, the fire had swept over and left nothing to sustain animal life. The cattle had been held in most instances upon the coarse, dry, unnutritious grasses, hoping to find a purchaser, until they had become poor in flesh and weak from sheer starvation. Finally, when the last hope of selling had expired or passed, they were put upon the buffalo grass regions, and when suitable locations unoccupied were found,

worth, 28,500; Abilene, 40,000. In addition to the above shipments by rail, large numbers of cattle, probably 150,000 head, were bought in this market and driven on foot to Missouri, Iowa, Nebraska, Montana, Colorado, Nevada, New Mexico and other states and territories." David R. Gorden, station agent of the Kansas Pacific Railway at Abilene, stated that 2500 carloads of cattle (or nearly 50,000 head) were forwarded from Abilene by rail during 1871. *Abilene Chronicle,* Jan. 25, 1872.

put thereon into winter quarters. The buffalo grass is so short that prairie fires make but slow progress consuming it, but are easily extinguished.

Before the herds had scarce arrived at their destined wintering ranges, a great rainstorm set in, and a keen cold wind sprung up at a brisk rate from the northwest, freezing the water into ice soon after reaching the ground. The whole surface of the earth had become thus encased to the thickness of two or three inches, covering and freezing the short buffalo grass up solid with sheets of ice. Then the furious gale of piercing wind continued, accompanied with sleet and snow, and lasted for three days and nights. Many men and horses froze to death; and as for the cattle, they perished by the thousand or, it might be truly said, tens of thousands. It was impossible to hold them in any given bounds. They were driven before the storm, or, in cattleman's parlance, "drifted" with the gale. Wherever the poor brutes stopped to rest and laid down, many were found frozen stark stiff and dead, often in just the position that they had taken when they first laid down. It was wholesale death to the stock and widespread ruin to the owners. Many drovers lost more than their all; others, who previously [228] regarded themselves as being worth seventy-five to one hundred thousand dollars, found themselves suddenly made bankrupt. It was a disaster amounting in the aggregate to millions of dollars. Perhaps one-third to one-half of the dead animals were skinned after the storm abated and the weather moderated; the balance were permitted to rot unmolested, save by the hungry wolf or wild varmint. At one railway station twenty thousand, at another thirty-five thousand, at another near fifty thousand hides were collected and shipped east. A single firm placed upon the Republican river over thirty-nine hundred head of cattle and in the following spring could muster only one hundred and ten head of living cattle. Numerous other instances of equally disastrous loss could be cited. The winter of 1871 will long be remembered by many drovers as one in which they met reverse, loss, and financial ruin. It has been estimated that fully two hundred and fifty thousand cattle and many hundred cow ponies perished. It gave a great check to the business of wintering

on the range, or for that matter, upon hay, for the feeders
lost heavily also.

In the spring of 1871 the Atchison, Topeka and Santa Fé
Railroad Company completed their line as far west as the
sixth principal meridian. At a point on the cattle trail sixty-
five miles south of Abilene was located the town of Newton.[339] Early in the spring the railroad company, through
its general manger, made arrangements with a cattleman
living near Topeka, Kansas, to erect and run a good stockyard near Newton, and establish a shipping depot. He, in
turn, employed the Illinoisan to do the work for him, agreeing to give him the earnings of the yards for his services,
there being other considerations in the trade with the railroad company of which the Topeka cattleman was to have
the benefit. In pursuance of this agreement the Illinoisan set
about stopping the incoming cattle herds near the new town
of Newton and succeeded in locating more than one hundred
thousand head.[340] After about three months' work a fine
[229] shipping yard was completed.[341] When about one
hundred and fifty cars had been loaded, and it was probable
a good fall's business would be done, the Topeka cattleman
began to devise means to break up the arrangement with the

---

[339] During the summer of 1870 the Atchison, Topeka and Santa Fé Railroad selected a site for a station, or town, which it soon named Newton,
after Newton, Massachusetts. Settlers arrived there at least as early as March
and April, 1871, after which the place grew rapidly. Writing from the new
town on May 24, 1871, one of the pioneer residents stated: "Four weeks ago
today, the first building was commenced, and we now have twenty houses
almost finished." The railroad reached Newton about the middle of July,
1871, when the shipping of Texas cattle began. *Kansas Daily Commonwealth,*
Mar. 28, May 30, 1871; Robert W. P. Muse, "History of Harvey County,
Kansas," *Harvey County Clippings,* I, 88-124, K.S.H.S.; *History of the State
of Kansas* (1883), 771-781.

[340] Since Newton was on the cattle trail from Texas to Abilene, very little
"locating" was necessary.

[341] About the middle of August, 1871, a newspaper correspondent described the stockyards as follows: "About one mile and a half from Newton
are stock yards erected by the railroad company, into which cattle are driven
that are to be shipped. These yards contain six 'shoots,' through which the
cattle are driven into the cars. The area of these yards is 300 by 450 feet,
and their capacity is four thousand head. . . They were designed by and
erected under the immediate supervision of Joseph G. McCoy, mayor of
Abilene." *Kansas Daily Commonwealth,* Aug. 15, 1871.

Illinoisan and possess himself of the shipping yards. He was not long in finding a man who was willing to be a pliant instrument in his hands to accomplish his dishonorable scheme, being too cowardly himself to face the job. By securing the coöperation of the general manager of the railroad by false representation, they accomplished their dishonorable purposes. An amount of deceit, lying, and mean, underhand collusion was resorted to, to accomplish this feat of repudiation and bad faith, that was anything but creditable to the parties engaged in it. Indeed, the whole affair was one beneath the dignity of decent, honorable men, and one that would have been least and last expected of the parties engaged in it. A moderate business only was done at Newton, which gained a national reputation for its disorder and bloodshed.[342] As many as eleven persons were shot down on a single evening, and many graves were filled with subjects who had "died with their boots on." [343]

The year of 1871 was the last one in which a cattle business was done at Abilene. The trade was driven away by the schemes and concerted actions of a trio of office seekers. Just how this was done or brought about will require a retrospect to the year 1868, in which Abilene was visited by a brace of town-site seekers, forerunners of a band of ministering angels who came from the far-off land of Mendota, Illinois. Finding the proprietors of Abilene in a selling humor, they were not long in deciding to purchase and in closing a contract for the entire town site. Soon after this was accomplished, they desired to establish a weekly newspaper. After casting about for a suitable person to publish a journal, not finding one in Illinois, they sent to northern Ohio and procured a biped of the genus editor, although but a feeble and doubtful specimen. Soon [230] after the necessary contributions were made to defray the expense

[342] As early as the middle of August, 1871, the *Kansas Daily Commonwealth* called Newton "The Wickedest Town in Kansas." *Ibid.*

[343] About two o'clock on Sunday morning, August 20, 1871, a shooting affray at Perry Tuttle's dance house in Newton resulted in the immediate death of one man, the ultimate death of three more, and the wounding of about six others. "This was one of the bloodiest affrays that ever occurred in our State," asserted the *Emporia News* (Aug. 25, 1871). See also *Kansas Daily Commonwealth*, Aug. 22, 27, 1871.

of shipping the editor and his press to Abilene, he arrived; then the villagers were as proud and put on as vain airs over the new acquisition as they did when the railway company whitewashed the "ample depot accommodations." [344]

The editorial oracle had been duly installed in his new

[344] During August and September, 1869, Jacob Augustine, of Mendota, Illinois, bought from Charles H. Thompson and Joseph G. McCoy "the undivided one half of all the lots in Thompson and McCoy's Addition to Abilene" and "the undivided one third of all other lots in the said addition." C. H. Lebold, of Tuscarawas county, Ohio, where Augustine formerly lived, furnished him with much of the money and in return received an interest in the purchase. Augustine and Lebold then began to induce their friends in Mendota and Tuscarawas county to move to Abilene or its vicinity. Reaching their new homes in the latter part of 1869 and during 1870, the emigrants from Illinois and Ohio settled in Abilene or a short distance north of it. The most important group of these settlers was the Buckeye Colony, organized by Vear Porter Wilson, of New Philadelphia, Tuscarawas county, Ohio. Although a few members of this organization came to Dickinson county as early as December, 1869, and January, 1870, the main body started from Uhrichsville, Ohio, on April 5, 1870, and reached Abilene three days afterward. Additional emigrants belonging to this colony arrived later in the same year. Most members of the Buckeye Colony settled north of Abilene, in what is now Buckeye Township, Dickinson county, but a few located in Abilene itself. Wilson, the colony's organizer, was born near West Newton, Westmoreland county, Pennsylvania, April 1, 1828. Later he moved to New Philadelphia, Ohio, where, during the sixties, he published a weekly newspaper called the *Tuscarawas Chronicle*. After, or before, organizing the Buckeye Colony, he decided, or was induced, to bring his press to Abilene and publish a newspaper. Calling it the *Abilene Chronicle,* he issued the first number in February, 1870, before his arrival there. Wilson, who brought his wife and eight children to Abilene shortly afterward, described his vocation as "Universalist Minister and Printer" to an enumerator for the United States Census of 1870. "Abilene may well be proud of her editor and his paper," wrote a correspondent of the Topeka *Kansas Daily Commonwealth* about July 1, 1870. Wilson died at Colorado Springs, Colorado, February 14, 1899, but was buried in Abilene. Ninth Census of the United States, Dickinson and Doniphan Counties, Kansas, MS., K.S.H.S.; Dickinson County, Deed Record C, 27, 241-242, MS., Recorder of Deeds Office, Abilene; *ibid.,* Deed Record J, 173; Vear Porter Wilson, Annals of the Buckeye Colony, MS., Homer W. Wilson, Abilene; Homer W. Wilson, Statement, August, 1938; *Abilene Chronicle,* Mar. 3, Apr. 21, May 19, Sept. 1, 1870; *Kansas Daily Commonwealth,* May 19, June 2, 1870; *Leavenworth Times & Conservative,* June 21, 1870; J. B. Edwards, "History of Early-day Abilene," *Abilene Daily Reflector,* June 12, July 3, 1938; Little, "Early Days of Abilene and Dickinson County," in Roenigk, *Pioneer History of Kansas,* 32-35; *History of the State of Kansas* (1883), 686-691.

quarters but a brief space of time before he affiliated with certain county officers, and they soon formed a ring, or clique, which, with consummate presumption, undertook to manipulate all public matters, even assuming to dictate who should and who should not have public offices, or in any manner have ought to say about matters of a public nature. Anyone who dared act or aspire without first consulting them would be denounced, maligned, and slandered in a malicious manner. The sacredness of one's family circle would not be regarded or respected, but innuendoes and dark hints of a base nature, always wholly untrue, would be manufactured and published in the newspaper, or otherwise industriously circulated.[345] If any person was thought to be, or probably would be in the future, in their way, or was likely to indulge a desire to hold an office no matter how humble, who did not bow to them or acknowledge their assumed authority, he was assailed in the most malignant manner. And if the people chose, as they occasionally did, to elect such one, he was the object of their special malevolence, and no matter what he did, whether good or bad, he was weekly denounced, misrepresented, and slandered in unmeasured terms and in the most vindictive spirit. This trio were as unscrupulous about the means by which they made money as they were about acting in an indecent manner.

They thought they could blackmail the cattle business on a large scale, as they had already done on a comparatively small one. Accordingly, they hit upon the plan of publishing a notification, signed by themselves, to the drovers not to come back to Abilene, as they would not be tolerated in the

---

345 Wilson and McCoy were bitter enemies. As soon as the latter became mayor, Wilson, through the medium of the *Chronicle,* launched an extremely vitriolic personal and political attack upon him, accusing him of extravagance, corruption, immorality, and indifference to the welfare of the people. He charged McCoy with "vileness," "reckless extravagance," "boyish silliness," and "un-mayor-like conduct," and called him "poor, corrupt man," "scapegrace," "contemptible," "unscrupulous man," "poor, fallen creature," "unprincipled mayor," "worse than beastly mayor," and "skunk." At no time did Wilson present any adequate proof to substantiate these charges. McCoy never made any replies to the accusations, or Wilson refused to publish any in the *Chronicle. Abilene Chronicle,* Apr. 6, May 4, 18, 25, June 1, 15, July 6, 27, Sept. 7, 1871, Mar. 14, 1872.

county.[346] They had a double purpose to serve by this; one of which was to cater to [231] certain farmers who had suffered small grievances from the presence of the cattle trade and thus secure political strength; the second object was to place themselves in open hostility to the cattle trade, expecting the following spring to be bought off. But the drovers took them at their word and turned their herds to other points farther west on the line of the Kansas Pacific Railway, or stopped at some eligible point on the Atchison, Topeka and Santa Fé Railroad.

But few months elapsed in the following spring before the suicidal effect of the step taken by the politicians was painfully visible in Abilene. Four-fifths of her business houses became vacant, rents fell to a trifle, many of the leading hotels and business houses were either closed or taken down and moved to other points. Property became unsalable. The luxuriant sunflower sprang up thick and flourished in the main streets, while the inhabitants, such as could not get away, passed their time sadly contemplating their ruin. Curses both loud and deep were freely bestowed on the political ring. The whole village assumed a desolate, forsaken, and deserted appearance. The remaining inhabitants betook themselves to suing each other with a vigor equalled only by the famous Kilkenny cats. Some of the best citizens became entirely bankrupt from the sudden stagnation of trade; while others, with cadaverous cheek and weird eye, watched any ominous ripple in the sunflower, to see if perchance a homesteader was making his entrance into the dead village, bringing farm products which could only be bartered off at very low prices, if sold at all. It would be difficult to describe the revolution – the waking up to a realizing sense of where their former great prosperity had come from – that occurred in the public mind. During the summer of

[346] This "circular," written by Theodore C. Henry, was as follows: "We the undersigned members of the Farmers' Protective Association and Officers and Citizens of Dickinson County, Kansas, most respectfully request all who have contemplated driving Texas Cattle to Abilene the coming season to seek some other point for shipment, as the inhabitants of Dickinson will no longer submit to the evils of the trade." *Abilene Chronicle*, Feb. 8, 15, 22, 1872; Henry, *op. cit.*, 307.

1872 petitions were freely circulated and numerously signed, praying, inviting, begging the cattlemen to return with their herds, but alas, it was too late! The trade had been turned to western points, which were only too glad to profit by Abilene's suicidal folly.

The editor busied himself with making excuses for the [232] decline of Abilene's business and pretending that the cattle trade was of no benefit.[347] He was an adept at making pretensions as well as insinuations. There was nothing so sacred or profane that he would halt or shrink from assuming or pretending to be, if it but promised him future political preferment. Every secret society that would receive him upon any terms, he joined and sought to place himself at the head thereof.[348] In fact, there was nothing he would hesitate to prostitute to his own selfish purpose – that of aiding himself to get an office. It was his thought by day and his dreams by night; the rule by which all his acts were squared; the overshadowing, all-prevailing ambition of his being. No stone was left unturned or unplaced that would, no matter how remotely, aid him to obtain an office. As to talent, or even average ability, he had little or none. Low cunning, shrewd wire-pulling, and cheeky presumption, coupled with loathsome flunkyism, and vindictive, unscrupulous hatred of all whom he could not manipulate, constituted his make-up and capital. A closer inspection of the personal appearance of the editor caused the gravest discussion and doubts in the minds of the villagers whether he was a real human or only an extremely well-developed specimen of the ape family. The disposition and degree of manhood, or rather lack of manhood, that he soon developed, fixed the conviction that if at some time in the distant future some enterprising phrenological Darwin should chance to exhume his cranium, it would be regarded as a rare specimen and as conclusive proof of the soundness of the Darwinian theory

---

[347] "The town of Abilene is as quiet as any village in the land. Business is not as brisk as it used to be during the cattle season – but the citizens have the satisfaction of knowing that 'hell is more than sixty miles away.'" *Abilene Chronicle*, May 30, 1872. See also *ibid.*, Mar. 21, 1872.

[348] In 1870 two fraternal organizations established lodges at Abilene – the Odd Fellows and the Masons – and Wilson was a charter member and the first treasurer of each. *History of the State of Kansas* (1883), 689.

— an undeniable connecting link between the animal and human race. However, as the cranial formation would show but little brains before the ears, and still less above the eyes, but an enormous development behind the ears, where the bump of self-esteem and ambitious proclivities to seek office are supposed to be located, it would doubtless be classed as of doubtful origin or classification, and labeled "A what is it."

He [233] spent many years in Ohio unsuccessfully intriguing, planning, and scheming to obtain office — a kind of standing candidate. After practicing diligently his well-learned tactics in Kansas for three or more years, he came forward for the office of state senator from his district. On the meeting of the nominating convention, he found that he was in the minority. But not to be daunted or defeated in his predetermination to serve and represent the people, whether they desired him or not, he, aided by the political clique, or cabal, set about influencing the delegates by promises of future promotion or by threats of vengeance and political ostracism. By such means, in connection with his misrepresentations and falsehoods concerning his opponents, he succeeded in securing the nomination by a bare majority. He freely used whiskey and other unfair and indecent means to secure votes. His majority was near fifteen hundred less than that of his ticket. A presidential campaign only saved him from utter defeat.

Soon after his election he became suddenly interested in a little town site, laid out near a water mill, built by a little Dutchman who had just previously held the office of county treasurer. It is surprising how, after holding the office of county treasurer for one or two terms in Kansas, even a pauper can build expensive mills or palatial residences. But the public were at a great loss to understand of what earthly use a state senator would be to the owner of a water mill. But soon after he took his seat in the legislature, he quietly introduced a bill (number 151), which was for an act, the provisions of which would have practically and completely placed the entire milling privileges of the river and county in the hands of the little Dutch miller, thus creating an [234] oppressive monopoly. This measure was quietly passed through the senate, the senator making a flaming speech in its behalf; then tried to prevent his constituents from getting hold of it, but without success. The leading citizens of Abilene sent one of their number to the capital to look after the mysterious senate bill number 151. Before it had passed the house and become a law, the delegate extraordinary from Abilene arrived and lost no time in privately showing the members of the house the infamous intent of the measure; and they made short work of it. Thus the senator's nice little scheme not only failed, but was ventilated and exposed to the eyes and understanding of his constituents. A more disgusted, exasperated, and enraged people are not often seen. All over the county public meetings were held, the senator denounced and called upon to resign.

When the senator found his nice-laid plans to sell out [235] the farmers' interests had miscarried, his anger and furious passions knew no bounds. Upon returning to his home at Abilene, he was publicly hooted and hissed by a host of boys yelling "milldam" in his ears. He was demoniacal in his rage and frantic in his wrath. He denounced everybody connected with his exposure and humiliating downfall; especially the delegate sent down from Abilene was the victim of his special vindictive malice. But the people had got their eyes thoroughly opened, and understood the animus of his vindictive, malicious charges and the object of their publication. A few of Abilene's leading business men established another paper, which fast supplanted the senator's. The community loathed him as a traitor and corrupt, dishonest legislator. The following fall the people of Dickinson county elected Doctor J. M. Hodge to the house, greatly to the disgust of the senator; the very man whom he had villified so monstrously. This they did because the doctor was a good, able man, the one most capable of watching the senator and protecting the people's interest from the senator's dishonest schemes; and for the additional purpose of rebuking the senator in unmistakable terms. Finally the senator sold out his paper and home, and left the district in disgust, but entirely unlamented. The tedious notice of the senator has been somewhat prolonged that the reader could see what an unprincipled, hypocritical scalawag can

THE SENATOR SELLS OUT.

"YE LOCAL EDITOR."

YE EDITOR.

get into office in Kansas, and how he will try to enrich himself at the expense of his constituents; and how, in time, he meets his merited downfall. This great ex-editor and ex-senator had a soft-brained son, out of which he tried to make a local editor, but the boy's mental imbecility, in connection with his inordinate [236] love of whiskey, made the effort prove a failure. While under the influence of his daily quart of inspiration he could write locals of one to three lines in length, but the habit of "inspiring" grew too fast, and he failed totally as a local editor; but he became a profound success as a whiskey guzzler.

Early in the spring of 1872 the Atchison, Topeka and Santa Fé Railroad was extended west from Newton up the Arkansas river valley; also by a branch road in a southerly direction to Wichita, a thriving frontier town of near two thousand inhabitants located on the banks of the Arkansas river.[349] It is favorably situated for the cattle trade, and when the branch railroad was nearly completed to it, many of the citizens became anxious to have the cattle trade centered there.[350] Accordingly, a well-known Texan drover who had remained over winter in the county, and the Illinoisan,

349 Wichita, named after the Wichita Indians who resided there during the middle sixties, was first settled by whites in 1867. On August 28, 1869, a resident wrote: "Our town affords four stores, only one saloon, one blacksmith and saddlery shop and twenty families." On August 13, 1870, the *Wichita Vidette*, the first newspaper, stated: "E. H. Durfee established a trading post at this place in 1867, and Lewellen one on the Chisholm Creek, 1½ miles east, in the same year. In 1869, Judge Greenway came back again and opened a general stock of supply goods for the Texas cattle trade. . . In 1868 Gen. Lawrence, Durfee, Munger and others began talking about laying out a town; but it seems the land could not be obtained for that purpose. A year later Mr. Munger got a title to a part of the old town, and laid it off in lots. He had several buildings put up, which gave it the appearance of a town. Little else was done until about 3 months ago, when Wm. Griffenstein laid off a town south of the old town, since which time buildings have been going up as fast as mechanics can do the work and building material furnished. At an early day steps were taken to secure the publication of a newspaper, the first number of which is before you." See also *Junction City Weekly Union*, Sept. 4, 1869; *History of the State of Kansas* (1883), 1384-1402.

350 The first passenger train reached Wichita on May 11, 1872. The first shipment of Texas cattle, consisting of eighteen carloads, left Wichita for Chicago on June 8, 1872. *Wichita City Eagle*, May 17, June 14, 1872.

of Abilene, were employed: one to stop as many cattle upon the good grazing lands near Wichita as possible; whilst the other put forth every effort and put in practice every advertising method with which he was familiar to draw cattle buyers to the point. The success attained was beyond the most sanguine expectation.[351] During the first season nearly four thousand cars, containing nearly eighty thousand head of cattle, were shipped. Indeed, there are few towns better located to do a good cattle business than Wichita.[352]

During the same year (that of 1872) the cattle trade of the Kansas Pacific Railway was done from a point west of Fort Harker, fully sixty-five miles west of Abilene, a point with a grazing country inferior to that surrounding Abilene.[353] Indeed, time and experience has proven that no other such point as Abilene for the accommodation of a large cattle trade has or can be found. The folly of permitting or aiding it to be driven therefrom is yearly more apparent. We doubt not that the stupidity and bad faith of the old management of the Kansas Pacific Railway has cost the road the loss of more than five thousand cars of freight worth near a quarter of a [237] million of dollars, besides placing it at a serious disadvantage compared with what it once had and might have maintained in the western cattle trade by an upright, judicious, honorable line of conduct and manner of dealing.

It is the purpose or intended scope of this work to give due notice and attention to every prominent cattle interest in the West, and not to be specially devoted to what is often termed the long-horned, or Texan, cattle interests, which, although of very great magnitude both in numbers and value, is by no means the only valuable or large cattle interest in the West. The Durham, or short-horned, cattle, raised and fed so extensively and profitably throughout the North-

---

351 For McCoy's activities in behalf of the Texas cattle trade at Wichita, see the introduction to the present volume.

352 From June 8 to December 31, 1872, the Atchison, Topeka and Santa Fé Railroad shipped 3530 carloads of cattle, or about 70,600 cattle, from Wichita. This number was not exceeded by any town or city in Kansas during 1872. *Kansas Daily Commonwealth*, Jan. 8, 1873; *Wichita City Eagle*, Jan. 23, 1873.

353 The principal Texas cattle shipping point of the Kansas Pacific Railway in 1872 was Ellsworth. Kansas Pacific Railway, *Seventh Annual Report*, 18; *Ellsworth Reporter*, Oct. 17, 1872.

west and West, are in almost every respect more valuable and profitable stock to breed and handle than any other throughout the entire West. The Durham blood is sought by breeders, and of late years shrewd, enterprising Texan ranchmen have been sending young graded Durham bulls to their ranches for the purpose of improving their stocks in blood and quality. They plainly see that Texas must improve her cattle in blood and quality if she would longer compete successfully and profitably in the beef markets of the Union. It is beginning to dawn upon the understanding of the Lone Star ranchmen that his only hope, as well as imperative duty toward himself, lies in improving the blood of his stock, even at the expense of numbers. While it is a well-established fact that Texan cattle can be fatted upon corn, yet it is not so easily or successfully done as with the Durham; although it is quite as well established that Texan cattle will fatten better upon grass than the native, or shorthorn. Now inasmuch as cornfed and cornfatted beef invariably brings better prices than the grassfatted, it becomes a matter worthy of note to the producer to secure such grades of cattle as will make the most valuable beef. It is also an item worthy of consideration to the ranchman to breed that class or grade of cattle which the [238] cornfeeder desires and for which he will always pay good prices.

In Colorado it is made by statute a punishable offense to permit a Texan or scrub bull to run at large, and ranchmen are authorized to shoot down such whenever and wherever they may meet them upon the commons. This law, in connection with the private enterprise of her ranchmen, is fast changing the form and appearance of Colorado native cattle. Indeed, it is astonishing, as well as highly encouraging, to note the marked improvement in color, form, and weight arising from a cross of Texan cows with Durham bulls, although the latter may be common grades only. In many instances the ordinary observer will scarce believe or recognize that the cross, or half-breed, has any Texan blood in it. But little trace of the mother is transmitted to her offspring, which sell upon the eastern markets quite as well as other Durham grades of equal fatness bred in the Northwest. There is nothing else which holds out the hope and sure promise of so great reward for the investment to Texan ranchmen as the crossing of their cows with grade Durham bulls. If the cattlemen of that state would import one car-load of yearling bulls of Durham blood for each one thou-sand head of cattle they export annually, the lapse of time would be brief before a marked difference would be seen in the quality of their stock and the prices realized for Texan cattle. It is to be hoped that the ranchmen of that state will speedily realize the importance of improvement in blood of their herds. The great number of Texan cows and heifers that have been placed upon ranches throughout the West, coupled with the irrepressible desire for improvement, has given considerable impetus to the breeding of thoroughbred and grade bulls throughout the Northwest, and especially in the country adjacent to Kansas City. The interest in thoroughbred shorthorn cattle continually increases, as is plainly indicated by the sales that have occurred during the year 1873. The [240] demand from Colorado and western Kansas for superior bulls has been, and still is, large.

No one has been more fortunate in establishing a large fine herd of shorthorn cattle at the opportune time and at just the right locality than Andrew Wilson of Kingville, Kansas. Few cattlemen comparatively so young, are so widely known as he. Few have had the experiences, the suc-cesses, the failures, the advances, the reverses, the ups, and the downs that have fallen to his lot. He is widely known throughout Kansas, Colorado, and the West, alike for his eccentric character, as well as for his fine herd of shorthorns and his extensive operations in Texan cattle. Mr. Wilson is a native of Ohio but was reared in central Illinois, where he early imbibed the notions and ideas of live stock specula-tions. In war times, when money was plenty, there was no difficulty in commanding as much money as was desired, and he sallied forth to western Missouri and essayed to try his hand in live stock operations. Within the space of three years' time he made a series of ventures, such as only a bold, almost reckless operator could or would make, in which he was remarkably fortunate. Indeed, the profits were so large that money ceased to have value in his estima-tion, and he scattered it as freely as he had made it. There existed no kind of an operation or investment from a faro bank to a purchase of ten thousand head of live stock, that

HERD OF SHORT-HORNS—PROPERTY OF A. WILSON.

RESIDENCE OF ANDREW WILSON, NEAR KINGSVILLE, KAS.

he hesitated to invest in. Everything was advancing at a rate commensurate with the abundance and depreciation of the currency. It was only necessary to buy and hold, or buy to receive in the future, and a large profit was sure to be realized. It only required nerve, and of this he had more than a supply; indeed, he was all energy and nerve, and had no caution or fear of results whatever. It has been said with truth that to be successful in the first speculation is infinitely worse in the long run for a young man than a severe reverse or heavy loss. Be this as it may, success was not a blessing, unless one in disguise, to Andrew [241] Wilson. However, he probably could not appreciate it as such.

In a series of ventures he had made near one hundred thousand dollars; but he was caught with twelve or fifteen thousand hogs in the shipping pens on line of the railroad by one of those terrific winter storms occasionally experienced in the West, wherein men and animals freeze to death in great numbers. His hogs froze to death by the thousand, and for weeks the railroad company was unable to put through a train of any description. This unforeseen disaster swept away his former profits even more rapidly than they had been acquired. When the storm abated and the weather had moderated, the frozen animals were disposed of, realizing but a trifle compared with their cost. After spending a few months in sour, blue meditations, in which he took a careful and accurate reckoning of his whereabouts, condition, and standing in the business world, and the causes that had most contributed thereto, he resolved to make a change of base, and at the same time leave behind him the dissolute, reckless habits that had contributed so surely to his downfall and ruin. Accordingly, he gathered his meager effects, and, crossing the Missouri river, set his face toward the capital of Kansas, near which he has ever since made his home. Soon after arriving in Kansas, he was most fortunate in obtaining the coöperation of a stockman who had credit and means. In a short time he began to make himself known in the state of his adoption by his live stock operations; however, not so much on a line of shipping and speculation, as in his Missouri operations, but more on a basis of legitimate business transactions.

Soon he began to form the nucleus of a herd of thoroughbred shorthorn cattle. This herd he has steadily increased by purchase and breeding until it holds rank as the largest and best in the state, and has repeatedly taken many first premiums at Kansas state fairs, as well as at various other competitive exhibitions. As a successful breeder of fine, [243] pure-blood cattle, he has shown great skill and good judgment, and that peculiar fitness or adaptation to the business; that keen sense of fine points and good qualities so necessary to a successful breeder. All admit and accord him merited success. His herd became so large that a public sale during the summer of 1873 was determined upon, and such as could be spared were sold; also a number of graded animals. The venture of a public sale of thoroughbred cattle in Kansas had never before been made and was regarded extra-hazardous by many; but the result of this one proved that new as is the state, and poor as are most of her citizens, yet there is money to pay for and appreciation of fine stock. The gross amount of the two days' sale aggregated over twenty-four thousand dollars. Single animals sold for over one thousand dollars. So great and growing is the demand for blooded bulls to place upon cattle ranches with Texan and Indian cows, that the business of producing the full-bloods and grades is becoming very large and lucrative. In the foremost rank of breeders, Mr. Wilson has established a reputation and a herd second to none in the West. After securing a long lease upon one of the largest and best improved farms, of two thousand acres, in central Kansas, he has spent many thousand dollars in erecting improvements, such as pastures, yards, and barns, for the complete protection and care of his thoroughbred cattle. He purposes in the future to make his the largest and best herd of cattle in the West, and to furnish annually large numbers of grade bulls to ranchmen. This line of business will in the future be profitable and pleasant, and in pursuit of it a man can confer great benefits upon humanity, besides securing lasting fame and fortune.

This branch of business, although large and important, is but a fraction of Wilson's interests. From his first entrance into Kansas he has been interested in large live stock operations, principally stall-feeding, wintering, grazing, and fat-

ANDREW WILSON, OF KINGSVILLE, KAS.

ting cattle, both native and Texan. Notwithstanding the great financial embarrassments under [244] which he entered the state, he has ever had the good fortune to meet with men of credit and means who have stood by and sustained him in carrying to successful issue many large operations; and it matters not what the fate of anyone who is interested with him may be, so soon as he steps aside, another comes forward to tender his aid. Thus it has ever been; so that each year has only witnessed larger and larger operations, until long since he has been accorded the position of Kansas' heaviest feeder. During the winters of 1872 and 1873 he "roughed" about five thousand head of Texan cattle through the winter and fatted them the following summer on grass. Not content with the magnitude of this operation, the following fall season he formed new business alliances, and bought seven thousand five hundred head of Texan cattle at panic prices and put them into winter quarters near Topeka. His chosen method of handling Texan cattle is to winter them principally upon cornstalk fields, which he buys in great abundance at low prices, usually from twenty to fifty cents per acre, after the corn has been gathered therefrom. Upon these fields the cattle are turned in herds of one to five hundred head. As soon as one field is depastured, another is provided, so that the labor of feeding or care for the stock is small and light. When the approach of spring is near, it is found to be good practice to feed corn for several weeks, so as to strengthen up the stock and start it to improving in flesh and heart; so that when the new grass comes in the spring, the cattle fatten rapidly and without delay, or loss from death, as is often the case when the animal is weak and poor in flesh. This style or manner of wintering cattle is called "roughing," and the feeding of corn in the spring is termed "warming up." It is one of the most successful and profitable methods of handling Texan cattle. Inasmuch as little or no loss by death ever occurs, it is economical, especially when the corn crop of the region has been good, and, as a natural result, the stock fields abundant, good, and cheap. It is claimed that by roughing through the winter, the cattle can [246] be made fat upon grass at an earlier date, and be ready to go to an earlier and better market than by any other method of wintering.

In central Kansas by far the larger portion of the corn crops are harvested by husking, or snapping the corn from the stalk, leaving the immatured ears and nubbins on the stalks with the fodder. These make good feed for the stock steer, upon which he thrives nicely so long as he is able to get sufficient thereof. When spring comes and the natural grasses become abundant, the cattle are taken from their winter quarters and, in herds of five hundred or less, are herded until fat, which requires from two to five months' time. Cows and young cattle get fat much quicker than aged steers. A great gain both in weight and value is thus secured. But many feeders prefer to fullfeed their cattle with corn, and make them fat by the opening of spring, when beef is scarcest and hence commands the highest prices.

There are few methods of handling cattle Mr. Wilson has not tried, in all of which he has won the name of being an able, efficient cattleman and a good feeder. As a man he has few equals in energy and natural resources. Indeed, it has been said that it was impossible to conceive a difficult situation, or complicated or adverse circumstance, which he could not surmount, and from which he could not extricate himself and always to his own advantage. His business principle seems to be that the end justifies the means; hence he is not overscrupulous as to the means adopted or resorted to, in order to compass his purposes. He is shrewd, deep, cunning, and unlimited in natural resources and expedients; abundantly calculated to take care of himself and to make his own way through the world; is entirely honorable in meeting and paying his written obligations, but his verbal agreements are held at his pleasure. Nevertheless, he has unlimited energy, liberal ideas, and comprehensive plans, and is capable of undertaking and carrying to a successful issue [247] large business transactions; and seldom fails to bend everything and everybody to his own purposes, and thereby further his own schemes. There are in Kansas few better judges of live stock than he, and none will outstrip him in the race for fortune and honorable distinction in business.

XIII. THE PANIC OF 1873 AND ORGANIZATION OF THE LIVE STOCK ASSOCIATION

Near three hundred and fifty thousand head of cattle arrived in western Kansas during the year of 1872,[354] scarce more than one-half as many as were driven during the previous year. This fact alone is quite suggestive of the widespread loss and disaster of 1871, the year often termed "bad medicine" by western drovers. There was great rivalry between Wichita and cattle points on the Kansas Pacific Railway. There was a vigorous effort made to draw a portion of the drovers with their herds to Coffeyville, on the Leavenworth, Lawrence and Galveston Railway.[355] The cattle season of 1872 was a good one for the drovers, although they did not receive other than fair paying prices for their stock; yet, in consequence of the bountiful corn crop throughout the Northwest, creating an immense demand for cattle for feeding purposes, the drovers were able to sell out at moderately good prices.

The good results of the season had the effect in 1873 of a marked increase in the number of cattle driven. At the opening of the season three different railways competed for the cattle trade — the Kansas Pacific, the Atchison, Topeka and Santa Fé, and Leavenworth, Lawrence and Galveston Railways. It was evident, even before the opening of the cattle season, that the drive would be very large. The utmost

---

[354] This estimate is identical with the one made by McCoy for the United States Census of 1880, where, however, he stated inaccurately that all the cattle were driven to Wichita and Ellsworth. *Tenth Census of the United States,* III (*Agriculture*), 975.

[355] As early as June, 1871, the Leavenworth, Lawrence and Galveston Railroad, which had just been completed to the northern boundary of Indian Territory, advertised the advantages of shipping Texas cattle over its line. *Dallas Herald,* June 3, 1871.

activity was manifested on the cattle trail by parties working in the interest of their respective roads or points, all of which poured out money freely in order to secure cattle business. How different was this to the conduct of the [249] railway company the first three years of the existence of the cattle trade, when it was first being established. Then it required both money and labor, coupled with faith and nerve, to do the task – to overcome the multitude of obstacles that successively arose, mountain high, to oppose and almost overwhelm the enterprise undertaken at Abilene. In the years of 1872 and 1873 the Kansas Pacific Railway Company were willing to pay numbers of men snug sums of money to use their influence and to work in favor of their line, and then pay handsomely to have the stock loaded upon the cars from shipping yards built by the railway company at many thousand dollars' cost, while in the years of 1868 and 1869 they did nothing to aid the business. When parties secured the cattle and loaded them upon the cars from yards built, maintained, and operated at private expense, the railway company had only repudiation of its contract to offer as recompense for services.

In 1873 near four hundred and fifty thousand head of cattle entered western Kansas,[356] besides about fifty thousand which turned off of the trail to the eastward and went to Coffeyville,[357] making an aggregate of near one-half million head of cattle.[358] Of this number, fully three-fifths were stock cattle, that is, cows, heifers, yearlings, and steers younger than four years old.

The season was marked as the first in which there was nearly no demand from any source for stock cattle. Scarce a single buyer from any of the territories put in an appear-

[356] In the United States Census of 1880, McCoy estimated that 405,000 longhorns were driven to Wichita and Ellsworth during 1873. This figure, which has been copied by all writers on the cattle trade, is probably a typographical error for 450,000. In McCoy's census estimate for 1873, as for 1872, he erred in asserting that all Texas stock were trailed to Wichita and Ellsworth. *Tenth Census of the United States*, III (*Agriculture*), 975.

[357] In December, 1873, an estimate was made that over 80,000 Texas cattle had been driven to Coffeyville during that year. *Kansas City Journal of Commerce*, Dec. 10, 1873.

[358] The *Kansas City Journal of Commerce* (Jan. 18, 1874) estimated that 500,000 longhorns had been driven north from Texas in 1873.

ance; but, on the other hand, it was reported that they were supplied with cattle, and that instead of being buyers, they would be for years to come extensive sellers. Thus, instead of relieving the western Kansas cattle market of its surplus or excess, they were pressing to the front, shoulder to shoulder, as competitors in the eastern markets, in which they had a decided advantage from the fact that the territorial cattle had been wintered North, and not being [been] driven to disturb or prevent them from fatting. The result of the [250] situation which developed in 1873 was that such herds as failed to get into the Indian contracts were held upon the range, and an attempt was made to fatten them for the fall market. In order to do this, large sums of money had to be raised by borrowing of such banks as were disposed to accommodate the cattlemen. Many drovers were in debt in whole or in part for their herds, while others did not have means to pay off their surplus men on arriving in Kansas or buy necessary camp supplies. Resort was had to borrowing money, instead of selling cattle at such prices as were offered. This was done to a very large extent. On the first of September, Texan drovers in Kansas were in debt fully $1,500,000. The greater portion of this amount was due and payable during the month of October.

About the middle of September the great panic of 1873 began in the eastern cities, and by the first of October had reached the Northwest and West in its full force, paralyzing every business to a greater or less extent. Perhaps no business in the West suffered so much as the cattle trade. There was an unprecedented number of cattle awaiting the opening of the packing season and the general fall markets, and their owners were as a rule largely in debt to the banks, which debts matured during the month of October. Owing to the distressed condition all the banks found themselves placed in, it was impossible to grant extensions, and there was no other alternative than to put the cattle upon the market in order to pay the debt for which the live stock was in many instances pledged. The short corn crop had reduced the number of buyers fully fifty per cent as compared with the previous year, and the panic had the effect of further reducing the number of would-be purchasers fully one-half;

so that there were scarce one-fourth the number of buyers for cattle in the fall of 1873 that there were in that of 1872, whilst the number of cattle for sale was much larger. In addition to the foregoing, the season had been rainy and the grass coarse, soft, and washy; consequently the cattle had [251] stampeded much and fatted little, so that more than ninety per cent of them were unfit to be packed or to go to eastern markets. In fact, they were only fit to be fed during the winter and marketed the following year.

To a man whose sympathies ran with cattlemen, it was like attending a funeral of friends daily, to stand upon any of the cattle marts and witness the financial slaughter of drovers and shippers constantly occurring. Many cattle that were forwarded east did not sell for scarce more than freight and charges. A single firm lost one hundred and eighty thousand dollars in three weeks' shipments. It was common to hear a shipper say, pointing to his cattle, that every horn in sight was losing a five-dollar note, or ten dollars per head. Indeed, money was lost as fast and completely as if a bonfire had been made of it and kept burning for forty days. It is estimated that the panic lost Texan drovers fully two millions of dollars. No such calamity ever befell the western cattle trade. It is beyond the power of the writer to give by pen or word, even a faint description of the great calamity or tell of its widespread ruin. Men by the score could be named who were suddenly bankrupted, and it was very rare to meet a cattle drover, trader, or shipper who had not lost heavily. Many thousands of stock cattle, especially cows and rough, thin steers, were sold at from one to one and a quarter cents per pound gross weight, to be "tanked" – that is, the hide, horns, and hoofs taken off, and the balance of the carcass placed in a tank and rendered, or steamed; the tallow obtained, the balance was thrown away. Many thousand were disposed of in this manner, while by far the greater portion were taken by feeders; some of the best herds were taken by the packers. The year of 1873 was, taken as a whole, one of great disaster to western cattlemen, and will be long and vividly remembered by many whose fondest hopes, together with their fortunes, were dashed to the earth and broken. Of the half million cattle that came to Kansas during that year, fully two-fifths were [252] put in winter quarters in western Kansas or driven into Colorado; and of the remainder, perhaps one hundred thousand were put on feed in the northwestern states; and as many more went direct to market and were slaughtered; whilst the remainder went to the Indians and to be consumed in the more northern territories.

One thing may be regarded as effectually settled, that is, no more stock cattle are needed or wanted from Texas in the northern states or territories; and the sooner the stockmen of Texas recognize this fact and cease depleting their stocks at home, the better for them. We deem it now full time to urge Texan live stock men to stop driving off to northern markets other than beef cattle; and whether it is really best to drive them, or allow them to remain upon their native pastures until fat and then ship direct to market, is a proposition that will bear discussion.

About the middle of September, 1873, a mass meeting of live stock men was held and a banquet given at Kansas City. The purpose of this was to bring the northern and southern cattlemen together in social contact and intercourse, and, if possible, to inspire the drooping cattle trade with greater life and activity; and also to form an association of live stock men. The mass meeting and banquet was a great success. Near two thousand cattlemen sat down to the banquet, and addresses were delivered by Governor Woodson, of Missouri, and other prominent men representing the various sections of the West and Southwest. Many amusing incidents occurred, one of which we relate. An unshaven, unshorn, roughly clad cowboy fresh from New Mexico obtained a seat at the banquet table. He had often heard of the exhilarating effect of fine, pure wine, but had never tasted any. As soon as he was cleverly seated he clutched a quart bottle of champagne, saying: "What's this hur trick? I guess I'll try the critter." Popping the cork, he proceeded to pour one-half the contents of the bottle down his throat without stopping. Then, hesitating for a moment, [253] remarked: "This hur stuff is too d——d thin; it won't make nobody drunk; I could drink the Gulf of Mexico if it was like this, and not be drunk neither." Then guzzling the balance of the quart, he reached for a second bottle, which he was in the act of uncorking when the effect of the first bottle seemed to suddenly reach his brain. Hesitating for a moment, in which his eye was observed to tingle with a newly aroused wildfire, he arose to his feet; then suddenly jumped about two feet into the air and brought his ponderous fist down on the table with the force of a trip hammer, and screamed in tones near akin to the war whoop of a Comanche: "I'm a s—n of a b—h from New Mexico, by G—d! I'm just off of the Chisholm trail – wild and wooly – and I don't care a d—n! I can whip any shorthorn in America, by G—d!"– all the while jumping up and down like a caged wild demon, his long uncombed hair hanging a profused mass over his face, whilst his eye shot forth piercing tiger glances. Had he had his pistols, death's cold leaden pellets would have been distributed promiscuously.

The following evening a meeting was held and an organization was formed, which was named and styled The Live Stock Men's National Association. Officers: president, John T. Alexander, of Alexander, Illinois; corresponding secretary, Joseph G. McCoy, Kansas City, Missouri; treasurer, W. H. Winants, Kansas City, Missouri. The great panic of 1873 beginning soon after the instituting of the association, all efforts to extend the organization were temporarily suspended. But it is the determined purpose of interested parties at an early day to push and extend the organization, until, if possible, every live stock man in the United States is induced to become a member. All communications pertaining to the association should be addressed to the corresponding secretary.

It is a fact that every other branch of business or occupation, although often not of one-half the magnitude nor employing a fourth of as many men as the live stock [254] business, is organized completely; and by such organizations, aid and protect its members in a thousand ways, besides collecting statistical and other general information concerning their special business, as well as protecting their colaborers from oppression and outrage at the hands of strong monopolies, with which they are often individually brought into business relations. It is true that live stock men are, or have been heretofore, entirely unorganized, and as a result thereof they are not correctly informed as to the extent or magnitude of the business in which they are engaged. Nor do the stockmen of one state, as a class or as a rule, have any definite knowledge of the number engaged in like business in any other state or territory. This might be truthfully said of most stockmen as to their adjoining counties and often townships. Nor do they know or have any good means of informing themselves as to the number of live stock – hogs, cattle, or sheep – that are being prepared for market, or that are likely to be put upon the market at any given time in the future. And when they are prepared or ready to market their stock, if the nearest and most convenient means of transportation chooses to ask them exorbitant rates of freight, they submit, and although they will complain piteously about the extortion, they do nothing to prevent its repetition. Indeed, it has often been said that every stockman was an independent sovereignty in and of himself, and preferred to act for himself alone, free and independently, even if he does pay dearly for the privilege of so doing. It is idle to question the proposition that if stockmen would organize, they could have at least a part of the say in fixing rates of freight, yard charges, feed charges, commissions, and other incidental expenses to which the business is inevitably subjected. It would be next to impossible for railroads to effect and maintain combinations which the stockmen could not break. Corporations, by combination, would not successfully put up and maintain the price of freight fully thirty-three per cent over rates charged previous years, and that, too, when live [255] stock is selling at prices ranging from twenty-five to fifty per cent below those realized in former years. No such outrage could or would be attempted successfully, or tolerated, if live stock men would act in concert to obtain that, that they desire and of a right ought to have. Neither could stockyard companies insolently mistreat and abuse live stock, or charge exorbitant and outrageous prices for yardage, hay, corn, or for other services rendered; they would not dare to do it. But as matters now stand, the live stock men, entirely unorganized, each one by himself and for himself only, are subjected to the arbitrary restrictions and extortionate charges of conscienceless corporations. A stockman or shipper sees himself wronged, and his stock abused, neglected, and otherwise mistreated, but feels himself powerless as to remedies, and usually does nothing but mutter curses, not loud, but deep; then pass along, only to have the same outrages repeated as often as he attempts to go to market.

The only remedy suggested to the mind of the author for these and many other abuses and grievances is in organization. Then a potent protest that could and would be enforced and respected would issue against offending parties, and they be compelled to do right and act fairly with their patrons; or in the event of their persisting in oppressive practices, such retributive justice could be meted out to them as would compel a change in their conduct and manner of doing business, or the business would be taken entirely from them. Again, if the stockmen were properly associated together, a statistical bureau would be established for gathering and disseminating such information as would enable the members of the association to form correct estimates as to the amount of stock in every section of the country, and the probable number that would be marketed each month of the year. It is not difficult for the practical cattleman to see wherein such information would be of inestimable value in forming business calculations, and a correct judgment of the probable [256] future status of the business and markets. Besides, a great aid to both buyers and sellers would be thus created, and a general business register of the wants or desires of live stock men would exist, to which any member might refer at his pleasure; and thus save much time and money which would otherwise be spent in rambling over the country seeking, without knowing just where to look, for that which he desired. The advantages of organization or association are so numerous and so great that it is time spent idly to urge them upon the attention of thinking, discerning live stock men. But if they continue to bear without effort to remedy, the many evils, abuses, and extortions which have been heaped upon them in the past, then are they degenerate dunghills and unfit to bear the proud distinction to which as a class they aspire.

But we hope and apprehend the day is not distant when there will be found organizations of live stock men in every state and in many counties, all of which may be made auxiliary to a general or national association. When that day does come, live stock men will be subjected to fewer losses, and be able to conduct their business in an intelligent, systematic manner, just as is every other industry or vocation in the United States. It is in no sense for the lack of intelligence among stockmen that effectual organization has not before been effected, but from a habit of doing and acting in an independent, individual capacity. The benefits to accrue from association are not thought of or realized; but the day now is, when their numbers and their interest alike, behoove them to organize for their own mutual benefit, information, and strength.

Some of the most intelligent of the land, both of the East and the West, are found in the live stock business. Impaired health often drives eastern born and educated men into the vocation of live stock; in the outdoor, pure-air exercise, they find restored health. Men who are familiar with the amenities of high social life, those who are fitted by nature and education to adorn the best walks of life, are often found [257] in the live stock business in the West. Such a one is Colonel O. W. Wheeler, who, in his native Connecticut home, received such a business education and training as fitted him for a commercial life; but that fell malady of New England, consumption, soon manifested its unmistakable presence in his breast, and he was not long in deciding to test the effects of a trip by ocean steamer to the Pacific slope. Sorrowfully he bid an affectionate adieu to the loved home of his childhood, and to his parents, brothers, and sisters, and boarded a Pacific mail steamer bound for the Isthmus. This was before the Panama Railroad was completed, and the passage from ocean to ocean was made in canoes poled by natives up the Chagres river to the head thereof, thence on mules to Panamá harbor. Although that scourge of the tropics, Panamá fever, laid its heavy hand upon his debilitated form, yet he survived it, and after a passage of thirty-two days found himself upon the golden sands of California. Arriving in the year 1851, he was among the comparatively early settlers in that Eldorado. The very atmosphere was dense with excitement about the mines, of which new ones were being daily discovered, adding their volume to the constantly increasing wave of excitement. When the colonel's health was somewhat restored, his means being limited, he went to the mines, but upon a brief trial found that he was not physically able to endure the heavy labor incident to mining. Accordingly, he returned to Sacramento and engaged in mercantile pursuits, taking a position as head salesman in a large establishment. But having a disposition that prompted the desire to be in the open air, and having naturally a great love for live stock, he accepted the first good opportunity and went to trading in cattle. Going a few hundred miles east into the desert on the emigrant trail, he met an immense concourse of incoming caravans, consisting of teams and outfits en route overland from the states. Of course, many animals, oxen, horses, and mules were jaded out by their long journey over the plains, and [258] were comparatively valueless to the emigrants, who were only too glad to part with them for a small consideration either in cash or recruited animals, for one of which a half dozen jaded ones could readily be exchanged. The all-absorbing effort of the emigrant was to get through to the land of golden promise, and he knew not how soon he would be compelled to either halt or leave part of his outfit. This jaded stock only needed a few weeks' rest and recruiting; no other food was required than the natural grasses of the mountain valleys. This trade, as the reader might readily infer, was very profitable, and the colonel made several trips, reaping rich harvests.

When this trade was over or done, he outfitted several teams and went to freighting to the various mining districts. But not liking this business, he sold out, and meeting an excellent opportunity, he bought out a disgusted merchant and soon built up a lucrative trade, and then sold it out at good advantage. Finally, he met with an opportunity to buy a large flock of sheep which the owners did not know how to handle to advantage. The colonel, having been reared a practical farmer, had no difficulty in putting the flock in fine condition, soon after which he divided the wethers from the stock sheep, and sold the former to the butcher at twelve dollars gold per head; and for the stock sheep a little better price was realized. These sales, in addition to the proceeds of the wool clip, made the transaction highly satisfactory. Being the most successful in live stock, as well as best pleased with the business, he decided to go to Los Angeles in southern California and bring up a herd of cattle, which he did, and sold out at a splendid profit on his arrival at Sacramento. This operation proved so remunerative and congenial that he was prompted to repeat it, which he did; but owing to serious illness he did not succeed so well, yet he made money. While in southern California, two hundred miles south of San Francisco, he espied a large, fine ranch stocked up with over three thousand head of cattle, besides horses, of which [260] the owner had become tired. The colonel determined to buy the whole establishment, which he did without delay or trouble. But he did not hold the realty more than a year before receiving a fine offer for it, which he accepted, retaining the most of his cattle.

About this time he conceived the project of opening a wholesale meat market in San Francisco, which soon required the carcasses of forty bullocks daily. This soon exhausted his herd, but there was no trouble in getting a supply from others at such figures as afforded a fine margin.

The wholesale slaughtering and meat market was continued for two years, when the desire for a more roaming venture took possession of him. Accordingly, he made a trip by way of his Connecticut home to the northwestern states and purchased a herd of horses, which were started over the plains. This was in the year of 1861 and the plains Indians were all on the warpath, and crossing the plains was an undertaking fraught with great danger; especially as Mr. Lo was decidedly fond of horses and was not scrupulous about paying for them in coin or greenbacks. To prevent capture or robbery, if not worse, it was necessary to travel in large trains, or caravans, and maintain by organization a semimilitary defensive attitude. At the head of this organization the colonel was placed by the unanimous vote of a large number of emigrants and plainsmen. That trip was one of great peril and required persistent, eternal vigilance.

The experience and prudence of the colonel was equal to the occasion; and although the train passed through a country swarming with hostile redskins who were ever on the watch for an opportunity to attack the train unawares (the only mode of Indian warfare), and although the red devils hovered on the route for days, the entire train, comprising several hundred wagons and more than a thousand head of loose stock, was conducted through safely. After arriving in California, his horses were sold at a moderate profit. But not content to stop or abandon the [261] drover's life, the colonel embarked in driving fat stock from lower, or southern, California, to the various mining regions in the northern part of the state, and to those of the great silver regions of Nevada. This very profitable traffic was continued through summer and winter, through snow and sunshine, until the spring of 1867, when in consequence of the extreme scarcity of cattle – a result brought about by a drought which had prevailed on the Pacific slope – he determined, in company with Messrs. Wilson and Hicks, to go to Texas and drive a large herd of cattle from there to the mining regions of the Pacific slope.

In pursuance of this determination they visited the Lone Star State early in the year, and purchased a select herd of twenty-four hundred head of cattle and over one hundred head of good cow ponies, and employed fifty-four sturdy men, all of which they armed in the best manner with superior rifles. No more complete outfit or better herd of stock ever left Texas. This herd was the first to pass through the Indian Nation and broke the trail over which the drive of 1867 came. It was a year of constant rain and flood, and, as if to add to the distress of the situation, the Asiatic cholera made its appearance and swept away many cowboys and some of the drovers. When they had arrived in the vicinity of Abilene, a halt for consultation and for reconnoitering the situation was made. The Indians on the plains were extremely hostile and all on the warpath. After obtaining all the information possible, it was determined to stop at Abilene and dispose of the herd. To this course the colonel objected and earnestly urged his two partners to go forward as per the original program, but he was overruled. He was no theorist or dreamer desiring to attempt impossibilities, but having often been exposed to savage redskins, and being anything but a coward, he did not fear to go forward with the herd and fight their way, if need be, through the hostile Indian country. The fear of Indian depredations influenced his partners to take the course determined upon. This magnificent herd [262] did not get in good flesh during the summer season; nevertheless it was shipped to Chicago and packed upon the owners' account, which operation was not profitable. The colonel's plan was to winter the herd, when he found that his partners would not risk going through to California, but in this he was again overruled.

However, when their herd was shipped and packed, he returned to Kansas, and bought on his individual account a herd of fifteen hundred head of cattle, which he wintered in the southeast part of the state and fatted the following summer. Notwithstanding the Missouri mobs, he drove the herd to Quincy, Illinois, where he placed it upon pasture. This was about the time of the great excitement about Spanish fever, and a good opportunity occurred to buy Texan cattle at Quincy from panic-stricken shippers, which he was not slow in improving. Indeed, the colonel bears a well-established reputation as a shrewd, observing operator, whose keen eye always readily sees quickly an opportunity for a profitable investment. Many hundred were sent from the yards to his pasture and mingled with his wintered herd; then he went to Abilene and bought and held several thousand choice cattle. When the excitement subsided and the brisk demand (noted otherwheres) arose for fat Texan cattle for packing purposes, he was found right on hand with rousing fine herds, just ready to reap a harvest of profits. After closing up his summer and fall's operations, he went to Texas, where he bought five thousand head of cattle to be delivered in Nevada. When this contract was completed, he returned to Kansas; and whilst the parties with whom he contracted in Texas were driving the herds to Nevada, he bought and shipped about six thousand head upon the Chicago market.

Upon the arrival of one shipment, a genius named Milk

took upon himself to inform the board of health that the colonel was shipping "fresh Texan cattle." The board thought him a fit subject upon whom to try the recently enacted prohibitory legislation; accordingly, one day when the [263] colonel had about twelve hundred head upon the market, they (the board of health) arrested him for having Texan cattle in the state of Illinois. Before they took the cattle into possession, the colonel demanded a bond of indemnity, and then dug out of his convenient pocket a "certificate under seal," setting forth that the cattle were wintered; and just then the aforesaid board of health "saw it" and wilted. The superintendent of the yards revived them with sparkling champagne, over the effervescence of which the board not only revived but waxed liberal, and patting the colonel on the back, told him to bring all the cattle he pleased. This was esteemed an exalted privilege for an American citizen to enjoy in this free country. But the colonel is anxious to meet the man who set that board of health on him. He would make it warmly interesting to that fellow and would show him a peculiar variety of the "milk of human kindness"; but it is apprehended that that "milk" would not be appreciated. In all these shipping ventures he was successful. Indeed, his judgment was as unerring as his fortune was good; where others stumbled or fell, he cautiously but successfully trod.

In the fall season, at the appointed time, the colonel went to the designated point in Nevada and received, then disposed of, the five thousand head of cattle previously contracted for in Texas; the operation was only moderately profitable. In the year of 1870 he drove from Texas, and shipped altogether near twelve thousand head of cattle; and the following year he drove seven thousand head. This was the year in which occurred the great exodus of kine from Texas to Kansas, and was followed by the winter of disaster. The colonel succeeded in selling all his but one thousand head, which, with eighty-seven head of cow ponies, he put into winter quarters. Of the cattle, he lost twenty per cent, and every one of the ponies perished. He then determined in the future to drive less in numbers, but be more careful in selecting good ones. Accordingly, he only put two thousand upon the trail leading northward [265] the next year, but they were selected stock. After reaching Kansas, he bought five thousand head, mostly wintered cattle, and held them during the summer. He succeeded in making one sale of five thousand head to J. B. Hunter & Company for the snug sum of $125,000.[359] The remainder of his herds he managed to dispose of at paying prices. On returning to Texas the following winter with his cow ponies, and after looking over the situation, he concluded that too many cattle were being driven to be profitable. Accordingly, he sold his ponies and returned to Kansas, where, during the summer of 1873, he maintained a masterly inactivity – a mere spectator of occurring events. But, when a favorable opportunity to make an investment presented itself, he bought six thousand head of cattle and one hundred horses.[360]

The great panic beginning soon after, he was able to sell only about twenty-five hundred head at satisfactory prices and put five hundred head on slop feed in central Illinois; then placed three thousand head in winter quarters in western Kansas. The business of wintering cattle in western Kansas has attained great proportions, and life in camp, and in winter quarters, is much like that described under head of ranching and grazing.

After reading this, and the sketches of other cattlemen, the reader will rightly conclude that the life of the drover and dealer is one full of change, both in lines and character of business. Such is the fact, and in this fact – the perpetual changing of clime, country, scenery, men, and circumstances, coupled with the excitement ever incident to risk and ven-

[359] On October 31, 1872, the *Abilene Chronicle* published the following item: "Col. Wheeler has already shipped this season from Ellsworth 28 cars of cattle, and still has 67 car loads to ship from that point. He has also shipped 47 cars from Abilene, and 8 from Junction City, besides 300 head of stock cattle driven to the vicinity of Manhattan and other points east of Abilene, for the purpose of wintering them. Altogether Col. Wheeler has already sold during the present season over 4000 head of cattle – 3000 of which were bought by Mr. Hunter of Kansas City, the largest sale made by any dealer in the market."

[360] Wheeler arrived in Ellsworth during the latter part of May, 1873. *Ellsworth Reporter*, May 29, June 5, 1873.

ture — is to be found the fascination of the life and business of a drover, the key to the impetus which ever drives and animates him to greater and greater efforts and larger and larger risks. So deep and firm does the habit and incentive to trade and speculation take hold upon its votaries, that few men, after beginning, are ever willing to quit the business of stock trading and shipping, or exchange it for any [266] other business. If, from financial inability, he is compelled to take up some other vocation, he is ever longing to again try his fortune in live stock operations. If he succeeds, no matter how well at first, it only stimulates him to greater exertions and greater risks. If he does not succeed, it only serves to make him determined to retrieve his losses in the same vocation in which he sustained it. Bankruptcy and financial ruin is the only means that will put a stop to his operations. These observations are more applicable to shippers of live stock than to ranchmen, or to that other class of dealers who conduct their operations altogether in the country and seldom go to market, [and] then only with their own production. This class of operators are not only more safe and successful, but almost invariably accumulate wealth, for they can remain at home when the market is not good and hold their stock off, or await the coming of a shipper or speculator to whom they sell when the prices offered are satisfactory. To this latter class belongs Colonel Wheeler.

Northwestern Kansas is a superior stock country, and abounds with fine buffalo grass upon the uplands and bluestem or bluejoint grass in the valleys, affording abundant hay and winter range; also water, fresh and salt, and timber and other shelter exists in abundance. In these regions the colonel has chosen his wintering grounds; and when the herds are once located and become quiet and content, they are not herded, but outriding the country instead, is practiced. Substantial dugouts were constructed for the comfort of his men, and everything provided to render them as snug and content as possible under the circumstances. The colonel's employees are to a man loud in praise of his generous liberality, and everyone of them would fight and, if need be, lay down their lives for him or his interests. When

COL. WHEELER COUNTER-BRANDING A HERD, PREPARATORY TO PUTTING IT INTO WINTER QUARTERS.

WINTER QUARTERS OF COL. O. W. WHEELER'S COW-BOYS, ON THE SOLOMON RIVER.

the winter is passed, the cattle are gathered together and put under herd, and camps established; this is done to prevent the cattle from straying off or being stolen. [268] The frontier of Kansas, like all other frontiers, is subject to the depredations of thieving bands of desperadoes, a lot of outlaws who cannot live in a country or district where civil law can be enforced, but hover on the frontier ever ready to prey upon the honest frontiersman. These bandits do not hesitate to run off any number of cattle or ponies that the negligent herder may permit to come within their reach.

There are many comforts enjoyed in camp life out on the Great Plains in the summer season, not the least among which is the delightsome breeze which so gently sweeps over the land, bringing health, vigor, and "the balm of a thousand flowers" upon its wings. The freedom and abandon which naturally abounds, coupled with the jovial hilarity inevitable to robust health, to which may be added the often-recurring sharp appetite for the feasts of game often provided by the skill of some semi-Nimrod herder, all conspire to render camp life upon the broad plains a joy forever. When any attention whatever is paid to camp comforts and the most ordinary sanitary regulations, sickness is almost unknown, but the opposite – vigorous health, energy, and a keen appreciation of life with its ever-changing vicissitudes – is realized. It is true that many drovers are apparently indifferent to the health and comfort of the cowboys in their employ; not of this class is the colonel. The welfare and comfort of his employees are scrupulously looked after, and as a consequence he receives in return faithful service, besides the highest esteem bordering on veneration from his men, of which he employs constantly a dozen or more.

There are few men in the western live stock trade more widely or more favorably known than is Colonel Wheeler; a Puritan in blood, tracing his lineage direct to an honorable soldier of the War of 1812, whose forefathers were among the hardy band of Pilgrims that landed upon the historic Plymouth Rock. His manner of doing business is such as will bear favorable comparison with the most scrupulous and exacting. His business principles are of the loftiest order, [269] and none more heartily condemns and loathes a low, mean, or arbitrary act, than he, and none would be farther from performing a dishonorable deed; prudent and close, yet bold and daring, in his business transactions; punctual in meeting his engagements; shrewd and correct in finances; cordial and courteous, withal dignified but not bigoted, in his manner and intercourse with men. He is the universal favorite of a large circle which embraces the entire personnel of the western live stock trade, besides many honorable gentlemen in other walks of life. All recognize in him the generous, chivalrous gentleman, whose impulses are ever true and good, and whose sympathies are ever with the worthy and deserving.

COL. OLIVER W. WHEELER.

XIV. CREATING A LIVE STOCK
MARKET IN KANSAS CITY

As the territory of the United States has been gradually developed by settlement and cultivation, new live stock markets have sprung into existence and grown to such magnitude as their location and the permanence of the necessity for them warranted. Thus, scarce more than fifty years since, the entire live stock product of the nation was produced east of the Allegheny mountains, and Philadelphia, Baltimore, New York, and Boston were the only live stock marts of note. But in later years Albany, then Buffalo, and finally Chicago on the northern lines, and Pittsburg, Cincinnati, and St. Louis on the southern and central lines, became markets of great importance. It is quite within the memory of many living stockmen when both St. Louis and Chicago, and particularly the former, were in their infancy as live stock markets. St. Louis being located on a river, formerly the only means of transportation, is the more ancient as a live stock market.[361] The years are few since both these cities were not only regarded as extreme frontier markets, but so much so that it was not thought possible or needful to ever attempt a permanent live stock mart west of them. But upon the development of the country, accelerated by railroads, it became [271] apparent that the area of the production of cattle must be that of the Far West – that tract of country east of the Rocky mountains which our infant minds were taught to regard as a desert, but which proved upon closer inspection and experiment to be *par excellence* a live stock producing country.

As the region immediately tributary to the Missouri river for a distance of near one hundred miles on either side be-

---

[361] For an account of the early live stock trade of St. Louis, see the introduction to the present volume.

came developed, it proved to be very superior corn-growing lands, not excelled as such by famous central Illinois. Upon the establishment and recognition of this fact, the area in which cattle and hogs could be profitably fatted on corn became greatly extended, and the business of raising cattle for the feeder correspondingly stimulated but pushed still farther westward. And so the business of breeding and rearing of live stock, especially sheep and cattle, has extended to the base of the Rocky mountains; and after occupying its parks and valleys with live stock ranches, turns back over the plains to occupy every available location for a distance of five hundred miles in breadth, and more than two thousand miles in length from north to south, covering the vast plains in due time with bleating flocks and lowing herds. From the nature of the country and its climate and seasons, the positions now fast shaping will of necessity be permanent. The corn-producing belt cannot be extended farther west, not at least sufficiently profitable to ever become an extensive competitor to exclusive live stock production. The Great Plains are fast becoming peopled with hardy herdsmen, whose flocks and herds will soon cover the whole of the rainless belt. In the very nature of things, and in obedience to the same commercial law or necessity that impelled the building of live stock marts at St. Louis and Chicago, there must be a mart, a point of common center, of sale and interchange somewhere in the valley of the Missouri.

This self-evident fact being admitted, the question naturally presents itself — what point on the Missouri river is the [272] best one; and as naturally answers itself — the one that is most eligibly located and that furnishes the best facilities for doing the business; the point that has the most tributary lines of supply, as well as lines of outlet; the point which concentrates the greatest number of buyers and sellers. It should be the one where a number of points are competing for the same branch of commerce, that makes the greatest efforts to establish the necessary facilities and financial accommodations, besides such establishments as manufacture live stock into commercial commodities, such as packing and rendering houses, which require immense capital to construct and operate. Taking all these prerequisites into considera-

VIEW OF KANSAS STOCK YARDS, KANSAS CITY, MO.

VIEW OF KANSAS STOCK YARDS.

tion, it is easy to see that Kansas City is preëminently the point on the Missouri river at which a live stock mart ought to be established, and by the united exertions of western stockmen, sustained. Stock marts, like cities, are not made in a day or by a single man, but by persistent and continued efforts of many parties in interest. So if the western live stock men desire a market nearer their home than St. Louis or Chicago, it is their duty to themselves to aid in making such a one. They should second the efforts already put forth and still being made to create a good, complete live stock mart at Kansas City, because the point fills, in a marked degree, all the essential requirements necessary to make a complete market. The history of the beginning and development of some of the facilities for doing a large stock trade, and the manner in which the business is conducted, with sketches of some of the representative men engaged therein, forms the purpose and scope of this and the succeeding chapter.

In 1867 the cattle shipped from Abilene went by way of Leavenworth to Chicago, but no good facilities for transferring over the Missouri river existed, and but little desire to retain the business was manifested by Leavenworth; so the following spring it went to Kansas City. There the Missouri Pacific Company had built small yards sufficient to [274] accommodate only ten cars of stock, but which had previous to that season never been full. As soon as the river was bridged, the Hannibal and St. Joe Railroad Company built small yards, but they soon proved inadequate to accommodate the business, which was yearly growing larger.[362] In the spring of 1871 a joint stock company was formed for the purpose of erecting and operating a complete feed and transfer yard. A suitable tract of land was secured, and during 1871 quite a large portion of the ground covered with yards, lanes, alleys, scales, barns, and a building for business offices. Every railroad entering or departing from Kansas City soon connected with the yards; and business

---

[362] L. V. Morse, superintendent of the Hannibal and St. Joseph Railroad, who was primarily responsible for the establishment of these stockyards, "mapped off and fenced in five acres of ground, divided it up into eleven pens, built fifteen unloading chutes and put in a small pair of Fairbanks scales." Powell, *op. cit.*, 15.

from the beginning was brisk, crowding to their utmost capacity all the facilities provided, and necessitating additional yards, hog sheds, stables, and office room, until at the present the entire tract of land is occupied. Ample room exists for seven thousand head of cattle and six thousand hogs at one time without overcrowding, but in a case of emergency fifty per cent more could be taken care of. Water fresh from the Kaw river is conducted by pipes laid under ground to troughs provided in each yard; also mangers for feeding hay in cattle yards; and floored pens, covered with roofs for shade and shelter, are provided for the hogs and sheep.[363]

The first year, that of 1871, 120,827 cattle, 41,036 hogs, 4,527 sheep, and 809 horses were received, of which but a small per cent were sold, for Kansas City was then naught more than a feeding and resting point, no effort having been put forth to make it a market. During the year of 1872, 236,800 cattle, 105,640 hogs, 2,648 horses, and 6,071 sheep were received at Kansas City, and a successful effort was made to create a market. Its creation sprang from the necessities of the situation. Parties failing to sell upon the prairies naturally desired to sell at the first point at which it was possible. Purchasers from the East naturally preferred buying at Kansas City to going to the prairies; especially [276] was this the case when the frontier points of rendezvous for cattle became numerous and distant apart. Large pack-

---

[363] These stockyards, which were located in Kansas City, Kansas, just beyond the state line, were begun early in 1871 and completed during June and July of the same year. At first called the Union Stockyards, after the Union Stockyards in Chicago, they were renamed the Kansas Stockyards in September, 1871, when they received a charter of incorporation from the legislature of Kansas. Powell wrote: "The yards covered only twenty-six acres, but were provided with pens and chutes and was a trading place for the western cattle then seeking a market here. The Exchange Building was even less pretentious than the yards, being a one-and-a-half story frame structure at the end of Twelfth street and without Commission men's offices, yet it was a shelter and a warming and drying place in cold and wet weather. . . The year 1872 saw many changes. Early in the spring of that year an upper story was added to the Exchange Building and it was divided into offices, giving the Commission men their first quarters." *Ibid.*, 17-18. See also *Kansas City Journal of Commerce*, June 5, July 12, Oct. 4, 1871; *Kansas Daily Commonwealth*, Feb. 8, 1871, July 10, 1877; *History of the State of Kansas* (1883), 1241.

ing houses were located at Kansas City, and its superior advantages in location and climate for doing a successful and profitable packing business had become established; and thus a considerable demand occurred, aside from that of northwestern feeders and grazers. All these influences gradually developed and created a market, which, since its beginning, has grown rapidly.

During the year of 1873, 238,825 cattle, 201,113 hogs, 6,056 sheep and 3,961 horses were received, of which by far the larger proportion were sold. The financial panic reduced the receipts of cattle fully 100,000 during 1873.[364] It is a fact that although the prices which ruled at Kansas City during that season of financial distress were extremely low and unsatisfactory to the drover and shipper, yet they were much better than were realized farther east, freights and charges being deducted. This is proven by the fact that of the parties who bought in Kansas City market and shipped forward to eastern markets, ten lost where one made money, showing conclusively that they had paid too high for the stock. Again, it is a fact that shippers who refused to accept offers for their stock at Kansas City, but shipped it forward on their own account, almost invariably realized less net for it than they had refused at Kansas City. It has been abundantly demonstrated that at Kansas City a good and complete live stock market can be created or established; one that will be alike beneficial to the western and southwestern live stock producers and to the northwestern feeders and grazers; and it certainly is alike desirable and profitable to both parties that such should be. A near, home market is essential to the producers of all marketable commodities, and to none more so than the live stock man, be he breeder, feeder, grazer, or shipper.

The Kansas Stockyards are under the management of [277] Superintendent Jerome D. Smith, who has been in

---

[364] Powell, who obtained his figures from the Kansas City newspapers, stated that in 1871, 120,827 cattle, 41,036 hogs, 4527 sheep, and 809 horses and mules were received at the Kansas Stockyards; in 1872, 236,802 cattle, 104,639 hogs, 6071 sheep, and 2648 horses and mules; and in 1873, 227,680 cattle, 221,815 hogs, 5975 sheep, and 4202 horses and mules. Powell, *op. cit.*, 38, 49, 57, 66. See also *Kansas City Journal of Commerce*, Jan. 3, 1872, Jan. 7, 1873, Jan. 18, 1874.

charge since the organization of the company. J. D. Smith has certainly a right to claim a cattleman's blood. His father was one of the most widely known cattle shippers in the Northwest, having persistently shipped cattle for forty-two consecutive years, and in that space of time was "busted" ten different times — a comprehensive and suggestive commentary upon the business of live stock shipping. J. D. Smith was born and reared to the age of seventeen in Newark, New Jersey; then came to Illinois; and after completing his education, engaged in the live stock trade on his own account in Kansas and Missouri for two years; then went to Chicago, where for six years he acted in the capacity of live stock agent for the Michigan Central and Great Western Railways. Finally, upon the organization of the Kansas Stockyard [278] Company, he secured the position of superintendent, which he has filled to the satisfaction of the company. Mr. Smith is a congenial, jovial young man, who has, by energy and application to duty, worked himself into an honorable lucrative position, and by diligence and sober deportment has won the esteem of many friends and the kindest respect of his employees, all of whom indulge the fondest hope and confidence in an honorable future for him.

But the success of the Kansas Stockyards is quite as much due to its late secretary and treasurer, George N. Altman, as to any other officer connected therewith; for it is evident that his was a position that required capacity and ability to administer, as well as one of no small degree of responsibility; for it was upon him rested the labor and responsibility of keeping, not only the accounts of the stockyards' own business, but of all the railroad live stock deliveries and shipments. His books must [279] show the receipt of each and every carload of live stock, from whence received, and how disposed of, whether carred or driven out, and upon whose account — in short, the entire workings and business of the yards. Besides the duties as a secretary, that of treasurer imposed the collection of all freight charges and the disbursing of the same. The positions of secretary and treasurer are such as require positive exactness in accounts and impose great responsibility. The position of secretary

GEO. N. ALTMAN.

JEROME D. SMITH.

EXCHANGE BUILDING AND BUSINESS OFFICES OF KANSAS STOCK YARDS.

was given Mr. Altman at the first organization of the stockyard company, and after the first year the position and
duties of treasurer were added; in all of which he acquitted
himself to the entire satisfaction of the company and to his
own great credit. Mr. Altman, for several years previous
to his connection with the Kansas Stockyards, was book-
keeper and cashier to a live stock commission firm in Chicago, who did a large business, and was the one that sold
the first trainload of Texan cattle that was shipped from
Abilene, the account of sale of which was made by Mr.
Altman. Previous to that, he held honorable positions of
trust in the telegraph and ticket department of the M.S. &
N.I. Railroad. Mr. Altman was a quiet, mild, accomplished
gentleman, who had by energy, honesty, and real ability,
merited and obtained positions of honor and responsibility,
and had won scores of friends and admirers, all of whom
esteemed him highly, alike for his many good qualities of
heart as well as his persistent, laborious attention to the
interest of the company. When, upon a bright morning late
in the year of 1873, it was announced that Mr. Altman was
dead, fallen a victim of incurable consumption, a deep sadness pervaded the habitués of the stock mart, and the tear
of sorrow glistened in many eyes unaccustomed to weeping.

The manner in which live stock are received, fed, watered,
rested, and otherwise cared for, and the manner in which
they are handled, sold, weighed, and delivered, may be of
interest to the general reader; therefore, to this his [280]
attention is invited. As soon as a train bringing stock arrives
at the yards and is drawn up to the platform for unloading,
the employees of the yard company (of which there are
many) at once open the car doors, put down a small bridge
from the car floor to the platform, and drive the stock out
and down the inclining platform into the alleys, along which
they are hastily driven to a yard of proper size, into which
they are turned. Soon after, they are watered and fed according to order of shipper. Large barns for storing baled
hay and corn are provided, and a shipper can have his stock
fed either or both, and only has to pay for the amount he
orders; and if no sale of his stock is made, no charge is
made for yardage or reloading, which is done by the yard

company. Only in case of sale are charges of yardage made
for stock, which includes weighing. A large building is provided for the business offices. Some of the principal railroads
maintain special stock agents, whose offices are near-by. The
upper floor is divided off into small compartments, or offices,
which are occupied by live stock commission merchants. The
entire premises are under the control of the superintendent,
whose word or command is law to all the employees of the
yard company. If he is efficient, there is no minutia or detail
that he does not give his personal attention. There is great
need that he be a practical cattleman, with business capacity
equal to any emergency.

The business of live stock commission merchants is to
take care of, feed, water, sell, and render to the owner an
account of such consignments of live stock as he may be able
to obtain either from his patrons direct or from such as may
arrive with stock not consigned to any other house. It is a
part of his duties to keep himself fully posted as to prices,
not only in the market in which he sells, but of all distant
markets, besides always keeping a sharp lookout for live
stock buyers for all grades; and, in short, to keep and be
a kind of general intelligence office concerning live stock men
and matters; to which it might be truthfully added, to be a
[282] most obedient servant or convenience, to perform any
errand or office for a live stock man that may be desired.
There are few men who do as much work for so little pay
as the average commission merchant, and certainly none
who do more to create good markets than he; and notwithstanding that it is common to hear ignorant dolts mouthing
otherwise, they are, as a class, honest, fair business men.
Indeed, they could not be otherwise and succeed for any
considerable length of time, because the competition and
rivalry is so great, and competitors so watchful, that any
other than an upright, correct course or manner of doing
business would be exposed and published to the world.
Again, the rivalry impels them to work for the highest
prices, in order to please and hold their customers; and they
usually know better than one who has just arrived or is
seldom on market, the true value of all grades of stock;
besides, they know the man, if any there be who desires any

particular grade of stock. There are men engaged in live stock commission in every mart, and none can be cited where they are not found also; and as a body, do much toward establishing good markets.

Among the first, if not the first man to locate at Kansas City and attempt to establish a live stock commission house, was W. A. Rogers, who had been for two years previously, and still is, connected as a partner in the house of Robert Strahorn & Company, of Chicago. Soon after he decided to locate at Kansas City, he entered into a firm, which, after one or more changes, is now widely known as Rogers, Powers & Company. The experiment was a success from the first, and the close of the second year showed that a business of near two thousand cars of stock had been done annually. Mr. Rogers was born in Indiana, but while young was taken by his parents to Iowa, where he remained until he attained the years of manhood; after which period, farming and local live stock trading engaged his attention for three years. Finding the stock business more congenial to his tastes, he abandoned farming and formed his Chicago business [283] connections and went to Kansas, where for two years he bought, shipped, and fed cattle, always keeping a sharp lookout for chances to improve the business of his Chicago house. Finally, additional business relations and a permanent location at Kansas City were decided upon. Perhaps few men so young are so widely known in the West as Mr. Rogers; young, energetic, shrewd, and quick, never slow to discern an opening or an opportunity for a profitable business operation, and untiring in his efforts to increase his business; a good judge of the quality and value of live stock; a close observer of human nature, readily reading a man's thoughts in the expression of his countenance, and never at a loss to know how to turn it to advantage. Fortune has dealt liberally with him and success crowns most of his undertakings. With his ability, experience, and already-acquired capital, it is easy to see that the future is full of hope and bright promises for him. [284] Both firms (as now constituted) with which he is connected present combinations of capital and practical adaptability to the business rarely met with, and insures the utmost good faith and responsibility.

It is not often we meet, permanently located at a market, aged men; men whose heads bear nature's silvery crown of honor, whose patriarchal beard reminds the beholder of the ancients, and in whose presence one intuitively feels the reverence due to venerable experience and wisdom. But ever and anon we do meet such an one; such is J. L. Mitchener, who stands at the head of the capable house of Mitchener & Son. His life has been a varied one – one ever cast in busy exciting scenes. [He was] born and reared to manhood in Pennsylvania, where, with his father, he was annually engaged in large live stock feeding operations, being thoroughly schooled in the manner of handling, feeding, and marketing stock. Whilst yet a [285] young man not above a score in years, he incidentally visited the state of Ohio. So soon as he perceived the great advantages for live stock operations that that new state then offered, he determined to realize their benefits. Accordingly, after spending a short time in making needful preparations, he entered the (to him) promiseful Buckeye State, and within her borders made his home for seventeen years; two-thirds of which time was devoted to a profitable live stock business; and the remaining third to manufacturing product of live stock in the city of Cincinnati, in which and in other products he was a heavy operator. But in time he became restless in the pent-up city and longed for the freedom of the country, for the vocation of the stock farm; and having tasted the unrestrained exciting life peculiar to a new country, concluded to try Illinois, and in 1854 took up his abode upon a good farm of seven hundred acres, which he had previously bought.

After spending five years in his rural home, engaged successfully in extensive live stock operations, he went to St. Joseph, Missouri, at the solicitation of a St. Louis packing firm, and aided in conducting a large packing establishment. Here, again, the Great New West, the mighty predestined valley of the Missouri, enraptured him; thinking that he could foresee the day, which to him looked as one not distant, when the onward, westward march of civilization would develop that rich, new country into a garden of beauty, an Eldorado of health; and with a ken little short of

J. L. MITCHENER.

WILLIAM A. ROGERS.

GEORGE R. BARSE.

JOHN SALISBURY.

prophetic saw and believed in the coming greatness and commercial importance of Kansas City. Therefore, to that point he brought his effects, and it is said actually built the first packing house ever erected there. But the unforeseen war soon occurring, he was induced, out of motives to preserve his family, to return to Chicago, where he again connected himself with a prominent packing house. Soon thereafter the project of the Union Stockyards took shape; and to the enterprise he gave his aid, and was the first man to actually break dirt, setting the first post and nailing the first board in their [286] erection. And when the yards were so far completed as to be open for business, he accepted the position of division superintendent, which position he held until the year 1869, when he established the house of which he now stands at the head.[365] In a life in which fickle fortune alternates a smiling and frowning countenance, most men become in age morose and sour, or settle down in hopeless impotency, apparently only waiting the last summons, thus confessing life a failure, and life's rugged steeps too precipitous for them to reattempt to scale, since once attaining, have been hurled to the bottom. Not so with Mr. J. L. Mitchener; his voice is as cheery, his air as confident, his manner as open, frank, up and above board when in poverty's narrowest rut as when upon fortune's most gilded heights. With him it matters not; hope and manhood is high whether his purse be full or collapsed, for he believes "A man's a man for all that." The commission house at the head of which he stands is one among the reliable and capable established in Kansas City during the year 1872. Its business is steadily increasing, and its already long list of patrons is daily augmenting.

---

[365] By the latter part of 1864, Chicago had six stockyards. "Lying in different parts of the city, on different and diverging streets, in several instances two or three miles apart, these yards were found inconvenient for the transaction of business." To remedy this defect, the legislature of Illinois, early in 1865, incorporated the "Union Stock Yard and Transit Company," with a view to centralize Chicago's stock transactions. The company purchased 345 acres of swampy land on the south side of the city, just beyond the corporate limits, and began the erection of stockyards on June 1, 1865. The work was completed by the following December 25, when the first cattle were received. *Transactions of the Illinois State Agricultural Society*, VI, 314-324; Clemen, *op. cit.*, 85-87.

Most of the men engaged in live stock commission are either western born or western raised, and often both. Such is the case with George R. Barse.[366] Wisconsin is the state of his nativity, although he was educated at Detroit, Michigan. Then he went to Illinois and began business for himself as a grain and live stock dealer, which occupation he followed but too closely for three years. At the earliest call for volunteers he enrolled his name and served his country faithfully four years, fourteen months of which time he was a prisoner in the South, and was in nearly every prison pen in Dixie. Four different times did he escape, three times was he retaken; but the last time success crowned his efforts and he joined Sherman's "bummers" on their way to the sea. When peace was restored, he returned to Illinois and resumed his old business, which he followed with varying fortune until the year of 1871, in which he formed connections [287] with one of Chicago's most widely known live stock firms, and the following year came to Kansas City. But the great panic of 1873 had the effect of severing his connections with the Chicago house, and he formed other connections. Mr. Barse understands the practical management of live stock and is a good salesman. He is a whole-souled, good-tempered man, whose record for integrity, energy, and a conscientious application to the interests of his patrons is unspotted.

Some of the Chicago commission houses have established branch offices at Kansas City, which are usually conducted under the same name as the original house. Such is the case with the well and favorably known house of Hough Reeves & Company, whose Kansas City salesman is John Salisbury – a man who was reared to the business, beginning at the 100th street, New York City, the city of his birth. After [288] selling for years in New York, he went to Albany and Buffalo, stopping for a year at each. He finally went to southern Illinois, where he occupied himself as a local trader until the outbreak of the war; at the close of which he returned to New York City and for three years continued his old first vocation; then went to Chicago, and after selling on

---

366 For a biographical sketch of George R. Barse, see Powell, *op. cit.*, 201-204.

that market for the house with which he now is, for two years, was transferred to Kansas City; where he has been for more than two years and where he expects to remain permanently. The house for which he acts as salesman is one of the most substantial financially and widely known firms in the West; and in the person of Mr. Salisbury they have an able, experienced salesman, who can discern at a glance the correct grade and value of a drove of cattle, and can sell them for every dollar they are worth on the market. It is only necessary for him to attend strictly to the business in which he is [289] engaged to make sure of abundant success and a prosperous future.

It might be supposed that a firm, one or more of whose members were Texans, would naturally attract and receive the patronage of southern drovers. Their suspicion of a northern man is deep and universal. Therefore they prefer to intrust one from their own state with their business. Accordingly, it is not infrequent that one or more northern men will associate with themselves one or more Texan men, and thus present a house unobjectionable to men from either section. W. H. Kingsbery, of the firm of Matthews, Kingsbery & Company, one of Kansas City's most enterprising live stock commission houses, is well known to Texans as being a member of the firm of Kingsbery & Holmsley, of Comanche, Texas. Born and reared to the age of sixteen in the state of [290] Georgia, he became so enraptured with the glowing accounts of the great new state of Texas that he determined to emigrate hither. Not having funds to travel by public conveyance, yet so determined was he to try his fortune in the distant Lone Star State that he set out afoot and alone, and tramped the entire distance from Georgia to the western frontier of Texas, where he promptly accepted the position of clerk in a country store. After many years of hard struggling, self-denial, and economy, he became enabled to establish a business for himself by purchasing a small branch store from his former employer. This opportunity was improved to the best advantage, and the foundation of a future substantial business and a sound, strong credit was carefully laid. Men who in their youth receive a thorough drilling in adversity, and thus not only learn the intrinsic value of a dollar but how to make and take care of one, invariably make earth's most successful business men, those who manifest actual talent and business capacity; and the rule holds as to the subject of this sketch. When the war came, he took part as a soldier and served actively for three years; but on receiving a severe wound he returned home, and as soon as he was able took up his vocation as a merchant.

At the close of the war, money was very scarce in Texas, everything being uncurrent except specie, and much of the business in the merchandising line had to be done in exchange for cattle. During 1867 and for two succeeding years Kingsbery & Holmsley found buyers at or near home for such stock as they had taken in exchange for goods. For the next four years they sent their herds to Kansas — first to Baxter Springs, then to Ellsworth, and lastly to Coffeyville. Their annual drives would average fully twenty-five hundred head. Finding it necessary for an agency at Kansas City, they opened a commission house there in 1872 under [the] same firm name as the Texas business was conducted. The following [291] year a new combination was made, and in Kansas City's stock mart the name of Matthews, Kingsbery & Company are as familiar as household words. As a firm they are liberal, straightforward, upright, and possess indomitable energy, coupled with integrity, financial responsibility, and good practical judgment in matters pertaining to live stock. The house is firmly established, and its business, already of enormous proportions, is daily increasing. Mr. Kingsbery is of that class of men to whom any vocation or community may refer to with pride.[367]

During the month of August, 1872, R. Nichols, who had formed connections with a prominent firm in Chicago, established a house at Kansas City under the firm name of R. Nichols & Company and flung his shingle to the breeze. He was already quite well known in the West, having been in [292] the western cattle trade for three years previously;

---

[367] During 1874, Matthews, Kingsbury (or Kingsbery) & Company were engaged, among other things, in introducing thoroughbred Durham bulls into Texas and crossing them with native cows in order to improve the breed of stock there. *Denison Daily News*, June 25, 1874. See also Powell, *op. cit.*, 177.

ROBERT C. WHITE.

WILLIAM H. KINGSBERY.

RANDOLPH NICHOLS.

"SCALPING."

besides having been an active local trader in Illinois, where
he was reared to manhood, although born in Ohio. Mr.
Nichols was not slow in establishing a lively paying business,
but the great panic dealt harshly with him, clouding his
bright prospects of honorable success. He is quick, shrewd,
sharp, and a good salesman, one who can always get fair
prices for his consignments. One would scarce suppose, to
look upon his youthful, boyish face, that he was a business
man of eight years' experience, yet such is the fact.

Such are the men who first engaged in the attempt to
create or establish a live stock market at Kansas City; an
attempt worthy of success, and one fraught with great good
to western and southern live stock men, as well as to Kansas
City, for it brings to her a lucrative commerce amounting to
many millions of dollars annually. But certain adjuncts or
aids of some commission firms may be of interest to the
general reader. Active men are employed to perform various
duties, but the particular class now referred to are the
solicitors – those whose duty it is to meet every train and
secure such stock as may not be consigned to any commission
house. So soon as an incoming train is announced nearing
the stockyards, the hurrying tramp of solicitors – vulgarly,
but not inappropriately, called "scalpers" – may be heard
hustling toward the unloading platform. If there is a shipper
on the train whose stock is not consigned, they proceed in
a cheeky, *sang-froid* manner to interview him, presenting
the business cards of the commission firms which have the
scalpers employed. Such oily, persuasive arguments as scarce
ever fell from mortal's lips are poured into the ear of a
newly arrived shipper. But the first scalper to reach the ear
of the shipper enjoys but a brief monopoly of his attention
before a second, representing another and competing house
or firm, puts in not only a presence but a lip also, and with
a coolness and self-possession beyond comprehension, plucks
the shipper to [293] one side and begins to pump him full
of the points in favor of the house, or firm, which Scalper
Number Two serves. But before the pleasant duty is half
completed, Scalper Number Three arrives and straightway
goes to the shipper, grasps his hand in the most cordial and
familiar manner, just as if he was an old schoolmate and

bosom friend, although ten to one Scalper Number Three never saw the shipper before, and cares little whether he ever does afterward; especially if he fails to get the shipper's stock turned over to the desired firm before Scalper Number Four captures the shipper, only to see Number One, who has recharged his mortar, retake the shipper, who becomes so dumbfounded and fuddled that he scarce knows his own name, much less where he is or what he wants. The scalper is a distinctive type of the *genus homo,* is supposed to be omnivorous and brimful of bland cheek, of which he has more than an army mule; but in this he does not excel more than [294] in facile, glib talk — genuine chin-music and cool impertinence. To say he has a conscience, much less is ever checked or restrained thereby, is to state a proposition without having an experienced, observing believer. He is *au fait* on all matters pertaining to his firm, as well as to all points against a competitor. Nevertheless, he is an "institution," a kind of necessary evil, about the propriety of maintaining which, commission men differ. However, when a covey of scalpers do unitedly beset a verdant country shipper, a humane man can but feel that they are a nuisance that ought to be speedily and thoroughly abated.

Sometimes a scalper will perpetrate a sharp practical joke on some comrade, such an one as may be late getting to a newly arrived train upon which there may be a car of horses, the shipper of which will be pointed out to the unposted scalper, accompanied with the remark that "that man has a load of stock for you." Then to see the scalper rush to the man and ask him if they are natives, if they are butchers or shippers, cows or steers, longhorns or shorthorns, through or wintered, and such other questions as the scalper imagines would betoken a profound, deep interest in the stranger's welfare! But when he learns that he is "sold," his indignation is only excelled by his loud curses. When the reader is told that Kansas City is not a horse market, and all those arriving there are only in transit to other points, he will comprehend the discomfiture of the scalper.

At the beginning of the year 1873 the conviction was firm and widespread that at Kansas City a complete live stock market was established beyond doubt. All the essential requisites and necessities existed for the creation of such a mart, and the results of the previous year had demonstrated its practicability. Early in the season several new firms and partnerships were formed, preparatory to a vigorous summer's campaign with the bovines and porcine grunters. Among the new firms established, none was more notable as being composed of substantial, practical, clear-headed business men than that of Hunter, Pattison & Evans, since changed to Hunter, [295] Evans & Company.[368] Each member of this firm is a successful live stock man of long experience, which, coupled with their individual responsibility, renders their house one altogether reliable and safe, and one which adds greatly to Kansas City's young, flourishing live stock mart.

But of all the commission houses established up to July, 1873, there was none which was known to, or composed in whole or in part of, local live stock men or such as were residents of western Missouri, or even known to the stock feeders of that vicinity. Of course, this condition or state of affairs made a good opening for the establishment of such a house, and R. C. White, long a resident of Kansas City and well known to every stockman in the adjoining country, entered the arena of the Kansas Stockyards and opened a live stock commission house under the firm name of White, Allen & Company. It did not require great forecast to see that his undertaking would be a success, [296] or a long lapse of time to demonstrate it. From the beginning, business offered, and as time progressed, it greatly

---

[368] During 1872, Edward W. Pattison and A. G. Evans, of Kansas City, founded the firm of Pattison, Evans & Company, a commission house for the sale of live stock at the Kansas Stockyards. Early in 1873, after Robert D. Hunter joined the organization, it was known as Hunter, Pattison & Evans. Pattison withdrew from the company in 1874 and was replaced by W. L. Harding, when the firm changed its name to Hunter, Evans & Company. During the same year it opened an office at the National Stockyards in East St. Louis, Illinois, which became the headquarters of the company after its withdrawal from Kansas City in 1877. Meanwhile, in 1876 it established the first beef canning house in St. Louis. *Parsons' Memorial and Historical Library Magazine* (Mrs. August Wilson, ed., St. Louis, 1885), I, 319-325; *Ellsworth Reporter*, Apr. 17, 1873; Powell, *op. cit.*, 179-181, 210.

increased until at the end of six months the firm stood among the first in the yards. Mr. White hails the state of Kentucky as that of his birth. When but a boy he left his native state, and after rambling through Texas he came to Missouri and made his home near Platte City, where his time was divided between his farm and local live stock trading. Finally deciding that Kansas City offered superior inducements, he moved his residence there, and for sixteen consecutive years followed diligently and with varying fortunes his chosen vocation, that of live stock trading, which embraced cattle, horses, mules, sheep, hogs — anything, no matter what, so it had four feet, either with or without horns; seldom shipping anything away to market, but nearly always selling to some professional shipper who preferred greater risk and less work. Nevertheless, Mr. White has experienced all the phases of ups and downs, fortune and adversity, so peculiar to stock traders, and that seems to be the inevitable fate of all live stock shippers. No matter from what source his misfortune came, whether by declining markets or by surety obligations, he stood square to the issue, and paid dollar for dollar till the last obligation was canceled. Such integrity, in time, always establishes unlimited confidence in he who exhibits it, and such is the case with Mr. White; a kind, courteous, true man, whose plain, straightforward manner impresses one with his exalted, unassuming manhood.

Such are the leading men who are seeking to make a great live stock market at Kansas City — men who are laying the foundations of a mart that is destined at no distant day to rank, in numbers of live stock received, the equal of any other in the United States. But these men are not alone or unaided in their great efforts. They have the moral and business support of every right-minded western live stock man, as well as the encouragement of Kansas City's leading business men, besides the aid and influence of the enlightened [298] management of every line of railroad entering the city, of which there is a large number. To conduct their business, each house retains in its employ a corps of assistants who are detailed to the various departments of business. Every well-regulated and successful commission house

CASHIERS AND ACCOUNTANTS.

L. M. HUNTER.

employs one or more good bookkeepers and accountants. These are usually young and middle-aged men of good business qualifications and steady habits, each of whom look eagerly forward to the day when they will establish a business of their own. Nowhere in the West can a galaxy of finer, truer young men be found than in the exchange building of the Kansas City live stock mart.

It is often asked why live stock shipping cannot be conducted, like any other ordinary business, without great losses. The reasons are various, some of which may be named. In the first place, the manner in which the business is conducted in the West necessitates the shipper to buy stock, often months in advance of shipping. It is the custom when a shipper determines to ship cattle during the year or season, for him to mount his horse, traverse the cattle-feeding district, and contract for various lots of cattle to be received at stipulated times in the future. The shipper usually manages to have about an equal proportion of the cattle he buys or contracts for, to be received each week, so that he may have a shipment on market being sold, another going forward, and still another being received and collected at the various shipping yards along the line of railway over which he is sending the stock. Now it is plain that unless he prearranges his shipments, he may occasionally be unable to obtain the stock, for if he has not bought ahead, some other shipper has entered the field and bought or contracted all the cattle. It is equally plain upon reflection that buying to receive ahead is much like gambling with the feeder on the future price or value of his stock. It may be compared, and not inaptly, to an insurance or guaranty business in which the shipper guarantees or insures the feeder a [299] certain price for his cattle, agreeing to take the excess realized over the price paid or stipulated, for his premium on the risk taken and for his services in marketing the stock. Of course, the feeder is not obliged to sell or contract his cattle in advance of delivery, and will not unless it is at a price that pays him a handsome profit, which often puts the cattle at such figures that the shipper cannot realize first cost. Again, a man who ships live stock, by his continual risk soon becomes reckless and imprudent, loses his caution, and "goes it blind." Again, the time between purchasing a drove of cattle in the West and the day they can be put upon the eastern market is nearly or quite two weeks, in which the market often declines heavily. It requires the most extreme speculative turn of mind to constitute a live stock shipper; none other would take the risks; none other would hazard so much for the chance of gaining so little. Persistent shipping engenders loss of [300] business prudence, and creates a feverish, speculative turn of mind in which there is little cool, solid judgment, but an ever-increasing desire for greater operations and greater hazards. Heavy losses incurred, alike with large gains, stimulate the shipper to renewed efforts; in the first instance to cover, in the last to increase, the amount already gained.

For one of his age it would be difficult to find a better specimen or illustration of cattle shippers than L. M. Hunter, who, although scarce more than one and a half score of years old, has shipped many thousands of cattle. Indeed, he is never so happy as when he is shipping from one to three thousand head of cattle weekly. Born and reared in Illinois, his father a life-long shipper, he began shipping when but a boy, and the passion has grown with and upon him until it is more than a part of his nature. After operating upon his own account for several years, in which he experienced all the phases, successes, and reverses peculiar if not inevitable to a life-long shipper, he associated himself with his father in the firm of J. B. Hunter & Company, and took charge of and conducted the business of the firm in the West, with office at Kansas City. There are but few western drovers who do not know him familiarly. No one ever entered the western trade that bought so many cattle as he, and few young men had so many friends among live stock men. He is the very embodiment of energy, seemingly never caring to rest, sleep, or scarcely to eat; sinewy, wiry, restless, always looking for an opportunity to trade, never idle for a moment, and always in a hurry; withal, a man of fair judgment about live stock, and a man of many good qualities of head and heart.

XV. PACKING HOUSES IN KANSAS CITY

Before Kansas City assumed to be a live stock mart — even before any fitting accommodation to feed or rest any large number of cattle in transit was provided — it attracted the attention of packers as being an eligible point for packing establishments. As early as 1868 the house known as the Stone House, now owned and operated by Messrs. Nofsinger & Company, was erected, and as soon as completed was occupied, first killing cattle, then hogs, and preparing the product thereof for commerce and consumption.[369] In a few years other and larger houses were built, until four [370] are now standing upon the banks of the Missouri river just where it makes the "great bend," turning abruptly from its southerly course, rolls onward in an almost direct eastward course across the state of Missouri, pouring its turbid waters into the Mississippi river. Two of the houses are in the state of Kansas, the other two are in the state of Missouri.

It is enough to say that the location for packing houses could not be improved upon or surpassed in the West. This may be truthfully said as to the exact grounds upon which they are built, as well as the point in the West at which they are located. For Kansas City — with her network of railroads already built and in process of building, being located in the center of a district of country fully three hundred miles in diameter which, as an inevitable result of its unparalleled fertility and its immense yield of corn annually, must

---

[369] The stone house was erected and used as a packing plant in 1868 by the pioneer packing establishment in Kansas City — E. W. Pattison & Company. It was located in "West Kansas City." *Kansas City Journal of Commerce*, June 23, Dec. 1, 1868. See also footnote 376.

[370] Plankinton & Armour; Ferguson, Slavens & Company; Nofsinger, Tobey & Company; and Thomas J. Bigger. *Ibid.*, Dec. 15, 1871; Powell, *op. cit.*, 86-88.

ever be a prolific hog country as well [302] as a great cattle-feeding district — must not only be, from the very nature of the situation, a good and great live stock mart, but also a choice point for packing establishments.[371] Just beyond the corn-producing area to the westward and southwest is the illimitable grass belt, which will ever furnish ample supplies of suitable cattle for packing purposes at prices and in con- ditions not attainable at other points. Again, its proximity to the plains and mountains will, in consequence of the pure air, enable it to put up meats successfully at times and tem- peratures which would forbid operation at any other packing point east of it. These reasons, in connection with the fact that large establishments for packing cattle exclusively can- not be profitably maintained, insures the future permanency of the beef packing to it. Shrewd, practical operators, seeing these truthful reasons and advantages, have occupied the grounds in part.

Now as large and prosperous packing houses arranged for handling both cattle and hogs are already in operation there as can be found on this or any other continent, and that, too, without likelihood of ever being removed or ex- celed by any other point. Among the largest and most com- pletely equipped and operated establishments is that of Messrs. Plankinton & Armour's, an establishment which covers an area of land equal to three acres, with capacity to handle one thousand cattle and three thousand hogs per day. Built of brick, its massive walls rise up in imposing strength and extent, like the battlements of some ancient fortified city. There are few, if any, superior establishments of the kind in the United States. It is but one of three packing houses owned by the same firm — one being located in Chi- cago, the other in Milwaukee, Wisconsin. Their brands and trade-marks are favorably and widely known throughout the United States, and not unknown in the Old World.[372]

[371] As early as January 20, 1866, the *Kansas City Journal of Commerce* prophesied: "The dozen railroads that will center here within the next five years, will afford transportation facilities in every direction, and the result will be that a number of packing houses will be built at this point." At this time Kansas City had a population of about 7500. *Ibid.,* Jan. 24, 1869.

[372] In 1863, at Milwaukee, Wisconsin, John Plankinton and Philip D. Armour founded the firm of Plankinton & Armour, which slaughtered and

The other Kansas City packing establishments have an aggregate capacity equal to that of Plankinton & Armour's, so that in a single day it is possible at Kansas City to slaughter and dress two thousand [304] cattle and six thousand hogs, and in the same time to cut and salt the carcasses of as many more.

The country surrounding and tributary to the point, when developed, can furnish annally one-half million cattle and two million hogs. It is evident to the thoughtful observer that the Missouri valley must develop some metropolitan live stock mart — some point at which her live stock production can be converted or manufactured into merchantable commodities. Such a point Kansas City seeks to be, and if the brief past shall be a criterion whereby to judge the future, success may as well be conceded. But for the purpose, if possible, of conveying to the reader a correct idea of how meats are prepared for market and export, a few pages are devoted to the packing business, or the mode and manner of transforming live stock into merchantable product. The illustrations, so far as practicable, were made from sketches and photographs on the ground, and are from scenes at the establishment of Plankinton & Armour, their facilities being the most complete and extensive, embracing the very latest improvements and conveniences.

The hog crop, for packing purposes, is the most important, from the significant fact that the consumption of salt beef is annually decreasing and the use of fresh beef is increasing; while the use of salt and cured pork is annually increasing very perceptibly, and the consumption of fresh pork is diminishing in a marked manner. But the manner of

packed beef and pork on a large scale. Shortly afterward Armour, with the aid of his brothers, established similar houses in Chicago, New York City, and other places. During July, 1870, Plankinton & Armour opened a plant in Kansas City, Missouri, renting the stone house in which that city's first packing had been started a few years before. But in 1871 the firm moved to Kansas City, Kansas, just beyond the state line, where it was housed in a building of its own. This structure measured 160 by 180 feet and had two stories and a cellar. The manager of the company in Kansas City was Simeon B. Armour, Philip's brother. *Kansas City Journal of Commerce,* July 27, Oct. 26, 1870, July 22, 1871; *History of the State of Kansas* (1883), 1241; Powell, *op. cit.,* 86-91; Clemen, *op. cit.,* 149-154.

slaughtering and curing pork has of late been extensively illustrated, so that it has been thought best to give greater attention to cattle than hog packing, although in point of numbers and value it is inferior. Yet it is by no means an insignificant branch of commercial industry. During the fall seasons of 1871 and 1872 over 68,000 cattle were packed at Kansas City, and at the same point during the single season of 1873 fully 26,500 were slaughtered and the product fitted for commerce. During the packing season of 1872 and 1873, 180,000 hogs were packed, and the number slaughtered during the [305] season of 1873 and 1874 falls not much short of 200,000. The panic of 1873 embarrassed the packing business greatly.[373]

The manner in which the porcines are hurried from the feed pen to the pork barrel is summary and expeditious. When they are made fat by the farmer, chiefly on corn— every well-to-do husbandman raising and fatting a herd of greater or smaller number, owing to his thrift, enterprise, and facilities – they are gathered together at the most convenient railroad stations and loaded upon the cars and hurried to market, where their stay is usually brief before they are sold and hustled to the establishment of some packer; in whose yards they do not remain long before they are driven up an inclined plane or gangway securely boarded up on either side, reaching to the uppermost story of the building, where they are secured in a large pen, from which they are passed in little squads into smaller pens within the slaughter room. Overhead an endless single bar or rail track is firmly arranged, upon which are movable single-wheel pulleys, to which are attached self-tightening grappling hooks or chains. Before piggy is aware of it, one of those clamps is around one of his hind legs, and he is hoisted by steam power off the floor. Thus suspended, he is rolled over a platform arranged to receive and carry off his gore; upon which platform stands a muscular, active, and skilled fellow

---

[373] About 4200 cattle were packed in Kansas City in 1868; 4450 in 1869; 21,000 in 1870; 45,543 in 1871; 20,500 in 1872; 26,549 in 1873; 42,226 in 1874; 26,372 in 1875; 26,765 in 1876; 27,863 in 1877; 18,756 in 1878; 29,149 in 1879; and 160,290 in 1887. *Kansas City Journal of Commerce,* Jan. 3, 1872, Jan. 7, 1873, Jan. 18, 1874, Jan. 3, 1875, Jan. 1, 6, 1876; Jan. 12, 1878, Jan. 4, 1880; *Kansas City Times,* Jan. 6, 1877; Powell, *op. cit.,* 82-83.

PLANKINTON & ARMOURS PACKING ESTABLISHMENT, KANSAS CITY, MO.

GREAT BEND OF THE MISSOURI RIVER—SHOWING PACKING-HOUSES.

who grasps the suspended, frightened, struggling pig by the
fore leg with his left hand, whilst with his right he thrusts
a keen blade to the pig's heart letting out lifeblood copi-
ously, at the same instant giving him a heave toward the
scalding tub. An inclining chute terminating in the scalding
tub receives his dead or dying body the instant his foot is
disengaged from the grappling irons by an ingenious con-
trivance. Down the chute he glides, and in an instant is sub-
merged in the hot, scalding water, which is maintained at
just the required temperature by means of steam pipes.
Over and over he is rolled until near the other end of the
scalding vat, where in a twinkle he is thrown up by mechanical appliances onto the scraping table, [307] or platform,
toward the other end of which he never ceases to be rolled,
all the while being scraped by the score of laborers who
speedily denude him of his coating of hair. When the lower
end of the cleaning or scraping table is reached, he is under
another single-track railway, upon which run single pulleys
with a flat hook attached suitable to receive a gammon
stick, each end of which is inserted beneath the strong leader
of his hind legs. So soon as the gammon is placed, piggy
slides lightly off the platform and hangs by his hind legs.
A push and a whirl, and he is in the presence of the butcher,
who, with an expedition incredible, disembowels the subject
almost in a moment; an insertion of the knife, twist of the
wrist, a rip down piggy's belly, and his entrails are out, fly-
ing through the air en route to the tables where they receive
proper attention; whilst steaming, disemboweled piggy's
carcass goes spinning off on its easy moving pulley to the
cooling room. It is there placed upon guys and permitted to
hang over night to cool.

On the following day the carcass is taken down and
thrown upon the cleaving block, and is speedily cut into such
shaped pieces as are desired. Meats for certain markets and
for certain purposes are cut different to those intended for
other purposes or different markets. After cutting, sorting,
and trimming, the meat passes down inclining chutes to its
proper salting room below, where it is salted in bulk or barreled as desired. The reader should bear in mind in following a single subject in its quiet transit from the living pig to

salt pork, that the way is thronged by a host of others following in close succession. The establishment from which the illustrations are taken, when run to its full capacity, employs near five hundred men — active, muscular fellows, who, under the direction of a foreman, move things at a very lively rate.

A story illustrative of the expedition with which business is dispatched at a packing house is told of an old territorial farmer, of Illinois, who declined current prices for his [309] little squad of long-nosed hazel-splitters, but concluded an arrangement with a packing firm which was doing a large business, to have his hogs slaughtered and packed on commission. Accordingly, he placed them in the yards belonging to the establishment, and essayed to watch what become of them and so prevent any stealing, or substituting mean hogs for his good ones, which he was very suspicious would be done. But the process through which his hogs were taken was so unexpectedly rapid that he was thrown into unutterable confusion and bewilderment. When he saw great, burly, stalwart, powerful men with iron hooks, hurling his indistinguishable porkers, with others, over a partition into, he could not tell or find out where, he became wild with excitement and fear, but finally gave up in despair and rushed to the office of the establishment. Sinking heavily down into a chair, he exclaimed in a voice expressive of ruin and despair: "Mr. Clerk, I cast myself upon your honor. Yes, sir, right upon yer honesty. If you ever do find them thar hogs of mine and can get anything outen em, jist let me know. Jist now I want to go home — I feel so bad! Oh, so bad! I want to see my wife, then go to bed, I do. Yes, Mr. Clerk, upon your honesty — I trust upon your honor — oh, dear me!" The old farmer rushed from the office to his "old mar" and was off for home, fully determined next time to sell out his "crap" of hogs and leave the business of packing to those who could understand it.

But the manner of slaughtering and dressing cattle, they being much larger animals, differs greatly from that of hogs. Cattle packing is chiefly done in the late fall and early winter months, when a supply of grassfatted stock can be had, and the weather is sufficiently cold to thoroughly cool

KILLING CATTLE—PLANKINTON & ARMOURS, KANSAS CITY, MO.

SLAUGHTERING HOGS—PLANKINTON & ARMOURS, KANSAS CITY, MO.

the meat. It is only grassfatted cattle that can be had at prices sufficiently low to justify packing. For this reason cornfatted cattle are seldom, if ever, packed. Hence, a point near the plains where cattle are cheaply bred and fatted, at which a supply of hogs can also be had, is the one most likely to [310] do the principal portion of cattle packing. Such a point Kansas City rightly claims to be.

When a herd of cattle is placed in the yards adjoining a packing establishment for the purpose of being packed, they are separated into squads of two or three, and driven through a long, larrow lane and forced into a small box pen, the gate being securely fastened behind them. A dozen or more of those box pens are located side by side, all connected with the main lane, or driveway, so that the men in the yards always have empty pens to fill. So soon as a pen is filled, a man standing upon a narrow gangway just above the cattle's heads, with a rifle loaded with fixed ammunition, shoots the bullocks in the head. The ball ranges down into or through the brain, producing instant death. Of course the bullock instantly drops, only to receive the falling body of his comrade. Formerly a long pike was used, with which the brute was speared just behind the horns, or forehead, upon the top of the neck, where the vertebræ joins the head. But this method of killing was abandoned as being less humane than the rifle. Often when good aim was not taken, or the animal at the critical moment moved its head, it would be mangled horribly, but not killed without repeated blows. So soon as all are shot down in any one pen, a rising door which divides the pen from the inner portion of the establishment, is hoisted, and a man enters from within the house, dragging a long chain with a noose formed at the end thereof. This chain extends back and around certain pulleys, and up to a revolving drum, or windlass, which is driven by steam and governed by means of a lever in the hands of a person whose sole duty is to manage the machine, stopping and starting it instantly at the call of the man who handles the chain. This he drops over the bullock's head, around his neck or horns, as may be convenient, then calls for power, which the man at the lever at once applies; and the bullock is drawn out on a narrow floor, inclining toward a gutter or [312] drain, near to which the head of the bullock is stopped. The chain loosened, the drawing-out operation is repeated upon the comrade, which is left lying beside him. Then the chain man shifts his chain into the next pulley and enters the next pen.

So soon as the bullock is stopped upon the narrow inclining floor, a butcher opens the skin on the underside of the neck and cuts both jugular veins, thus letting the hot blood run freely upon the floor, thence into the drain, which conducts it from the building and empties it into the river. Even before the blood is done flowing and before the bullock is quiet in death, the butchers begin dressing it; one taking off its head, first denuding it of the skin; another peels the hide down the legs to the knees, then adroitly separates the joint, throwing the feet and shins upon the floor, from whence an urchin removes them to the proper room. The bullock is then turned upon its back, being propped by a short pointed brace, and another pair of butchers take it in charge; and whilst the first two are beheading and unlimbing the next bullock, they quickly strip the hide from belly, quarters, and sides of the animal. Then comes one or more men and insert a strong gammon of four or more feet in length in the hocks beneath the hamstrings of the hinder legs. In the middle of the gammon stick a flat iron hook is adjusted, which is attached to a strong rope running over a pulley aloft, and is wound up on a windlass so rigged and geared that a muscular man can raise slowly upward the carcass of the bullock, which is fast relieved of its hide and entrails whilst so moving. So soon as the hide is off and the inwards taken out, the carcass is split in twain, dividing the backbone with a broad-bladed ax, save a small portion of muscle at the back of the neck. The hide is dragged off to a small hole in the floor, through which it is tumbled to the salting cellar below. The paunch and entrails are dragged with hooks of steel to their proper rooms, whilst the lungs are thrown into the drain with the blood and other filthy waste, and passes out of the building. In the meantime the [313] carcass is windlassed to a height which brings it clear off the floor, and [which brings] the gammon level with a series of skids, a distance apart equal to the length of the gammon, the ends of which groove into smooth

SAWING UP THE CARCASS.

DRESSING BEEVES—PLANKINTON & ARMOURS, KANSAS CITY, MO.

slots. The hook and rope being relaxed, the carcass rests upon the skids, which run parallel the entire length of the cooling room at right angles to the dressing floor. Upon the skids the carcasses are permitted to hang in close proximity until they are thoroughly cooled and the fatty parts become hard and firm, which occur as soon as all animal heat is out.

When the reader bears in mind that of the fourscore or more of men engaged, each one has a certain part only, which he performs and then passes to the next bullock – one assisting, some throwing feet, others dragging off heads, others scraping and cleaning the floor, whilst others are doing various duties – and that the space over which the work is done is more than one hundred feet in length, and that a score or more of bullocks are being operated upon at the same time, he may rightly conclude that the scene of cattle dressing is one of entirely too great activity, life, and space for one illustration to do ample justice.

When the carcasses are properly cooled, the work of cutting up may begin. This requires a large number of men to do the work expeditiously. However, of late years the saw propelled by steam is largely substituted for the cleaver and knife. A full complement of saws to do all the different styles of cuts comprises five, each of which is operated in a separate frame and driven by a belt which receives its motion, or power, from a shaft and pulley overhead, which is driven by steam power. These saw frames stand in position describing a flatiron; the first one being next to the hanging carcasses, at the opposite end of the large cooling room from which the cattle are dressed; the other saw frames stand two and two, just opposite to each other and behind the first frame; still farther back the remaining pair of saw frames are stationed. Trimming tables are near, and also suspended [315] platform scales for weighing of each barrel or tierce of beef, care being taken to have as near the same pieces and the exact weight in each package as possible. Near-by, the barrels are brought and a given amount of salt provided to each. Meats for certain brands and markets are cut in uniform shape and size, and from certain portions of the carcass.

Quite a large number of men are required to operate all

the saws, to bring the carcasses, handle the meat on the frames, trim on the tables, weigh up and pack in barrels, bring up salt, empty barrels, and take away full ones. The quarters of beef are brought one at a time and thrown upon the first saw frame, where two men adjust the quarter and pass it up to the saw, which divides flesh and bone in a jiffy; and the pieces pass on to the next saw and over trimming tables and then to the scales, thence to the barrel. When the reader remembers that the capacity of the house from which the illustrations are taken is one thousand bullocks per day, making four thousand quarters to be handled and cut within ten hours, he will not hesitate to believe that the corps of laborers is large, and that each man moves quick and steady; no dilly-dallying, no playing, no foolishness, but work quick, fast, and constant is the order of the establishment. The fat, or tallow, is trimmed off and rendered in large tanks, which are heated by steam. The hides are usually salted, packed in large heaps or piles, then, after draining for a few days and taking salt, they are rolled up in a snug bundle, tied with a strong cord, and are ready to go forward in bulk to the tannery. The entrails are emptied of their contents, washed, heaved into a tank, and steamed out into grease used for mechanical purposes. The hoofs and horns go to the glue and comb makers. The stomach, or manifold, is carefully saved, cleansed, and prepared for tripe. Thus nothing is lost; almost everything is utilized pertaining to the bullock.

A great part of the beef packed is consumed in the lumber regions, and aboard sailing vessels, whalers, and naval [317] vessels. A part is consumed in Europe, for which the best grade, called "India mess," is required. The fleshy part of the ham is put up in various shapes, but is mostly salted, then dried; by far the largest portion of the dried beef seen in provision and grocery establishments is prepared in this manner.

It requires a large capital to build and operate a packing establishment of great capacity. Inasmuch as the hog and beef product is, like cotton, a staple article of commerce and consumption, therefore always in demand, it is not diffi-cult in ordinary times to hire abundant capital with which to prepare the crop of the West, which in these later years has become immense, especially of hogs. Yet the full capacity of the country for their production is not now, nor never has been, taxed or developed to one-half its abilities.

Of the enterprising firm [374] from whose house the illustrations herein presented were taken, little need be said. Their meats are well known in most of the world's markets; and their manner of dealing with their fellow men is such as to inspire confidence in their patrons, and a respect bordering on veneration in their employees, to whom they pay promptly liberal wages, and among whom the firm, in the year 1872, is reported to have distributed as a gratuitous present the sum of twenty thousand dollars. One thing worthy of note which strikes the observing stranger on entering their establishment, either when it is in operation or standing idle, is the perfect neatness, cleanliness, and good order in which everything is kept and done, and the entire absence of the stench and filth so common to similar establishments. This is not by accident, but by vigorous, persistent attention to cleanliness, to preserve which many men are constantly employed scraping, scrubbing, and washing all parts of the house in use. This fact alone should make a preference for their product over houses run in the usually unsavory, not to say stinking and filthy, style. No blood or filth is allowed to so much as dry up within the [318] house, much less to decompose and fill the air with its repugnant effluvia. Their success has been great and as deserved as great.

The first person who engaged in packing pork at Kansas City was Thomas J. Bigger, in the fall of 1868. This gentleman is a native of Belfast, Ireland, and came to New York City for the purpose of preparing meats especially adapted to the Irish market. After engaging in business for five years in the American commercial metropolis, he determined to change his base to the source of supply, the Great West. Accordingly, after carefully looking over the country for a suitable, favorable location, he finally selected and located at Kansas City.[375] After five years' residence, and as many

374 Plankinton & Armour.

375 In 1893, Powell wrote: "[Thomas J. Bigger] rented what was later

years' business, he has no occasion to regret his selection of location. Although his establishment is not so imposing as others, yet it is ample for his present business, which ranks [319] second to but one in the city. It is a fact of which Kansas Cityans may well boast that one of the packing establishments of which she is so justly proud is engaged almost exclusively in preparing meats especially for a particular foreign market, to which they are shipped direct. As every market requires its peculiar cuts, so does the Irish market, and for this Mr. Bigger prepares his product. During the great panic, when other packers' financial arrangements were deranged, his, being with European houses, was undisturbed. This gave him substantial advantages of which he was not slow to avail himself, and the close of that season showed a goodly number of hogs to have met death and dissection in his establishment. Mr. Bigger is an affable, unassuming business man — one who has many friends, and whose successful career is regarded with interest and pride by every true Kansas Cityan.

However, there were others who engaged in pork packing the same season at Kansas City, prominent among whom was Edward W. Pattison, who is a Kentuckian by birth, but in early childhood his father removed to Indiana (then a new, heavily timbered country) and engaged in the laborious and tedious task of clearing up a farm. He was so successful that he was enabled to give his son Edward the benefit of a good common school education. When Mr. Pattison had attained the age of seventeen, he engaged in driving live stock to Cincinnati, the principal market for that portion of the country; which business was continued for ten years. Having acquired a snug capital for those days; and becoming familiar with the mode of packing cattle and hogs, he determined to build a packing establishment in Indiana and try the business upon his own account. After operating for two years, the canal (his only means of sending the product to market) was destroyed, and he moved to Cincinnati and there opened a commission house for the sale of provisions,

known as the DuBois hide house, on St. Louis avenue just west of Hickory street, and packed hogs during the winter of 1868-9 in a small way. The following year he bought ground and built a house of his own where the Fowler packing plant now stands." Powell, *op. cit.*, 82.

THOMAS J. BIGGER.

EDWARD W. PATTISON.

especially the product of live stock. But not liking this business, he went to Indianapolis and for ten years engaged in live stock shipping, and, during the winter [320] seasons, packing pork, occasionally stall-feeding cattle in eastern Illinois. Returning to his former business, he erected at Indianapolis a packing establishment of capacity to handle three hundred cattle or one thousand hogs daily, which was for that day and generation a large establishment.

After conducting the packing business for five years, he went to western Kansas in the fall of 1867 and formed a company at Junction City, put up a packing house, and slaughtered five thousand head of Texan cattle. The following year he decided to locate in Kansas City, and joining one or two associates in business, they erected the first packing house of note ever built at that point [376] — one of capacity sufficient to handle daily four hundred cattle or fifteen hundred hogs. After three years devoted to operating this establishment, he sold out and purchased land and established four stock ranches in Ellsworth county, Kansas, upon which he placed in the fall of 1871 five thousand head of Texan cattle. The [321] reader will remember that was a cold, stormy winter, one of widespread disaster to cattlemen; and Mr. Pattison lost many cattle, although his losses were not so severe as were those of many other parties engaged in wintering on the buffalo grass. Nevertheless, they were such as determined him to change his business. Accordingly, the following summer he bought and shipped eight thousand head of cattle to market. The succeeding spring he formed connection with and took charge of the St. Louis branch of

[376] During September, 1867, Edward W. Pattison, of Indianapolis, began the erection of a beef packing plant in Junction City, Kansas, which, under the name of E. W. Pattison & Company, began operations on the following October 9. Moving to Kansas City, Missouri, in 1868, Pattison joined with William Epperson, of Indianapolis, and J. W. L. Slavens, of Kansas City, to found the firm of E. W. Pattison & Company, the first packing house in that city. The company purchased three acres of land in "West Kansas City" and erected a three-story stone building that measured 88 by 138 feet. The estimated cost of the structure was about $20,000. During the first season (1868) E. W. Pattison & Company packed approximately 4200 cattle and 13,000 hogs. *Junction City Weekly Union,* Aug. 31, Oct. 12, Nov. 30, 1867, Mar. 21, 1868; *Kansas City Journal of Commerce,* June 23, Dec. 1, 1868, Jan. 19, 1869; Powell, *op. cit.,* 86, 205.

a prominent live stock commission house. At the end of one year he opened a house upon his own account at the National Stockyards, East St. Louis. If the reader has read this sketch closely, he will not doubt that Mr. Pattison ought to be posted in all the phases of the live stock business, which is a truth. He is a high-minded, honorable business man — one whose experience qualifies him to fill the station he now occupies to the satisfaction of all reasonable patrons. He is a man of the kindest impulses, and one who has experienced every phase of fortunes; one whose eventful, ever-changing life has led him to entertain the most kindly, charitable feelings for his fellow man. Indeed, he means and deserves well, and is a man of integrity and perfect rectitude of purpose.

XVI. FINANCING THE CATTLE TRADE

It has been truly said that money is the sinews of war. It is equally as true that it is the sinews of the live stock trade – the motive power which drives as well as oils the mighty yet intricate system upon which the live stock commerce, both in the living and the product condition, is done. Immense sums of money are paid annually for live stock, for consumption and other purposes. But few of the civilized world's inhabitants do not daily consume more or less meat, either fresh or cured; and of the few who do not so daily use it, poverty, more than a dislike or lack of desire for it, prevents them from using it also. Often in single live stock transactions as much as fifty to one hundred thousand dollars changes hands, and transactions reaching from one to twenty thousand dollars are of almost hourly occurrence in every live stock mart of note within the country.

It is common in transacting live stock business to borrow large sums of money, usually upon short time, say thirty to ninety days. Not one operator – whether he be drover, feeder, or shipper – in a thousand ever has money sufficient of his own to conduct all his business operations without borrowing capital. If he had so much of his own, he would not need to operate at all, for he could and would live at his ease. The reader may rest [323] assured that it is the hope of gain, and not the love of the business or the labor connected with it, that impels the operator to take the risks, endure the hardships, and perform the labors which he does. Drovers, shippers, and feeders of cattle are almost unavoidably heavy borrowers of money. The banking institutions are the most common source from which they obtain loans. In every live stock mart or section of stock country, be it great or small, there is, and of a necessity there must be, one or more financial institutions which are able to supply the requisite accommodations and make a specialty of accommodating the stock trade.

As every other great center or geographical division of the live stock trade has its leading financial institutions, so has the live stock trade of the West and Southwest. It is useless to tell a western reader that that institution was for many years the First National Bank of Kansas City alone, for every stockman knows it. The officers of this bank at an early day saw, as with a prophetic eye, the future greatness, importance, and the lucrative nature of the live stock trade, and its value as a commerce to such banking houses as secured it. Seeing this so plainly, they put forth early and effective efforts to secure it to their institution and to Kansas City. At first they had little or no competition, for few other banking houses cared to take such as they deemed extreme, extra-hazardous discount risks, as they regarded loans to the uncouth, sunburned drovers who claimed to have herds grazing on the prairie, somewhere out on the uncertain frontier of civilization. At first but few drovers wanted money, save for expenses or to pay off extra help on arrival at Abilene, for they had purchased their cattle on time, payable when the cattle were marketed and returns were realized; this limited amount needed could in most cases be obtained in Abilene or Junction City. But as the volume of trade grew, the necessity for money grew also, because the time for payment for their herds in [324] whole or in part, became shortened, it often being at the time of arrival at Abilene, whether sale of the stock was made or not. This, of course, increased the demand for loans, which soon outgrew the supply at Abilene and other western points; and in such cases it was the custom of the Illinoisans to direct the drovers to the First National Bank of Kansas City for funds, or for eastern exchange to take back to Texas. Indeed, it was common to advise, and often urge, returning drovers to take New York exchange instead of currency back to Texas, [and] thus avoid the danger of robbery or permanent loss whilst en route home. Often those who declined to act upon the advice rued it when too late; in several instances they were robbed and sometimes mur-

dered for their money whilst going through the Indian
Territory to Texas. The drovers were not slow in learning
what financial institutions were disposed to afford them
needed accommodations. It is true that in a certain sense,
banking with cattlemen is extra-hazardous, from the fact
that their herds are distant, often in different states and
counties from the one in which the bank is located; and being
a class of assets that has the power of self-transportation,
could be hurried off in a short time to regions in which force
and the pistol is the only recognized law. This being the
fact, the bank that affords them discounts must do it as
much upon the drover's honesty and honor as upon his financial
responsibility. And this, of course, requires in the
banker a keen, shrewd judgment of human nature; one who
has faith in humanity; one who does not imagine every
applicant for accommodation to be a thief or swindler; one
who is willing to let go his ducats without exacting a pound
of flesh as surety from next the heart of the borrower; a
banker who understands the financial necessities of live stock
men and the nature of their business; one who regards the
major part of business men as being honest and not as ever
seeking to swindle somebody. Such are some of the requisite
traits for banking in the western cattle trade; such a one
has ever [325] been at the head of the affairs of the First
National Bank of Kansas City.

It is related that at an early day in the opening and development of the cattle trade, when the personnel of the
droving fraternity was but little known in Kansas City, a
certain now well-known major who had just arrived at
Abilene with a large herd of cattle, and needing a loan,
after having made unsuccessful applications at other banking houses of Kansas City, went into the First National,
and, unheralded and without formal introduction, went
abruptly into the president's room and bluntly announced
in a full, audible voice: "My name is Major ——; I have
a herd of two thousand head of cattle at Abilene, Kansas;
I want ten thousand dollars for ninety days; can I get it
here?" He was asked by the president if he knew anyone in
the city, or if there was anyone who knew him or that would
probably endorse his note; to which the blunt drover frankly

replied, "No." After talking a few moments, in which the banker put various questions to the drover, and scanned his countenance closely as if he were looking into his inmost soul and noting whether its impulses were honest or otherwise, the drover was dismissed with direction to call again the next morning. Promptly at the hour designated the drover went to the banking office; he had nothing but his stock; nevertheless, he was told to sign a plain note of hand, upon which he received ten thousand current dollars, less the interest. It is needless to add that the note was [326] paid promptly at maturity, just as western drovers are in the habit of doing. A hundred similar instances might be related where money has been freely loaned to the drover without other than personal security. Yet, as a rule, to which the exceptions are rare indeed, the notes have been paid on or before maturity.

The First National of Kansas City was established and opened for business in 1865, with a capital of $100,000, and has gradually increased in capital and strength until it now ranks second to none west of St. Louis. In 1868 it began to cultivate the acquaintance of and extend accommodation to western and southern cattlemen. Those at the head of that institution early saw the importance, magnitude, and profit of the cattle commerce then just beginning to develop, and with rare business tact reached forth a helping hand to aid, secure, and build up the great commerce; and richly have they been rewarded for their foresight and efforts. By the year 1870 their business with the drovers had so materially increased that they opened an office at Abilene under the able management of W. H. Winants,[377] a capable and popular young business man who has long been honorably connected with the institution, and by this means secured the lion's share of business. Indeed, but a small fraction of the banking business of the western cattle trade was done in other financial institutions. So much has this been the case that it is justly regarded as a part and parcel historically of the western live stock trade; hence the space devoted to it. It never seemed too limited in

---

[377] Winants arrived in Abilene during September. *Abilene Chronicle,* Sept. 15, 1870.

its ability to accommodate drovers and dealers, and never unwilling to aid liberally any upright man who was making honest efforts to conduct his business. It has been influential in a marked degree in securing and aiding the various packing establishments found at Kansas City. Among stockmen it has many patrons, from the Rocky mountains on the west to the Gulf on the south, who regard it as their best friend and most ready helper.

As may rightly be supposed, when the great panic of [327] 1873 burst upon the country, this institution, like every other one that was doing an extended business, felt its fury severely. For sixty days during that unprecedented stringency it kept open and paid more than one million of its obligations. At the beginning of the panic, of its assets, were live stock men's notes to the amount of over one-half million dollars. In nearly every instance they were met and paid at maturity, although to do so caused the sacrifice of thousands of cattle upon ruinously low markets. Indeed, it may be said that that institution has found, upon the severest of tests, that banking with live stock men has been eminently satisfactory and safe, instead of extra-hazardous as it appeared to be in the beginning.

During the prevalence of the panic, which depressed the live stock interests of the West more disastrously than any other branch of commerce, the various marts were the centers at which the greatest distress imaginable was daily manifested. Indeed, it may truthfully be said that for many weeks to be upon a live stock market was, to one in sympathy with the operators, like witnessing a daily calamity. So depressed was the business and so severe were the losses sustained, that whole days would be passed without one being able to hear a lively or jovial remark or [see] a smile upon the universally sad and gloomy countenances of the dealers. This was emphatically the case upon the Kansas City market during those memorable weeks of financial darkness and ruin. But when it was known that the First National Bank was ordered into liquidation by its stockholders and officers, who had in the previous sixty days struggled so persistently that in sheer exhaustion they adopted the course as a means of shelter and relief from distress and overtaxation — when the fact became known among stockmen at the yards, a gloom little less in its density than Egyptian darkness settled upon every one, and a sadness such as one experiences on hearing of the loss of a friend was depicted upon every countenance. Men spoke in inaudible accents, and sorrow was [329] manifested upon all sides. Many could scarce talk of the event, so deeply were their sensibilities touched. It was conceded by all to be the greatest and crowning disaster of the many that had occurred. That day was the gloomiest ever experienced in Kansas City.

After a few brief days, during which business men recovered from the paralyzing shock, a petition went up, numerously signed, to the directors of the bank, asking them to reopen, and pledging aid and support in any reasonable amount or manner. When, after the elapse of a few weeks, it was announced that the bank would reopen, with its capital increased to $500,000, a feeling of joy and relief was manifested on all sides. Now that resumption with double capital is fully accomplished, the live stock dealers look forward to the future with buoyant hopes and sure confidence that both they and the bank will be mutual coworkers to the accomplishment of a great and good destiny.[378]

The gentleman who has been at the head of this institution nearly from its beginning is so widely and well known among western stockmen, and has been so closely identified with the developments of the live stock commerce of the West, that its history would be incomplete without a brief sketch of him. Howard M. Holden [379] is a native of Massachusetts, in which state he was reared and educated, the latter including a thorough, practical business training, to which is due in no small degree his subsequent success in business. Soon after attaining the years of manhood, not meeting opportunities to suit him in his native state, he turned his face toward the West, whither goes so many capable young men to better their fortune and aid in developing those great new states. Iowa was the state to which he di-

---

[378] The First National Bank of Kansas City failed in 1877. Powell, *op. cit.*, 98.

[379] On July 13, 1873, McCoy sold Holden some land in Kuney and Hodge's Addition to Abilene for $2700. Dickinson County, Deed Record G, 409, MS., Recorder of Deeds Office, Abilene.

HOWARD M. HOLDEN, PRESIDENT.

DAVID W. POWERS.

FIRST NATIONAL.

rected his steps, and at Des Moines opened a bank which he conducted successfully for more than three years. Meeting an opportunity, he sold out, and removed to Washington in the same state and opened a bank, which was a branch of the State Bank of Iowa. This he conducted for six years with [330] marked success. But when by national legislation its circulation, in common with that of all other private banks, was taxed out of existence, he sold out and came to Kansas City and bought nearly the entire stock of the First National Bank, which had a few months before been organized but had not got fairly under way, and of course had made little or no progress or impression on the business community. So soon as he became identified with the institution, he industriously looked about to increase its sphere of usefulness by building up a business. The opening of the cattle trade, with other new enterprises then developing, afforded superior opportunities, which he was by no means slow to improve. The lapse of time was brief before his institution took rank among the first in the city, and began to make its power felt throughout an immense area of country, greatly to the accommodation and benefit of the business men thereof, as well as to Kansas City. As the city has grown and its commerce expanded, his acquaintance and influence has extended coequal, and that invariably to the benefit of the city of his adoption.

He is personally, in every sense, an enterprising, liberal, appreciative business man, one who has naturally an endowment adapted to the business in which he is engaged and fully understands. He appreciates the wants, necessities, and nature of live stock operations and of live stock men. His affable manner and ease of approach render him popular with the live stock dealers. His willingness to aid them, alike with his easy, smooth manner of declining their requests when not convenient or desirable, are alike unoffending, if not pleasing. He is a man who possesses rare faculties which contribute to his popularity and success – one who has hosts of friends and but very few enemies. Complaints are rare indeed, of unfair, oppressive, or arbitrary dealing, or of haughty or harsh treatment at the hands of Mr. Holden. Standing as he does at the head of the strongest financial institution in the Missouri valley, his [331] power is immense to do great good unto many men, as well as to his adopted city, and it is not doubted that he will be equal to his opportunities, and so wield the power that his name will descend to future generations as one among Kansas City's greatest benefactors.

For the more perfect accommodation and the greater convenience of Kansas City's constantly increasing live stock trade, the First National established an office at the stockyards and placed Mr. Winants in charge. This office has been of great benefit and an appreciated convenience to live stock dealers. The success and profitable results accruing to the First National in its long experience in banking with live stock men, has fixed the determination to continue to seek and accommodate that branch of commerce in the future, as in the past. Its greatly increased capital of half a million dollars will proportionately augment its ability to accommodate a larger proportion than heretofore of the constantly increasing demand for financial accommodation. The institution rightly claims the credit of being, in a financial sense, the founder and promoter of Kansas City's live stock commerce. None will dispute the claim, and none are so historically connected with the western stock trade; hence this extended sketch.

But it is not the only banking house that has in later years successfully sought to extend its line of business to stockmen. The directors of the Mastin Bank, during the early part of the year 1873, turned their attention toward the stock trade. They have been successful to a degree so highly satisfactory that at the close of the first year they determined to continue. This institution also established a branch office at the Kansas Stockyards, under the management of M. R. Platt, which has extended facilities and accommodations to a large number of stockmen, and its patrons are increasing daily. In the association constituting the Mastin Bank are some of Kansas City's oldest, most wealthy, and prudent business men, and its entry into the [332] vast field of live stock commerce is warmly welcomed by stockmen. There is ample room and use for its large capital in the chosen field, without intruding upon the preoccupied ground of other financial institutions. The First National and Mastin Banks will in the future be able to extend ample financial accommodation to the patrons of Kansas City's growing live stock mart, and may be regarded as the central financial institutions – the heart of the immense stock trade centering there.[380]

Whilst upon each line of road centering at Kansas City from the west and south (at such points where southern cattle are driven for sale and shipment) other and minor financial institutions are established which afford accommodations and facilities (although generally in a comparatively small way, yet aggregating immense sums), in all cases a round interest is charged the drover and dealer, who are, as a rule, scrupulous about paying up their bank obligations. A breach of faith upon the part of one would to a great degree effect the credit of all, so that other than an honest honorable course is as a matter of self-protection frowned down by all stockmen; and the one who would attempt to defraud his banker would be made to feel uncomfortable beyond endurance.

Messrs. Noah Eby & Company, private bankers at Coffeyville, Kansas, give close attention and liberal financial accommodation to the live stock trade centering at that important point. They have never experienced serious trouble in loaning a large amount of capital at good rates, or the least difficulty in securing prompt payment. By a shrewd arrangement they manage to be posted on what herds of cattle leave Texas for their point, and the financial standing of the owners. The Messrs. Eby were large and successful live stock operators in northern and central Ohio, but on going to Kansas decided to enter the banking business, as in it there was little competition and a broad and inviting field. They are well pleased with the chosen vocation, as well as the point selected. They have contributed largely to Coffeyville's [333] recent success as a cattle mart, and after a full test are satisfied that banking with western drovers is both safe and very profitable. At Wichita, Kansas, the First National of that place was the first bank which extended accommodations to stockmen. It entered the field, and by

---

[380] The Mastin Bank failed in 1878. Powell, *op. cit.,* 99.

liberal accommodations and shrewd management was able to do an enormous and lucrative business with stockmen, greatly aiding the point to build up and retain a large cattle trade. But it did not have the field to itself but one year. The second season the Savings Bank, under able and obliging management, was opened, and from the first had many warm friends and patrons among the stockmen. To the liberal policy pursued by Wichita's bankers, as much as to any other one source, is that point indebted for its wonderful success as a cattle market and shipping depot.

Among the solid and successful cattlemen of Kansas none are better known than D. W. Powers, whose residence is at Leavenworth but whose principal place of business is Ellsworth, where he stands at the head of the banking house which does the financial business of the Kansas Pacific's cattle trade. In this banking house are associated his nephews, who attend to the office duties whilst the principal and senior member devotes much of the time to his live stock interests and operations.[381] Mr. Powers is in every sense a self-made [334] man. Not liking the restraints of his Kentucky home, at the early age of sixteen he departed for the state of Virginia and began life upon his own account. But in after years he removed to Missouri, where he engaged in farming and stock dealing. In those days there was a great demand for suitable cattle for oxen, to be used in freighting over the plains, and into this ox trade he gradually grew until he became one of the principal purchasing agents of extensive freighters in the days of prairie schooners. He was not long in getting initiated into the profits of the freighting business, and determined to start an outfit as large as his means would admit, on his own account. Accordingly, after raking together all his means, and investing it in wagons, teams, and necessary outfitting, he found that three teams of four or five pairs of oxen each was the result, and represented his available [336] worldly assets. But not daunted by its limited appearance, rather pleased

---

381 During 1870, David W. Powers opened a bank in Salina, Kansas, under the name of D. W. Powers & Company, but early in May, 1873, he moved it to Ellsworth. The owners of D. W. Powers & Company in Ellsworth were D. W. Powers, J. W. Powers, and D. B. Powers. *Ellsworth Reporter,* May 8, 1873.

BLUFF CREEK RANCH—PROPERTY D. W. POWERS & CO.

that it was as much, he took in his own hands one of the ox whips, and, to use the parlance of early days "whacked bulls" many trips to Denver and Salt Lake. In this business he gradually acquired a start in this world's goods, got something ahead for which he owed nothing. But this lucrative although hard business did not last very long. Soon the construction, or rather the completion, of the Pacific railways superseded freighting by ox teams, and prairie schooners became institutions of the past – institutions about which cling many reminiscences of events interesting and thrilling.

But the departure of the days of overland freighting did not leave Mr. Powers without means or a knowledge of good, paying business opportunities. In wintering his freighting teams, which in time grew to be large herds of oxen, he learned the advantages and facilities of central Kansas as a live stock country. As early as 1866 he bought many Texan cattle, and wintered and fatted them to his great profit. Having practical experience at so early a date, he improved his opportunity by purchasing four superior locations for live stock ranches, one of which is upon Bluff creek at its junction with the Smoky Hill river, twelve miles southeast of Fort Harker.[382] This ranch is one of four owned by D. W. Powers & Company, upon which they annually winter about three thousand head of cattle and sufficient cow ponies to handle the stock. Over two thousand acres of good, tillable land is included in this ranch, of which more than one-fourth is substantially fenced with posts and boards. A large part of the enclosed lands are under cultivation, Hungarian, millet, oats, and corn being the chief products. Although the uplands furnish unlimited grazing, partly of buffalo grass, yet they deem it prudent, if not necessary, to provide a good supply of hay and other food; with such facilities and good preparations their wintering operations are uniformly a success, and heavy losses by storms comparatively unknown. Several hundred acres are annually sown to Hungarian grass, and the [337] hay thus produced is of the very best for cattle feeding; it is easily raised and harvested, the land yielding abundantly. When properly cut and cured, it forms the best and cheapest feed

---

382 For a description of this ranch, see *ibid.*, Apr. 30, 1874.

that can be secured by cultivation. It will keep Texan cattle thriving and in good heart during the worst winters known in Kansas.

The ranches are each under the supervision of a foreman, under whose direction are enough herdsmen and other laborers to conduct business and take proper care of such stock as the proprietors may purchase. Mr. Powers's business, as may be inferred, is large and varied, and requires a good business man to successfully manage it; this he has shown himself to be. He has engaged in almost every branch of business pertaining to live stock, as well as every manner of handling it, having cornfed, grazed, ranged, shipped, and packed cattle; besides, for one or two years fed the Lo family on the upper Missouri river country. In nearly all these departments he has been successful and now ranks among Kansas's most responsible men. He is an unostentatious, matter-of-fact, everyday-style man, whose solid judgment and long, varied experience enables him to plan and execute business operations with unerring skill and certainty; quiet, kind, and mild in disposition, he has many friends and an irreproachable credit. Few men have labored more diligently and perseveringly for success, and few have been more amply rewarded for their labors than he.

FIRST NATIONAL.

XVII. STOCK RANCHING IN THE WEST

The business of breeding and handling live stock in the West is one of deep interest. Most young men, no matter where living or what doing, think and feel that if they were West engaged in the live stock business, they would wake up some fine morning to find themselves wealthy. Just how it would be accomplished they scarcely know, but nevertheless that such would be their happy lot, they have a profound confidence. How the business is conducted they do not know, yet are anxious to learn. If by perusal of this volume their information is increased or corrected, a part of its objects will have been accomplished.

Cattle or sheep ranching in the West does not differ materially in manner from the same vocation in Texas. There is an immense belt of country along the Rocky mountains and extending eastward about four hundred miles, with a length of near two thousand miles which, from its character, climate, and comparatively rainless seasons, is preëminently adapted to sheep husbandry and the breeding of cattle. This vast area is covered with a fine species of grass known as buffalo grass, which is equally nutritious in winter as in summer. Either cattle or sheep not only live well but fatten fast so long as they can get an abundance of buffalo [339] grass. No matter how cold the air may be, so warming and nutritious is this grass at all seasons of the year that cattle or sheep do not care for hay or other feed in winter. Running from the mountains eastward are various small streams of water which, falling together, form rivers whose numerous tributaries from either side, water and drain the whole country sufficiently for stock purposes. Numerous rivers, such as the Republican, Saline, Solomon, and Smoky Hill, rise in the midst of the plains, many miles east of the mountains, upon whose tributaries many eligible locations for extensive live stock ranches can be found. The great Platte river has unlimited stock country tributary to and drained by it. The North Platte, or Black Hill, country of Wyoming is excellent for cattle and famous for its nutritious bunch grasses, which are unexceled for stock purposes.

The Territory of Colorado has a deserved fame as a stock country, to which it would be difficult to add.[383] Within her bounds are forty thousand square miles of grazing lands; lands that are well fitted for grazing and fitted for nothing else; lands that cannot be irrigated or made available for agricultural purposes; lands upon which grows the rich buffalo grass, covering its entire surface like a soft velvety carpet. Many extensive live stock men from all parts have been attracted to her border. Within her limits can be found immense cattle and sheep enterprises in successful operation. Some of the largest operators in cattle are from Texas.

But just what a man may expect to do and endure if he attempts to establish a live stock ranch, especially if his capital is limited, may be of interest to the reader whose eye and mind is upon the West with thoughts of making it his home, and the business of live stock growing his vocation. It may be assumed that he has not only decided to go West, but is already there and in the act of locating a stock ranch. His first care will be to select a location that has living or running water, as much timber and other shelter as [340] possible, with a large tract of unsettled and untillable country surrounding it. It is important to choose such a location that when he has purchased a reasonably sized tract of land, he will own all the water and tillable land in the vicinity for miles around; otherwise he may have agricultural neighbors in such near proximity as to interfere with the free ranging and grazing of his stock. When the location is finally made, one of the usually first undertakings is the construction of a place of abode, which is generally a dugout, an institution in the construction of which little lumber and much dirt is used, and the principal tool employed is the

---

[383] For a detailed account of the cattle business of Colorado, see Peake, *The Colorado Range Cattle Industry.*

spade. It is simply a covered excavation on the bank of some creek or ravine, resembling an outdoor cellar for the preservation of roots and vegetables. The dirt taken out in excavating the room serves to form the roof, which is supported by rude, strong pieces of timber, mere round logs or poles. The front is formed of cut sods laid up like blocks of rock, or is made of split boards or posts much after the fashion of a stockade. A flue is cut in the back wall and often terminates upward with an empty salt barrel for a chimney stem. The cooking utensils are few and primitive. The dry condition of the ground renders the dugout entirely free from dampness, and not only warm and comfortable, but entirely healthy.

The dugout done, the next job that would engage the attention of the new beginner is the construction of a corral – a large, strong, rudely built affair, with a small subdivision for branding his stock (that is, his purchases), which process is called "counter-branding." When the dugout and corral are done, the ranchman brings his herd of cattle and the necessary number of cow ponies upon the grounds, and after branding them, begins the work of getting the stock attached to and contented with its new home. But this is not a difficult task, especially if the weather is fine and feed is plenty.

But let no one delude himself with the idea that cattle ranching – either breeding and rearing, or only wintering and [341] fatting, or handling live stock in any manner peculiar to the West – is a business wherein the poetic or sentimental aspects of life or labor abound to any alarming extent. Indeed, it is a life and business which, aside from its phase of independent freedom, has few other aspects than those of diligent labor, watchfulness, care, and risk, combined with great self-denial, privations, and lonely hardships. He must be the servant of his herds, to attend to and provide for their every want. When the weather is stormiest, and a comfortable seat in a snug corner by a warm fire would be most congenial to feelings, and perchance health also, then is the very time the would-be successful ranchman must be out with his herds and to them give double ordinary attention with extra feed and shelter. Anyone can attend live stock in fine weather, when the sun shines out mild and warm, and the stock can and will feed and care for itself. But when the cold, driving storm sweeps across the plains, piercing the animal world by its chilling blasts, then is when it requires the "man to the manor born," or one adapted by nature and stimulated by a love of the vocation. A man must have a natural adaptation and taste for the business and the life, to succeed. It is not a vocation wherein starched shirts, fashionable-cut broadcloth, polished boots, faultless set mustache, or latest style of hairdressing will flourish or scarce be in order for a single day. But long-legged stogy boots, huge spurs, strong corduroy pants, a thick, colored woolen shirt, a leather belt around the waist, no suspenders, a sombrero or other broad-brimmed hat, a soldier overcoat, and a pair of heavy blankets constitute the make-up, the necessary habiliments, the usual personal outfit of the practical ranchman or cowboy. And the daily fare almost of necessity is meager and of the commonest varieties of food, cooked in the simplest style of the art usually by one of the men who knows but little about culinary matters, and is not overanxious to learn more than he already knows, be that ever so little. [342] However, death from dyspepsia is never feared by the ranchman, for his daily labor and exercise give him a sharp appetite and a vigorous digestion.

If a young, energetic man, one who desires to make a name and a fortune for himself, and to be one among the substantial men of the new and great West, can make up his mind to endure the privations, hardships, and lonely life of labor and exposure incident to a ranchman's life, there are great opportunities offered and to be had for the taking in the broad, free West. Lands are cheap, the climate mild, the natural advantages good and great. The stock with which to begin is abundant and at reasonable prices. The process and means of improvement in blood, as well as in numbers, are at hand. The plainest and best of results invariably attend every effort made in crossing Durham bulls with Texan heifers and cows. An improved animal is obtained of nearly or quite double the value of the Texan. As a paying, reliable, certain occupation, there is none that is more so than stock ranching. But it requires time, labor, patience, energy, grit, and perseverance to make the begin-

JOHN HITTSON.

JOSEPH P. FARMER.

ning, and to carry it through to profitable fruition. But there are few vocations in any new country, or old one for that matter, that do not require the existence and exercise of the same qualities in order to achieve success. When it is remembered than annually more than two hundred million dollars changes hands for live stock for purposes of consumption alone, it must be potent that the production of the live stock is a staple, money-making business, full as much so as is the production of cotton. That the reader may have a glance at the appearance of some of the sturdy men who have made a success of stock ranching in Colorado, the portraits of Mr. J. P. Farmer and others, with illustrations, are presented.

Mr. Farmer is a son of the Emerald Isle, from whence he emigrated at an early age; and after attaining years of manhood, he went to Colorado in 1861 and established a stock [343] ranch on the Bijou, a small tributary of the South Platte, near which the Kansas Pacific Railway has established a station of the same name. His herd of cattle was very small at the beginning and was Texan stock. Indeed, it may truthfully be said that he began at the foot of the ladder, and by industry, perseverance, and determined labor, climbed up round by round to a substantial annual income and a competence that might with propriety be desired by anyone. This he has attained by energetic application to business, [by] closely studying the situation, and by taking advantage of the great opportunities afforded in the New West. He gives his stock business close personal attention, and constantly labors to render his herds more numerous and valuable. He now owns a tract of six hundred and forty acres of land, covering all the water in the West Bijou, upon which and adjoining lands he keeps a herd of stock of twenty-seven hundred head of cattle and [345] fifty head of horses. Of his cattle, one thousand are steers of three years of age. Of the remaining seventeen hundred head of cows and stock cattle, the half are grades or half-breeds, that is, a cross between Texan cows and Durham bulls. Mr. Farmer regards Colorado not only a good cattle country but as *par excellence* a good horse country. He takes great pride and pains with his horses, of which he has many good strains of blood. He keeps superior-blooded stallions as well as good grade bulls. It is his constant effort to improve his stock in blood as well as numbers. He feeds neither cattle or horses, except his saddle ponies, which are used in looking after the stock. He does not herd his cattle, but designates certain bounds within which the employees permit the stock to range at will. This manner of holding stock is termed "outriding" the country. Mr. Farmer has put upon the Kansas City market some of the fattest grassfed cattle that has ever entered that mart, for which he obtained the highest market prices. He is a solid, matter-of-fact, every-day-style man; one who has fine business judgment and takes great delight in his live stock; one who has laid the foundation wall of a substantial fortune, the full realization of which will be his at no distant day. He is among that class of self-reliant, hardy ranchmen that have done much to develop and demonstrate Colorado's superior facilities and advantages as a stock-growing country, and by his faithful persistence and enterprise, won and merited golden success.

But perhaps no live stock man in northern Colorado is so widely known as John Hittson, who went from Tennessee, the state of his birth, to Texas, and settled in the county of Palo Pinto, on the frontier. He located a stock ranch, and began in a small way to gather the nucleus of a stock of cattle which at one time reached the number of one hundred thousand head. His brand was put upon eight thousand calves in the year 1873, but the Indians continuing exceedingly troublesome, he sold out a part of his stock and his [346] ranch, and proposes to make his home in Colorado. At the close of the Civil war he began driving largely to Colorado, where he has annually marketed about eight thousand head of cattle. In sending his herds from Texas to Colorado direct, the Pecos trail, which runs through New Mexico and crosses the Arkansas river not a great distance below Pueblo, is traveled, instead of the trail via western Kansas. In order to facilitate his immense trade, he purchased a ranch on the Middle Bijou, known as the Six Spring ranch, which is located at a very eligible point for extensive live stock operations, and is near Deer Trail Station on the Kansas Pacific Railway. It was only necessary

JOHN HITTSON'S RANCH ON THE BIJOU IN COLORADO.

JOSEPH P. FARMER'S RANCH, BIJOU, COLORADO.

to own one-half section of land in order to possess all the water existing for many miles in all directions. Upon this tract of land are temporary buildings, corrals, etc.; but it is his purpose to place thereon a good class of improvements at an early day, and to make it his [348] permanent home instead of a mere trading post as heretofore. During the year 1873 eleven thousand cattle were driven from Texas and placed upon the ranch, to be followed by about twenty thousand more the succeeding year; and when fitted and stocked up according to his plans, it will be one of the best and largest stock ranches in Colorado, if not in the West.[384]

As has been stated, Mr. Hittson is one of the most widely known stockmen, both in Texas and the West. He is a man of commanding appearance and great experience – a man who has lived long on the frontiers and has acquired habits of bold self-reliance. He was largely instrumental in breaking up the predatory thieving incursions from New Mexico which had become so intolerably frequent in western Texas. With a party of men, and armed with authority from the governor of Texas, he went into New Mexico and recaptured many thousands of stolen cattle and drove them to Colorado, where they were disposed of for the benefit of the original owners. He is a man of great energy and determination, and one altogether capable of taking care of himself in any country; and in a land that abounds with opportunities, will make money fast, which, when made, he will freely spend for the benefit of his friends. Few men are better calculated to open up and develop a new country than he, and yet there are few men engaged in the live stock business more social, jovial, and hospitable than John Hittson. Like other extensive Colorado ranchmen, he outrides the country instead of close herding his stock. Of course, occasionally a small squad of cattle will escape or stray beyond the designated bounds, whose trail escapes the vigilant eye and Indian cunning and proficiency of the herdsman or outrider. The stock will not wander far before it finds such

---

[384] Claiming that he owned 100,000 head of cattle, John Hittson, in 1873, asserted: "I intend to divide my herds, and keep one-half in Colorado hereafter, on the Bijou and Platte rivers. There is plenty of grass and cattle will do as well there as in Texas, and then there is freedom from thievery in a comparative degree." *Ibid.*, 197. See also *Dallas Herald,* Dec. 10, 1870.

place as will tempt it to stop, if it is not met and turned into some neighbor's range. In many instances when great storms occur, as is sometimes the case, the stock will be driven from its proper location and scattered over a vast scope of country [350] and hopelessly mingled with neighboring cattle which have been scattered by the same causes. In such cases little or no effort is made to regather them before spring, when, by concerted efforts of all parties interested, a general round-up is made. This accomplished, each ranchman cuts out all bearing his own brand and returns them to his ranch. When one section of country has been thoroughly overhauled and the cattle gathered and sent to their proper ranges, another section is surrounded and another round-up is made, and so on, until the whole country has been thoroughly searched. By this means a great amount of labor and much hard riding is saved, for a single animal or small number thereof is hard to drive without much racing, which, of course, fast uses up the cow ponies.

Perhaps in no state or territory in the Union are the stockmen so wide-awake to their interests or so completely organized as in Colorado, where there now exists the leading state or territorial organization of stock growers,[385] the president of which association is Joseph L. Bailey, of Denver. The secretary, by whose exertions, more than that of any other man, the association was formed and is kept alive and in effective, beneficial working order, is William Holley, of Denver, a man of fine energy and abilities, and one who takes special delight in performing all the duties and kind offices which his position or opportunities place within his power. He has rendered great services to the live stock men and their interests in Colorado, and deserves well at their hand. The association and the live stock men's interest are largely promoted and benefitted by the *Colorado Farmer,* and also the *Colorado Agriculturist and Stock Journal,* two neat, enterprising weeklies published in Denver.

The president of the Stock Growers' Association, J. L. Bailey, is one of the recognized leading stockmen of the territory, in whom all stock dealers have the most explicit

---

[385] The Colorado Stockgrowers' Association, which was first organized at Denver in 1867. Peake, *op. cit.,* 126.

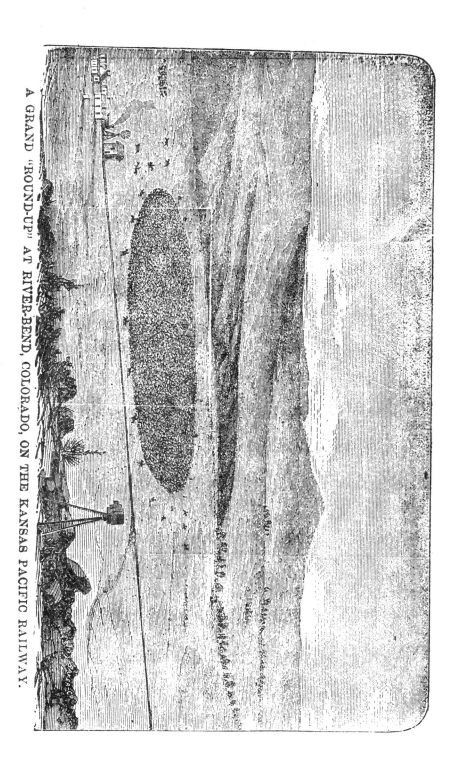

A GRAND "ROUND-UP" AT RIVER-BEND, COLORADO, ON THE KANSAS PACIFIC RAILWAY.

JOSEPH L. BAILEY.

confidence. It is at his office that you can see in a brief time every stockman in northern Colorado. For a visit to [351] Denver without seeing and exchanging items with Mr. Bailey, is not to be thought of, much less practiced, by any stock grower. In 1865 he established a number of corrals and named the place "Bull's Head," and it is there that the largest live stock market of the territory exists. There the various railroads centering in Denver receive and deliver their live freights. By fair dealing and close attention to business he has gained the patronage and confidence of his fellow man in a marked degree, and has acquired a substantial fortune. He has held various positions of credit and trust, and regards the live stock interests of the territory as paramount to all others. Mr. Bailey hails from Philadelphia, and after spending a few years in Kansas, went to Colorado, and was one of the pioneers of that rapidly developing and marvelous territory. Personally he is an affable, courteous gentleman of great business energy and activity, whose fortune is pleasant to [352] contemplate. He has ever been closely identified with the history of Denver, and is regarded on all hands as one of her most substantial, worthy citizens, and has from the first organization of the Stock Growers' Association held the position of president thereof.

Colorado abounds with many unoccupied locations for stock ranches; many millions of acres of its grazing lands are still untrod save by the migratory buffalo. Within its borders may be found locations for vast herds of common cattle and sheep. Eligible situations abound in great numbers for fancy or fine stock breeding. Along the base of the mountains, from whence come rivulets of pure, cold water, are many picturesque locations admirably adapted for thoroughbred stock ranches, where one could spend life in daily view of craggy peaks and beneath the shadow of lofty pines. It is more than worth the price of a ride over the Denver and Río Grande narrow gauge railroad to behold not only the grand scenery but also the beautiful, lovely landscapes through which the road passes. Certainly no road in the United States passes through and near so many desirable situations; and what will astonish the beholder still more, that comparatively so few are occupied. Of all the delightsome locations in bewildering profusion seen on the American continent, none will excel those found along the line of the Denver and Río Grande Railway, which speeds along the eastern base of the Rocky mountains from Denver to Pueblo, and destined soon to reach the Río Grande river, if not the City of Mexico. To the amateur live stock man, the breeder of thoroughbred stock, the country along the eastern base of the Rocky mountains presents the most desirable, charming location, not only for the business itself, but for beautiful, romantic, healthy homes, also.

Colorado, for a territory, is well supplied with railroads, the principal one of which is the Kansas Pacific. It was the first line built and the first one to do a large traffic in live [353] stock freights. Under the present practical management, which is the antipode of its predecessor, the live stock traffic is great and flourishing. From the beginning of their administration dates a new and better era in the live stock affairs of that line; an era when a live stock man was recognized as having rights which a railroad company might, with profit and propriety, respect; an era when a business man is regarded other than legitimate prey, to be ruthlessly crushed and his substance devoured. A railroad official is in a certain sense a public servant, and as such is generally well paid for his services; and when he has done well his whole duty, does not merit particular commendation on that account. Nevertheless, it should be recorded that the present practical management and operation of the Kansas Pacific Railway is a decided improvement upon the former. This company has other minor lines leased, the most important of which is the line from Cheyenne to Denver, beginning in and passing through a fine stock country; and the line lately constructed from Carson to Las Animas on the Arkansas river. This also begins in and passes through a fine stock country. Farther east it has other short branch lines, all of which contribute largely to increase the business of the main line, especially in live stock freights.

The main line passes for near four hundred miles through what may be truthfully termed a live stock growing country, if not such exclusively. Upon either side of this line for an

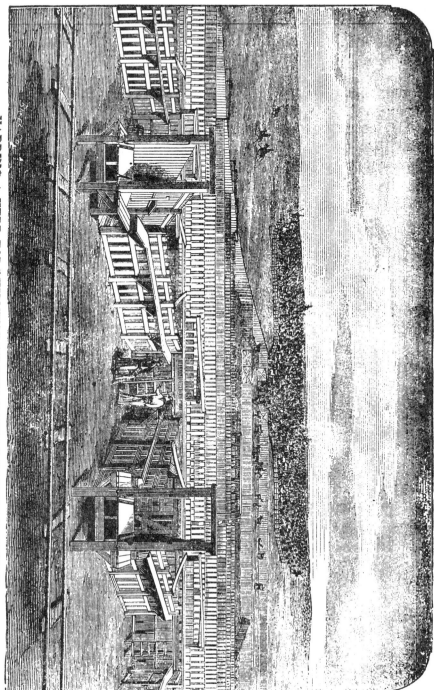

YARDING A HERD FOR SHIPMENT ON THE KANSAS PACIFIC RAILWAY.

RESTING YARDS—ELLIS, KANSAS, ON THE KANSAS PACIFIC RAILWAY.

indefinite distance, most suitable, if not superior, locations for live stock ranches can be found. Locations with nice running water, timber in limited supply (besides other natural shelter), and grazing in unlimited abundance are to be had for the taking and occupancy. In the more easterly portion of the live stock belt, and within the state of Kansas, the creek and river valleys afford great abundance of bluestem natural grasses, furnishing an unlimited supply of hay. Those regions will be preferred by many as affording the means to provide against [355] the contingencies of storms that may occur during the winter seasons. It is upon this belt the railway company have established, at a point west of Fort Harker and distant over two hundred miles west of Kansas City, its shipping depot for Texan cattle, and here annually many thousands are driven; and if not sold to go otherwheres, are, after being grazed a few months, shipped eastward. The line enjoys the advantage of being the only one reaching out into the buffalo grass regions and terminating, without change, at Kansas City. The grazing facilities along the line of this road are very good and great, and so are the facilities of the company for transporting live stock. No pains are spared to accommodate an immense live stock commerce, both from Texas, Colorado and New Mexico. The cattle from Colorado and New Mexico going east on this line are provided with a comfortable resting yard at Ellis, midway distant between Denver and Kansas City. There the cattle are rested, watered, and either fed hay or grazed on the buffalo grass, as the shipper may elect. The run from there to Kansas City is easy, and two-thirds of the distance is down a nearly level valley devoid of grades and sharp curves. The country for two hundred miles west of Kansas City along the line of the Kansas Pacific Railway is adapted to agriculture and mixed husbandry, and better adapted to raising grain and fatting live stock than to its exclusive growing. The next or third hundred miles west comprises some fine stock country, as well as occasional good sections or belts of farming lands. Within that area and along the line of the railway, extensive schemes for colonization and settlement of the country are on foot.

As such, none are more worthy of note, both from mag-nitude of design, extent of country embraced, and liberality of plan, than that known as Victoria Colony, the center and headquarters of which is Victoria Station on the Kansas Pacific Railway. The originator and promoter of this enter-prise is George [357] Grant, Esq., a retired London (Eng-land) merchant, and a Scottish gentleman of reputed sub-stantial wealth. He has purchased of the railway company the odd numbered sections of a tract of land twenty miles in width by twenty-five in length, each section containing six hundred and forty acres. The purchase exceeded one hundred and fifty thousand acres of land. The even num-bered sections belong to the government and were subject to homestead and preëmption. This tract of land is finely watered, sparsely timbered, and is covered with a vigorous growth of buffalo grass upon the up or rolling lands, and an abundant supply of natural hay on the broad, rich valleys found along all streams in Kansas. A vigorous little river named the same as the colony runs from west to east through the entire length of the tract, and frequent tributary creeks put in from either side, thus affording good drainage and an abundant supply of living stock water. The soil of both valley and upland is good, rich, and deep, and will produce all the cereals common to the latitude. The tract of land taken as a whole is exceedingly valuable, especially for the purposes of live stock and wool production. The uplands are gentle, undulating, and the valleys smooth and wide. The timber, which is abundant for that portion of the state, is good for fuel and the construction of temporary buildings only. It is also ample to shelter as much stock as would depasture the lands. It would be difficult to find in the state, noted for fine appearing lands, a more beautiful and withal naturally valuable tract of lands than those of Victoria Colony. It is unquestionably a healthy country; no malarial diseases prevail; indeed no swamps or pools of stagnant water exist. The winters are mild, the climate temperate and sunny. The tract of land lies on either side of the rail-way, which company is disposed to extend every facility to encourage and aid the enterprise.

Although the soil is ample for the production of all

VICTORIA STATION—HEADQUARTERS VICTORIA COLONY, KANSAS.

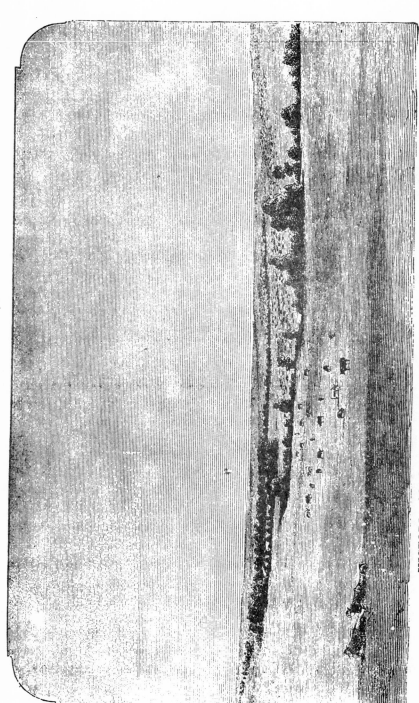

VICTORIA COLONY LANDS—PROPERTY OF MR. GEORGE GRANT.

needed grains and vegetables, yet it is evident upon reflection that the growing of cattle and horses, as well as sheep [359] and wool, will yield the greater profit. This is evident for various reasons, among which might be mentioned: its distance from market; the uncertainty of rainfall, which is always ample, but often occurs at such times of the year as prove too late to save the crops of grain, especially corn, from drouth, although wheat, oats, rye, barley, millet, and Hungarian grass can be grown with a reasonable certainty every year; again, the lands are already well and closely set with buffalo grass on the uplands and bluestem grass in the valleys, and stock can be kept in good condition of flesh during the entire year with but little greater expense than that of herding. Cattle can be cared for the entire year when held in moderate-sized herds, for two dollars per head per year, and sheep in proportion. Indeed, the state of Kansas offers no finer location for profitable, easy, and abundant production of mutton and wool than at Victoria. The dry nature of the soil, its freedom from mud and standing water, the purity and dryness of the atmosphere, the excellence and adaptableness of the buffalo grass to the wants and nature of the sheep, both in winter and summer — all conspire to make it preëminently a sheep and woolgrowing country unsurpassed. Horses and mules can be easily and profitably raised at an annual expense scarce above that of cattle. It is believed that the man who gives his exclusive attention to live stock, and particularly sheep, will grow rich much quicker than he who devotes his exclusive attention to farming; of this there can be no intelligent question; although an energetic agriculturist will soon make himself comfortable and above want by tilling the soil.

The purchase of Victoria Colony lands has been consummated scarce more than a year, yet their proprietor has made commendable progress in preparation for extended experiments with all kinds of live stock. To this end he has imported many thoroughbred sheep, cattle, horses, and hogs, besides buying largely of superior-blooded animals both in [361] Canada and the United States, with which he is placing Texan heifers and proposes to place Mexican ewes and native mares. Among the rare, noticeable importations are a number of black hornless bulls of pure Galloway blood, which have all the beef qualities of the Durham, maturing fully as early, and possessing, in addition, habits of industry, and are extremely hardy and thrifty. They are expected to prove a valuable acquisition to stock growers on the plains. Among his extensive importations of thoroughbred sheep are some remarkably fine specimens of Shropshires, Leicester, and Lincolnshires. The latter are very superior and of great promise in the future. Besides the above, he has put upon Victoria lands several thousand sheep of common or native blood, and proposes to test thoroughly the adaptation of the locality for wool and mutton growing. No intelligent man at all cognizant of the situation doubts for a moment the successful issue of the experiment. It requires no great tax of the imagination to forecast the situation of affairs at Victoria Colony half a score of years hence, when the lines of industry as well as the kinds of stock that experiments now being made will have proven to be the most lucrative and best adapted to the locality, shall have been pushed into the highest development the situation will admit of, which will in no respect be inferior to that of any other point or section.

It is easy to foresee that a happy, prosperous people, rejoicing in their new homes, abounding with all comforts and many luxuries of life, will in future time gratefully remember the man through whose munificence and enterprise they were induced and enabled to enter Victoria Colony. Mr. Grant has undertaken a laudable and, in a certain sense, a benevolent enterprise; one in which great permanent good can, and doubtless will, be done many of his countrymen; who, through his aid and encouragement, will be assisted and directed to a land in which a home of their own and manly independence [363] can be attained in a goodly country beneath a temperate, healthy clime, where the most ordinary economy and industry will bring the fatness of "a land of milk and honey." It is no mere land speculation upon his part, although his own interests are not lost sight of. But it is an honest, commendable effort to so invest and use a large capital in such a manner as will confer substantial, lasting benefits upon a large number of worthy, enterprising

THOROUGHBRED IMPORTED SHEEP—VICTORIA COLONY.

VICTORIA COLONY LANDS—PROPERTY OF GEORGE GRANT, ESQ.

persons who, unaided, could never raise themselves above positions of dependence, much less to the ownership of lands and homes of their own. No young, able-bodied Briton who has energy and ambition to do something worthy and good for himself can fail to better his condition materially by joining Victoria Colony. Its founder is animated by high motives, and with his great wealth is prepared and willing to do a great, good work for a large number of his country-men. He is, like many of his own isle, a lover of finely-bred live stock. He demonstrates by his liberal purchases of ele-gant thoroughbreds in this country and Canada, as well as by his importations of superior animals, his entire willing-ness, his earnest purpose, to enable his colonists to have the advantage and benefit of the best-obtainable strains of blood — and all this, too, at little or no expense to the colonists. It is his purpose to substantially aid all deserving colonists to establish flocks and herds of their own at an early day. Certainly no greater advantages, in fact none half so great, has ever been offered the sturdy Briton to seek and establish a home of his own beneath a sunny sky upon the richest of lands, where obstacles are so few, the advantages so great, the aid so substantial and so easily obtained, as are offered in Victoria Colony.

Its founder and proprietor is a shrewd business man and knows what he is doing; and although the remainder of his life might have been spent in ease and luxury, without know-ing an unsupplied want, yet he prefers to use his fortune in developing an enterprise, the intent and inevitable result of which cannot be other than substantial benefit to all who choose to avail [365] themselves of his magnificent scheme and investment in Kansas lands. Mr. George Grant is a quiet, retiring, dignified gentleman, whose kind, hospitable manner inspires one alike with respect and confidence. But a few brief hours in his presence will suffice to impress one with his courteous manhood and his keen appreciation of the really good and deserving, as well as how completely his heart is rapt up in the welfare and success of his colony.

The belt of country in which Victoria Colony is located, is, for a hundred miles in width from east to west and stretching across the state of Kansas, regarded as unsurpassed for stock purposes, and has attracted some of the shrewdest and closest-observing ranchmen from all sections of the Union, even from far-famed California; among whom is Mr. Shaeffer, who at the full years of manhood went from Ohio, his native state, to California. After successfully trying his fortune at mining, packing, or freighting, he finally settled down and established a live stock ranch in northern California. But after a brief time he began driving live stock to Idaho, also to Nevada, which he followed with success for four years. Then after operating in quartz mines for a short time, he turned his face eastward (after spending nineteen years on the Pacific slope) and selected central Kansas as a desirable place where he could engage in his favorite vocation — that of stock ranching. However, before he made a final location, he went to Texas, and from that state drove a large herd of cattle via the Staked Plains, Fort Sumner, Fort Union, and the Ratón mountains to Nevada, where, after a lapse of eighteen months from the day he started after the herd, he sold it at $52 (gold) per head. Of course, this operation made money; his ventures always do, for he directs his affairs with consummate skill, and is seldom at fault in judgment about when, where, and how to plan, begin, and execute a speculation or live stock operation. Indeed, he is often termed by the unobserving and unthinking, the lucky operator. At all events, [366] success seems to crown his every move. He seldom fails to make money upon everything he handles.

After looking over and experimenting in various parts of central Kansas, he selected and purchased a location and established his ranch. It is a tract of about four thousand acres of land situated upon the Saline river and one or more of its tributaries. Here he has running salt and fresh water, besides divers springs affording an unfreezing supply of water; timber and abrupt bluff lands constituting shelter in abundance. Upon the valley lands of his purchase, an unlimited amount of hay can be annually put up, costing only the cutting and labor of saving it. But upon the uplands the buffalo grass abounds in the greatest profusion and of the most luxuriant growth. Upon this ranch he annually winters about twenty-five hundred head of cattle, and keeps about

WM. SHAEFFER'S RANCH.

WILLIAM K. SHAEFFER.

GEORGE GROVES.

forty head of ponies, which he uses for saddle purposes. The cattle are fed [368] nothing other than the buffalo grass, unless it is when a protracted storm occurs, and then hay is given them, often only to be tossed about and played with, instead of eaten. So long as the stock can get the half of a supply of buffalo grass, although they may have to root in the deep snow to get it, they care but little for hay, be it ever so good an article thereof. Of the horses, none are fed grain save those that are under the saddle daily.

For location, and all essential conditions and surroundings, Mr. Shaeffer's ranch is a model, unexcelled for extensive stock handling. He does not put forth any effort to raise cattle or horses, but buys fresh-driven Texan cattle every season; and after wintering, grazes them the following summer upon the range (of which there is an immense supply) until fat; then they are sold and the operation repeated. In this line of business he has been successful and has made no losses, for his plan takes little or no risks; and by purchasing his cattle when they are thin and consequently very cheap, he cannot but make a profit by increasing their flesh and condition. Then selecting a propitious time to place them upon the market, he never fails to get remunerative prices; often very profitable sales are made. He estimates by actual expense accounts kept that it does not cost him above two dollars per head actual outlay to winter a bullock and fat it fit for the New York market. It is easy to compute the transaction. If he buys, say 2,500 head of fresh-driven Texan cattle at two cents per pound, or $20 per head, they amount to $50,000; to this add $2 per head expense of holding, or $5,000; also add $10,000 interest on money invested; then allow $2,500 for supplies in camp, loss, and incidental expenses. The fatted herd has cost $67,500; but it is worth three cents per pound and will weigh 1,250 pounds on an average and bring $37.50 per head, making a total, for the herd, of $93,750 – a net gain of $26,250, or something near fifty per cent on the capital invested. It is safe to count on receiving one cent per pound gross advance on purchase [369] price when the cattle are made fat.

Texan cattle of proper age become very fat upon the

natural grasses of central Kansas, especially after having been wintered. He keeps four men at an expense of twenty-five dollars per month wages (board not included), who are sufficient to attend twenty-five hundred cattle; for the stock is neither herded or lotted, but simply kept within bounds by outriding the country; and the time is brief before the stock becomes contented and "homed" to the locality, and lose all disposition to ramble or stray off. Stock held in this manner does far better than if close herded and confined nightly in corrals. Mr. Shaeffer is a man of superior judgment on all matters pertaining to live stock operations and is a man of convivial, jovial habits; one whom success does not elate; one who has many warm friends among stockmen. Who does not, if but fortunate in his operations, and the name of successful is bestowed upon him?

It is a proposition upon which cattle feeders differ, whether it is most profitable to fullfeed Texan cattle on grain; or "rough" them through (or "range" them upon the plains during winter, and fat on the grass the succeeding summer). The advocates of each method can offer substantial and, to their own minds, conclusive reasons in support of their favorite method. We apprehend that locality is the key to the correct solution of the problem. Very profitable operations are made cornfeeding Texan cattle when the feeder is a practical man and thoroughly understands his business and gives it his daily attention. Such a cattle feeder is George Groves, of Williamsville, Illinois.

At Chicago, Illinois, is the largest and most complete live stock market in the Union. It is an unanswerable argument in favor of union and concentrated effort, whereby three-quarters of a million of cattle and nearly five million hogs, with other live stock in proportion, are annually brought into one set of yards and one market. There are, undoubtedly, [370] great advantages, both to buyer and seller, gained by this concentration. Perhaps at no other point in the United States are so many commission merchants located as at Chicago. Many of them do almost a fabulous business in the aggregate, and most of them are good live stock men of excellent judgment, and well adapted to the business in which they are engaged. In some cases

they are of the most substantial cattlemen of the country —
feeders, grazers, traders, and shippers.

Of such is Mr. Groves, senior of the firm of Groves
Brothers, who is known in central Illinois as a large landowner, a successful farmer, an excellent feeder, and a
genuine good cattleman. He is a native of Pennsylvania,
but came with his father to central Illinois at the age of
fourteen. This occurred in the year 1836, when that state
was comparatively new and lands therein cheap. He early
saw and believed in the future value of the rich soil of those
[371] regions, and spared no honorable effort to acquire
a goodly number of broad, fertile acres, which he owns at
the present time. He began life poor, and worked himself
gradually into the possession of a princely estate. From his
earliest manhood he has been engaged in handling live stock,
seldom shipping, but annually feeding often several herds
or lots of cattle and hogs. His reputation as a superior and
successful feeder is unexcelled, especially as a feeder of
Texan cattle. Some of the finest and best-fatted cornfed
Texan cattle that were ever received at Chicago were from
his farm. Few men understand handling and feeding that
class of stock better than he. Indeed, no one will excel him
as a judge of that class of stock. In the fall of 1872 he
decided to go to Chicago and establish a commission house
for the sale of live stock, greatly to the pleasing of his many
friends, and to the cattle dealers of central Illinois, to whom
he is well known. As a man, he is plain, old-fashioned,
matter-of-fact in style, and possesses a cool, correct judgment, with unquestioned integrity of character. Besides, he
is substantial, reliable, brimful of "stock sense," and altogether responsible. He bids fair, at no distant day, to rank
among the most successful of Chicago's live stock men.

CHARLES GOODNIGHT'S RANCH

XVIII. CATTLE IN NEW MEXICO AND SOUTHEASTERN COLORADO

We have formerly had much to say concerning men and live stock interests of Texas, the Northwest, Kansas, and northeastern Colorado, but we now propose to devote brief space to New Mexican and southeastern Coloradoan live stock matters.

New Mexico, although comprising an area of more than 121,000 square miles and a population of near 100,000, and although it is now knocking for admission as a state into the Federal Union, is comparatively little known. This arises largely from the fact that no line of railroad has yet penetrated that territory. Nor until within quite a recent date has one been operated to a point sufficiently near to render the journey other than one of great hardship, requiring weeks of time traveling by tedious and uncomfortable modes of conveyances, over a monotonous, dreary country, under a burning sun. Now the speedy locomotive and luxurious car carries the tourist nearly to the northern line of the territory, and before many summers wax and wane, one or more lines will penetrate the heart of the heretofore secluded land of the Aztecs.

The territory, with other domain vast in extent, was acquired by conquest and treaty with old Mexico, as the mother country is termed in contradistinction to the New Mexico. Long before it came under the jurisdiction of the United States its adaptability to live stock production, [373] especially sheep husbandry, attracted many persons pastorally inclined. At the time of its conquest certain distinctively Castilian families had made it their home and were engaged in woolgrowing upon an extensive scale. The leading families did not lose but rather augmented their prestige after the change of rulers, and ultimately became, in a sense, dukes and princes of the land, having under and dependent upon them many thousand human beings of the lower order; many of whom, under a system of peon laws, were but a few removes from actual slavery — a system of customs and laws whereby a person could sell his services and himself for a stated period of time. Long before the stipulated time expired, necessities, real or imaginary, would arise, and an extension of the peonage would be fixed for a small sum in hand, perhaps a trifle in amount. So from year to year the person would be bound to work for his master, who controlled, ordered, and drove him as absolutely and as remorselessly as though he were — as practically he was — a veritable slave. But the new order of things arising from this has done away with peonage in New Mexico.

The average New Mexican is a bad mixture of Spanish, Indian, and sometimes Negro blood, producing in that warm, sunny clime a degenerate, unenterprising, go-easy specimen of the *genus homo*, who is in his seventh heaven when he can get enough to eat and an opportunity to "trip the fantastic toe" nightly at the fandango to lascivious music, in company with maidens to whom virtue is an unknown and unrespected grace, and to whom modesty is a lost sensibility. The race, as a whole, is, and has been for centuries, at a standstill. The same rude agricultural implements that their remote ancestors used, they cling to tenaciously, resisting all innovations of improved machinery. The wooden plow, mowing hay with a hoe, the ox harnessed or yoked by his forehead, grinding done by hand, transportation on little stupid donkeys scarce larger than a Newfoundland dog, are [374] seen everywhere. In short, a population almost, if not absolutely, impervious to progress either in business, science, education, or religion; their daily fare coarse and meager, their necessities few, their ambitions none. Far different is the case with the families of pure Castilian blood, who own most of the live stock found in the territory. Sheep constitute the principal live stock interest, and in numbers aggregate many millions; and in value, as in numbers, they outrank cattle and all other classes of stock.

Along the watercourses a sparse and stunted growth of reddish prairie grass affords a limited supply of hay; but as there is good grazing the entire year, hay is not extensively made or needed. Of that made, by far the greater portion is mown with the common field hoe. Imagine a troupe of men going to the hayfield with hoes in their hands, and ask, "Can this be in the United States and in the Nineteenth Century?" The uplands and plains are covered with grama grass, with an occasional tract abounding in the buffalo grass peculiar to Colorado. The grama grass is superior food for sheep, and in that winterless clime can always be had in abundance. But a small portion of country is under cultivation, and that along the streams in the valleys, where irrigation is practicable and easy. The upland, embracing by far the largest portion of the territory, is used, if at all, only for grazing purposes. It belongs principally to the General government. Some large tracts are held under old Spanish or Mexican grants made prior to the Mexican war of 1848 and confirmed by treaty of cession.

Upon the vast, almost limitless plateau, range countless thousands of degenerated sheep in flocks of three thousand or less, cared for by one person, a greaser, accompanied and aided by one or more sagacious, powerful shepherd dogs, which maintain a perpetual vigilance over the flock. With the speed of a racer they go to obey the command of the shepherd and turn the flock as directed. The dogs are reared with the sheep, sucking a ewe in puppyhood; and the [375] flock is lost without its attendant dog and guardian. Woe betide the unlucky coyote that essays to feast on mutton! If the shepherd dog is apprised of its presence, he will speedily annihilate his wolfship. They are very strong and rugged, and as brave as they are muscular. They are an indispensable adjunct of sheep husbandry in New Mexico. A greaser shepherd will sigh to lose his friend; groan if his wife or child dies; but if his dog is lost by death, his grief is overwhelming and his anguish cannot be assuaged. The flocks are enclosed in corrals at night, the shepherd sleeping with them, whilst the faithful, vigilant dogs maintain constant guard outside the corral. The corrals are located in the center of a large grazing district, and as many as eight, ten, or twelve flocks of three thousand each, nightly rendezvous in the same center, going out in different directions in the morning. The grown wethers are kept in separate herds from the stock sheep and lambs, and are usually sent out to the most distant herding posts.

The fare of the shepherd is very common, coarse, and scant, being a little coarse meal, goat's milk, and kid's flesh, all served in the rudest manner and highly seasoned with native pepper, used in every dish by Mexicans. Onions are the favorite vegetable, which grow to wondrous size and in the greatest profusion. Flocks aggregating thirty thousand are under the general control and supervision of an overseer, or major-domo, who is required to look after the general interest of the whole and see that all needed supplies are provided. He receives about $25 per month; the shepherds from $10 to $15 per month in specie. Your Mexican to this day has no use for the greenback, and cannot see any value in a national bank note; hence will accept nothing but gold or silver coin. The greasers are the result of Spanish, Indian, and Negro miscegenation, and as a class are unenterprising, energyless, and decidedly at a standstill so far as progress, enlightenment, civilization, education, or religion is concerned. The rudest and most primitive modes of life and of making a [376] living, such as their ancestors practiced five hundred years since, are entirely satisfactory to the present generation; and they look with profound, suspicious indifference upon any proposed innovation of ideas, modes, or implements of husbandry, such as mark the advancement of progressive nations of the nineteenth century. Such being the situation, but little progress in breeding superior-blooded stock is not to be found or expected in New Mexico.

It is claimed that their flocks of sheep are descended from imported Spanish merinos. There is nothing in their general appearance or fleece that would go to substantiate the assertion. But upon the other hand, the general appearance, the fleece, and the form of the Mexican sheep would indicate that its relation to the pure-blooded Spanish merino of the northern state is as distant as the era of creation.

Nevertheless, there is one strong argument in favor of the proposition, that is, that when the Mexican sheep is crossed with the pure-blood merino, the offspring will approach the type of the pure-blood at an astonishingly rapid rate. Indeed, it is claimed that a far superior flock of sheep can be secured by the first cross, as above, than from a similar cross with the common coarse-wool natives of the North. So satisfactory have the results proved to those who have tried on a large scale the crossing of Spanish merino bucks and Mexican ewes, that it is confidently claimed and asserted that a superior sheep for the western plains can be produced in this manner over any other. It is claimed that the Mexican ewe, like the Texan cow, when crossed with pure-bloods, transmits its hardy constitution and, above all, its energetic industry to the offspring, which inherits the form, size, appearance, and condition of the male. We believe it is a conceded fact that for ranching in Colorado and western Kansas, that Mexican ewes as a base are superior to all others. This may and perhaps does arise from the fact that Mexican sheep are cheap, hardy, industrious in seeking food, and perfectly adapted to living on the grass the year [377] round, without other food or any special care or attention other than to prevent their destruction by wild animals.

Many thousand ewes can be had for from 50c to $1.25 per head, taken at the Mexican ranches, and can be bought delivered in Colorado at $2.00 to $2.50 per head. An average flock of wethers will weigh about 70 pounds gross, and dress about 35 pounds of mutton, which, it is claimed, is superior in flavor, juiciness, and tenderness to northern mutton.

A limited number of families, mostly pure Castilians, have absorbed and now own nearly all the flocks of New Mexico. Prominent among the number is the Armijo family, whose flocks are estimated to aggregate fully two hundred and fifty thousand head of sheep. The number of greasers required to take care of, herd, shear, and mark this great number is over one thousand, [378] who, allowing five persons (women and children) to be dependent upon and belonging to each man employed, would aggregate six thousand human beings, and would constitute a city of pretentious numbers.

The late Pedro C. Armijo, a young, enterprising gentleman of Albuquerque, opened up a considerable trade in sheep with Colorado, driving from ten to twenty thousand head annually.[386] There was no trouble in disposing of the flocks to the mining towns and cities, or to parties desiring to embark in woolgrowing in Colorado. Señor Armijo had established a lucrative trade, one that afforded bright prospects for great profits. In an evil hour he perished. Charity for the living and pity for the dead alike forbid us to mention the cause of his untimely death. He was a young man of enterprise and the possessor of a bright, vivacious intellect, whose future prospects, so far as wealth could go, were as golden as the heart could have wished. He was thoroughly educated at St. Louis, Missouri, and when through with college, went to New York and took a position in a Wall Street banking house for the sole purpose of securing a complete, practical business education. At the end of four years he returned to New Mexico and enthusiastically engaged in woolgrowing and droving to Colorado.

Flocks of Mexican sheep shear, on an average, about two pounds of wool, which sells in Philadelphia for twenty to forty cents per pound, owing to its cleanliness and fineness. As no expense whatever is incurred on account of feed, and but little for labor, the business of woolgrowing is very profitable in New Mexico; it will be tenfold more so when full-blooded merinos are thoroughly introduced. The wool is baled much like cotton, and freighted with ox teams to the railroads in Colorado, and shipped principally to Philadelphia. Certainly no finer opening exists in the West than in southern Colorado and New Mexico in woolgrowing. To one whose tastes, habits, and bent of mind will permit him to [379] embark and continue in sheep husbandry, a sure reward and great wealth is almost certain.

There are, comparatively, but few cattle in New Mexico. Although it is in many respects a good cattle country, yet

---

[386] Armijo drove about 12,000 sheep to Denver in 1873. He was in Kansas City on November 1 of that year, when he declared that there was "nothing in the world to prevent a man from getting rich at sheep raising in five years." *Ellsworth Reporter*, Nov. 6, 1873.

CHARLES GOODNIGHT.

SEN. PEDRO C. ARMEJO.

it is better adapted to sheep. There are, however, some large stocks of cattle. It is claimed they do full as well as in Texas.

That portion of the Territory of Colorado lying east of the Rocky mountains has a natural subdivision constituting two distinct districts. This natural line of separation is the watershed, or Grand Divide, between the waters flowing into the Platte, Republican, and Smoky Hill rivers and the waters that flow into the Arkansas river. It starts out from the mountains just north of Pike's Peak and is traceable almost to the state of Missouri.

That portion of country south of the Divide constitutes southeastern Colorado, and as a distinct section deserves more than passing notice. It is watered by the Arkansas and numerous tributary rivers and creeks, and, as a whole, is one of the finest, if not the finest, live stock country on the continent. The winters are very mild, the air pure, the climate healthy, the grass fine – in short, nature seems to have exhausted herself in favorable combinations in its make-up. In this district are located many of Colorado's grandest live stock enterprises, including both cattle and sheep. It is a question upon which the present population is greatly exercised, and party lines are closely drawn – whether it is better for sheep or cattle, and which interest shall control and possess the country. An incipient war has been waged between the two factions for several months, which has greatly hindered the development of the country. But all matters of dispute are likely to be speedily and amicably settled. The region is penetrated by the Kansas Pacific Railway, the Atchison, Topeka and Santa Fé, and the Denver and Río Grande Railroads. The two latter lines will soon be extended into New Mexico.[387] Southeastern Colorado is more nearly stocked up to the full capacity of the country with cattle and [380] sheep than any other quarter of the territory; but yet there is abundant room for more. The original stocks were from Texan cattle and Mexican sheep; upon the former of which have been crossed Durham bulls, and upon the latter merino bucks, in both instances with the most satisfactory and profitable results.

387 The Santa Fé Railroad reached Trinidad, Colorado, in 1878, Otero, New Mexico, in 1879, and Santa Fé in 1880.

Nearly the entire Arkansas river front for a distance of one hundred miles east of Pueblo is already taken for stock ranches. Many young men of energy and determination have successfully established themselves and laid broad foundations for great wealth in southeastern Colorado, some of whom have already attained creditable success and distinction.

Among the latter may be named Charles Goodnight, resident six miles west of Pueblo City, upon the banks of the Arkansas river, near the foot of the mountains.[388] He is a native of Illinois, from which state, at the age of eleven years, he went to the northwestern frontier of Texas, where he remained until years of maturity. He was born upon a farm, and was reared to a full knowledge and experience of the hardships and toils peculiar to that vocation. That fitted him, to no small extent, for the privations and labors incident to a wild frontier life; such as was inevitable to a life in that section of Texas, which was subjected to the predatory and bloody incursions of hostile Indians upon one side and bands of lawless Mexican banditti upon the other, rendering life and the prosecution of business a continual hazard – a perpetual excitement. But young Goodnight was determined to do something to raise himself from poverty's humblest rut, and was prepared to forgo the comforts and luxuries of life, and endure any necessary privations and hardships that lie in the path to honorable success and fortune.

After being in Texas a short time, he, in company with another young man, took a herd of four hundred and thirty head of cattle, mostly cows, to keep for a term of nine years, upon the shares, i.e., one-half the increase to be divided and branded annually. At the close of the first year they [381] had raised only sixty-four calves all told, the half of which was thirty-two; and the half of that was sixteen calves, worth about three dollars per head. The result was decidedly discouraging, and the young men were disposed to give up the enterprise; but upon being encouraged by their patron, they determined, although they did not have a cent

---

[388] For a biography of Charles Goodnight, see Haley, *Charles Goodnight*. An early biographical sketch of Goodnight's activities and career is found in the *Fort Worth Daily Gazette*, Sept. 26, 1883.

in money, to see the contract through. So, mounting their cow ponies, of which they had but one each, they again went to the range, determined to wrest success from Dame Fortune, and to carry out the contract to the letter whether it proved profitable or otherwise. It was a turning point in Mr. Goodnight's life — one that well illustrates the firm determination of character that has marked his career and has contributed to his honorable, future success. At the end of the stipulated term the young men had as their share of the increase, including some small purchases, 4,000 head of cattle worth $8.00 per head, aggregating $32,000 in value. His prospect to secure an ample fortune speedily was all that he desired.

But about this date the Civil war began, which dashed to earth the bright prospects of the young stockmen. The Confederates took large herds of their stock and of course paid the rightful owners thereof nothing for it. After serving a few months in the Federal ranks on the frontier of Texas, Mr. Goodnight decided to gather his stock and move it out of the state. Accordingly, he started his herds across the Staked Plains and drove them into New Mexico and southern Colorado, where, to his happy surprise, he met cattle buyers to whom he sold out at very remunerative prices. Mr. Goodnight's first venture as a drover was not only of itself a success, but it developed to him a channel or method through and in which he decided there was a golden harvest for him in the immediate future. Therefore, he lost no time in returning to Texas, where, with the proceeds of his Colorado sales, he was enabled to purchase the entire stock of his former partner, consisting of [383] seven thousand head of cattle. This purchase was made of his former patron instead of partner. As soon as the stock could be gathered, it was put upon the trail for southeastern Colorado. But the journey was not made without danger, exposure, and severe Indian fighting almost daily whilst crossing the Staked Plains, a distance of about four hundred miles. In one of these hostile attacks the Indians killed his partner and captured a large number of the cattle. With the remaining herds Mr. Goodnight sorrowfully made his way, through daily dangers and untold privation and hardships, into Colorado. The losses en route by Indians were so great that the advanced prices realized in Colorado for the remainder of the herds did not cover entirely first cost of the stock.

Not daunted by the bitter, sorrowful experiences of the previous year, Mr. Goodnight renewed and continued the business of droving for the three succeeding years, realizing a profit of $104,000, a part of which belonged to the heirs of his former partner. The year of 1871 he operated in connection with Mr. Chisolm [389] and cleared $17,000. He has retired from droving, and two years since put a stock of cattle upon his ranch amounting in cost value, including $3,000 paid for Durham bulls, to $26,650. At the end of two years, by actual record kept for business purposes, the operations stand: Value of cattle now on hand, $27,950; amount realized from sales of stock, over and above the expense of keeping the stock two years, $17,925; which, added to present value of stock, aggregates $45,875; from which deduct the original investment, and the net profit for the two years' operation is $19,225, or $9,612.50 annually, or 36 2/3 per cent per annum – which ought to be a satisfactory per cent profit, and an equally satisfactory exhibit in favor of southeastern Colorado as a cattle country.

For the benefit of any reader who may be looking toward Colorado and indulging thoughts of entering its borders to become stock growers, we submit a [385] statement of Mr. Goodnight's live stock assets, as appears in an inventory upon his own books kept for business purposes:

400 Texan cows	$15 per head	$ 6,000
400 graded cows	20 per head	8,000
150 three-year old steers	20 per head	3,000
300 two-year old steers	12 per head	3,600
550 yearlings	9 per head	4,950
48 bulls	50 per head	2,400
1,848	Total value	$27,950

[389] John Simpson Chisum, the "cattle king" of the Pecos valley, New Mexico, was a native of Tennessee who moved to Texas and then to New Mexico. He died in December, 1884. *Historical and Biographical Record of the Cattle Industry*, 299-301; *Trail Drivers of Texas* (Hunter, ed.), 950-952.

The reader may rightly conclude that the above-estimated values per head are really lower than are warranted, but it is not the purpose to overdraw the business of stock ranching. These specific results are given in order that the reader may have a correct conception of the magnitude and profitableness of the live stock commerce between Texas and Colorado during that period, and the profitableness of stock growing in southeastern Colorado, and not in any sense for the purpose of boasting.

Having attained, at least to a reasonable degree, the goal of his ambition, to wit – a substantial competency won in an upright honorable business, in the pursuit of which he had spent twenty of life's brightest years, living at best in dugouts, cabins, and tents, and often day and night in the open air, enduring hardship, privation, and deadly danger – Mr. Goodnight determined to settle down and seek the comforts and quiet repose of a good home, and to bring around himself those tender endearments without which wealth and life itself is but a blank and a failure. Accordingly, in 1871 he made a purchase of a portion of the Nolan Land Grant, situated south and west of the city of Pueblo, Colorado, and well located for a large stock ranch and a desirable home. There he erected his residence, to which, soon after, he brought one of Tennessee's fairest daughters. Besides his present live stock interests, he stands at the head of the Stock Growers' Bank of Pueblo, an institution especially designed to accommodate the rapidly developing live stock interest of southeastern Colorado.

[386] From early childhood Mr. Goodnight's life has been spent upon the frontier, where educational facilities did not exist. Nevertheless, he has, by application since attaining the years of mature manhood, educated himself. Naturally he has superior talents and endowments, to which he joins a rigid and circumspect moral character, and a diffident modesty rarely met with in the West, which prompts him to shrink from rather than seek publicity. Indeed, it may be truthfully said that he despises notoriety and does not desire to appear conspicuously in print. Had the author been dependent upon him for the items concerning events of his history, this sketch would never have been

written. By nature he is gifted with a genius fitting him to command, even in a land of sovereigns. His life, although cast upon the wildest frontiers and subjected to the rudest circumstances, has been such that he has not lost the higher, nobler, tenderer feelings and sensibilities of an exalted manhood. The secret of his gratifying success is his diligent, persistent application to and study of his business until he was a complete master thereof both in theory and practice, coupled with an upright life and an unswerving integrity of character. He has no superiors in the Great New West, and his success has been as deserved as great.

It has often been truthfully observed that an inherited fortune ninety-nine in every hundred cases is an actual curse instead of a blessing to the legatee, especially if he be a young man who has never had to think or do business for himself. Whether this proposition is absolutely correct or not, one thing is certain — nine hundred and ninety-nine of every thousand successful business men in the West began life extremely poor in cash capital, rich only in energy and manly determination. It would seem to be a correct proposition that the best inheritance a young man can possibly receive is a clear, well-developed, and educated mind; good, fixed moral principles, energy, and an honorable ambition, with the necessity for self- [387] exertion before him. It seems to be true that no one is or can be born with correct ideas and knowledge of business. No matter how good a business man the father may have been, the son must needs go through a certain amount of trenchant drilling or experiences before he can comprehend or know how to conduct business successfully. And it is far better that the phases of business life and a knowledge of correct business principles be learned by actual experience when one is young and poor, than to begin life with hands full and in after years be compelled to begin anew, and not only learn correctly but unlearn all that has been erroneously acquired before. It is indeed more difficult to correct a faulty or false business education and fixed habits, and then learn or acquire a correct knowledge and habits of doing business, than to learn correct ones at the beginning. It does not seriously hurt the child if it totters and falls to the floor from the first stair step; but if it is carried to the top of the stairs and placed upon the highest step without a correct knowledge of the effort and manner of its getting there and the danger of falling, its fall to the bottom will be far more probable (and possibly painfully disastrous) than had it climbed up step by step unaided.

The reading public is interested in the history of the early, first efforts of a young man just starting out in the world for himself. The smallest incident or event that tests and indicates the metal of which he is composed is noted with deepest interest; far greater than is manifested in the largest business transactions successfully consummated in after life, when the trying reefs and shoals of poverty and temptation have been passed and the deep, serene harbor of great wealth fully attained. When a young, inexperienced boy of tender years is thrown upon the world to struggle and provide for himself, surrounded by every imaginable temptation, and allured by gilded vice and iniquity upon every hand, with no one to encourage his efforts toward the path of rectitude and success, [388] but a legion beckoning to ruin, we hail with joy the youth emerge unscathed, circumspect in morals, and strong in good, well-grounded principles, into bright, promiseful manhood and honorable success. We feel instinctively that for such the world has a sure and bountiful reward and humanity honorable plaudits.

Such an one is Dennis Sheedy, a young stockman well-known throughout the West and upon the Pacific slope. Born in Massachusetts, at the age of twelve years he was thrown upon his own resources, his father dying broken-hearted from financial reverses and losses which swept his ample fortune away, as the furious blast of the tornado sweeps the dust from the street. At this tender age the youth went to the state of Iowa and entered a large whole-sale and retail grocery store, in which he remained for five years. In that time he acquired a thorough practical knowledge of the business, including the minutest details. When he left that establishment, it was to cross the plains to Denver. He went in company with a number of teams loaded with freight for the mining districts. Paying a small stipend for conveying a limited amount of baggage, he walked nearly the entire distance. Arriving in Denver with but a few dollars in cash, he industriously set about obtaining employment, which he soon found in a wholesale and retail grocery and provision house doing a very large business. Although his salary was good, the expense of living was so great that he soon found no money could be saved in that situation, and he determined to abandon it, greatly to the disappointment of the proprietors.

He had went West to seek a fortune and not a mere living, and he determined to go to Montana and try mining. Accordingly, he set out over the mountains early in the spring before the snows were off, and endured great suffering and hardship from the cold winter storms. Yet he pushed on, arriving in Montana with only a few dollars, but in good time to begin mining in the spring of [389] 1864. Too poor and inexperienced in mining to begin on his own account, he went to work for a salary per diem. He was then but eighteen years old and unaccustomed to rough outdoor labor, and not of a rugged frame. There were several muscular miners employed upon the same work, and they thought it fitting sport to seek to overdo the young man and drive him from the situation. Upon one warm afternoon when they were wheeling over long gangplanks, heavy wheelbarrow loads of rock and débris, the young man, having drank too much water and becoming overheated from great exertion and labor, fell fainting and exhausted from the gangplank. This was the signal for coarse guffaws of laughter from the miners; but the young man soon revived, and to their astonishment, although he was pale and tremulous, remounted the plank and took his wheelbarrow and did do his part of the labor. This was an unexpected manifestation of genuine pluck, which elicited the admiration of the hardy, uncouth miners. Young Sheedy told them he came to Montana to mine, and he proposed to do it or die in the attempt; and he did not die, but continued to work for wages until he had earned a net $150.

Then he joined an experienced miner and bought a claim, which they soon resold at a snug profit; and another claim was bought and sold. He continued mining and trading in mines for three months; then bought a small stock of gro-

WINTER HERDING UPON THE UPPER ARKANSAS RIVER.—DENNIS SHEEDY'S CAMP.

DENNIS SHEEDY.

ceries and began business upon his individual account, which he conducted until fall. Then selling out, he went to Utah Territory, where, meeting an opportunity, he sold his gold dust at good figures. Taking an account of his financial standing, he found he had $7,000 in greenbacks as the result of seven months' operations in the mines, which he had entered almost penniless. This he regarded as a very encouraging exhibit. Having had a thorough schooling in adversity, he was fully apprised of the actual value and power of his means. It was the nucleus to which he could add daily; the key to [390] the Pandora box of future fortune; the trenchant blade with which to hew his way to wealth. Not wishing to spend the winter idly, he embarked in a general merchandising establishment to his great profit, and the following summer made two successful and remunerative trips to Montana, taking trainloads of supplies to the mines, each time selling train and freight at fine prices. Having acquired a snug capital and a thorough practical knowledge of business, he felt and foresaw the future need of a more complete knowledge of commercial law and the theories of commercial transactions. Accordingly, he went to Chicago, Illinois, and entered a commercial college of high repute. In six months, by diligent application to his studies, he advanced to the front of a class that had been one year in the college. His progress was unprecedented.

While trading in Utah, he had observed that the domestic labors of Mormon wives were almost universally performed with and by an old-fashioned, large fireplace. He concluded that a trainload of cookstoves would be a "hit." So upon leaving college, he purchased a cargo of stoves and necessary trimmings, also wagons sufficient to carry them; shipped the whole to Des Moines, Iowa, from whence he freighted them with ox teams to Utah. Single stoves that cost $24 each in Chicago sold readily in Utah at $125 to $175. Of course, the profits were enormous. Reloading his trains with supplies, he turned it toward Montana, in which, not finding a purchaser, he stored his goods and wintered his teams; and early the following spring reloaded the supplies and started for Idaho. He encountered deep snow and extremely cold weather in the mountains. Often his progress would be blocked for days by immense snowfalls and drifts. Finally, the summit passed and the perilous descent accomplished, a good market was obtained in the Lemhigh mining district. Returning to Montana, he sold his teams, and the following spring bid adieu to Virginia [392] City, so long his home, his center, his base, and went to the city of Helena, where he spent a year merchandising and trading. Then he put a loaded train on the road from Utah to White Pine, Nevada, where, upon arriving, he sold out at good figures, and then took a trip to California.

Feeling that he had seen and experienced enough rough, hard life clambering over mountains, enduring privations, racking hardships, and exposures of life and limb, and that he had acquired a reasonable amount of capital, he determined to look about and seek a country to his liking and settle himself permanently. In pursuance of this decision, he took two or three trips into southern California and Arizona, and one trip to Old Mexico, but without finding the goal of his desires. But while upon a trip in Arizona, he met several Texan drovers with herds en route to California, and from them heard with profound interest of the great numbers and low prices of cattle in Texas, and inwardly resolved to visit the Lone Star State upon a trading expedition. Accordingly, he took the train for New York City. From thence he leisurely passed to Texas by rail via [New] Orleans. Arriving in the stock-growing regions, he found, like the ancient queen, that "the half had not been told." Soon after arriving, he purchased two thousand good beeves and put them on the trail for California via western Kansas. But upon arriving at Abilene in the excellent season of 1870, he received such liberal offers for his stock that he decided to sell out, which he did – of course, at satisfactory figures. On returning to Texas the following spring, he found that full too many cattle were being driven, and decided that in western Kansas during the season would be the place to purchase cattle advantageously. His judgment proved, as usual, correct. During the summer he made a purchase of 7,000 head of mixed cattle. Meeting an opportunity to resell 3,000 head of his purchase, he put the [393] remaining 4,000 into winter quarters on the Arkansas river in Colorado near Fort Lyon.

Selling a part of his stock the following summer, he sent 3,500 head into Nevada, where, in the valleys of that state, he established a temporary ranch. The following year he marketed near 1,000 head of fat beeves, shipping by rail to San Francisco, a distance of 600 miles. He regards Nevada as a good cattle country, although subjected to heavy snowfalls endangering great loss by covering the feed, entailing starvation upon the herds. His herd has also increased by breeding near 1,000 calves. With the immature stock a remarkably fine development was made, the effect of transplanting them to more northerly climes and pastures. Indeed, this same improvement is plainly noticeable in young Texan stock transplanted to Kansan and other ranges north of Texas. A less growth of horn and better development of form and flesh are the improvements noted. During the fall of 1873, Mr. Sheedy made a purchase of 1,500 head of steers at panic prices and sent them into the upper Arkansas river country, and there placed them in winter quarters near Fort Lyon, Colorado. That portion of country along the Arkansas river for a distance of three to four hundred miles east of the Rocky mountains, is regarded as a very superior stock country and especially well adapted to wintering stock upon the range. Mr. Sheedy regards it as superior to any other known locality in Kansas or Colorado. In that district he has tested wintering cattle twice, both times escaping disastrous storms and serious losses of cattle. The winters being mild (no cold storms sufficient to warrant calling the season winter), but little other protection is needed for the comfort and convenience of the herdsmen than a common tent, such as is used in summer herding. Indeed, for many weeks in the winter months the weather would be as fine as that of September or May in other more northerly latitudes, the warm, [395] bright sun shining for scores of consecutive days. Water is abundant, the range unlimited, and of number one quality. Of course, the attempt to winter cattle under such circumstances could scarce fail of success.

Mr. Sheedy may be regarded as a cosmopolitan live stock man. His operations have extended and now are conducted upon both sides of the Rocky mountains, and he is familiarly known among stockmen in Texas, Kansas, Colorado, Ne-

vada, and California. And wherever known, [he] is regarded
as a prudent, cautious, thinking business man; one who will
not rush headlong into any operation whatever; and never
invests until he has fully calculated all contingencies and
sees his way through clearly; then never beyond his own
means. Having made the latter a rule of his business life,
never having signed more than three notes, he rightly at-
tributes his success largely to his persistent adherence to the
rule. Bank interest eats up the profits and substance of hundreds of stockmen annually. It is an insatiable leech, industriously sucking lifeblood both day and night; whether the
day is sacred or secular, sunny or stormy, or whether the
markets are good or bad, it matters not; the cry is "Give!
Give!" continually. Mr. Sheedy is by no means a timorous,
vacillating operator, but when his judgment endorses, he is
a nervy, bold trader. He is quite a young man, not having
entered his thirtieth year, although his experiences are as
great, trying, and varied as are those of many years his
senior. He may be justly proud of his success, wrought out
and attained unaided with his own hands and head. But that
pride is not of that vulgar stamp which often characterizes
young men of great wealth; but having bared his bosom in
the cause of fortune, and wrested success from adverse circumstances and untoward conditions by his own application,
energy, sagacity, and ability, he may well feel that life has
not been a failure. Having acquired a goodly fortune, he
now [396] seeks to adorn the mind and fit the man for a
walk in life upon a higher plane than that of the mere love
and acquisition of money, or the gratification of appetites
or passions. His ideas of the purposes and correct aims of
life are exalted; and his habits and principles, fixed upon a
firm basis and having been tried in the ordeal of western
life, are as irreproachable as unalterable.

Personally, he is impulsive and warm in his attachments,
suave and affable in his manner, kind and courteous, though
reserved and reticent among strangers. In all his wander-
ings in the Wild West, mingling with every class of characters and surrounded by innumerable temptations, he has
been superior to them, and is free from the most ordinary
and, we might say, universal vices which flourish luxuriantly

ALBERT CRANE'S STOCK RANCH, MARION COUNTY, KANSAS.

AVAILABLE STOCK RANCH LANDS OF THE A. T. & S. FE, R. R.

in the Great New West. His future is one full of promise and hope; his past, one worthy of imitation. His career stands out high and bold as a beacon light, and it may rightly be regarded as a pleasant oasis amid a limitless, dreary desert of innumerable failures.

The central portions of Kansas afford grand opportunities and landed facilities for extensive combined farming and stock growing operations. The districts drained by the Little Arkansas, Whitewater, Walnut, and Cottonwood rivers, abound with broad, undulating plateaus, whose deep, black, pliable soil is most easily brought into cultivation, rewarding the industrious, persevering agriculturist with generous yields of every cereal indigenous to a temperate climate. The amount of effort is small required to produce the most bountiful crops of corn, oats, wheat, and Hungarian grass, or millet on a large scale or upon vast areas of land. The entire district in its wild state is annually covered with a thick, rich growth of bluestem grass, affording unlimited summer range and millions of tons of hay for winter feed. The above section of Kansas may be properly classed as an agricultural and live stock country; one where both branches can be successfully and profitably conducted jointly; [397] feeding the grain products of the farm to the live stock; fitting it for any mart and thus marketing the grain also.

Within this vast area many large farming and live stock enterprises in various stages of development are located, among which none are more notable than that of Albert Crane, Esq., a resident of Chicago, Illinois, and a gentleman of liberal means. He has located his ranch enterprise in Marion county, Kansas, near the headwaters of the Cottonwood river, in the midst of a grand rich belt of faultless land. He has secured ten thousand acres of land and placed the entire tract under fence, mostly of post and board, the balance post and wire; and erected such houses, barns, cribs, sheds, and yards as enables both man and beast to shelter comfortably from the occasional storms; besides affording requisite conveniences and facilities for substantial living, and the easy handling of large numbers of stock. Already near eleven hundred acres are broken and under cultivation.

It is his plan to bring the entire tract of land into tame grasses – principally bluegrass – and to this end has sown one thousand acres of the unbroken, wild sod. The wild nature of the land, and the thick, firm turf of prairie grass caused this effort to result indifferently; however, in many places the bluegrass has taken hold and bids fair to succeed. Not to be daunted or thwarted, Mr. Crane is sowing timothy, clover, and bluegrass seeds mixed, upon one hundred acres of land, which has already been sown to oats or wheat. In this manner he confidently hopes for better success with the tame grass, and it is probable he will not be disappointed. He rightly believes that if he can but secure a good set of bluegrass upon all his land that then it will be easy to fatten or winter live stock without great labor or expense. When he has destroyed the wild nature of the land and fibrous roots of the native grasses, either by cultivation or depasturing closely and persistently, he will have but little trouble to get bluegrass to set and grow rapidly. Then his [399] highest anticipations of profitable live stock operations will be realized. With abundant bluegrass pastures, under the genial clime and mild winters of central southern Kansas, producing thick, fat cattle any month in the year inexpensively and without hard labor will be alike practicable and highly remunerative. No bank stock of the present day will pay such handsome dividends.

Mr. Crane has placed upon his ranch a herd of fine thoroughbred shorthorn cattle of the best strains of blood, one of which especially – the thoroughbred bull Prince Alfred, a genuine Booth – is unexcelled as a model animal in every respect. To this herd he proposes to add a score or more of select pure-bloods annually, until it takes rank among the leading ones of the West. Not by any means is his thoroughbred cattle his only live stock interest. More than one hundred of high-graded heifers, selected with great care in Illinois, are upon the ranch; which, crossed with thoroughbred bulls, will bring full-blood stock well fitted to any ranchman's requirements who is breeding to low-grade or Texan cows. It is Mr. Crane's purpose to give a degree of special attention to the production of superior-graded animals, and to induce, as far as possible, every

Kansas stockman to improve his herd; and to this end will place low prices upon his young-grade stock – a commendable spirit worthy of imitation, one that will bear fruits immediately and for all future time. Indeed, it is difficult to estimate the widespread substantial benefits accruing to a large community of stock growers by the location and development in their midst of an enterprise that includes among its purposes or aims the propagation and dissemination of pure-blood or high-grade stock at prices within reach of those of limited means.

But Mr. Crane's plans and operations are broader than yet indicated. Upon his ranch he keeps a herd of three thousand cattle of low or common grades, of which near one-half are cows and heifers; which brought an increase of twelve [400] hundred calves in the spring of 1874, all bred from thoroughbred bulls. The result of the first cross of this character is to lose every trace, both in form and color, of the southern mother; in short, brings such a class of stock as would pass for good native cattle in any mart. It is past all expectation, almost past comprehension, what wonderful good results are obtained by the crossing of Texan or Indian cows with full-blood Durham bulls. It is one of the grandest inducements to enter the safe and profitable vocation of stock growing in the Great Broad West, which affords so many inviting situations wherein are afforded every essential requisite to attain great wealth in the most healthful, honorable, and profitable of all callings. It is Mr. Crane's purpose to breed and rear cattle rather than to buy and sell them; in brief, to be a cattle producer and not a cattle speculator. He also proposes to make his live stock productions fit for the shambles of New York; and to this end cultivates yearly many hundred acres of corn, which is fed to the mature cattle during the winter. In short, he proposes to fullfeed every bullock for which he can produce sufficient corn. Each year a larger area will be planted to corn than on the previous. He proposes to soon add five thousand acres of land to his present estate, which will then embrace fifteen thousand acres in one compact tract. Upon this large estate we dare say that there are not five acres of waste land, but every acre is almost exhaustless in soil.

In southwestern Kansas are millions of acres as good as Mr. Crane's, in every way adapted to the joint uses of agriculture and live stock production, at prices ranging from four dollars to eight dollars per acre on long time at low rates of interest. It is true, to project and successfully develop an enterprise of the magnitude and upon the scale of Mr. Crane's, requires large capital, ability, and confidence in the capacities and resources of the country. Only a small per cent of men have sufficient capital to wield such immense enterprises. [402] But it is not essential to highly profitable ranch enterprises that they should be as large as Mr. Crane's. Live stock ranches and herds on a much smaller scale are eminently remunerative, and with only a proper degree of persistent application and patience will inevitably yield substantial comfort and independence, if not actual great wealth. But few men bring or send large capital to the West, and we deem it proper to point out the great field for capital and the need thereof in the western states and territories. There capital can earn great profit for its owner, besides doing good and conferring lasting benefits upon multitudes who are shaping and developing the young, plastic states of the West. Mr. Crane's ranch is within twenty-five miles of Florence on the Atchison, Topeka and Santa Fé Railroad, and will repay the time, delay, and expense of a visit. Besides, the hospitality and courtesy of its foreman, Mr. Reed, will make the heart glad; and a view of the princely estate and the massive herds will give enlarged views of the Broad New West, its privileges and possibilities.

XIX. THE RAILROADS AND THE LIVE STOCK TRAFFIC

Now that the live stock commerce of the West has become one of recognized importance and magnitude, it would seem proper that some mention at least should be made of the principal railway lines over which the larger portion of the live stock is moved to points of concentration; also, those which are the favorite and best routes over which the principal shipments are sent forward to eastern points. Of the latter, the Hannibal and St. Joseph, terminating at Quincy, where both Chicago and direct Buffalo connections are made, was the first to appreciate and encourage the western cattle trade. And it has never ceased to extend the utmost effort to secure and accommodate a large patronage. Its practical management has ever been, from the first opening of the cattle trade, of that farseeing, enterprising character which wins the appreciation and patronage of wide-awake shippers. It makes a specialty of the live stock traffic, and is particular to treat the stock shipper in such a fair, honorable manner as secures his warm friendship and patronage. It was the first road in the state of Missouri to place its stock trains practically under the control of its live stock shipping patrons, stopping to water, feed, rest, or, if need be, unload and reload any car of stock when necessary by reason of any portion of the stock shipping badly, at any station or hour that the shipper might demand. No employee of the road [404] could retain his situation after repeatedly violating this requirement. Of course, so humane and considerate a policy could only redound to the road's ultimate great advantage. Such appreciation of the stock shipper's interests bears its own rich reward to the company in a large list of friendly stockmen. But this line did not long enjoy a monopoly of the stock traffic.

Soon the St. Louis, Kansas City and Northern Railroad extended its line to Kansas City and entered the arena, bidding lively and with a great degree of success for a part of the rapidly-increasing live stock freights of the West. By securing a direct connection by way of Louisiana, Missouri (crossing the Mississippi river on a fine iron bridge) with the Chicago and Alton Railroad (thus reaching by a short, direct route the grazing and feeding regions of central Illinois, as well as the Chicago markets), it gave the St. Louis, Kansas City and Northern Road the double advantage of offering both St. Louis and Chicago marts to its patrons. Being a line of few gradients or sharp curves, but passing over a level route, it has been able to make quick time, and to carry live stock in such a manner as to deliver it in fine condition at its destination. The road with which it does its Chicago business, the Chicago and Alton, stands at the head of the list of Illinois roads as an unequaled live stock route. There are other railroads which carry live stock freights from Kansas City east, but the above named are the principal and favorite ones with stock shippers, and do nine-tenths of the forwarding of stock eastward.

Of the several railroads which gather the live stock from the western plains and concentrate it, the Kansas Pacific Railway is the oldest and the first in the stock traffic. But as it has been previously mentioned, possibly too often, in this work, it will here be passed, only remarking that its facilities to handle stock and its live stock resources are alike immense, and are rapidly increasing and developing.

The next road completed that bid for the southern [405] cattle trade was the Missouri [River], Fort Scott and Gulf Road, which made its cattle depot at Baxter Springs.[390] At that point it secured a large stock traffic for several years; but the habit of driving on more westerly trails was so firmly fixed with southern drovers that, coupled with other reasons, it did not succeed in securing and holding the stock business

---

390 The Missouri River, Fort Scott and Gulf Railroad, connecting Kansas City with Baxter Springs, reached the latter place about May 1, 1870. The shipment of Texas and Indian longhorns from Baxter Springs started shortly afterward. About 65,000 cattle were transported by this railroad during 1870. *Kansas City Journal of Commerce*, July 27, Nov. 2, 1870, Jan. 1, 1871; *History of the State of Kansas* (1883), 247.

at Baxter Springs to the extent that had been expected. Nevertheless, it still receives a portion of the Texan cattle traffic at Baxter Springs, besides no inconsiderable amount of stock shipped from Texas direct via Missouri, Kansas and Texas Railway. The country through which it passes is an elegant one, well adapted to stock growing and stock fatting combined with agriculture. For the latter the soil and climate is most propitious. In the fall and winter seasons all along the railway line can be seen numberless, well-filled corncribs and feed yards, in which are fullfed many hundreds of bullocks preparatory for market.

The third railroad completed to a point which gave it position to compete for the Texan cattle traffic was the Leavenworth, Lawrence and Galveston. This is operated from Kansas City to Coffeyville on the southern line of the state of Kansas, at a point sufficiently far west to enable it to enter into sharp competition with all other lines seeking patronage from southern drovers.[391] From the fact that the line was well built, and is so direct and short that only eleven hours are required to place stock in Kansas City from the Indian Territorial line; and the farther fact that it required less time driving from Texas to reach it than more westerly and more northerly points; coupled with the additional fact that the practical management of it has been in the hands of live, wide-awake men, who have taken especial pains to satisfactorily serve its live stock patrons — from all these reasons the line has been and is fast growing in decided favor among southern stockmen. Of all the lines seeking southern live stock traffic, this one is so situated that it can offer the lowest rates of freight and the [407] quickest time-table; hence can place its live stock freights in the Kansas City market in the best condition.

Reaching the very southern limits of the state, it has as a grazing district the entire Indian Territory, which near Coffeyville, its cattle depot, is principally prairie land covered with a bountiful growth of grass. Abundant water for stock and camp purposes, with ample wood for fuel, are

---

391 The Leavenworth, Lawrence and Galveston Railroad was completed to Coffeyville during the spring of 1871. *History of the State of Kansas* (1883), 248-249. See footnotes 355 and 357.

upon all sides. The whole region is one in which cattle can be held with the greatest ease and the least possible expense during the summer. The railroad company maintain ample, free shipping facilities, and is particular to leave nothing undone, the doing of which would add to the comfort, convenience, or accommodation of stockmen. The country surrounding the terminus within the state of Kansas is remarkably fine, closely settled, and in a high state of cultivation. Corn is largely grown; and cattle feeding, either full or "roughing through," is fast becoming a leading and profitable industry, and will in time develop to be a resource of great wealth to the shrewd agriculturist of those regions. In the Indian Nation on the south are broad valleys in which cane profusely abounds, which, keeping green during winter, affords unlimited food for wintering stock; while in the country west of Coffeyville it is hilly and broken, intersected with numerous gravelly, rocky, living streams of clear water, on either side of which in the valleys immense amounts of hay can be secured, costing only the labor of making it. Here, also, wintering advantages are afforded which are not excelled in southern Kansas. Into those regions in the fall of 1873 several thousand head of Texan cattle were put into winter quarters and cared for during the following winter without sustaining loss in flesh or numbers worthy of note. The railroad company owns many thousands of acres of good land, a large tract of which, situated farther up the line from Coffeyville, is held or reserved. Upon this well-watered [408] tract unlimited summer grazing is afforded to wintered Texan or to native stock. Taken as a whole, the Leavenworth, Lawrence and Galveston Railroad and its practical managers are deservedly listed among the western and southern stockmen's true friends, and bid fair to be classed among their benefactors.

Perhaps within the borders of no other state or territory has so great a proportion of the public domain been donated to railway corporations as within the state of Kansas. Besides the donations from the General government, divers large tracts of land formerly held as Indian reservations have passed for nominal considerations into the possession of railway corporations. As a result of the liberal, if not

ON THE GREAT HERDING GROUNDS, NEAR COFFEYVILLE, KANSAS.

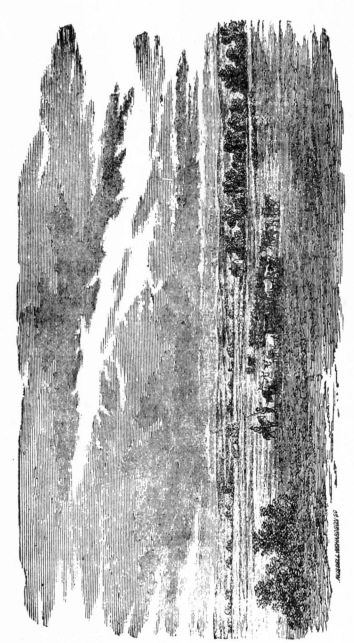

A NEW BEGINNER IN THE ARKANSAS VALLEY.

prodigal, policy of the Federal government, Kansas now has a munificent completed railway system far in advance of its settlement, population, or agricultural development. Indeed, the old order of building railroads into well-settled and developed districts has, by the stimulus of land subsidies, been reversed in the West; so that it has become almost impossible to speedily settle or develop a section of country through which there is not in operation one or more lines of railroad. The average American emigrant demands a railroad completed and in operation to carry him to the immediate vicinity to which he would go, as the necessary condition upon which he will graciously deign to accept as a free gift a quarter section of rich agricultural land as a home and a heritage. If Uncle Samuel fails to provide the prerequisite, a railroad, although it may cost a few million acres of his domain, why Jonathan will indignantly stay in the land wherein he is a dependent tenant. It is expected that the next generation will demand of the government a petit system of narrow-gauge railroads upon each quarter section of public land, centering at the most eligible spot upon which a homesteader would naturally be supposed to locate his grain bins, that his crops may be garnered without private expenditure of cash or labor.

[410] Of all the munificent land grants to railway corporations within the state of Kansas, none excels in number of acres, variety of country, quality and depth of soil, and salubrity of climate, the donation to the Atchison, Topeka and Santa Fé Railroad Company. As its name would indicate, the line begins at Atchison, Kansas, and passes in a southwesterly course through the capital city and through vast coal fields to the Neosho river; thence bearing more westerly, it reaches the great Arkansas river; up the level north side valley of which, to the western line of the state, it passes, aggregating a total length of four hundred and seventy miles. For two-thirds of its length a belt of rich farming and grazing land from ten to twenty miles in breadth is the munificent gift of the Federal government. But it is the province and scope of this work to treat only of such subjects as have a connection, bearing, or adaptability to the live stock business; or, using a phrase more

expressive than elegant, "look at everything through a cow's horn."

Of the Atchison, Topeka and Santa Fé land grant, the western third, situated upon the upper Arkansas river, may be regarded as being naturally fitted and adapted to exclusive stock growing, which, of course, includes woolgrowing. There is water, range, and shelter for hundreds of thousands [of] head of stock. The grasses are principally of the buffalo grass variety, with occasional broad valleys covered with bluestem. But a small per cent of the many good, eligible stock ranch locations, abundantly near the railroad, are as yet taken. This is true of the government lands, which can be had for the taking, as well as the company's lands. There are uncounted opportunities for live stock ranching operations of as large or small dimensions as the heart may wish; chances to grow cattle by the dozen or by the thousand annually; and equally as good opportunities to grow wool by the wagon or carload; in a sunny, almost rainless clime and in a winterless [412] latitude; upon lands to be had at extremely low prices, upon long credit with nominal interest; and all within sight of a railroad, the owners of which are as anxious to promote the general welfare of its patrons and the general development of the country as the settlers possibly can be. This line will be extended during 1874 in a southwesterly direction from Granada, Colorado, its present terminus, in the direction of Santa Fé, New Mexico. The country through which it will be located is unsurpassed on the continent for live stock growing. But to return — the remaining two-thirds of the land grant is located within that belt in which joint agriculture and stock growing and feeding can be most profitably conducted. The soil is very rich and deep. Water, bluestem prairie grass upon the bottoms or valleys, and buffalo and winter grass upon the uplands are abundant; indeed in limitless supply. Every specie of grain, vegetable, or other production peculiar to that latitude can be produced without limit and at the smallest possible expenditure of labor. The great Arkansas valley when fully settled and developed will produce more grain than any other valley in the world. It is in that valley that the railroad company have established

Ramsey, Millett & Hudson, Sc. K.C.Mo.

A.T. & S.F.R.R.

LOADING CATTLE AT WICHITA, KANSAS.

GREAT BEND CITY—CATTLE DEPOT ON THE A. T. & ST. FE R. R.

its cattle shipping depots for the concentration and shipment of Texan cattle. In the live stock traffic this line has been a determined and successful competitor of the Kansas Pacific Railway since the spring of 1871. Its first live stock depot was at Newton; but the rapid settlement of the country necessitated its reëstablishment, which was done at Wichita and at Great Bend. Both points are in the Arkansas valley, the first upon a branch railroad, the latter upon the main line.

At Wichita, during the first season after the road was completed to that point, a cattle shipment was made of near four thousand cars,[392] which amount was nearly duplicated during the following year.[393] So great a commerce thrust suddenly [413] upon the town created an unprecedented demand for business accommodations, storerooms, banks, hotels, etc. The town soon grew to the proportions of a city, and imposing brick and stone buildings arose upon all hands to accommodate the increased business; among which, the Occidental Hotel, an edifice that would do credit to rebuilt Chicago. The limitless, rich-soiled valley surrounding this point must ultimately become so thoroughly and compactly settled that a foreign cattle commerce will no longer be practicable. The settlement already extends fully twenty miles beyond the river; and only by an amicable arrangement made with the settlers before the cattle arrive in the spring can they be brought through the settlements to the shipping yards, of which the company has most excellent ones. Every needed accommodation exists in the way of able banking institutions, hotels, and large business houses, to accommodate an immense cattle trade; and the railroad is thoroughly equipped with superior rolling stock, motive

[392] 3530 carloads. See footnote 352.

[393] A total of 13,739 cattle were shipped by rail from Wichita between January 1 and September 1, 1873; but most of the longhorns which were driven to Wichita in that year were transported north after September 1. The Santa Fé Railroad shipped 98,058 cattle during 1873. It is probable that about forty or fifty thousand cattle were transported from Wichita in 1873, but this estimate is not based upon any definite figures. *Kansas Daily Commonwealth*, Sept. 16, 1874. During 1874 the railroad transported 2461 carloads of cattle, or 50,253 cattle, from Wichita. *Wichita City Eagle*, Apr. 1, 1875.

power, and all needful facilities to transport more than one hundred thousand head of cattle annually. Stock from New Mexico or southern Colorado are provided with a shipping depot at Granada, the present terminus of the railroad line.

Great [415] Bend, on the main line, is located near the river and immediately surrounded by a rich valley, which, upon either side, is bounded by millions of acres of upland covered with buffalo grass and watered by small living streams of water. This point is destined at no distant day to be recognized as the chief shipping depot for Texan cattle on the line of the Atchison, Topeka and Santa Fé Railroad.[394] By its location it is accessible from the best stock ranges in Kansas, and has had in the past no inconsiderable stock business from Colorado. Herds stopping in the vicinity of Great Bend have the advantage of the market and competition of the Kansas Pacific Railway, which is distant only about forty miles. This fact alone will secure it a good business. The adjacent country is such that it will remain unsettled for years to come, unless taken for stock ranches, for which the country presents magnificent opportunities and advantages. Parties seeking to purchase Texan cattle for market, feeding, or ranching purposes find Great Bend a point so located that from it all the southern and western cattle stopping near Wichita or near the Atchison, Topeka and Santa Fé Railroad, as well as all those stopping on the line of the Kansas Pacific Railway, can be seen without great difficulty or extremely long rides in the hot sun. This gives purchasers an opportunity to make selections of stock and find good bargains not equaled by any other cattle point in the state of Kansas. The shipping facilities are all that the most fastidious or the largest operators could desire, and the citizens are unanimous in the determination to promote and facilitate a large cattle trade.

The Atchison, Topeka and Santa Fé Railroad presents many advantages to the southern stockman; among which is its limitless grazing facilities, abounding in every variety

---

394 The Atchison, Topeka and Santa Fé Railroad was completed to Great Bend on July 13, 1872, and Texas cattle were first shipped from there on the following August 23. Great Bend remained one of the shipping points for Texas cattle until 1875. *Kansas Daily Commonwealth*, July 19, Aug. 28, Sept. 8, 1872, June 28, 1876; *Kansas City Journal of Commerce*, June 9, 1875.

HERD UPON THE GRAZING GROUNDS NEAR GREAT BEND, KANSAS.

of lands and grasses, with abundant living water in low, easy-banked, shallow, swift streams having sandy or gravel beds; the choice of two good, competing shipping depots and frontier marts; besides, offering the shipper choice of two routes — one by way of Atchison, thence by various lines to Chicago [416] and the East, or up into the corn regions of northern Missouri, Iowa, and eastern Nebraska — or to go by way of Kansas City and enjoy its numerous advantages. The practical management of this line has been, from the beginning, of that enlightened, liberal character that could not fail to secure and retain many patrons among live stock men. But a sketch of the Atchison, Topeka and Santa Fé Road would be incomplete that did not point out the great advantages offered by the vast country through which the road passes, for growing, wintering, and fatting live stock. The eastern third of the line passes through a corn-growing and stock-feeding section of great merit. The middle third is well adapted, if not specially designed, for joint stock growing and agriculture. The western third is among the best exclusive stock-[growing] and woolgrowing sections in the state of Kansas.

If the driving of cattle from Texas to Kansas must needs continue in the future, the drovers would act wisely to possess themselves of choice stock ranch locations, and hold their stock, if need be, over winter until it was fat, instead of putting it upon market whilst unfit by reason of its poverty. Too much cannot be said against the suicidal policy of shipping or marketing poor, thin stock. It is sure financial ruin and bankruptcy to those who persistently practice it. It is a common practice of southern drovers, and as unwise if not actually foolish as it is common, to ship their unfatted, immature stock direct to market, where they inevitably realize low, mean prices. Besides, the stock weighs next to nothing, and of course brings little, comparatively, above shipping and selling expenses. Millions of dollars are annually lost, or rather the means out of which to make millions of dollars, are annually sacrificed, lost, thrown away, by marketing thin-fleshed stock. It is like one burning his own resources. It is on a par with the wisdom which dictated the cutting open of the goose that laid the golden egg. It is a foolish sacrifice of great resources. It is like giving away one's opportunity to add fifty per cent to one's assets, or the [417] opportunity to double the value of one's property within a year. There can be no tenable justification of such conduct on the part of live stock owners. With millions of acres of grass and unlimited amounts of feed being annually burned up, or allowed to rot unused, or sold for a trifle above cost of production, nothing but a lamentable lack of business sense and thrift would ever allow or permit so many unfatted cattle and hogs to go to market, there to be sacrificed for nominal, unpaying prices, realizing scarce one-half the net sum that a little fat or tallow would make attainable. A reform in this respect is in order, if not imperatively demanded, by the best interest of western live stock men. Of the cattle coming from Texas, two-thirds are marketed when almost totally unfit for consumption, thus entailing comparatively immense losses upon the parties selling them. Rather than continue this foolish, wasteful, and ruinous practice, drovers had infinitely better buy stock ranch locations in western Kansas and Colorado, and there keep their stock until it is fat. When they comprehend their own best interests, they will see the force and truth of these observations.

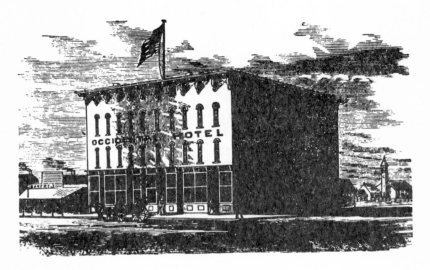

XX. THE MISSOURI, KANSAS AND TEXAS RAILWAY[395]

The Missouri, Kansas and Texas Railway, from its geographical location and its termini, is destined to become the chief Texas live stock route. This great road, with its present terminus in northern central Texas, is well located to command and accommodate the exportation of live stock from that broad state. The construction of the line commenced at Junction City, Kansas, in 1868.[396] The company is composed of an association of some of the best and most active business men and capitalists of New York – men thoroughly acquainted with the business wants of the country and possessed of the requisite knowledge of the demands of trade, to develop and successfully construct a line of railroad to meet all the various interests of cheap and rapid transportation from Texas to the seaboard and the northern lakes.

In a few months the line was extended down the Neosho valley to the southern line of the state of Kansas,[397] and a branch, destined to be the main line, was completed to Sedalia, Missouri, there securing complete rail connections for St. Louis. In a contest arising before the Interior De-

[395] McCoy has the following footnote at this point: "In explanation of the absence of illustrations in this chapter, it should be stated that the managers of the Missouri, Kansas and Texas Railway declined propositions to illustrate their line, preferring to revise and amend the manuscript."

[396] The Union Pacific Railway Company, Southern Branch, incorporated on September 25, 1865, started construction at Junction City late in 1868 and early in 1869. During 1870 it became part of a larger system – the Missouri, Kansas and Texas Railway. *History of the State of Kansas* (1883), 250-251, 1002.

[397] The Missouri, Kansas and Texas Railway reached the southern boundary of Kansas, a few miles south of Chetopa, about June 1, 1870. *Kansas Daily Commonwealth*, June 8, 1870.

partment, with another new line,[398] the right of way across
the Indian Nation was awarded to the Missouri, Kansas
and Texas Railway. This valuable [419] franchise secured,
the work of extending the line southward to Red river and
Texas was pushed energetically forward until, about the
first of January, 1873, it was completed to the flourishing
city of Denison, about five miles south of Red river in
Texas.[399] Before the southern extension was completed, a
line from Sedalia in a northeastern course to Hannibal,
crossing the Missouri river near Boonville, was projected
and vigorous work began. In less than six months from the
completion of the line to Denison, trains were run through
to Hannibal. This completed line from Hannibal on the
Mississippi river, where direct Chicago and Toledo connections are secured to Denison, Texas, is one remarkable alike
for its great length, for the brief space of time transpiring
in its construction, for the substantial manner in which
the road is built, and for the excellence of the material used
in its construction.

The climate is mild and healthy, and the country through
which the road passes produces cotton, wheat, oats, corn,
and all kinds of wild and tame grasses abundantly. In all
these respects it stands unrivaled by western railway lines.
But in another respect, one in which it is the province and
scope of this work to deal, it is none the less remarkable
and worthy of special note – that of it being a trunk line
over which the live stock freights of the great Southwest,
including not only a large portion of the state of Kansas
and Missouri, but the Indian Territory and the state of
Texas also, must find its way to profitable market. As a live
stock line it has a length of nearly eight hundred miles, and
not only runs through a great variety of fine stock country,
but passes through and into the home of nearly every grade
and breed of live stock. Beginning upon the margin of the

---

398 The Missouri River, Fort Scott and Gulf Railroad.

399 The Missouri, Kansas and Texas Railway reached Denison, Texas,
in December, 1872. The first through passenger train from the north arrived
there on December 25. Denison, named after the vice president of the railway, was laid out in September, 1872, and claimed to have a population of
about 2500 during the latter part of December of that year. *Denison News,*
Dec. 27, 1872; *Kansas Daily Commonwealth,* Dec. 22, 1872.

evergreen-growing regions of Texas, where exist uncounted thousands of cattle, lineal descendants of Cortes's importations into Mexico, which know not what it is to be fed by the hand of man — thence it passes in a northeasterly course through the Indian Territory. In the [420] Nation are found thousands of cattle whose progenitors were the old-fashioned American cattle, such as existed throughout the Union before the advent of the heavy-quartered Durham, whose rounded progeny are found in great numbers upon every farm in central and eastern Missouri. No other line of railway in the Union reaches so completely the natural homes of all classes and grades of live stock, as well as the countries best suited to the various modes of growing and fitting the same for market. Upon the great area situated at its southern terminus is found a country and clime where stock raising and fatting upon the rich native grasses is not only extensively but profitably done upon a large scale, and from whence an immense annual supply of beef can and will for years to come, be produced and put upon northern and eastern markets. In central Missouri a bluegrass and corn-growing region is traversed, in which stock feeding and fatting, rather than stock growing, is extensively and very profitably conducted upon a large scale.

For the accommodation of this trade, this great and growing commerce in live stock, the Missouri, Kansas and Texas Railway have made ample arrangements, both in the way of suitable rolling stock and motive power, and have provided suitable, complete loading and feed yards at such points along the line as will best serve the interest and convenience of stock shippers. At Denison, Texas, a substantial, commodious shipping yard is located, which is capable of affording accommodation for two thousand head of cattle, besides serving the additional purpose of a resting and feed yard for such consignments of live stock as may be received from the Houston and Texas Central Railroad. It is the intention of the company to enlarge their facilities for doing live stock business at Denison by securing for grazing purposes a large tract of prairie country west of Denison and convenient to the shipping yards. This prairie land is covered with grass the year round, and has fine,

clear water running in numerous branches [421] and creeks,
thus making it a very superior herding ground. But if the
stockman desires a larger territory upon which to hold his
herd, he is accommodated in the Chickasaw Nation, wherein
a large tract of prairie land has been leased by the railway
company expressly for the accommodation of cattlemen. In
the midst of this large tract, at Colvert Station, snug, substantial shipping yards have been established. At Denison
are located several first-class banks, one of which, the First
National, has a capital of $100,000; and the corporation is
composed of some of the best business men of Texas and
Missouri. The eastern connections of this bank are such
that accommodations at reasonable rates are given to stock
shippers in any amounts they may require in their business.
Other banks are also prepared to assist the stock trade, so
the shipper may be certain of being accommodated without
delay on his arrival at Denison. The hotels at Denison are
numerous, large, and commodious, and prices to stock shippers and dealers are made very reasonable.

At many stations through the Indian Nation are located
good shipping yards of capacity equal to the business offered.
All the shipping yards are owned by the railway company
and are free to the shippers. At Chetopa, on the Kansas
state line, a good feed and resting yard is located, wherein
are found ample convenience for both feeding and resting
stock. This point is about two hundred and fifty miles from
Denison, which distance is a good run from the latter point.
Chetopa is a point to which many cattle, before the completion of the railway to Texas, were driven across the
Indian Territory and there shipped to northern markets.[400]
Indeed, it yet enjoys a respectable amount of live stock
business, and perhaps will continue to do so as long as cattle
are driven instead of shipped from Texas. At Sedalia, Missouri, another good feed and resting yard is located, at
which such consignments as are destined for St. Louis are
fed, rested, and reshipped upon another [422] line; while
such shipments as are intended for central Illinois, Chicago,
or eastern markets, either with or without having been

---

400 As early as the latter part of October, 1870, Texas cattle began to be
shipped from Chetopa over the Missouri, Kansas and Texas Railway. *Republican Daily Journal,* Nov. 1, 1870.

rested and fed, go direct to Hannibal, where again ample facilities for resting, feeding, and reshipment are provided. At Hannibal the shipper has choice of good competing routes to Chicago or Buffalo, in addition to being in the midst of a large cattle-feeding and grazing district, which annually requires many thousands of imported cattle to consume the grass and corn crops of those regions. Certainly a very complete cattle market could be established at Hannibal; one that would be alike beneficial to the southern cattle producer as well as to the northwestern feeder and grazer; a market in which the Texan, the Indian, the old-fashioned native, the graded and full-blood Durham could be had in ample supply. Such consignments as are destined for Kansas City leave the Missouri, Kansas and Texas at Fort Scott, and reach that market via the Missouri River, Fort Scott and Gulf Railroad.

Thus it will be seen that no route from Texas or the Indian Nation offers such advantages as does the Missouri, Kansas and Texas Railway, reaching as it does from the Red to the Mississippi river. Coming north, the shipper can turn to the left and reach the Kansas City packing market; or turning to the right, go upon the St. Louis market; or going straight forward, can reach the central Illinois feed and grazing markets or go direct to Chicago, the greatest live stock market in the world. Over this route reasonable rates of freight and charges only are exacted – rates as low per car per mile as are afforded by any other route in the West, and that, too, without expensive, tedious, and risky drives, which always deteriorates the stock in value even more than it saves in prices of freights, not to mention the expense, risk, and labor of such long drives.

But there is another inducement, well worthy of note to Texan live stock men, located at Denison. The Atlantic and Texas Refrigerating Car Company, which has constructed one hundred new cars arranged and adapted to shipping fresh beef, has been [423] located and established at Denison for slaughtering cattle at the rate of five hundred daily. This company is prepared and was organized for the purpose of making a market at Denison for all good fat cattle that may be brought there. It will pay in cash good prices for cattle suitable for the eastern markets. They have capacity for shipping three trains each week, and the success they are meeting with will doubtless induce them to largely increase the business. To Texan live stock men, that ought to be and doubtless is an enterprise which should meet their approbation as well as hearty coöperation and patronage. Such a thing as a home demand and a home market, steady and reliable, is a desideratum they have never had but have long desired and needed. The establishment is complete in all its arrangements for slaughtering the bullock and cooling the carcass at a rapid, wholesale rate. When the meat is cooled, it is hung up by the quarter in a car specially arranged for its protection and transportation. Each car will hold double the number of carcasses of cattle that an ordinary stock car will hold of living cattle. Besides, the meat goes to market without bruising or delay, and in only about one-third the time and at one-half the expense required to market beef by the old methods. It has been successfully demonstrated that beef can be laid down in New York at reasonable prices and in fine, clean order by this mode of shipment. The great saving of freight is divided between the producers and consumers. If Texan live stock men have their own best interests at heart or have sufficient public spirit, they will hardly let that enterprise, which promises them so much timely relief and profit, go unaided and unsupported by their patronage.

In addition to the advantages enumerated for the rapid shipment of live stock to good eastern markets, the Missouri, Kansas and Texas Railroad are now having constructed a large number of cars that are known as the "Palace Stock Cars." [401] They are cars made longer than the usual stock cars now in use, and are so built that each animal is provided with a stall in which [424] it can lay down to rest. The stalls are provided with feed boxes and hay racks, also tanks for the purpose of watering the animals. In those cars fine beef cattle and blooded stock can be transported over long distances, and be taken from the cars as unfatigued as if they had not made a journey. Trains

---

401 Described in the *Denver Tribune*, Sept. 24, 1873.

of this kind will run regularly and the advantages to shippers cannot be overestimated.

But the question whether it would be more profitable and advisable for southern cattlemen to continue to drive their cattle to western Kansas and the territories, as has been their habit for the last seven or eight years, or leave them upon their native pastures until fat and then send them by rail direct to market, is becoming of more urgent importance daily, and is beginning to exercise the minds of southern drivers to a great extent. In view of the facts that the years of 1871, 1872, and 1873 have, taken in aggregate, entailed immense losses upon the southern drover whose herds have been taken to western Kansas; and again, that the western teritories have become so largely and completely supplied with cattle that, instead of being buyers of large numbers as heretofore upon the western Kansas market, they now are and hereafter will be large sellers; and inasmuch as they are able to send very fat cattle to market, their competition is not only great but disastrous to the driver of fresh Texan cattle – in view of all these facts, is it not full time that a change in the mode and manner of marketing Texan cattle be effected? Besides, the territorial demand in former years constituted one of the principal inducements to drive to western Kansas. Now since this inducement no longer exists but rather the reverse is true, it becomes a serious question, one which may be narrowed down to that of the profitableness of marketing fat and lean cattle. The observing, sensible drover, or the one who has experimented in shipping live stock, needs no words or figures to convince him that fat stock only can profitably be put upon the northern markets. Few business propositions are so little understood and comprehended [425] by Texan cattlemen as the fact that whilst a bullock which is fat may be worth many dollars, at the same time and upon the same market a bullock which is lean is almost worthless. If salable at all, it is only at mean, low prices, and when driven upon the scales, it weighs very light, almost nothing – hence brings little or nothing above expenses of marketing; whilst the fat bullock, although no better animal, only fatter, weighs heavy, sells at

high figures, and pays out a handsome price and profit above
cost and expense. No man living ever made a dollar by
shipping poor, thin cattle to market — many have lost thousands of dollars.

Now in view of these indisputable, well-known facts;
and in view of the fact that upon an average not one bullock
in ten when driven to western Kansas (unless wintered
there) becomes fat enough even for packing purposes; and
not one in a thousand becomes in such condition of flesh as
to be put on the eastern markets the same season in which
they are driven from Texas, and must for the very reason
named be sold at low prices — in view of these facts, in connection with the falling off of the demand for other than
fat cattle, is it not time the Texan should cease to exhaust
his herds of stock and breeding cattle, and reconstruct his
habits of driving and let his cattle remain upon their native
plains until fat, then send them direct to market. Take an
example. A thin-fleshed four-year-old steer does well to
weigh 900 pounds gross, and at 2c per pound (a price about
the average realized during the last three years) would
bring $18 per head, out of which driving and other expenses
must be paid, leaving but little net for the bullock; whilst a
bullock of the same quality and age, only actually fat, weighs
about 1,200 pounds, and is easier to sell at 3c per pound
gross weight, or upwards, than the thin one was at 2c, and
will amount to $36 per head, or twice as much as the thin
one; and the expense of marketing is nothing more but the
margin for profit is large. There is a lesson that live stock
men need [426] to learn thoroughly and perfectly — that it
pays to market fat live stock and only fat live stock — poor,
thin ones never.

If it be true that by driving their herds to Kansas, they
prevent them from becoming marketably fat, do they not
do themselves a financial injury by so driving, especially
since they have now a means of marketing their live stock
direct and quick from Texas to any desired northern market,
upon which they need not go until their stock is fat and fit
for the mart, and not then unless the market will justify?
When the rate of freight exacted from western points to

St. Louis or Chicago is compared with that asked from Texas over the Missouri, Kansas and Texas Road to the same markets, it will be found that the difference in favor of the western routes is scarce above one dollar per head – a sum that will hardly pay above one-third the actual costs of driving, not to mention the depreciation of the stock in flesh and consequent value, or rather the loss of the time and opportunity to appreciate its value by fatting the animals instead of driving them. In years gone by, before any railroad was built to Texas, when there was a great demand for cattle in the territories and upon the Pacific slope, and native cattle were scarce in the North, there was a necessity for and a profit in driving to western Kansas. But since the conditions are changed, and the demands from those sources has fallen off so that fat cattle only can be profitably marketed, it would seem to reasoning and reflecting minds that the day for driving cattle is past, and the time fully come when ranchmen in all sections should retain their stock at home until fat and then ship direct to market. The advantages of such a course are numerous and manifest: there need be no heavy loans of money, or loss of time in holding and fattening the stock; there would be no simultaneous running of many thousands upon the market at once, or within the space of a month's time; there would be no necessity to sell at the first approach of frosty weather, whether the cattle were fat or not, or the market good or bad. If the market should be unusually low, as has been the [427] case in former years, then the supply could be withheld for another year and better prices; again, the drover could enjoy the substantial comforts of home, with its thousand endearments, instead of hardships, exposure, and risks of a long drive, and the tedious, expensive holding in a country abounding in prohibitory legislation, dead lines, and herd laws.

THE SOUTHWEST HISTORICAL SERIES

Comprises the following volumes printed direct from the original unpublished manuscripts, and rare originals

Volume I. (1844-1847)

Webb (James Josiah), Adventures in the Santa Fé Trade, 1844-1847

From the original unpublished manuscripts

Volume II. (1854-1861)

Bandel (Eugene). Frontier Life in the Army, 1854-1861; translated by Olga Bandel and Richard Jente.

From the original unpublished manuscripts

Volume III. (1846-1847)

Gibson (George Rutledge). Journal of a Soldier under Kearny and Doniphan, 1846-1847

From the original unpublished manuscript

Volume IV. (1846-1848)

Marching with the Army of the West, 1846-1848. Comprising the following original unpublished journals:

Johnston (Abraham Robinson) Journal of 1846
Edwards (Marcellus Ball) Journal of 1846-1847
Ferguson (Philip Gooch) Diaries, 1847-1848
Muster roll of Company D, First Regiment of Missouri Mounted Volunteers, June, 1846

Volume V. (1849)

Southern Trails to California in 1849

Early news of the gold discovery
Advertising southern trails and routes
Routes through Mexico to California
Routes from Texas to the gold mines
· Routes through Arkansas and along the Canadian
The Cherokee Trail
The Santa Fé Trail

From various contemporary newspapers

Volume VI. (1846-1850)

Garrard (Lewis H.). Wah-To-Yah and the Taos Trail.

From the rare original edition of 1850, with extensive additions by the editor

Volume VII. (1846-1854)

Exploring Southwestern Trails, 1846-1854

Cooke (Philip St. George) Journal of the march of the Mormon Battalion, 1846-1847
From the original unpublished manuscript

Whiting (William Henry Chase) Journal of 1849
From the original unpublished manuscript

Aubry (François Xavier) Diaries of 1853 and 1854
From the original published 1853, in the *Santa Fe Weekly Gazette*

Volume VIII. (1687-1873)

McCoy (Joseph G.) Historic Sketches of the Cattle Trade of the West and Southwest

From the rare original edition of 1874, with extensive additions by the editor

Volume IX. (1859)

Pike's Peak Gold Rush Guidebooks of 1859

Tierney (Luke) History of the Gold Discoveries on the South Platte river; and a guide of the route by Smith & Oaks

Parsons (William B.) The new Gold Mines of Western Kansas: a complete description of the newly discovered gold mines, different routes, camping places, tools and